DEADMAN WONDERLAND
Volume 1
CONTENTS
Cartoon by JINSEI KATAOKA & KAZUMA KONDOU
Book design by TSUYOSHI KUSANO

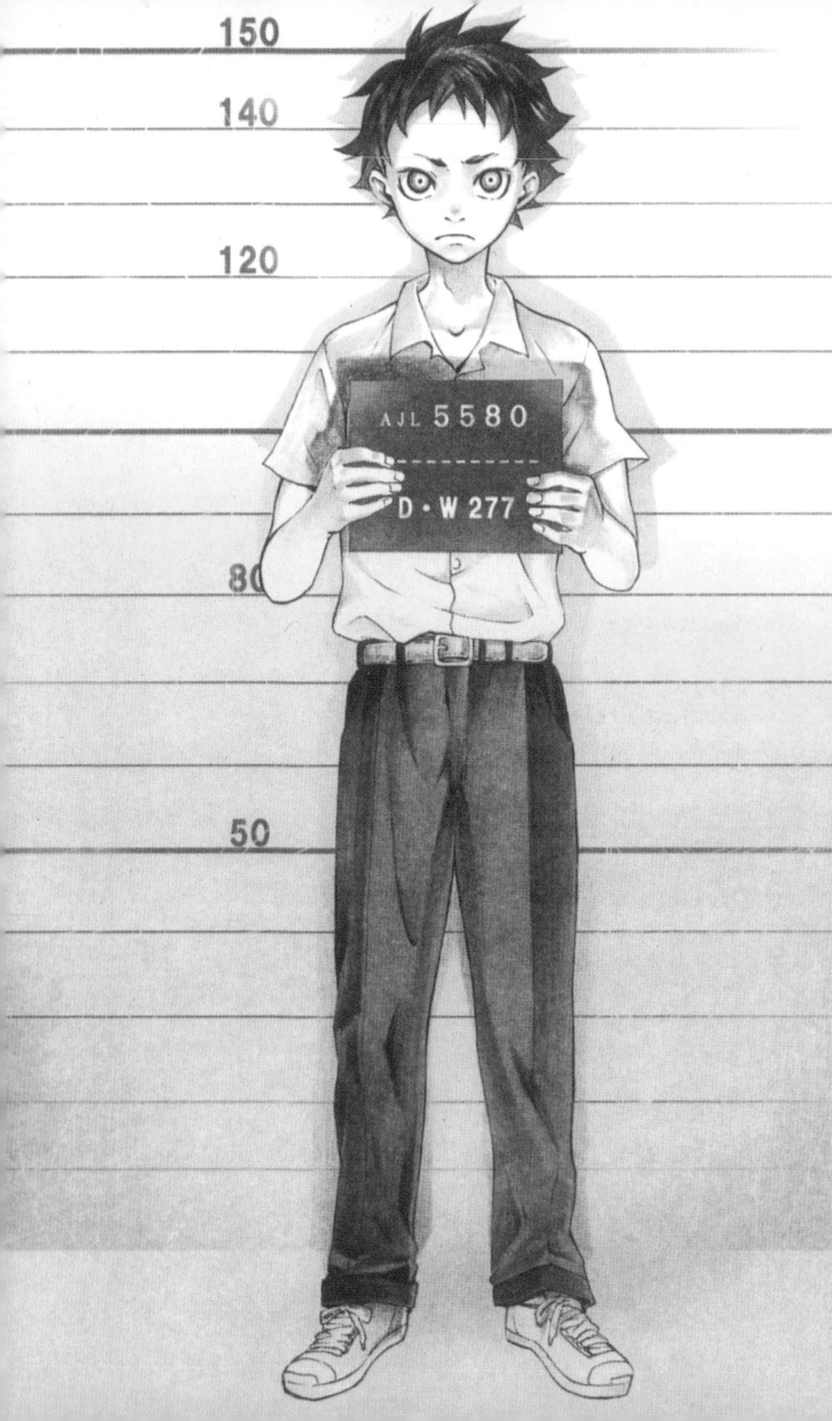
150
140
120
AJL 5580
D • W 277
80
50

BY JINSEI KATAOKA, KAZUMA KONDOU

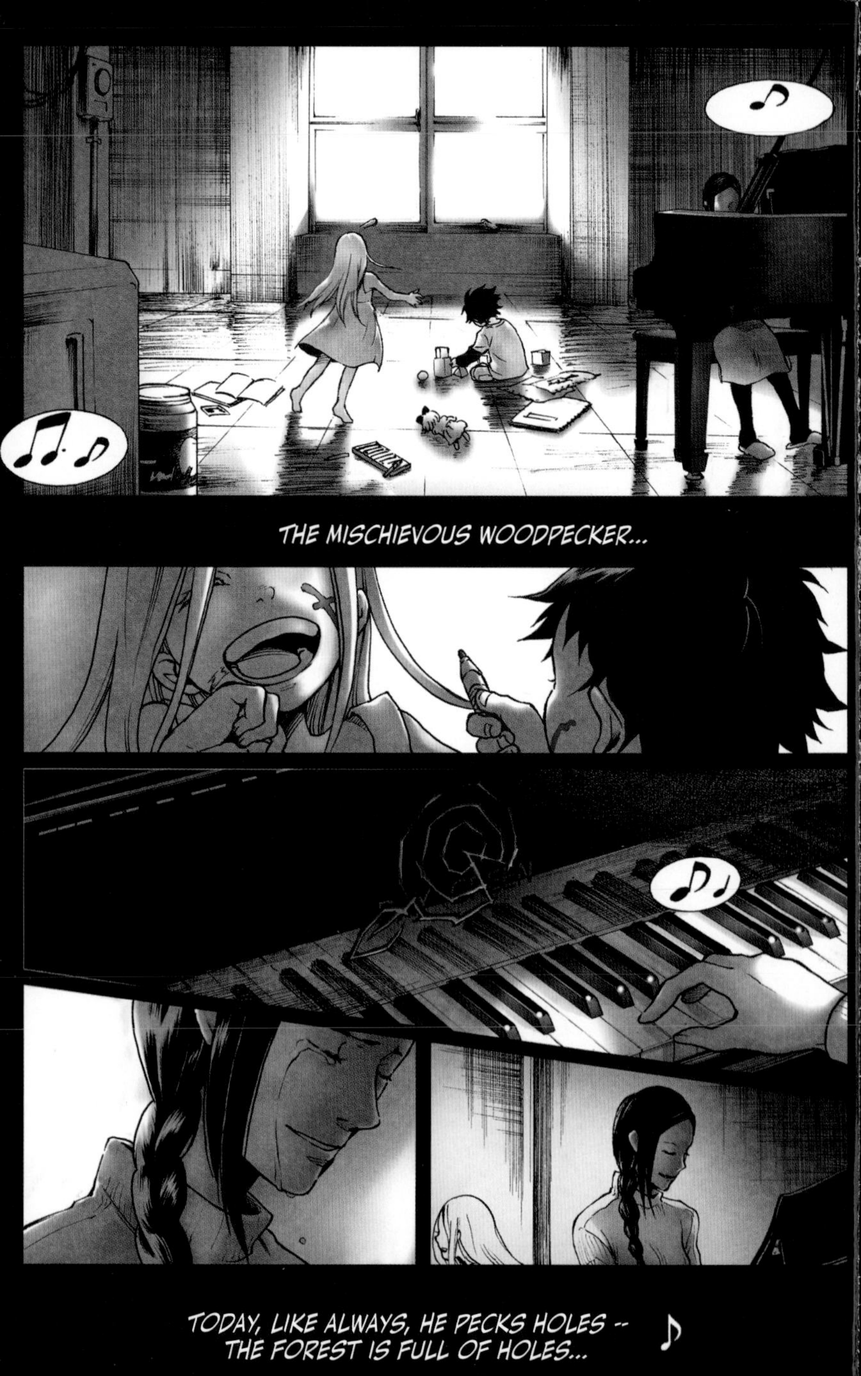
THE MISCHIEVOUS WOODPECKER...
TODAY, LIKE ALWAYS, HE PECKS HOLES -- THE FOREST IS FULL OF HOLES...

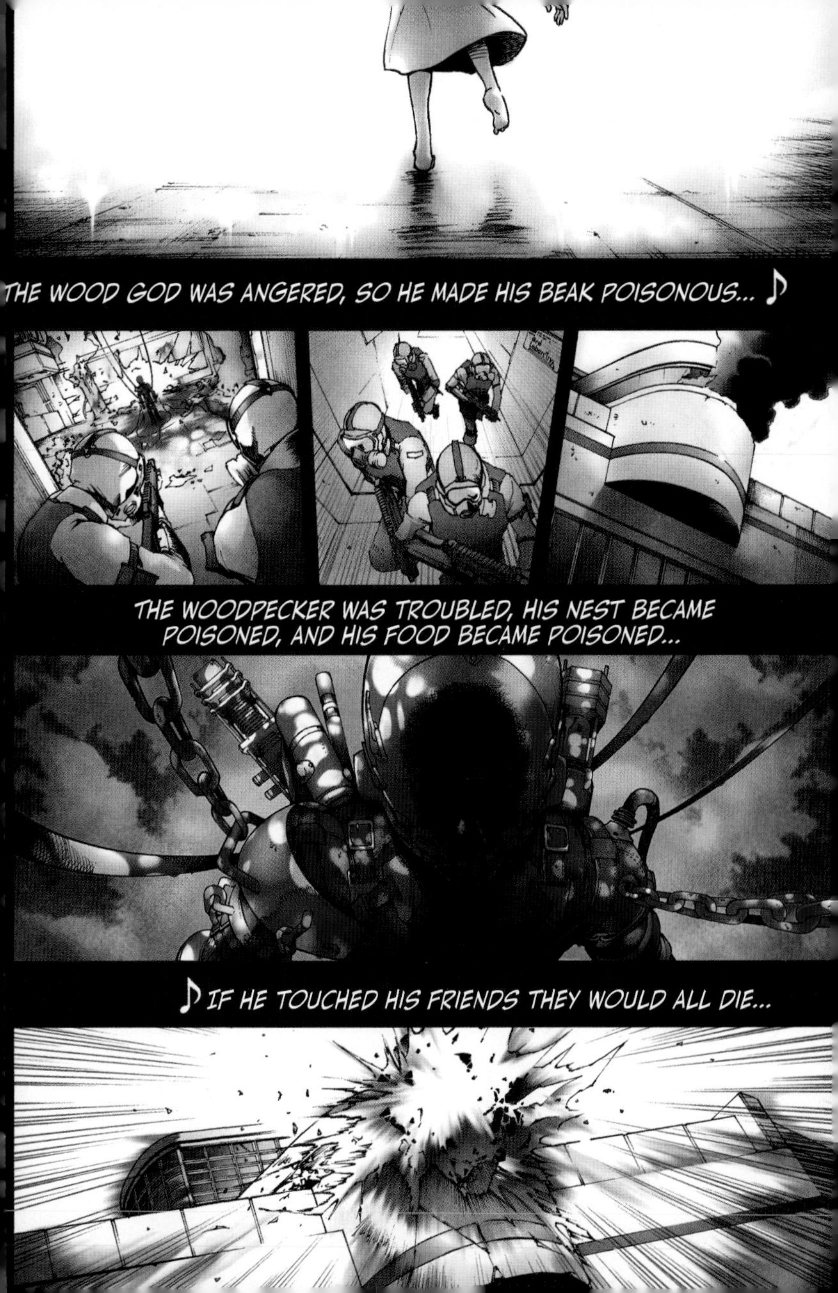
THE WOOD GOD WAS ANGERED, SO HE MADE HIS BEAK POISONOUS... ♪
THE WOODPECKER WAS TROUBLED, HIS NEST BECAME POISONED, AND HIS FOOD BECAME POISONED...
♪ IF HE TOUCHED HIS FRIENDS THEY WOULD ALL DIE...

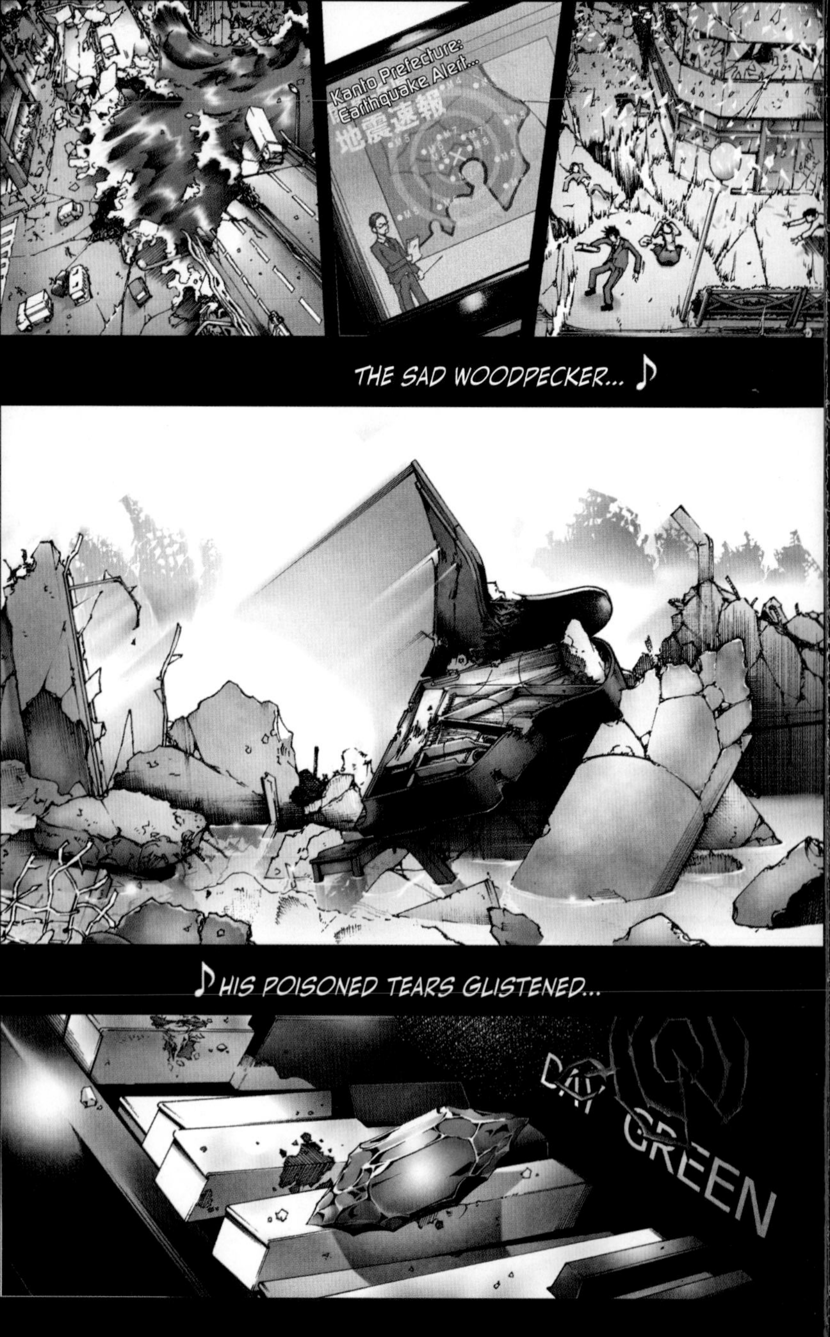
Kanto Prefecture: Earthquake Alert...
地震速報
THE SAD WOODPECKER... ♪
♪ HIS POISONED TEARS GLISTENED...
GREEN

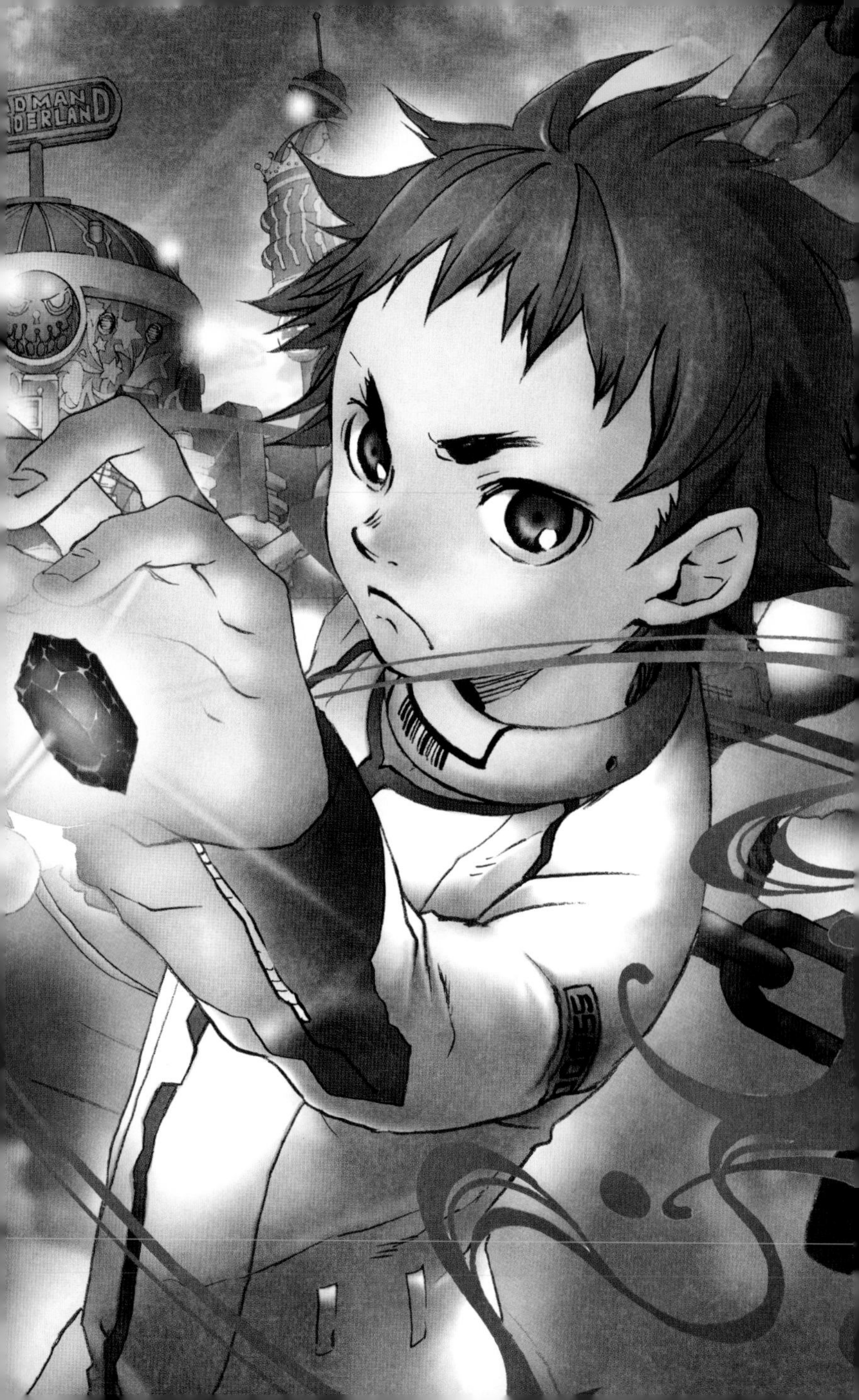

DMAN
DERLAND

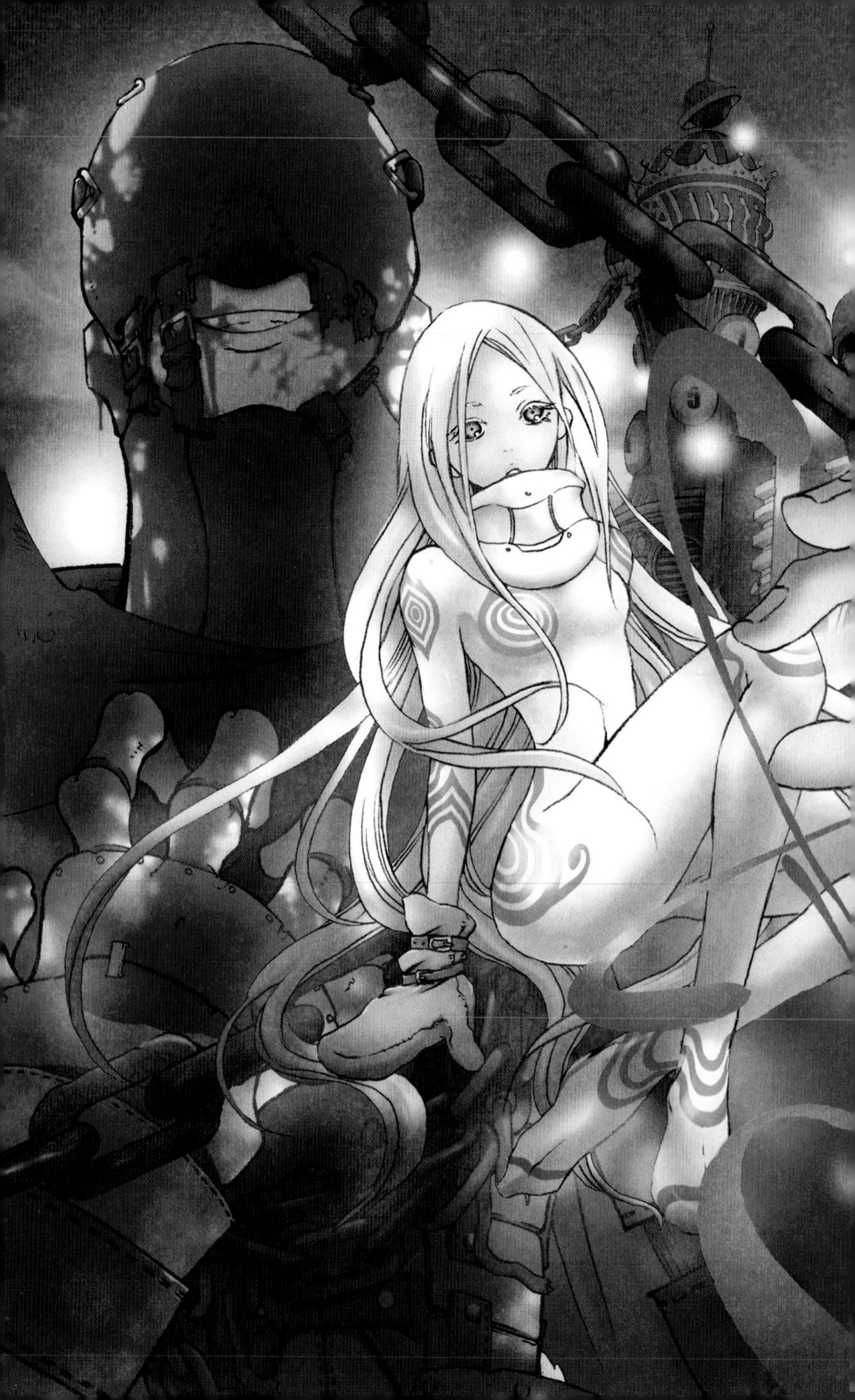

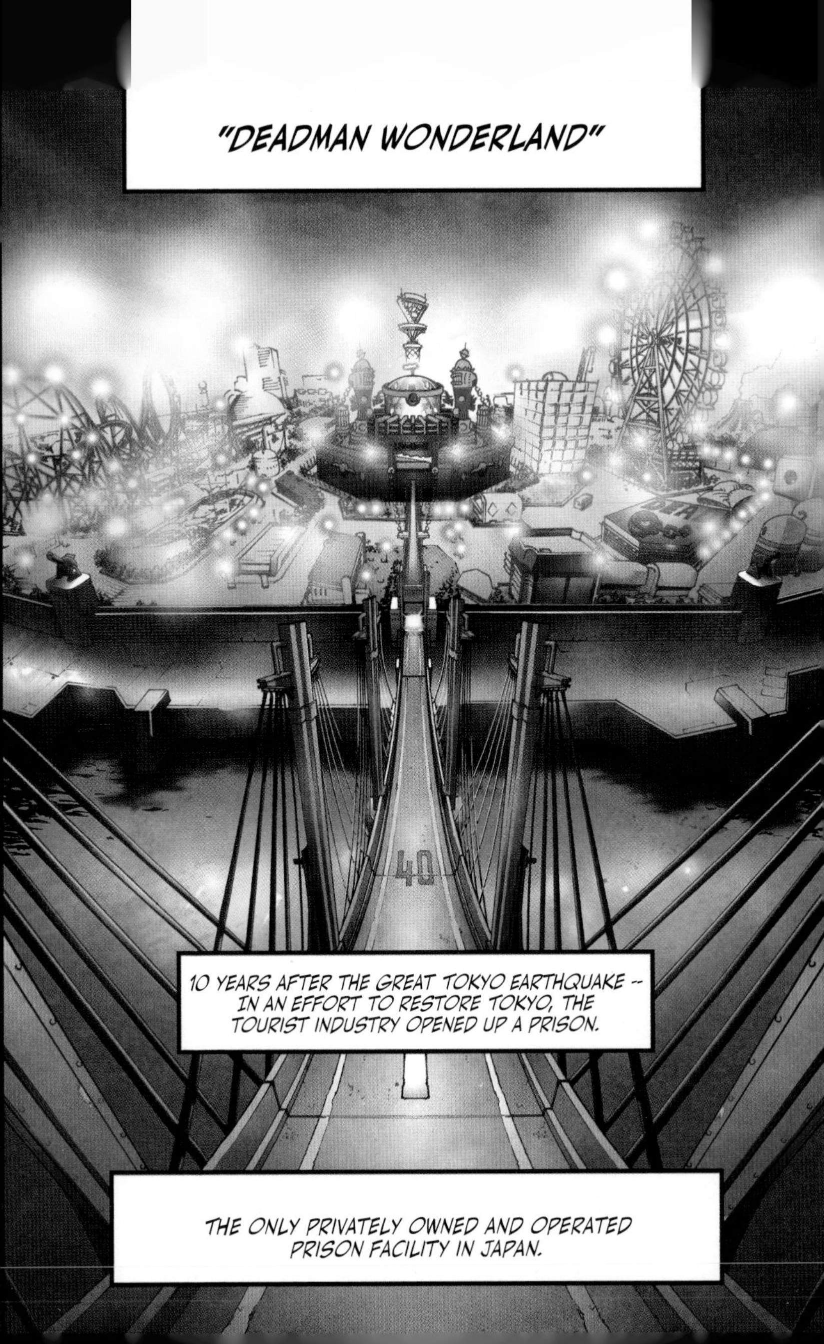
"DEADMAN WONDERLAND"
40
10 YEARS AFTER THE GREAT TOKYO EARTHQUAKE -- IN AN EFFORT TO RESTORE TOKYO, THE TOURIST INDUSTRY OPENED UP A PRISON.
THE ONLY PRIVATELY OWNED AND OPERATED PRISON FACILITY IN JAPAN.

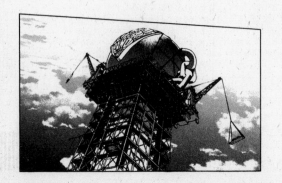

Deadman Wonderland Volume 1
Created by JINSEI KATAOKA, KAZUMA KONDOU

Translation - Ray Yoshimoto
English Adaptation - Bryce P. Coleman
Retouch and Lettering - Star Print Brokers
Production Artist - Michael Paolilli
Graphic Designer - Chelsea Windlinger

Editor - Cindy Suzuki
Print Production Manager - Lucas Rivera
Managing Editor - Vy Nguyen
Senior Designer - Louis Csontos
Art Director - Al-Insan Lashley
Director of Sales and Manufacturing - Allyson De Simone
Associate Publisher - Marco F. Pavia
President and C.O.O. - John Parker
C.E.O. and Chief Creative Officer - Stu Levy

A 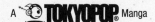 Manga

TOKYOPOP and 👁 are trademarks or registered trademarks of TOKYOPOP Inc.

TOKYOPOP Inc.
5900 Wilshire Blvd. Suite 2000
Los Angeles, CA 90036

E-mail: info@TOKYOPOP.com
Come visit us online at www.TOKYOPOP.com

DEAD MAN WONDERLAND vol.1
© Jinsei KATAOKA 2007 © Kazuma KONDOU 2007
First published in Japan in 2007 by KADOKAWA SHOTEN
Publishing Co., Ltd., Tokyo.
English translation rights arranged with KADOKAWA
SHOTEN Publishing Co., Ltd., Tokyo
through TUTTLE-MORI AGENCY, INC., Tokyo.
English text copyright © 2010 TOKYOPOP Inc.

ISBN: 978-1-4278-1741-9

First TOKYOPOP printing: February 2010
10 9 8 7 6 5 4 3 2 1
Printed in the USA

DEADMAN WONDERLAND

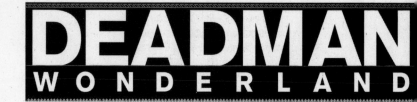

VOLUME 1

STORY BY JINSEI KATAOKA
ART BY KAZUMA KONDOU

TOKYOPOP®

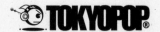

HAMBURG // LONDON // LOS ANGELES // TOKYO

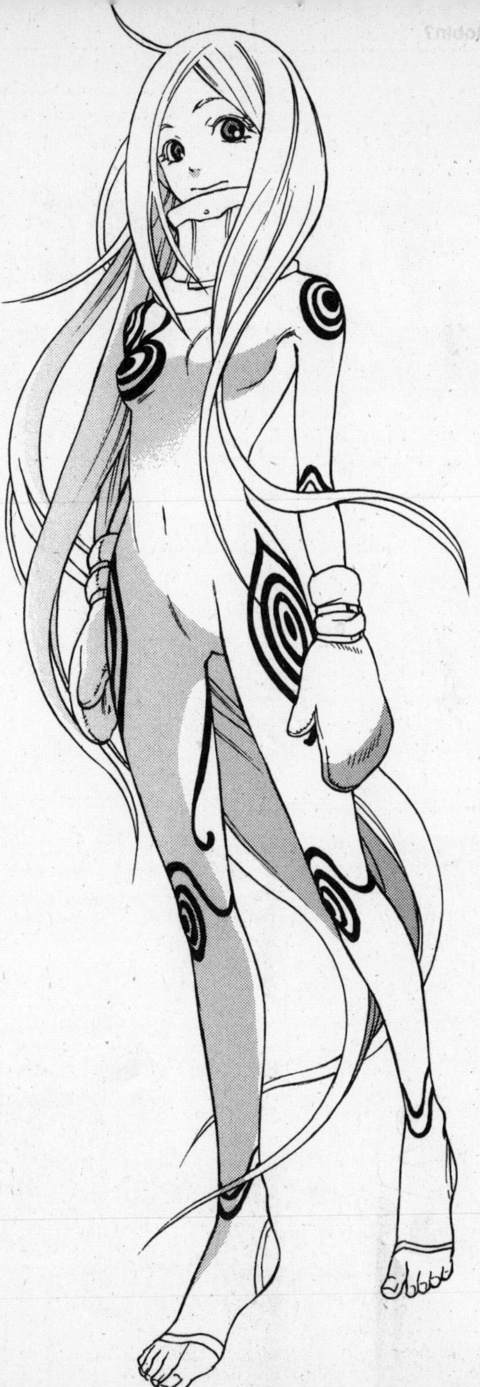

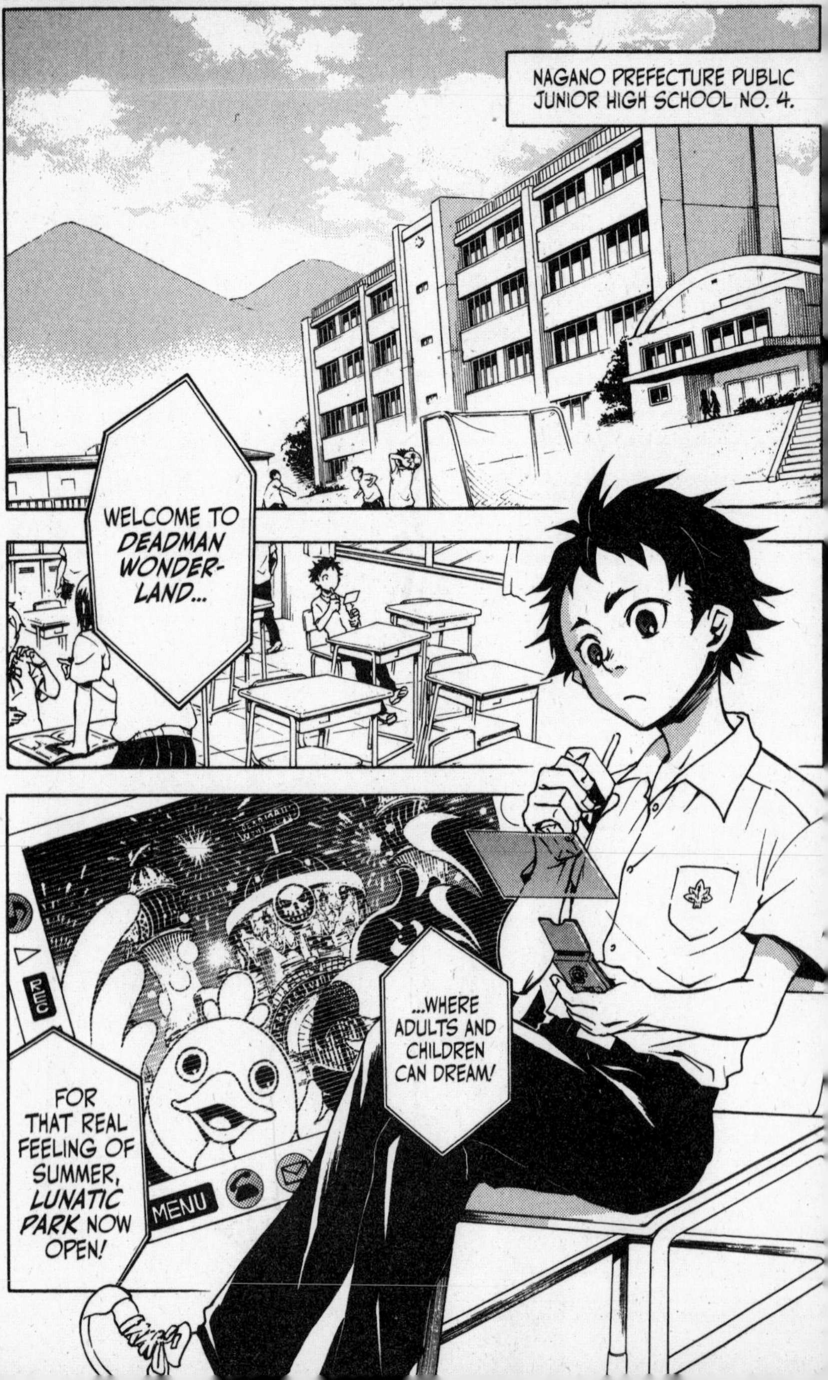
NAGANO PREFECTURE PUBLIC JUNIOR HIGH SCHOOL NO. 4.
WELCOME TO *DEADMAN WONDER-LAND*...
...WHERE ADULTS AND CHILDREN CAN DREAM!
REC
FOR THAT REAL FEELING OF SUMMER, *LUNATIC PARK* NOW OPEN!
MENU

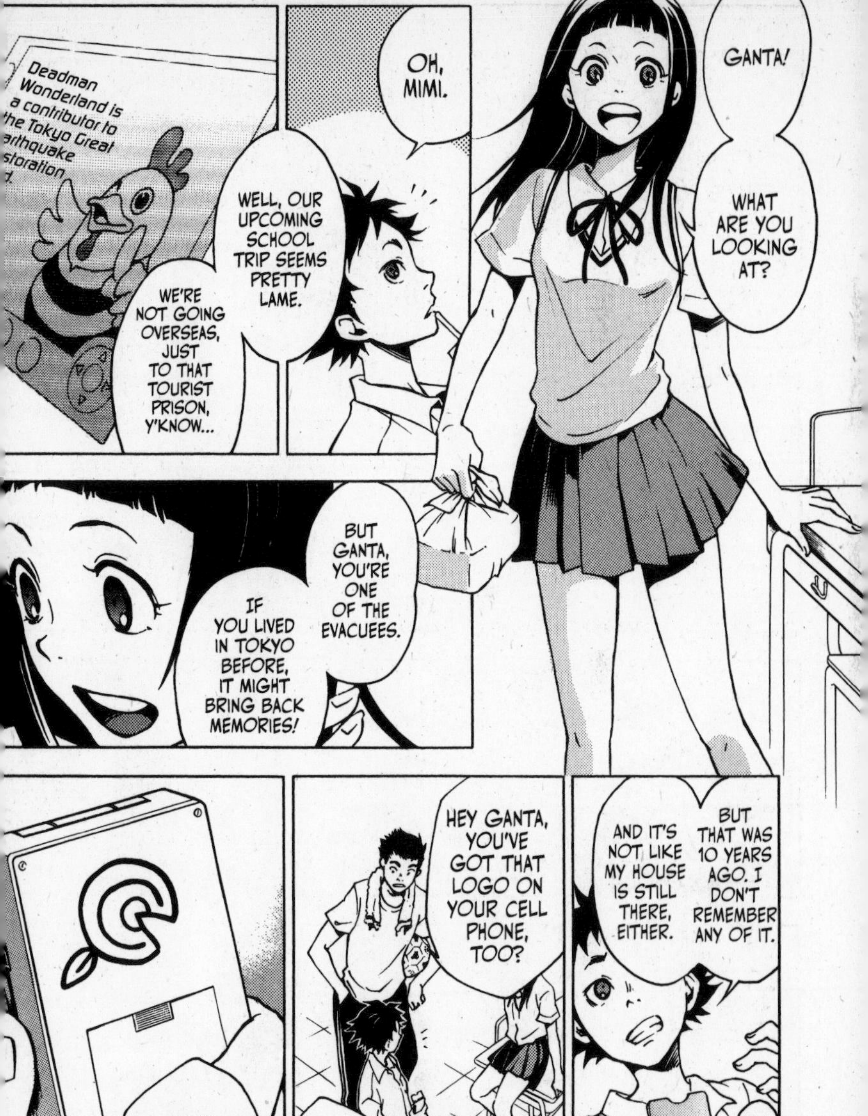
GANTA!
WHAT ARE YOU LOOKING AT?
OH, MIMI.
WELL, OUR UPCOMING SCHOOL TRIP SEEMS PRETTY LAME.
Deadman Wonderland is a contributor to the Tokyo Great arthquake storation d.
WE'RE NOT GOING OVERSEAS, JUST TO THAT TOURIST PRISON, Y'KNOW...
BUT GANTA, YOU'RE ONE OF THE EVACUEES.
IF YOU LIVED IN TOKYO BEFORE, IT MIGHT BRING BACK MEMORIES!
BUT THAT WAS 10 YEARS AGO. I DON'T REMEMBER ANY OF IT.
AND IT'S NOT LIKE MY HOUSE IS STILL THERE, EITHER.
FLIP
HEY GANTA, YOU'VE GOT THAT LOGO ON YOUR CELL PHONE, TOO?
WHAT, YAMAKATSU.
IT'S EASY TO RECOGNIZE, THIS "MARUTA" SYMBOL.

ANTA'S NAME CAN ALSO BE PRONOUNCED AS "MARUTA" = (TREE LOG).

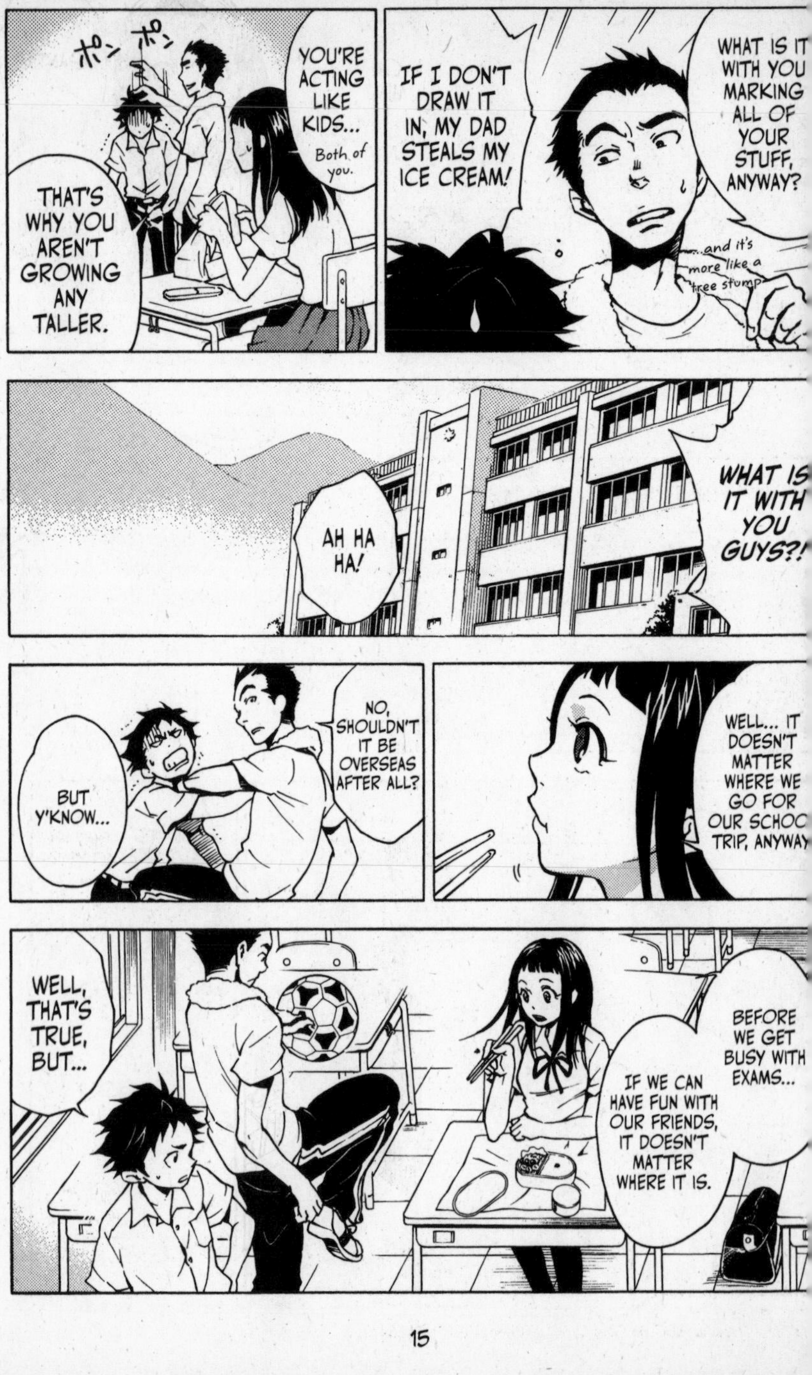
WHAT IS IT WITH YOU MARKING ALL OF YOUR STUFF, ANYWAY?
IF I DON'T DRAW IT IN, MY DAD STEALS MY ICE CREAM!
...and it's more like a tree stump
ポン ポン
YOU'RE ACTING LIKE KIDS... Both of you.
THAT'S WHY YOU AREN'T GROWING ANY TALLER.
WHAT IS IT WITH YOU GUYS?!
AH HA HA!
WELL... IT DOESN'T MATTER WHERE WE GO FOR OUR SCHOO TRIP, ANYWAY
NO, SHOULDN'T IT BE OVERSEAS AFTER ALL?
BUT Y'KNOW...
BEFORE WE GET BUSY WITH EXAMS...
IF WE CAN HAVE FUN WITH OUR FRIENDS, IT DOESN'T MATTER WHERE IT IS.
WELL, THAT'S TRUE, BUT...

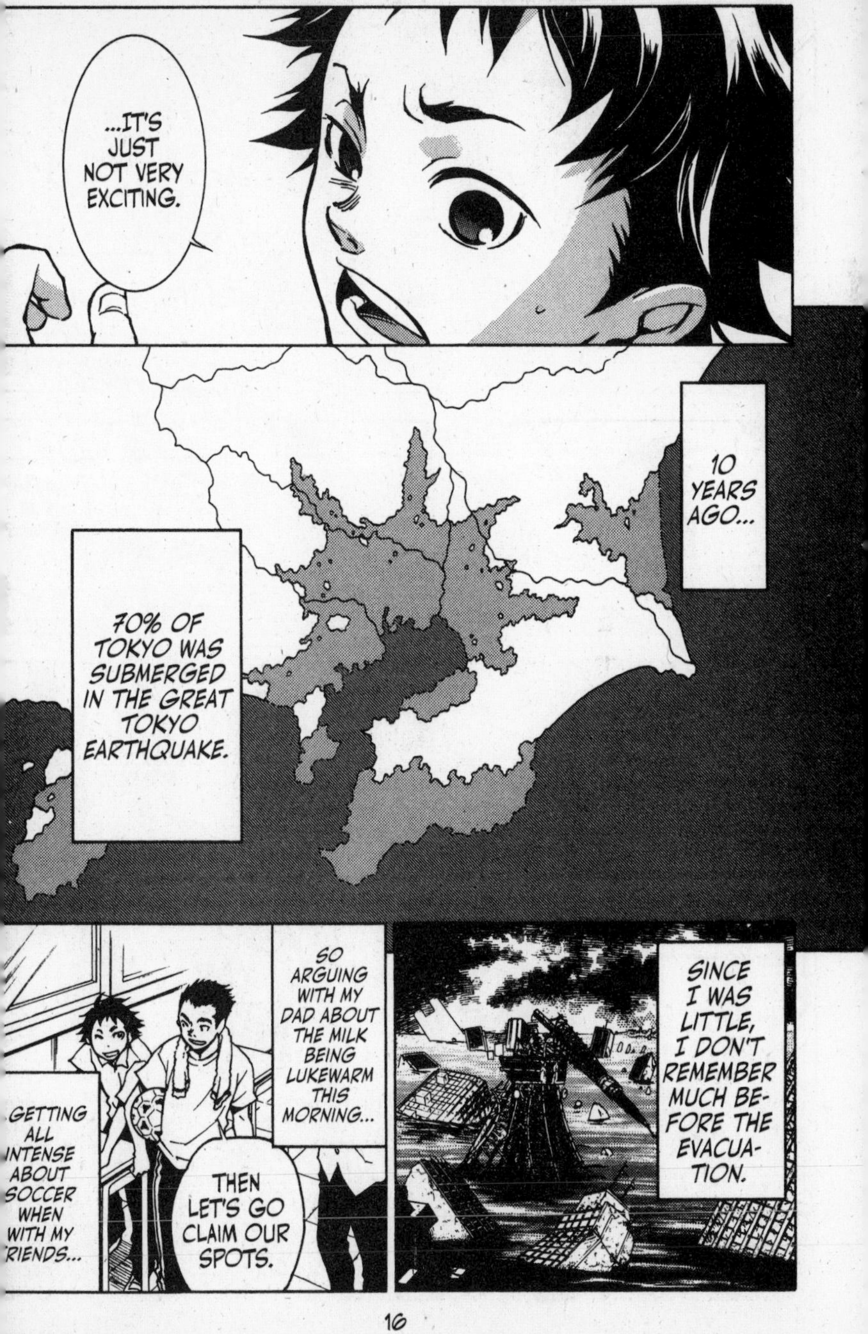
...IT'S JUST NOT VERY EXCITING.
10 YEARS AGO...
70% OF TOKYO WAS SUBMERGED IN THE GREAT TOKYO EARTHQUAKE.
SINCE I WAS LITTLE, I DON'T REMEMBER MUCH BEFORE THE EVACUATION.
SO ARGUING WITH MY DAD ABOUT THE MILK BEING LUKEWARM THIS MORNING...
GETTING ALL INTENSE ABOUT SOCCER WHEN WITH MY RIENDS...
THEN LET'S GO CLAIM OUR SPOTS.

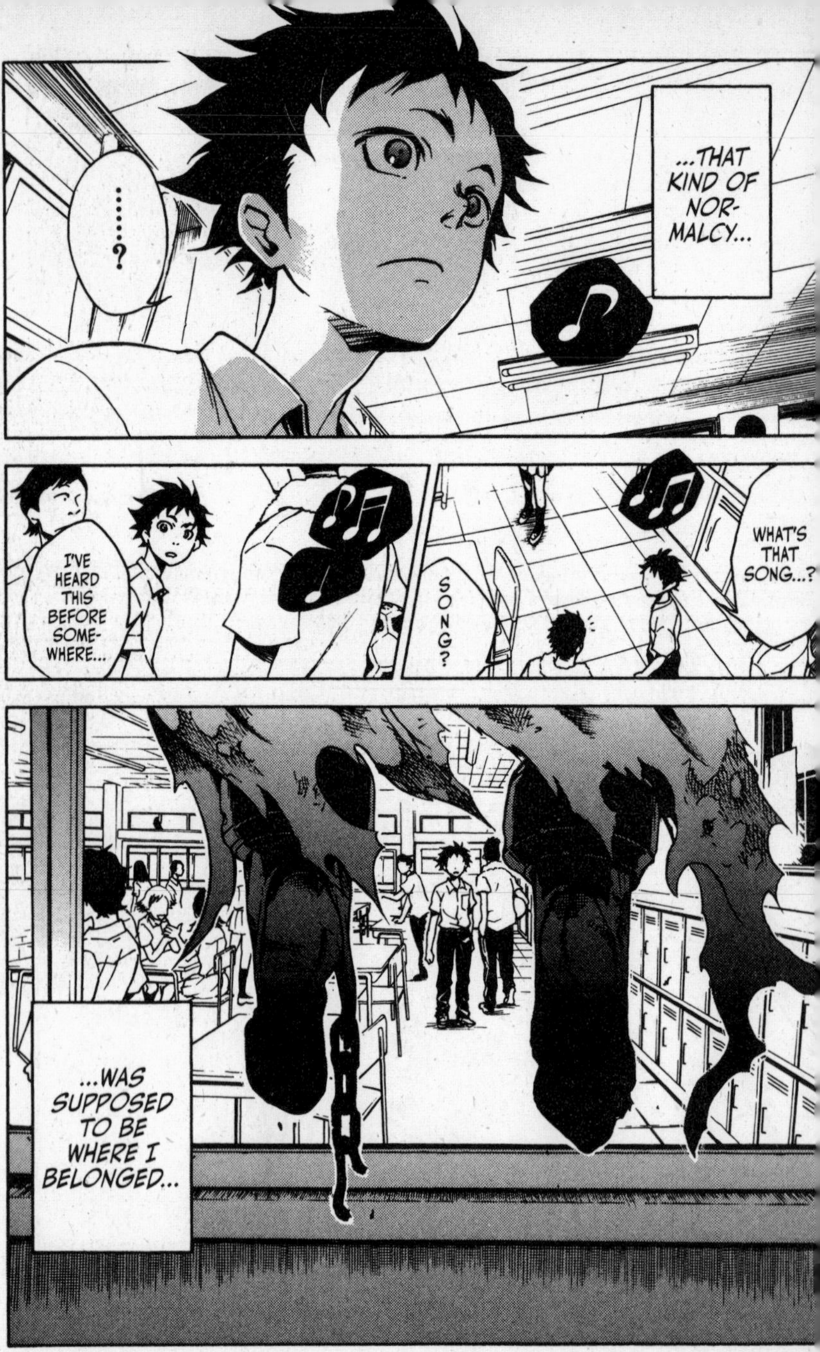
...THAT KIND OF NOR-MALCY...
......?
WHAT'S THAT SONG...?
SONG?
I'VE HEARD THIS BEFORE SOME-WHERE...
...WAS SUPPOSED TO BE WHERE I BELONGED...

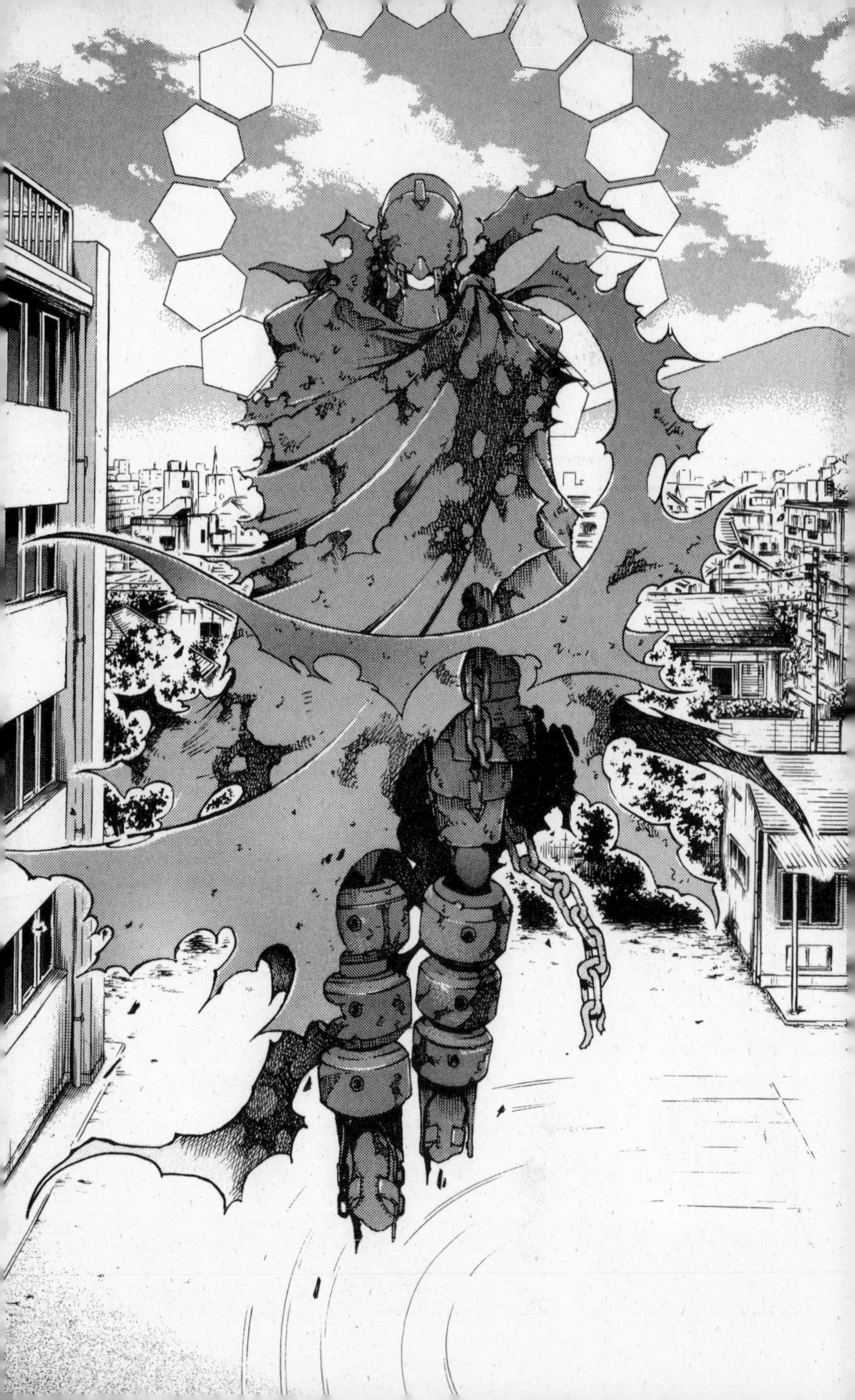

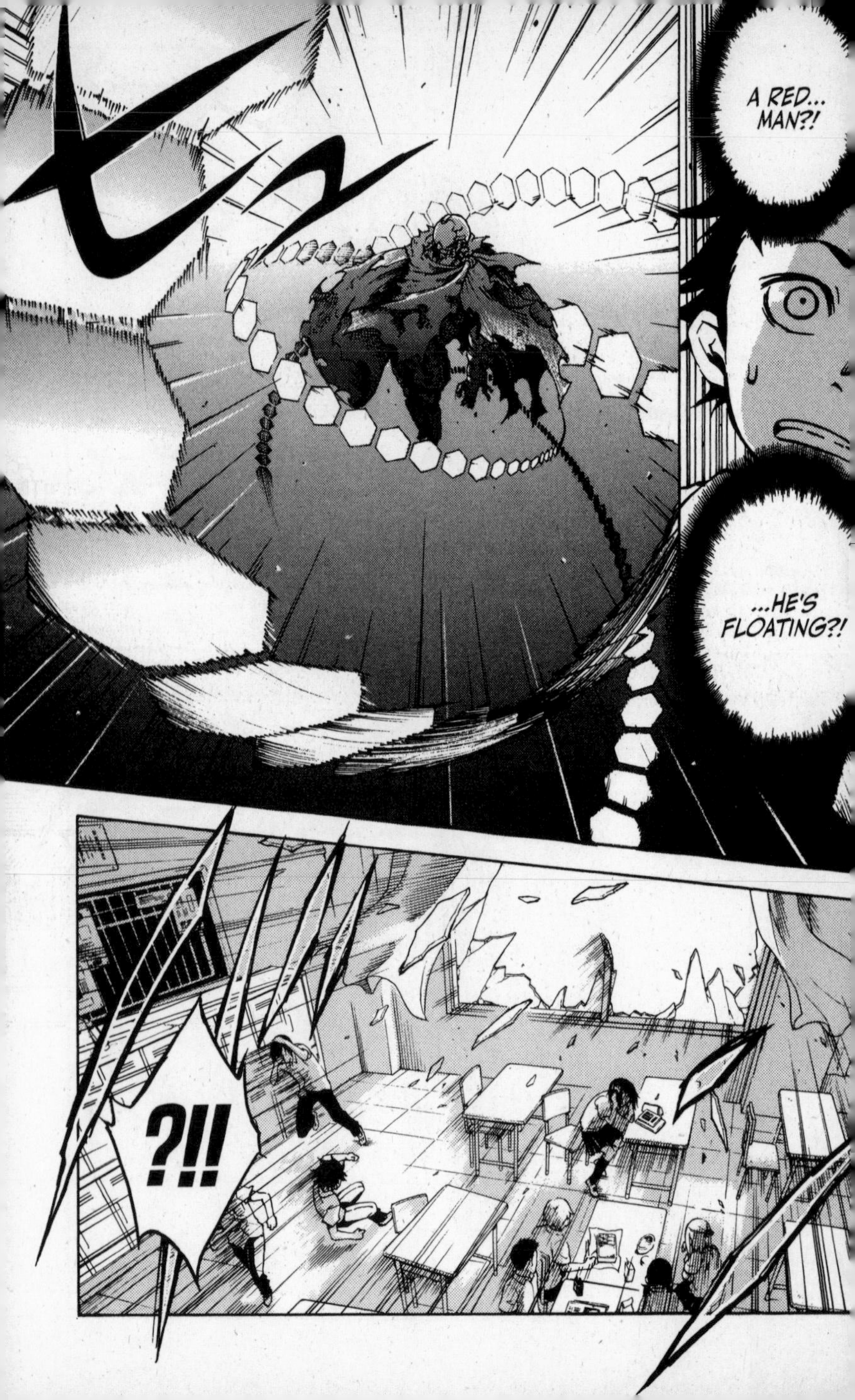
A RED... MAN?!
...HE'S FLOATING?!
?!!

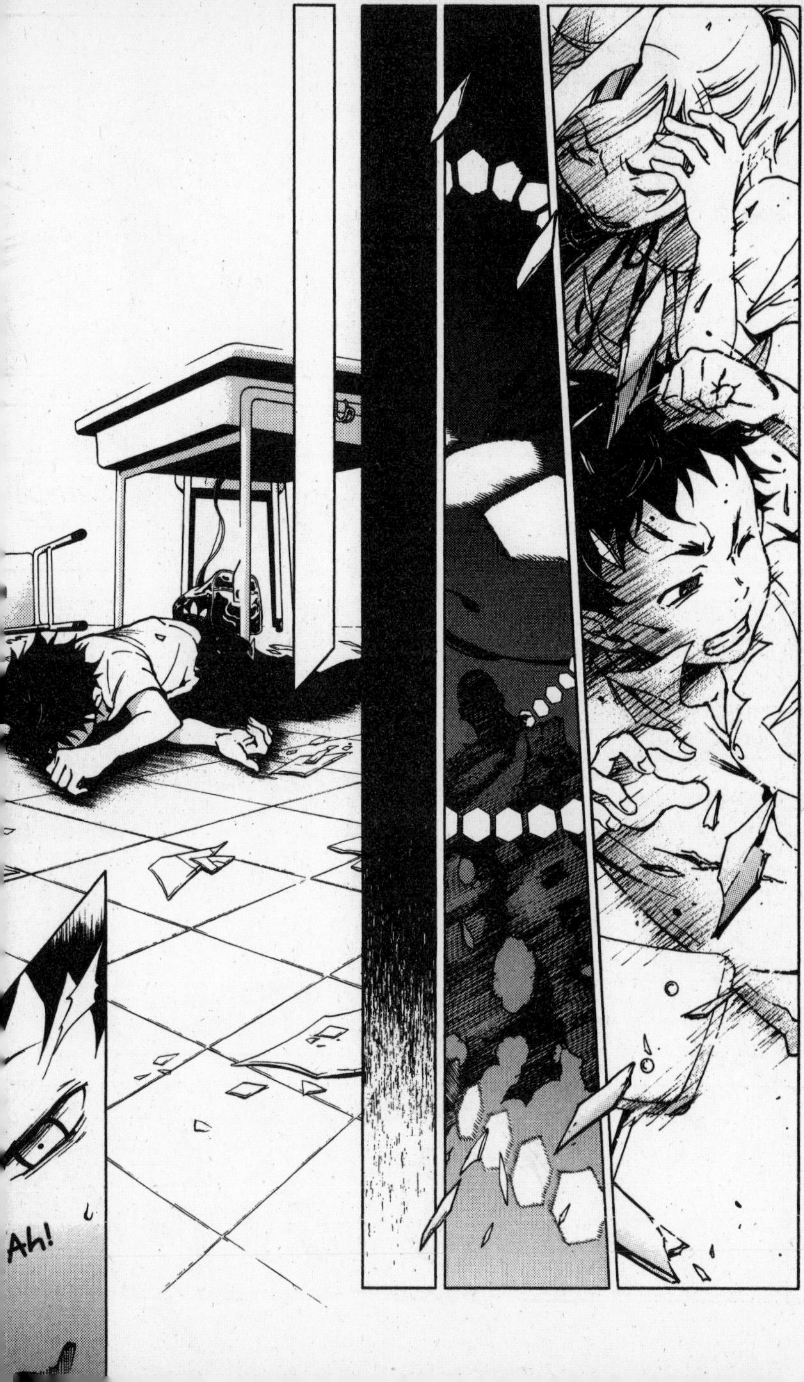
Ah!

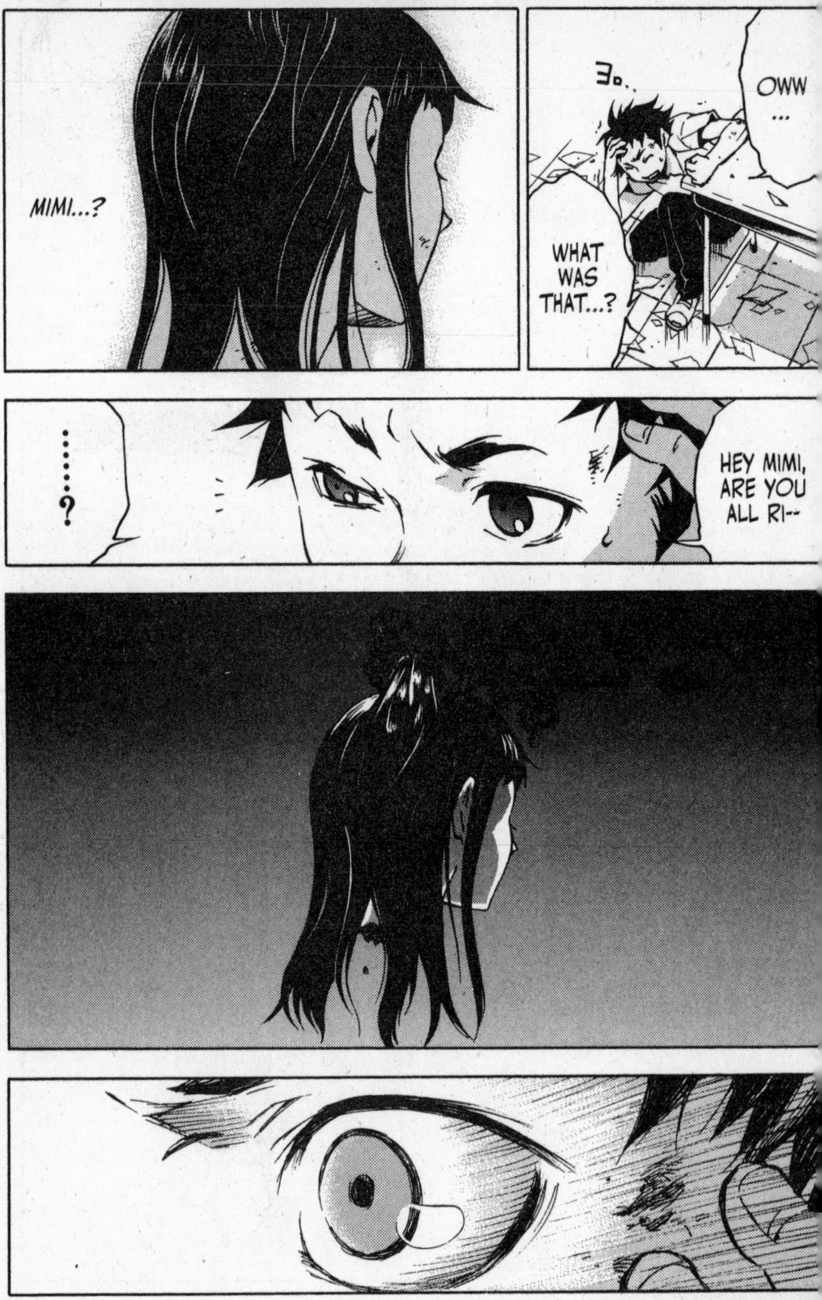
ヨロ..
OWW ...
WHAT WAS THAT...?
MIMI...?
HEY MIMI, ARE YOU ALL RI--
......?

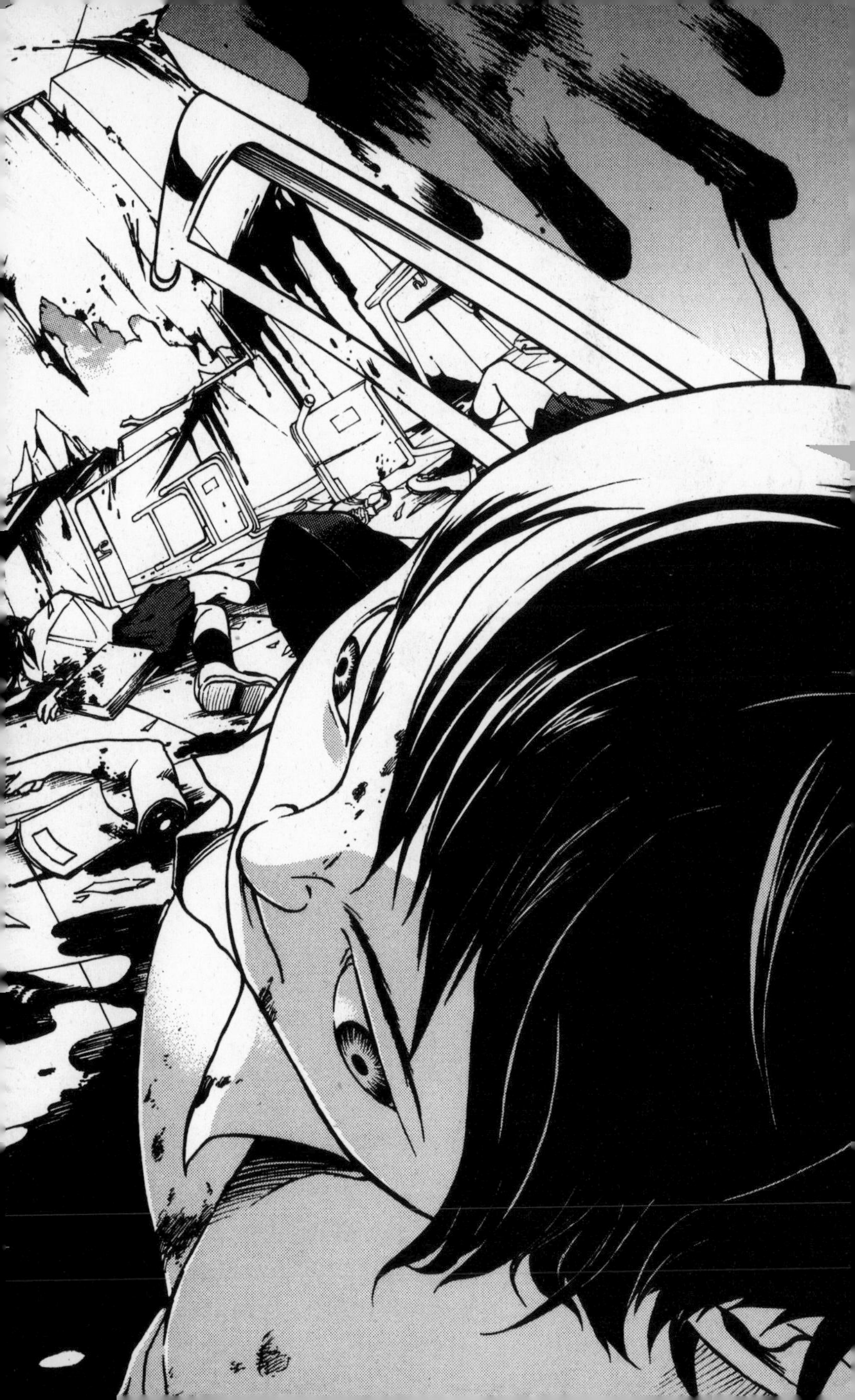

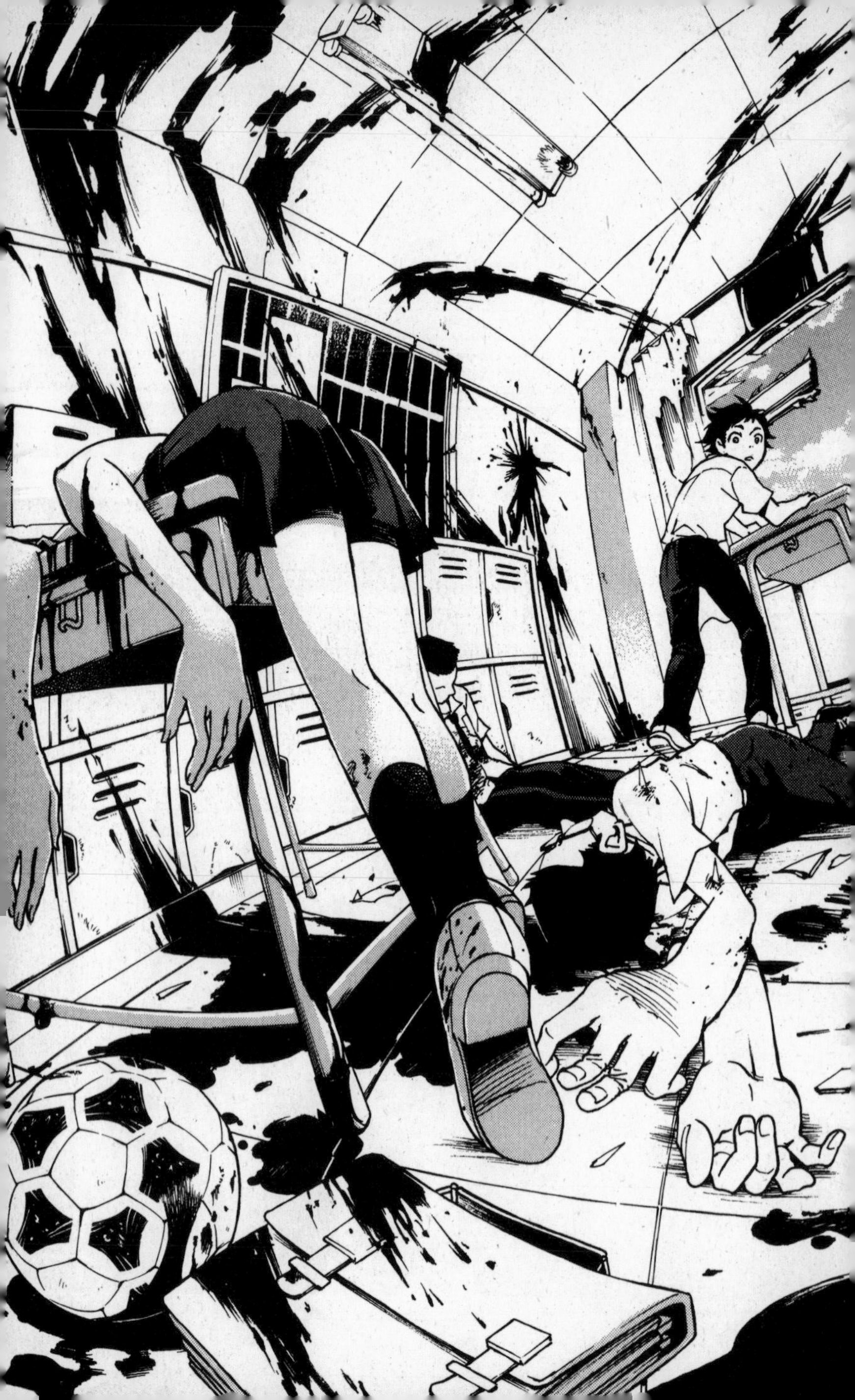

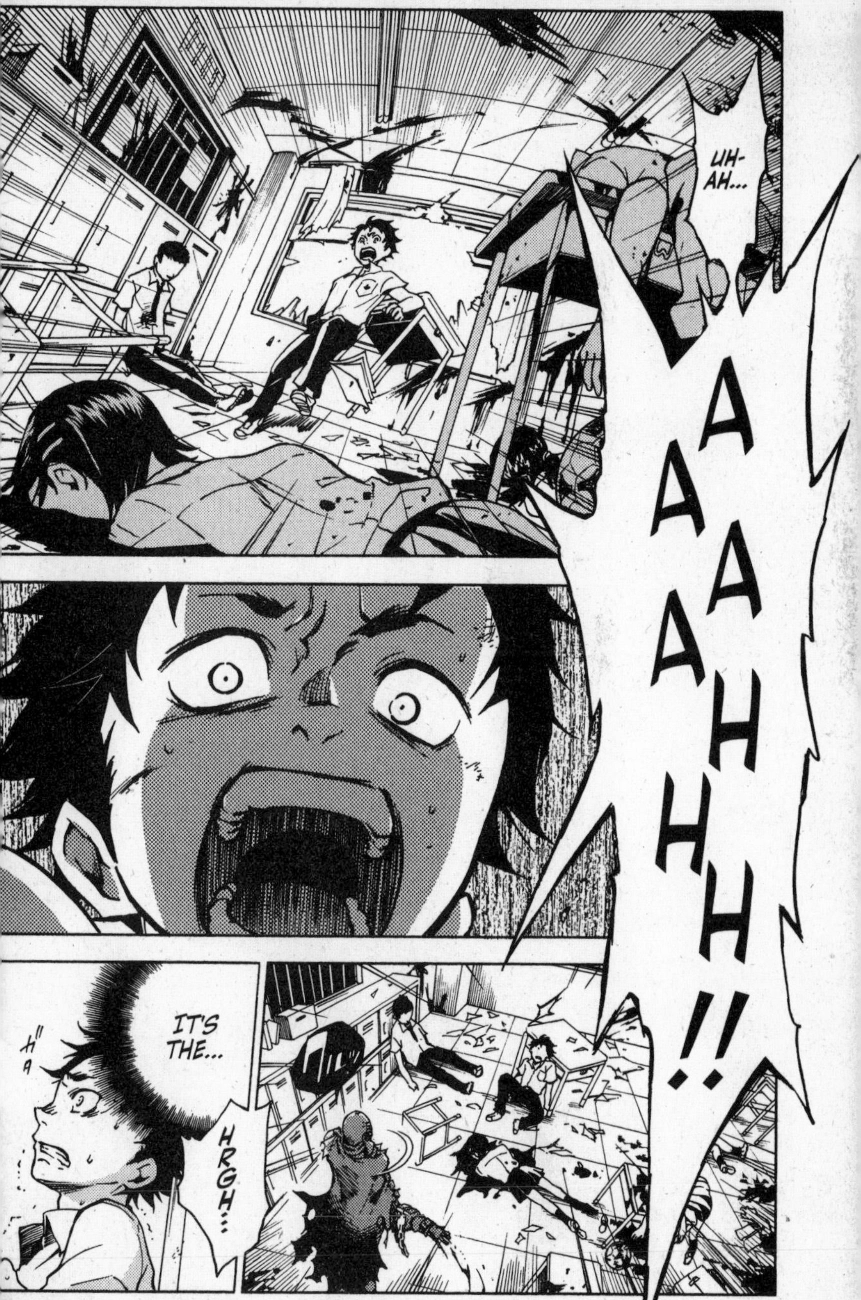
UH-
AH...
AAAAHHH!!
IT'S THE...
HRGH...
HA

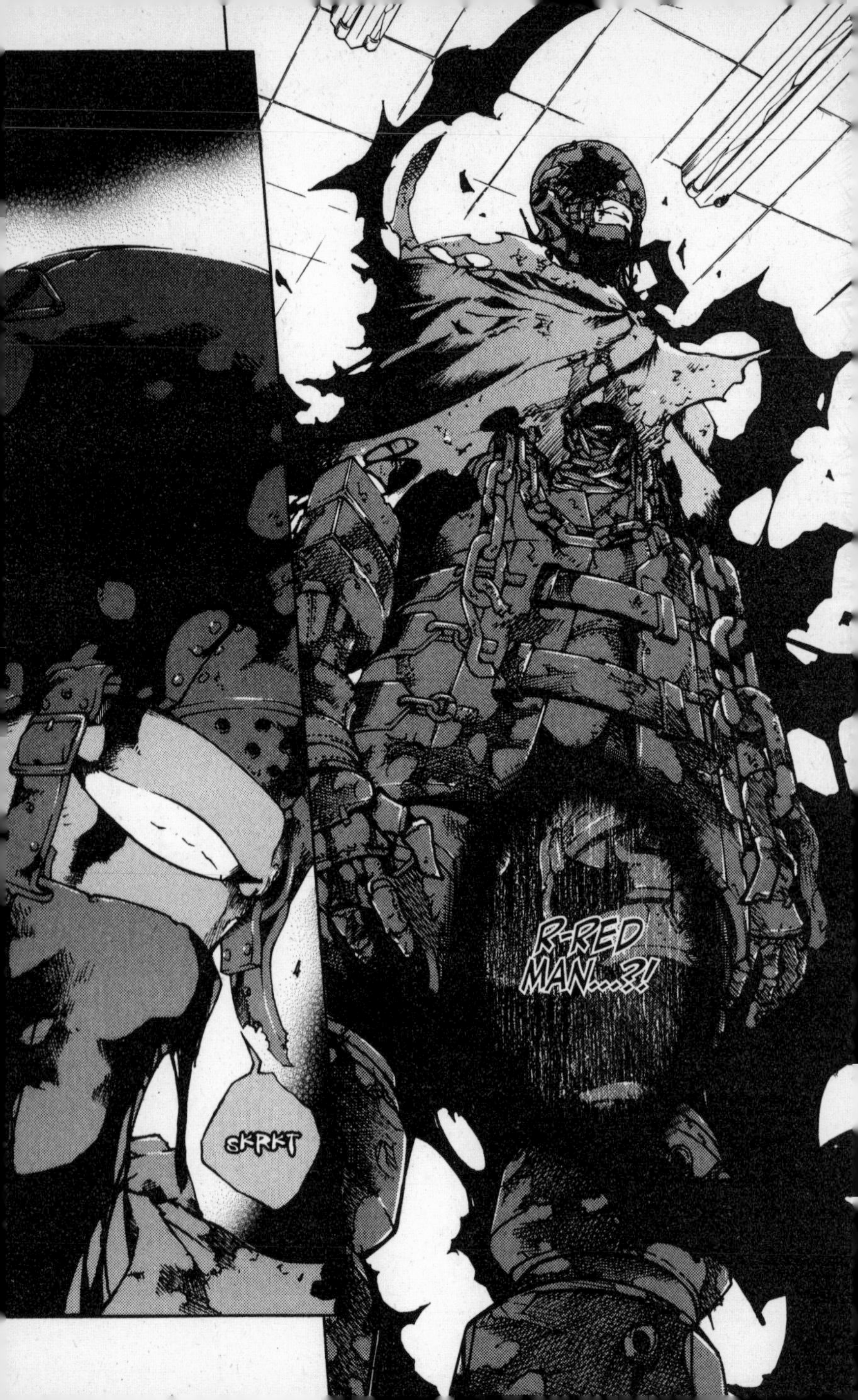
R-RED MAN...?!
SKRKT

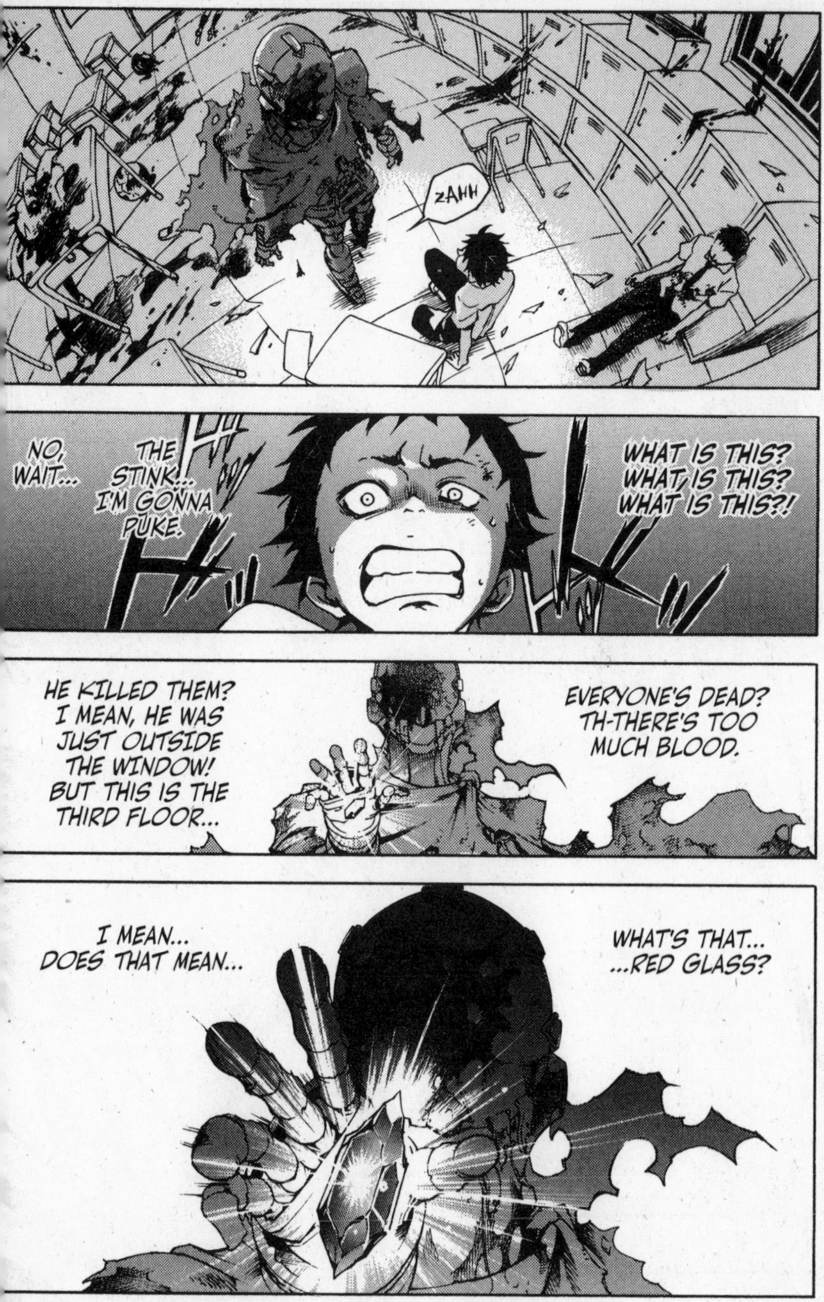
ZAHH
WHAT IS THIS? WHAT IS THIS? WHAT IS THIS?!
THE STINK... I'M GONNA PUKE.
NO, WAIT...
EVERYONE'S DEAD? TH-THERE'S TOO MUCH BLOOD.
HE KILLED THEM? I MEAN, HE WAS JUST OUTSIDE THE WINDOW! BUT THIS IS THE THIRD FLOOR...
WHAT'S THAT... ...RED GLASS?
I MEAN... DOES THAT MEAN...

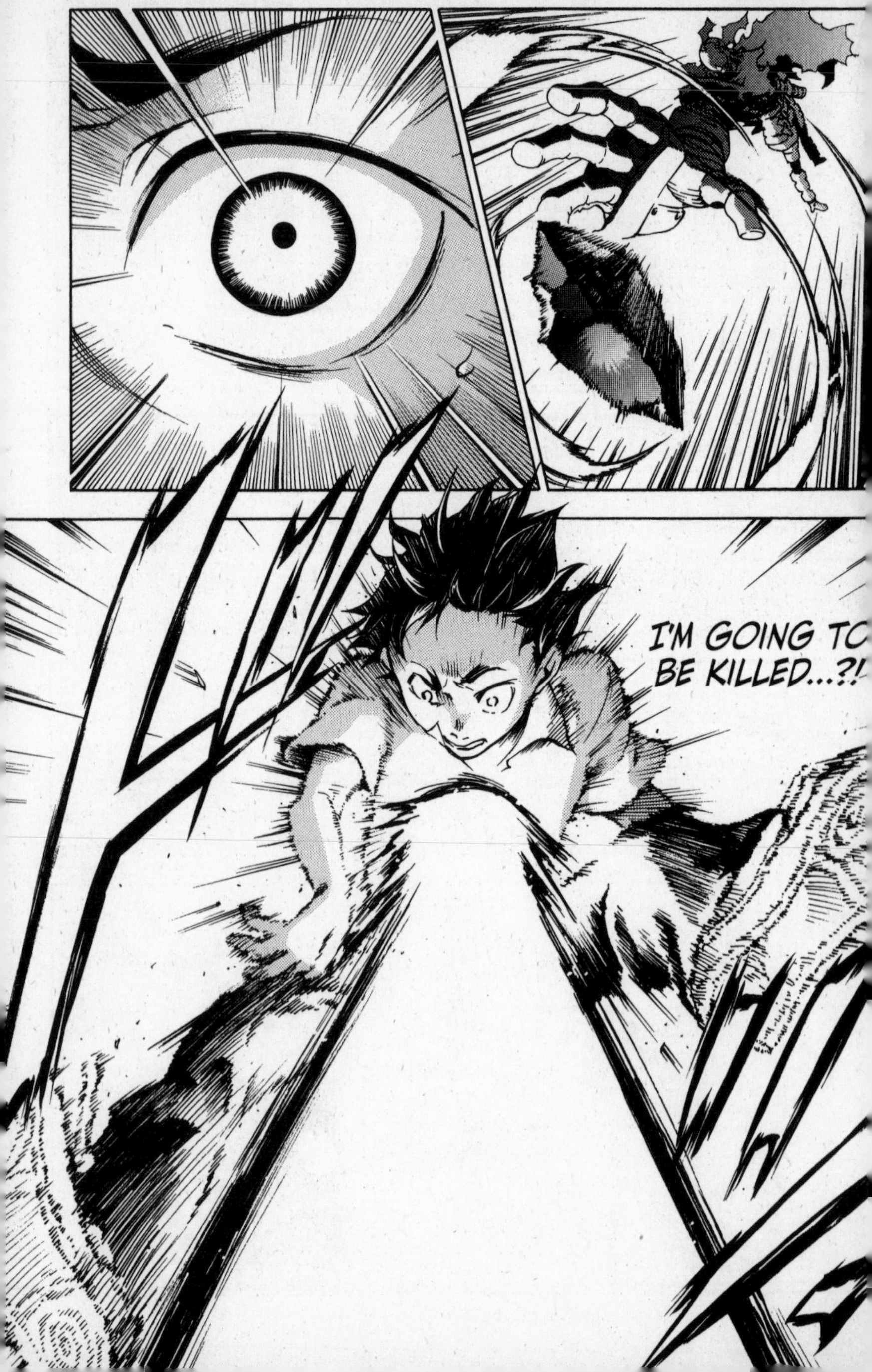
I'M GOING TO BE KILLED...?!

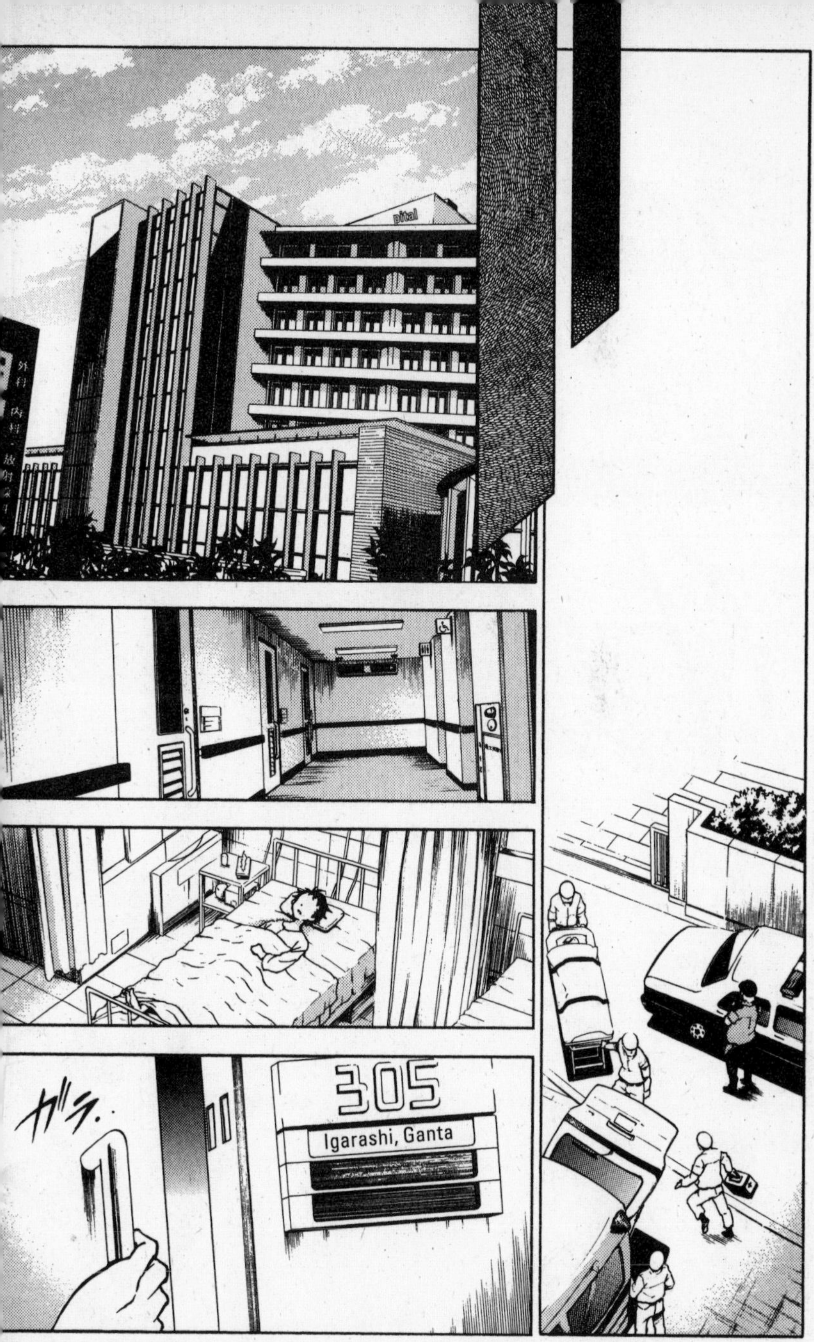
pital
外科
内科
ガラ…
305
Igarashi, Ganta

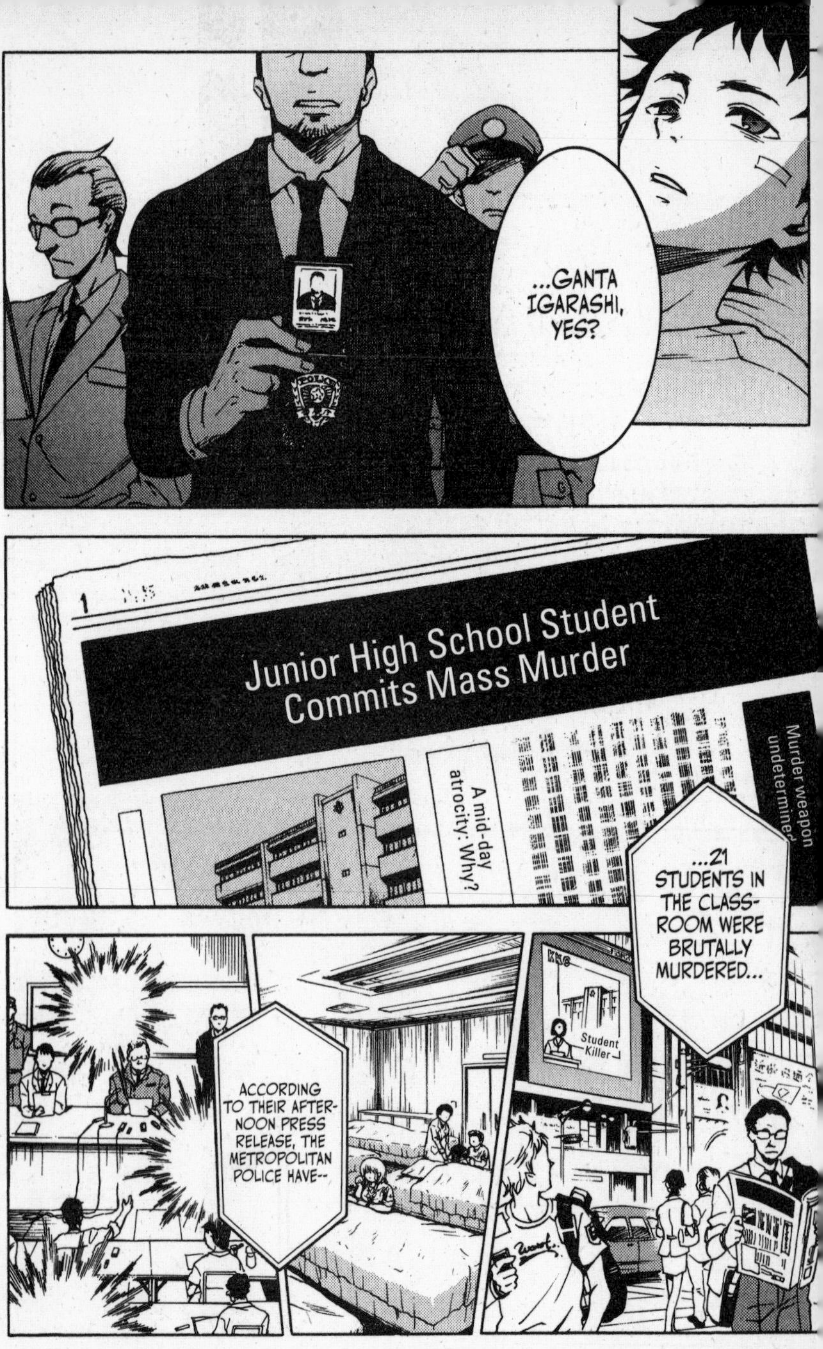
...GANTA IGARASHI, YES?
Junior High School Student Commits Mass Murder
Murder weapon undetermine
A mid-day atrocity: Why?
...21 STUDENTS IN THE CLASS-ROOM WERE BRUTALLY MURDERED...
Student Killer
ACCORDING TO THEIR AFTER-NOON PRESS RELEASE, THE METROPOLITAN POLICE HAVE--

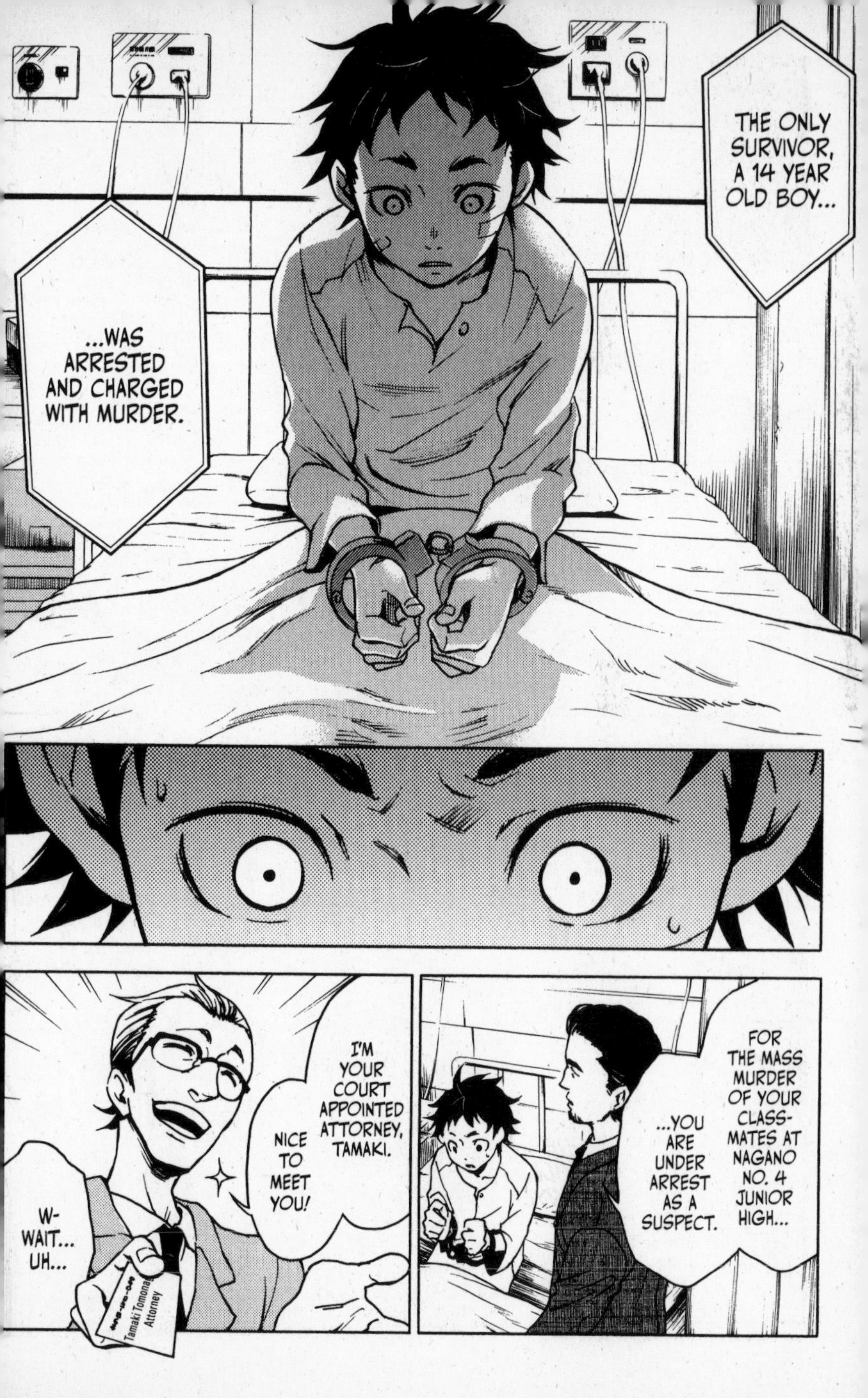
THE ONLY SURVIVOR, A 14 YEAR OLD BOY...
...WAS ARRESTED AND CHARGED WITH MURDER.
FOR THE MASS MURDER OF YOUR CLASSMATES AT NAGANO NO. 4 JUNIOR HIGH...
...YOU ARE UNDER ARREST AS A SUSPECT.
I'M YOUR COURT APPOINTED ATTORNEY, TAMAKI.
NICE TO MEET YOU!
W-WAIT... UH...
Attorney

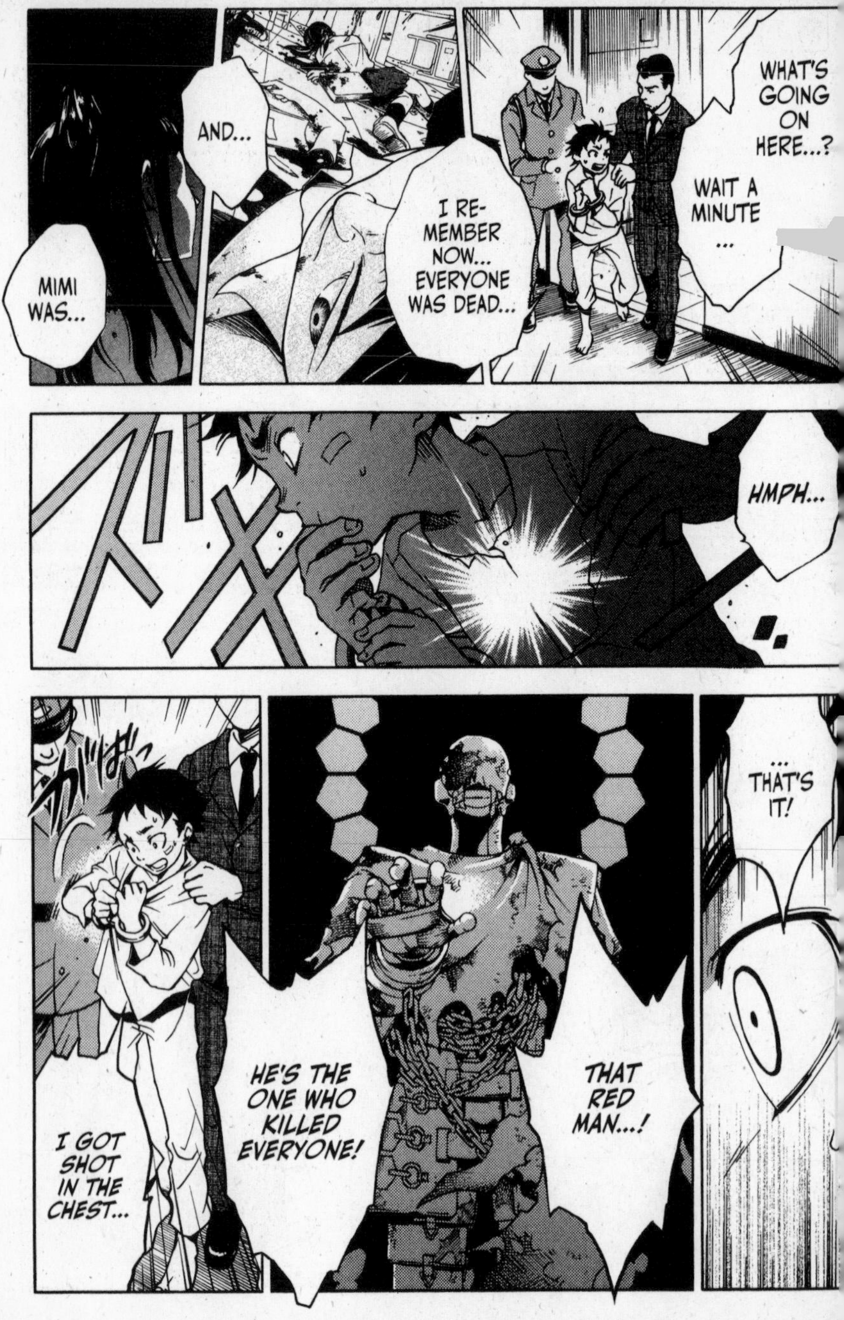
WHAT'S GOING ON HERE...?
WAIT A MINUTE ...
I RE-MEMBER NOW... EVERYONE WAS DEAD...
AND...
MIMI WAS...
HMPH...
... THAT'S IT!
THAT RED MAN...!
HE'S THE ONE WHO KILLED EVERYONE!
I GOT SHOT IN THE CHEST...

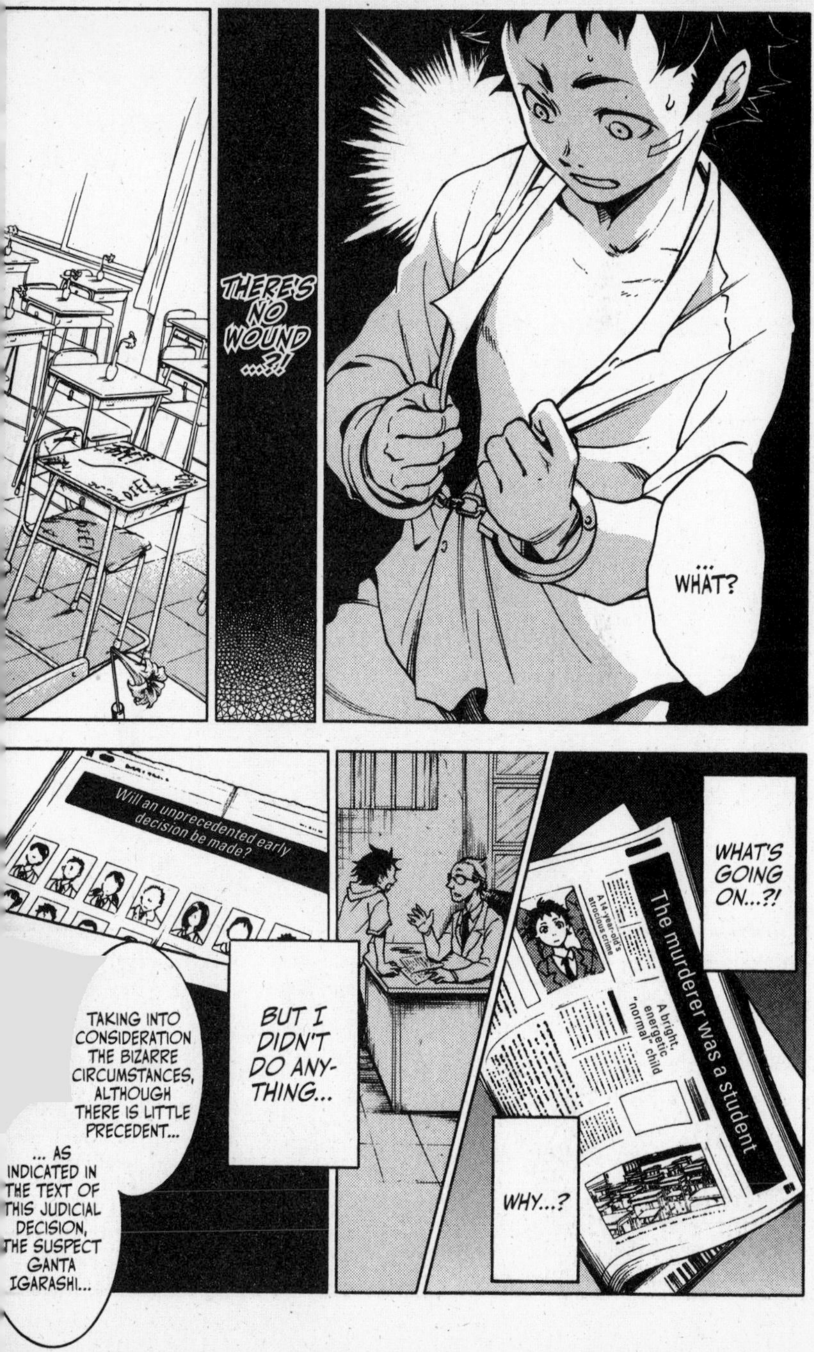
...WHAT?
THERE'S NO WOUND ...?!
WHAT'S GOING ON...?!
The murderer was a student
A 14-year-old's atrocious crime
A bright, energetic "normal" child
WHY...?
BUT I DIDN'T DO ANY-THING...
Will an unprecedented early decision be made?
TAKING INTO CONSIDERATION THE BIZARRE CIRCUMSTANCES, ALTHOUGH THERE IS LITTLE PRECEDENT...
... AS INDICATED IN THE TEXT OF THIS JUDICIAL DECISION, THE SUSPECT GANTA IGARASHI...

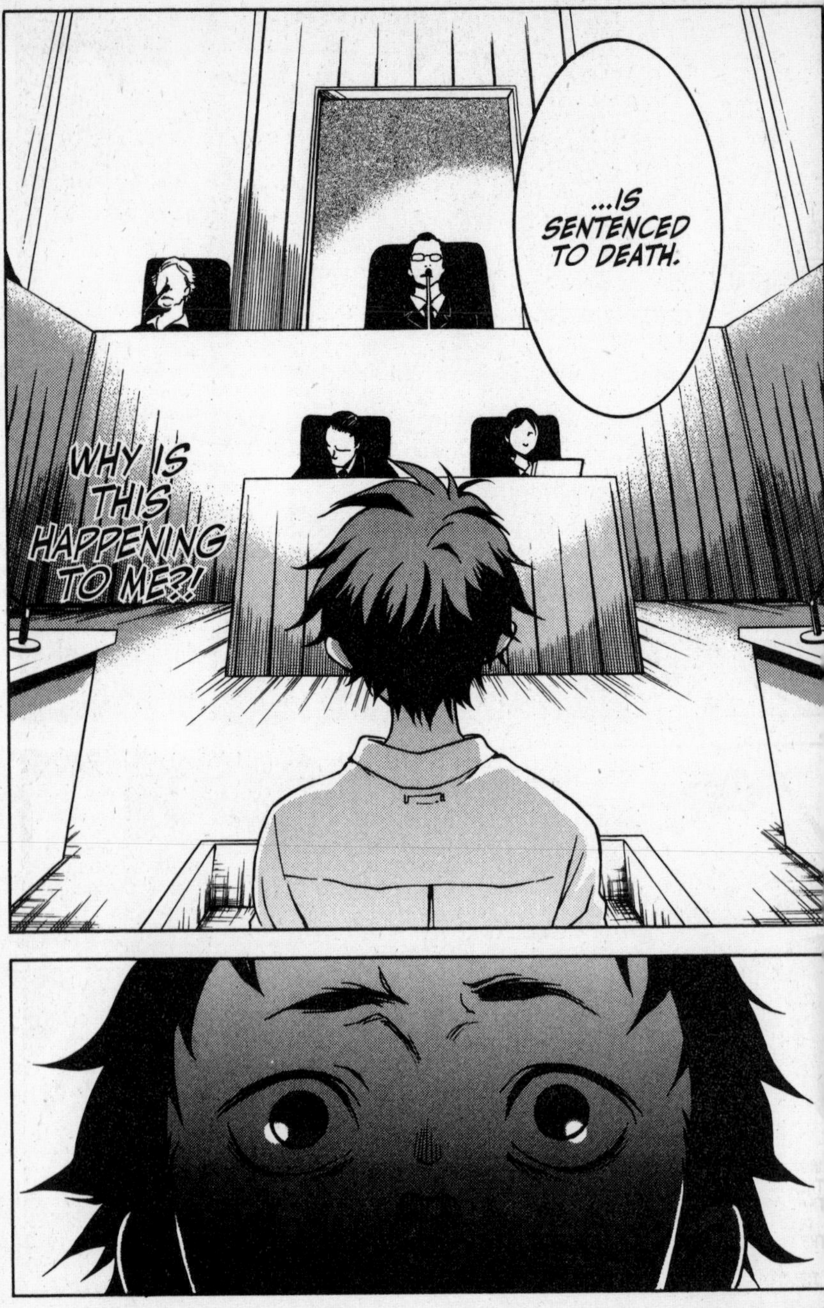
...IS SENTENCED TO DEATH.
WHY IS THIS HAPPENING TO ME?!

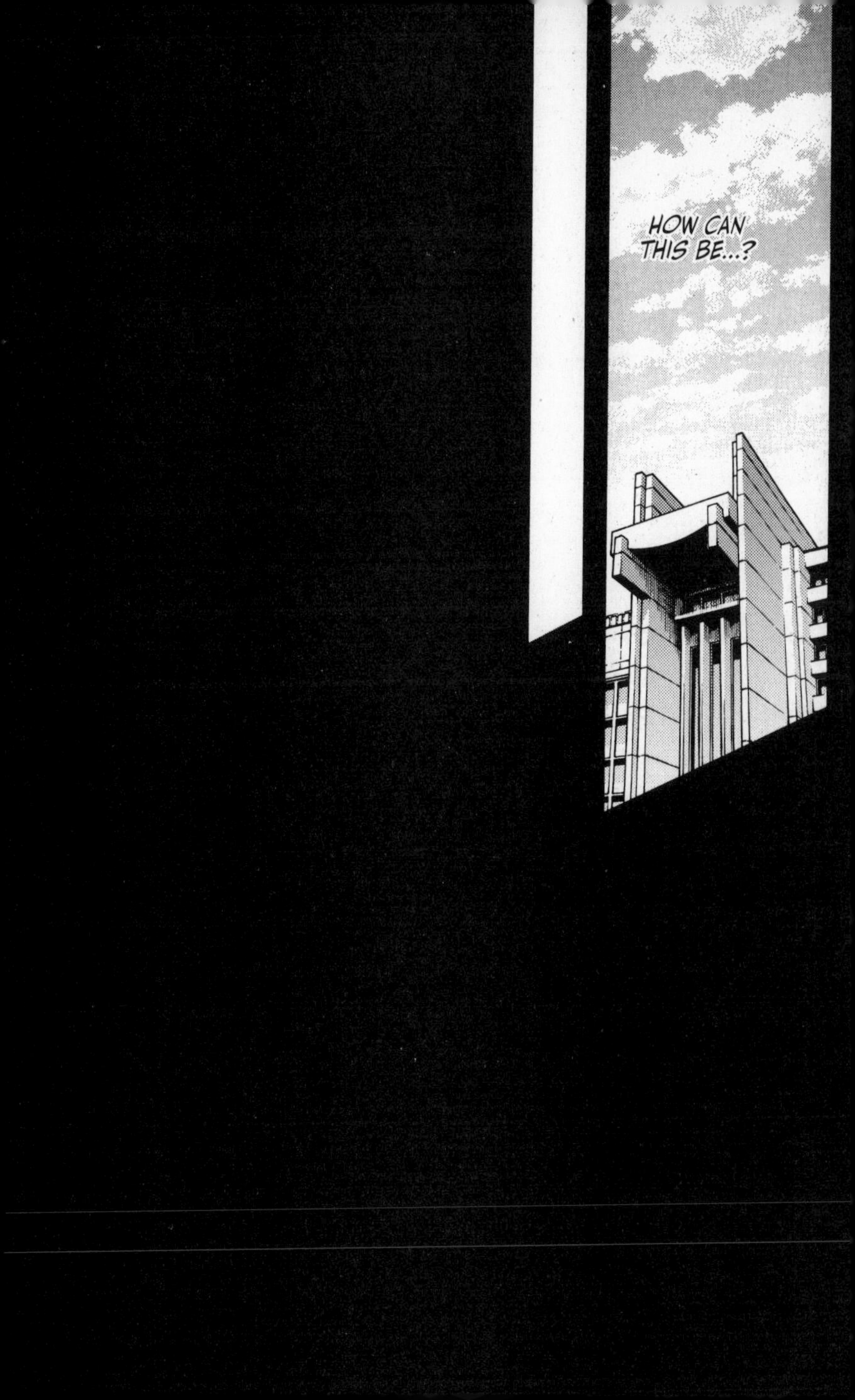
HOW CAN THIS BE...?

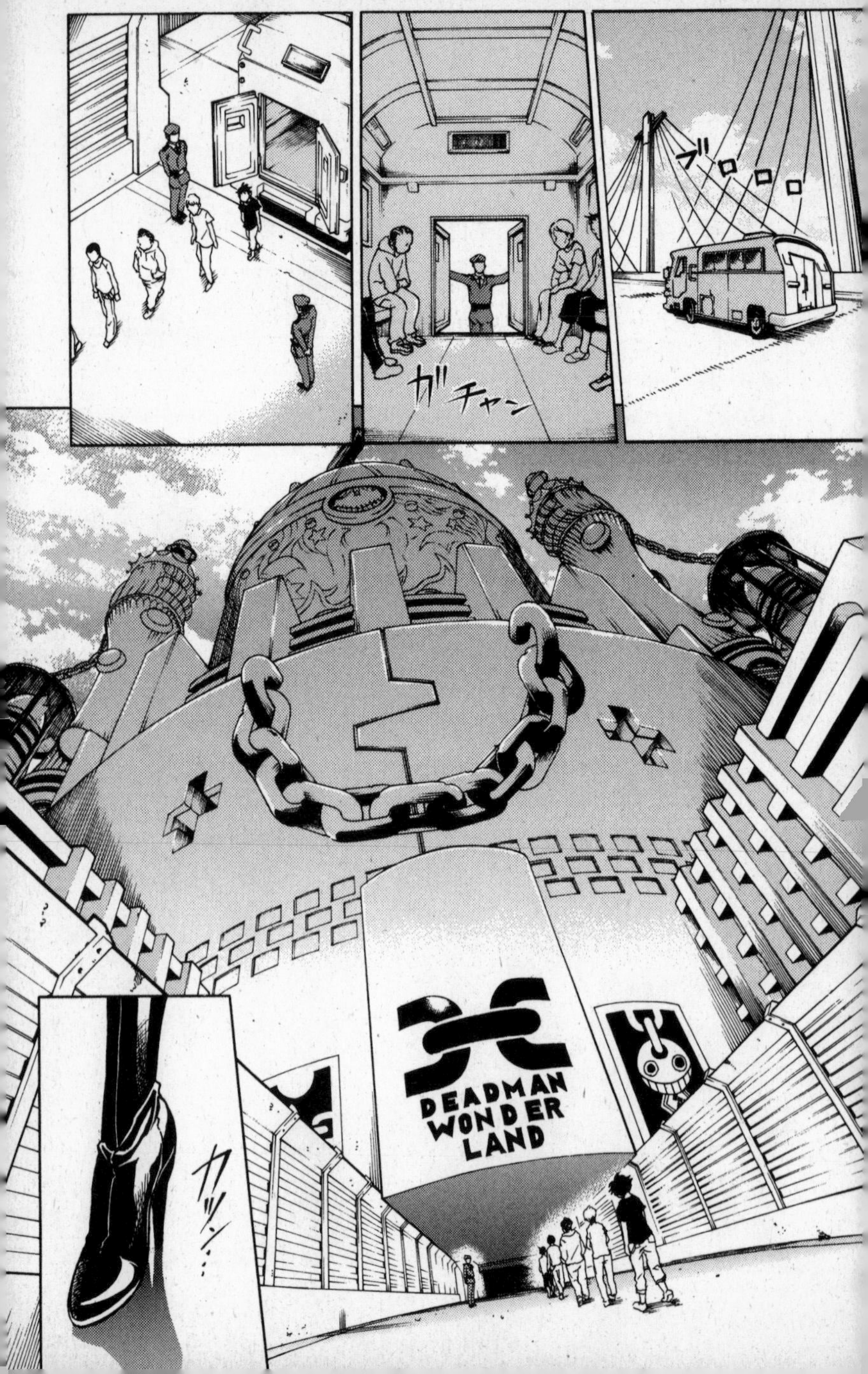
ブロロロロ
ガチャン
DEADMAN WONDER LAND
カツン…

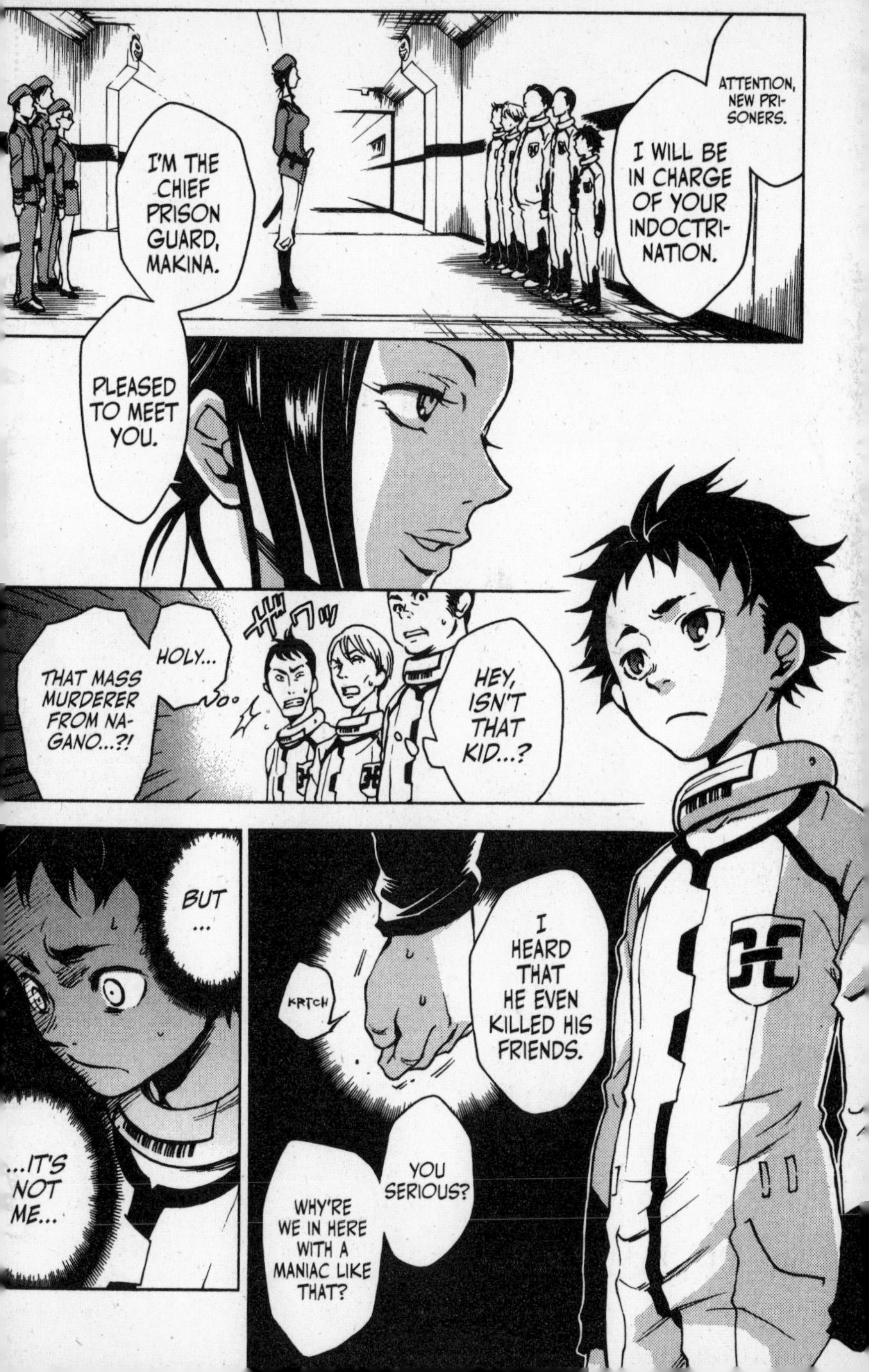
ATTENTION, NEW PRISONERS.
I WILL BE IN CHARGE OF YOUR INDOCTRINATION.
I'M THE CHIEF PRISON GUARD, MAKINA.
PLEASED TO MEET YOU.
ザワッ
HEY, ISN'T THAT KID...?
HOLY...
THAT MASS MURDERER FROM NAGANO...?!
I HEARD THAT HE EVEN KILLED HIS FRIENDS.
KRTCH
YOU SERIOUS?
WHY'RE WE IN HERE WITH A MANIAC LIKE THAT?
BUT ...
...IT'S NOT ME...

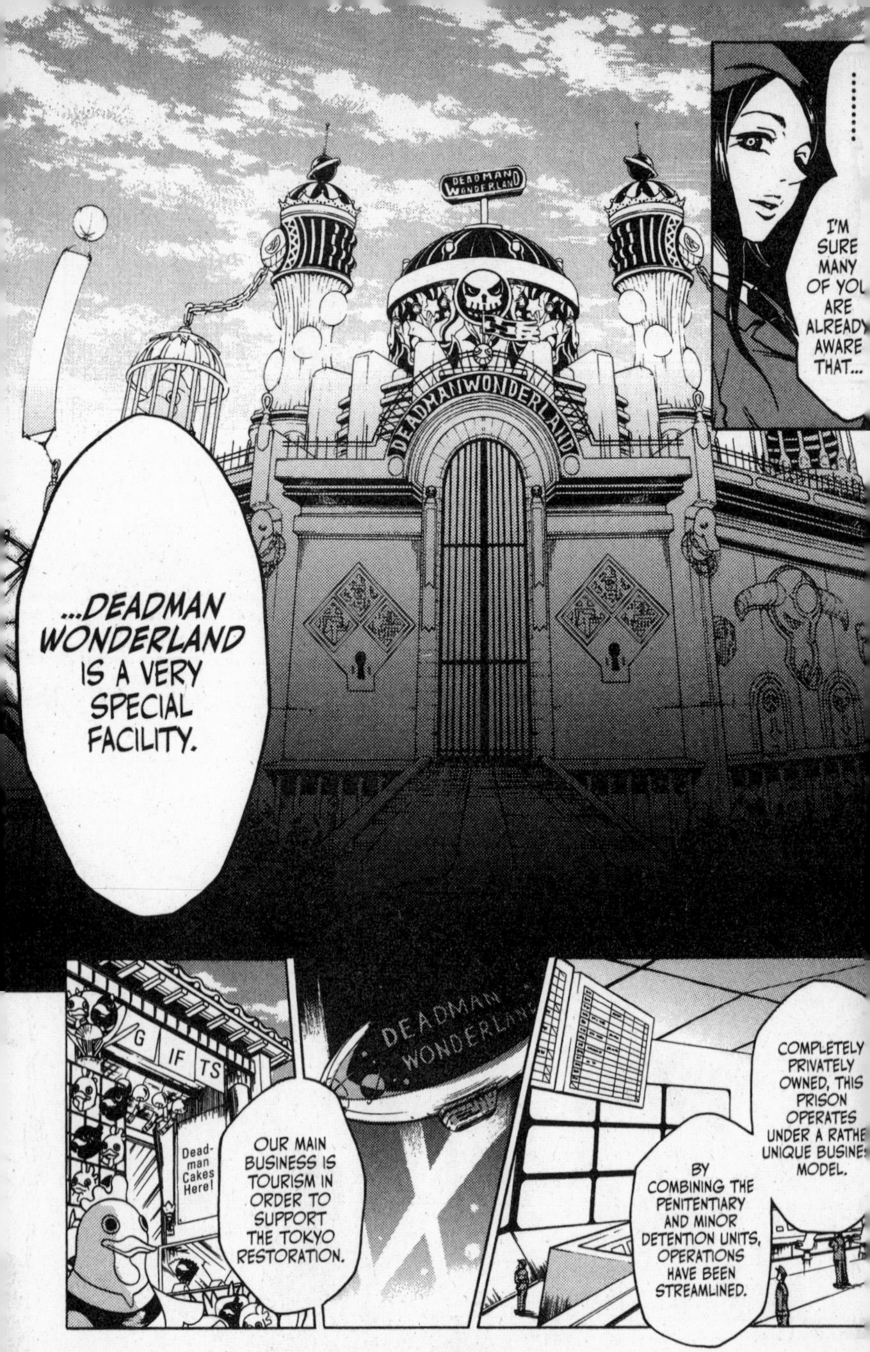
......
I'M SURE MANY OF YOU ARE ALREADY AWARE THAT...
DEADMAN WONDERLAND
DEADMAN WONDERLAND
...DEADMAN WONDERLAND IS A VERY SPECIAL FACILITY.
COMPLETELY PRIVATELY OWNED, THIS PRISON OPERATES UNDER A RATHE UNIQUE BUSINE MODEL.
BY COMBINING THE PENITENTIARY AND MINOR DETENTION UNITS, OPERATIONS HAVE BEEN STREAMLINED.
DEADMAN WONDERLAND
OUR MAIN BUSINESS IS TOURISM IN ORDER TO SUPPORT THE TOKYO RESTORATION.
G IF TS
Dead-man Cakes Here!

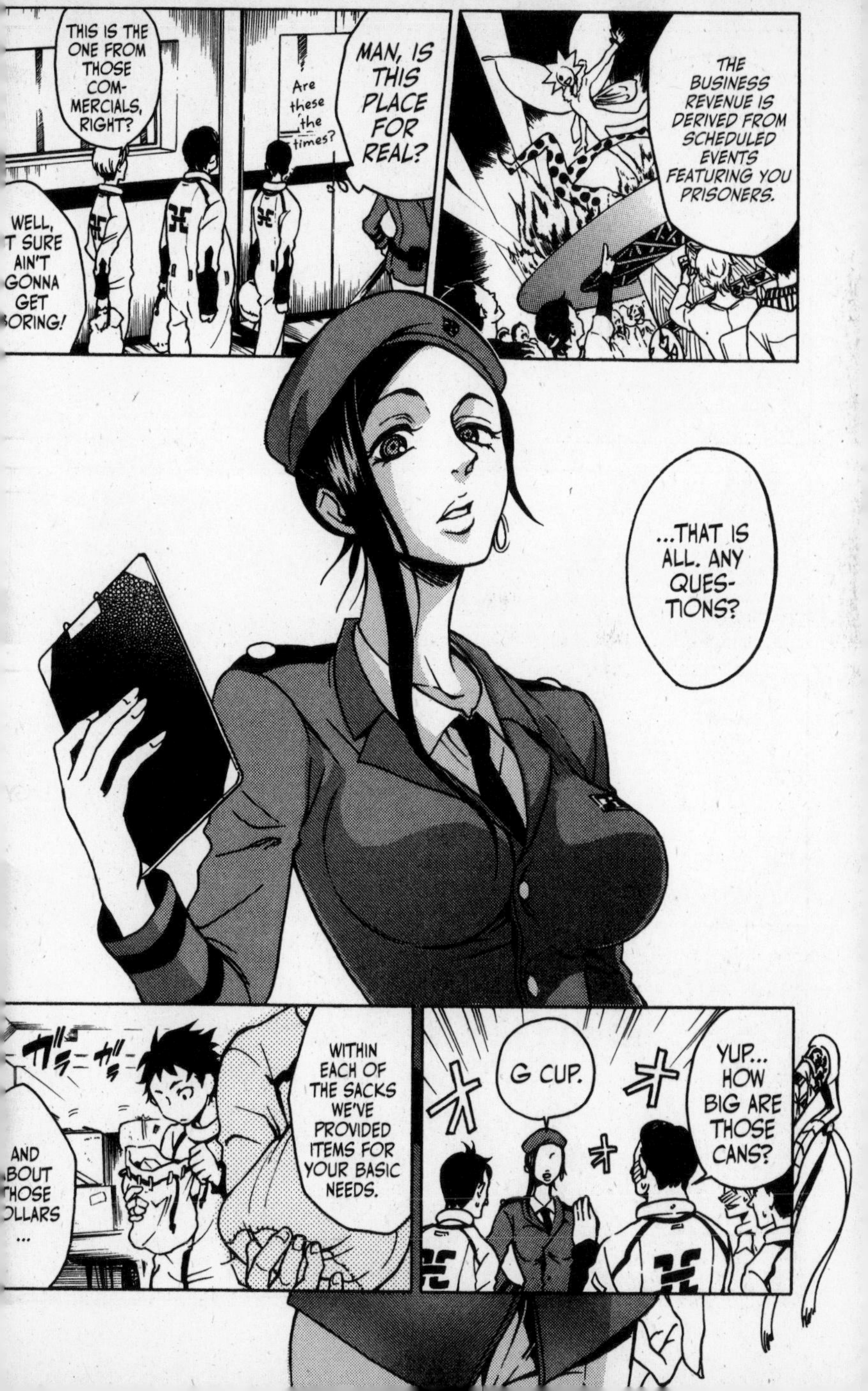
THE BUSINESS REVENUE IS DERIVED FROM SCHEDULED EVENTS FEATURING YOU PRISONERS.
MAN, IS THIS PLACE FOR REAL?
Are these the times?
THIS IS THE ONE FROM THOSE COM-MERCIALS, RIGHT?
WELL, T SURE AIN'T GONNA GET ORING!
...THAT IS ALL. ANY QUES-TIONS?
YUP... HOW BIG ARE THOSE CANS?
G CUP.
WITHIN EACH OF THE SACKS WE'VE PROVIDED ITEMS FOR YOUR BASIC NEEDS.
AND BOUT THOSE OLLARS ...

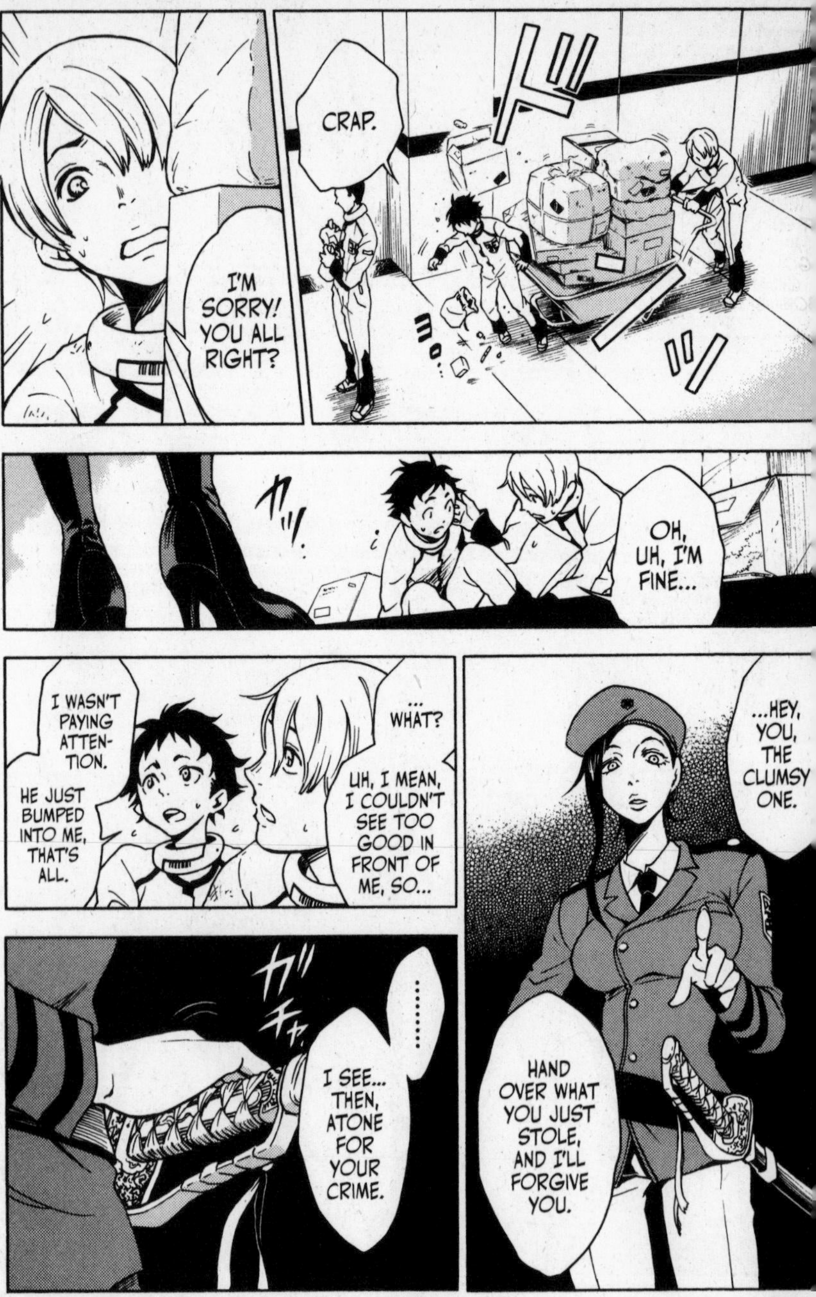
CRAP.
I'M SORRY! YOU ALL RIGHT?
OH, UH, I'M FINE...
...HEY, YOU, THE CLUMSY ONE.
HAND OVER WHAT YOU JUST STOLE, AND I'LL FORGIVE YOU.
... WHAT?
UH, I MEAN, I COULDN'T SEE TOO GOOD IN FRONT OF ME, SO...
I WASN'T PAYING ATTEN-TION.
HE JUST BUMPED INTO ME, THAT'S ALL.
......
I SEE... THEN, ATONE FOR YOUR CRIME.

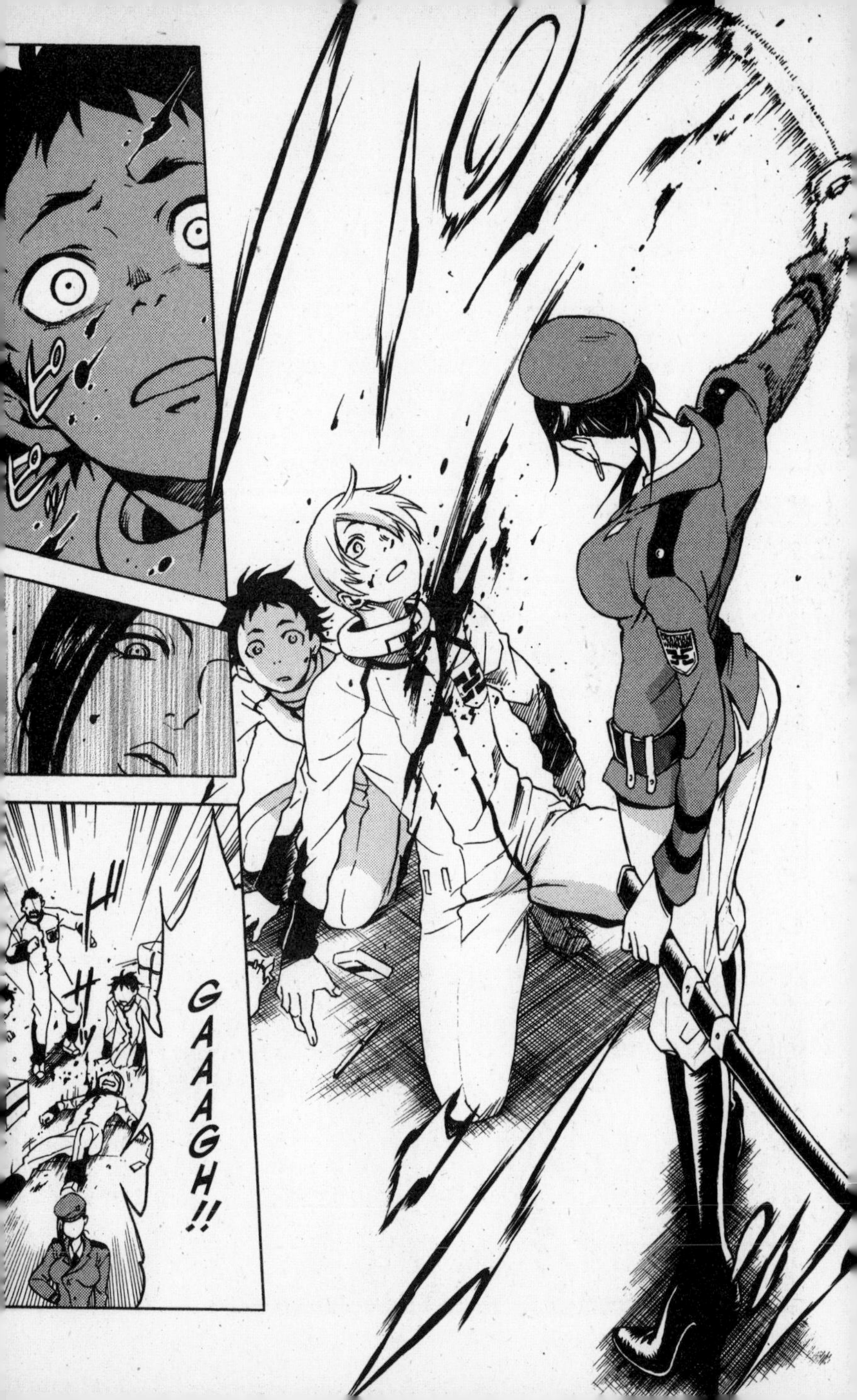
GAAAGH!!

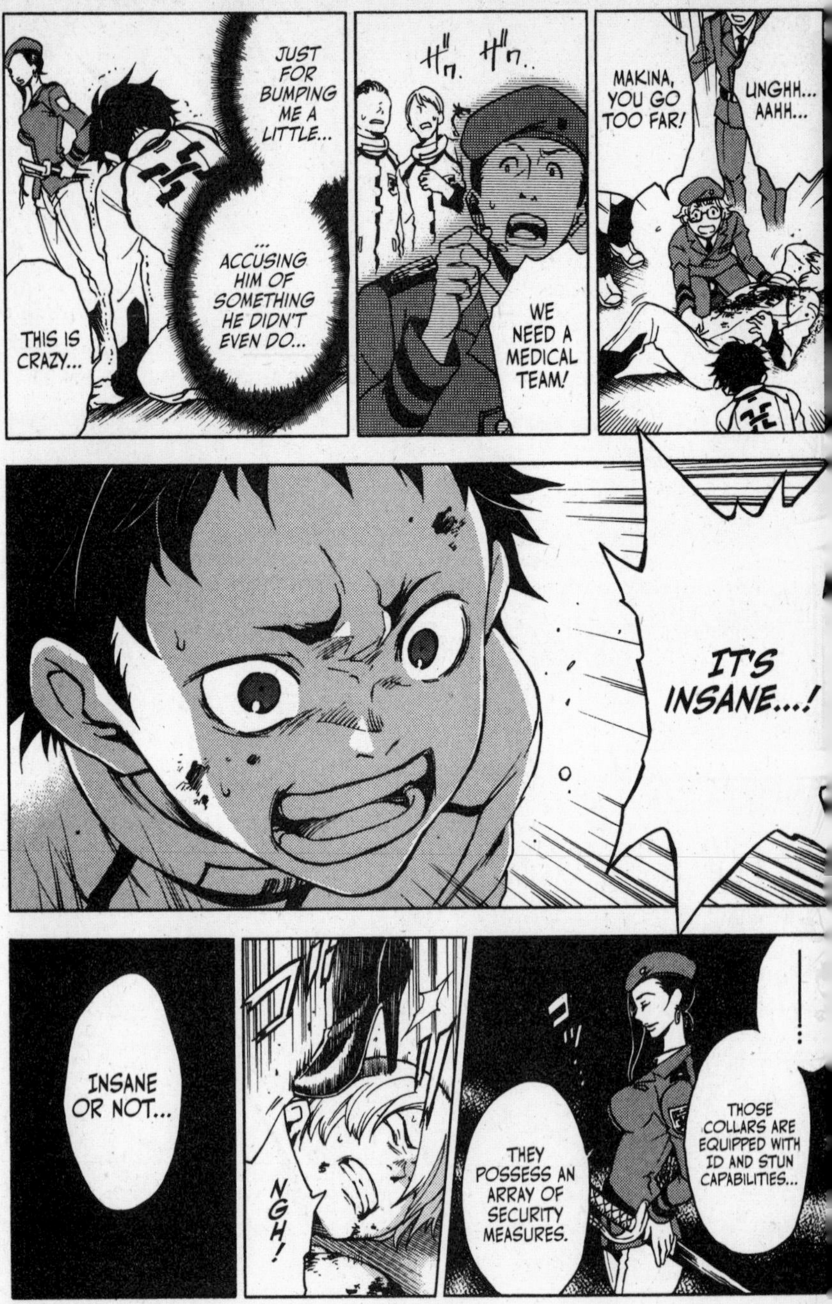
UNGHH... AAHH...
MAKINA, YOU GO TOO FAR!
ザワ ザワ
WE NEED A MEDICAL TEAM!
JUST FOR BUMPING ME A LITTLE...
... ACCUSING HIM OF SOMETHING HE DIDN'T EVEN DO...
THIS IS CRAZY...
IT'S INSANE...!
THOSE COLLARS ARE EQUIPPED WITH ID AND STUN CAPABILITIES...
THEY POSSESS AN ARRAY OF SECURITY MEASURES.
NGH!
INSANE OR NOT...

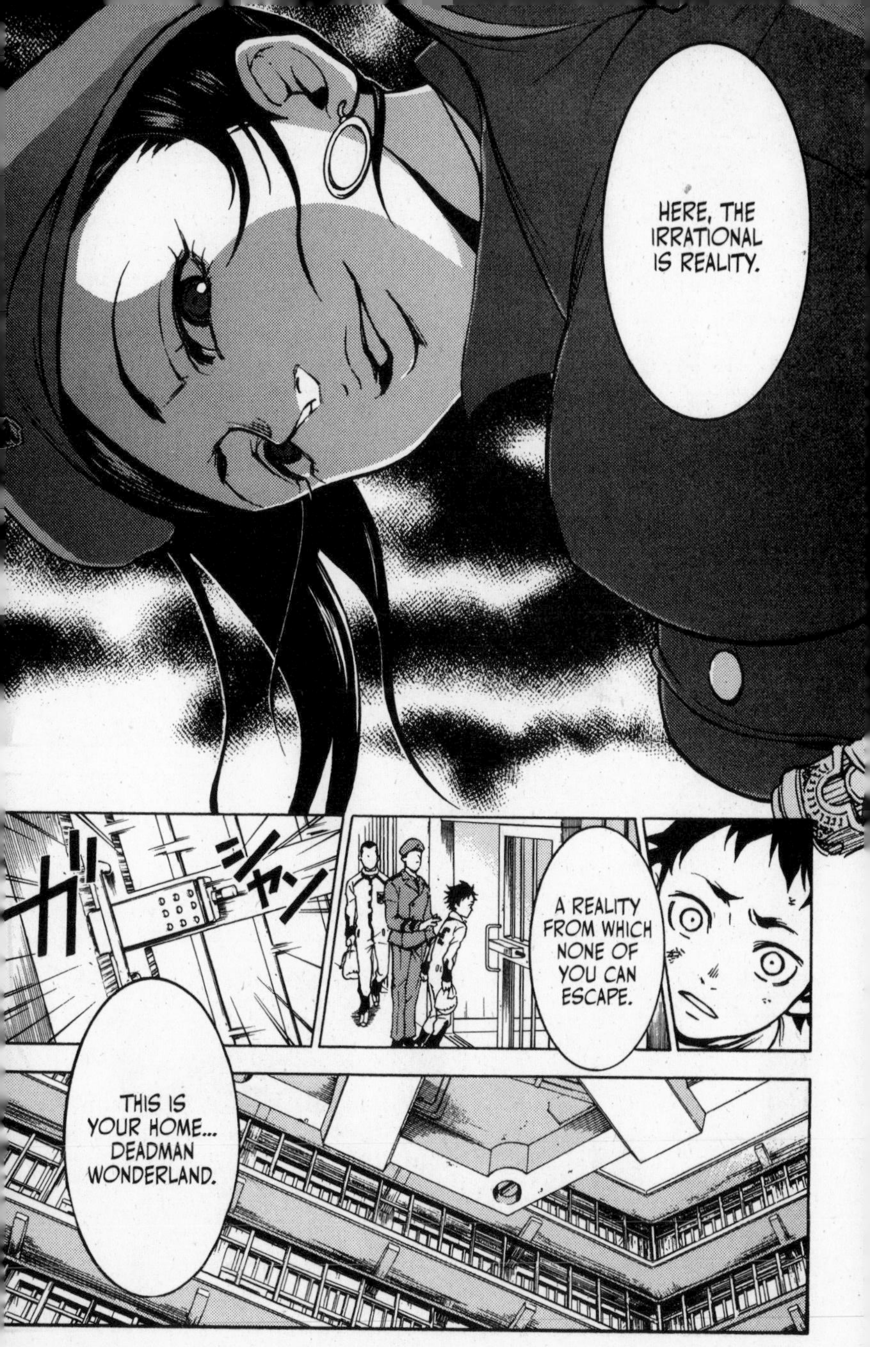
HERE, THE IRRATIONAL IS REALITY.
A REALITY FROM WHICH NONE OF YOU CAN ESCAPE.
ガシャン
THIS IS YOUR HOME... DEADMAN WONDERLAND.

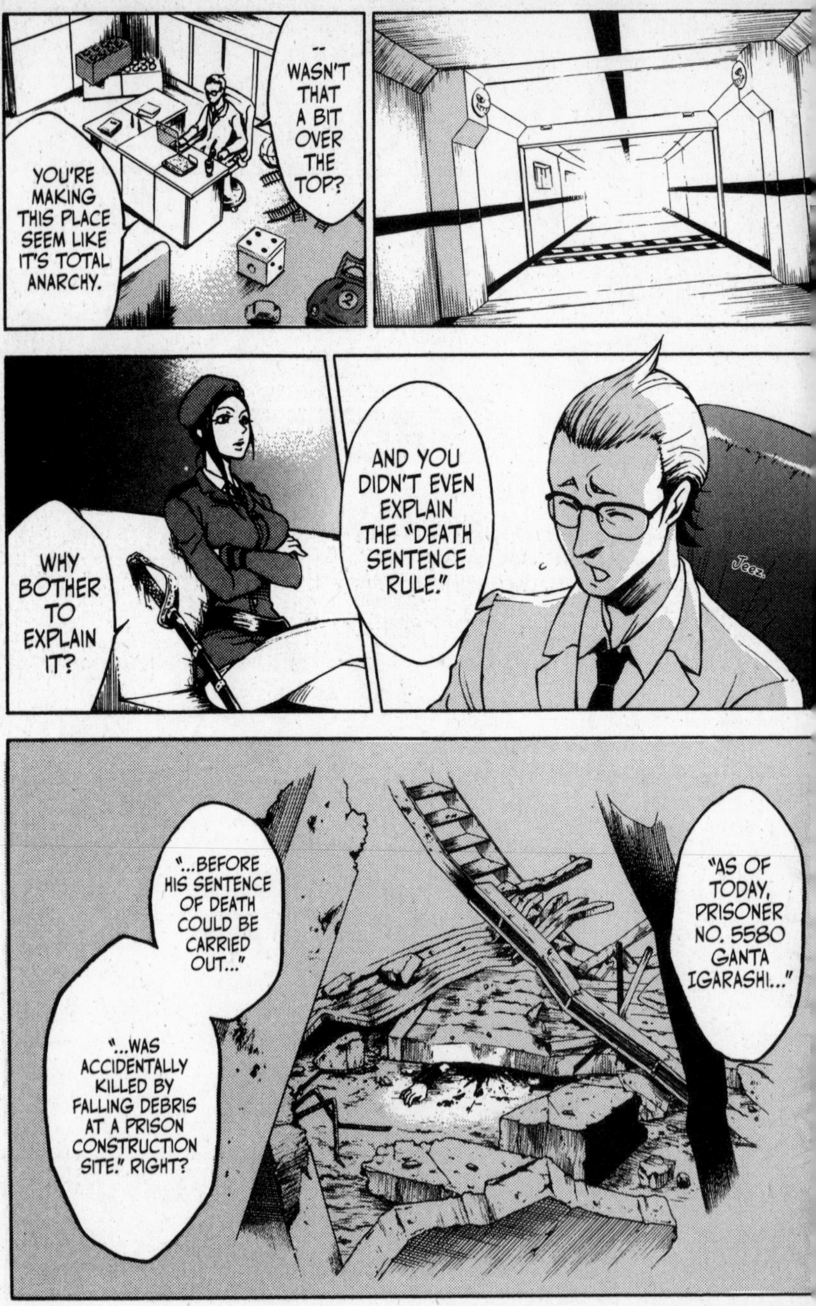
-- WASN'T THAT A BIT OVER THE TOP?
YOU'RE MAKING THIS PLACE SEEM LIKE IT'S TOTAL ANARCHY.
AND YOU DIDN'T EVEN EXPLAIN THE "DEATH SENTENCE RULE."
Jeez.
WHY BOTHER TO EXPLAIN IT?
"AS OF TODAY, PRISONER NO. 5580 GANTA IGARASHI..."
"...BEFORE HIS SENTENCE OF DEATH COULD BE CARRIED OUT..."
"...WAS ACCIDENTALLY KILLED BY FALLING DEBRIS AT A PRISON CONSTRUCTION SITE." RIGHT?

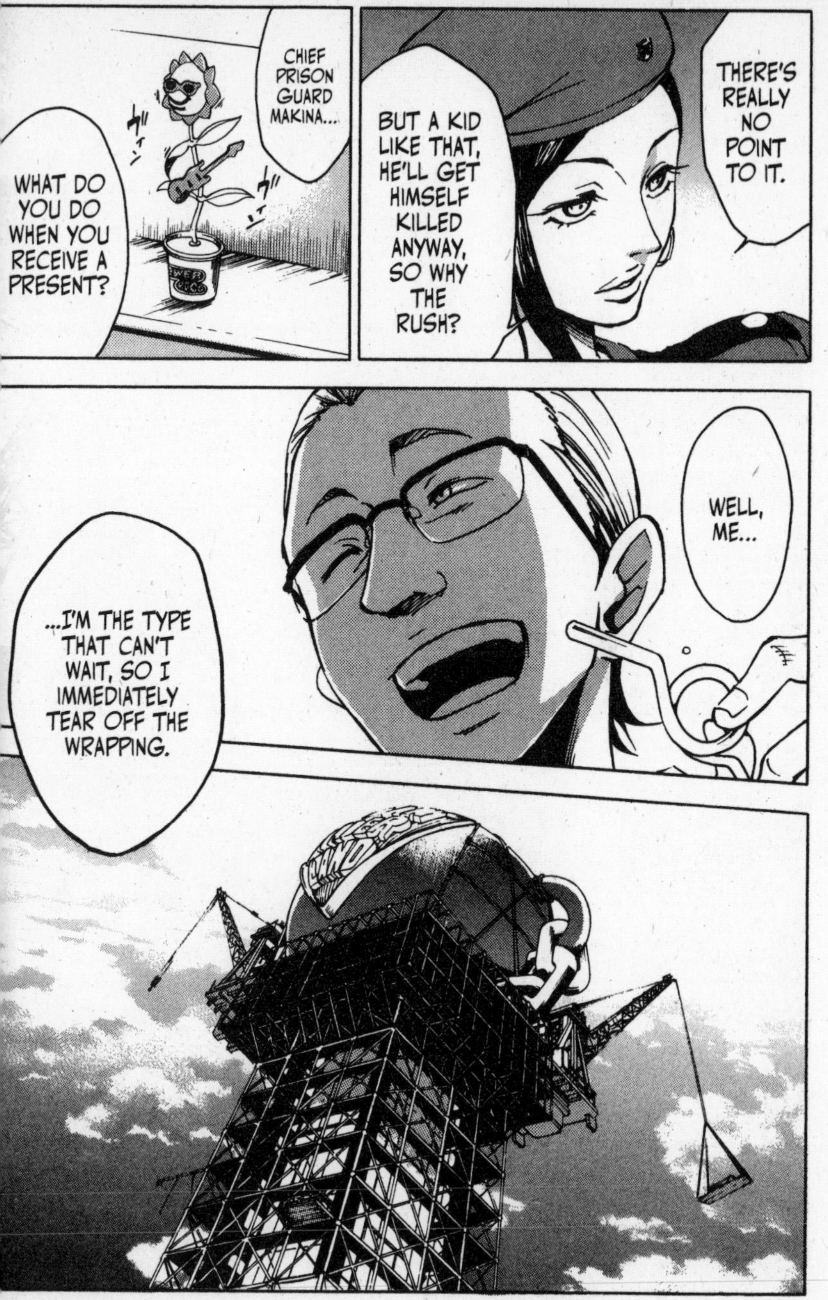
THERE'S REALLY NO POINT TO IT.
BUT A KID LIKE THAT, HE'LL GET HIMSELF KILLED ANYWAY, SO WHY THE RUSH?
CHIEF PRISON GUARD MAKINA...
WHAT DO YOU DO WHEN YOU RECEIVE A PRESENT?
WELL, ME...
...I'M THE TYPE THAT CAN'T WAIT, SO I IMMEDIATELY TEAR OFF THE WRAPPING.

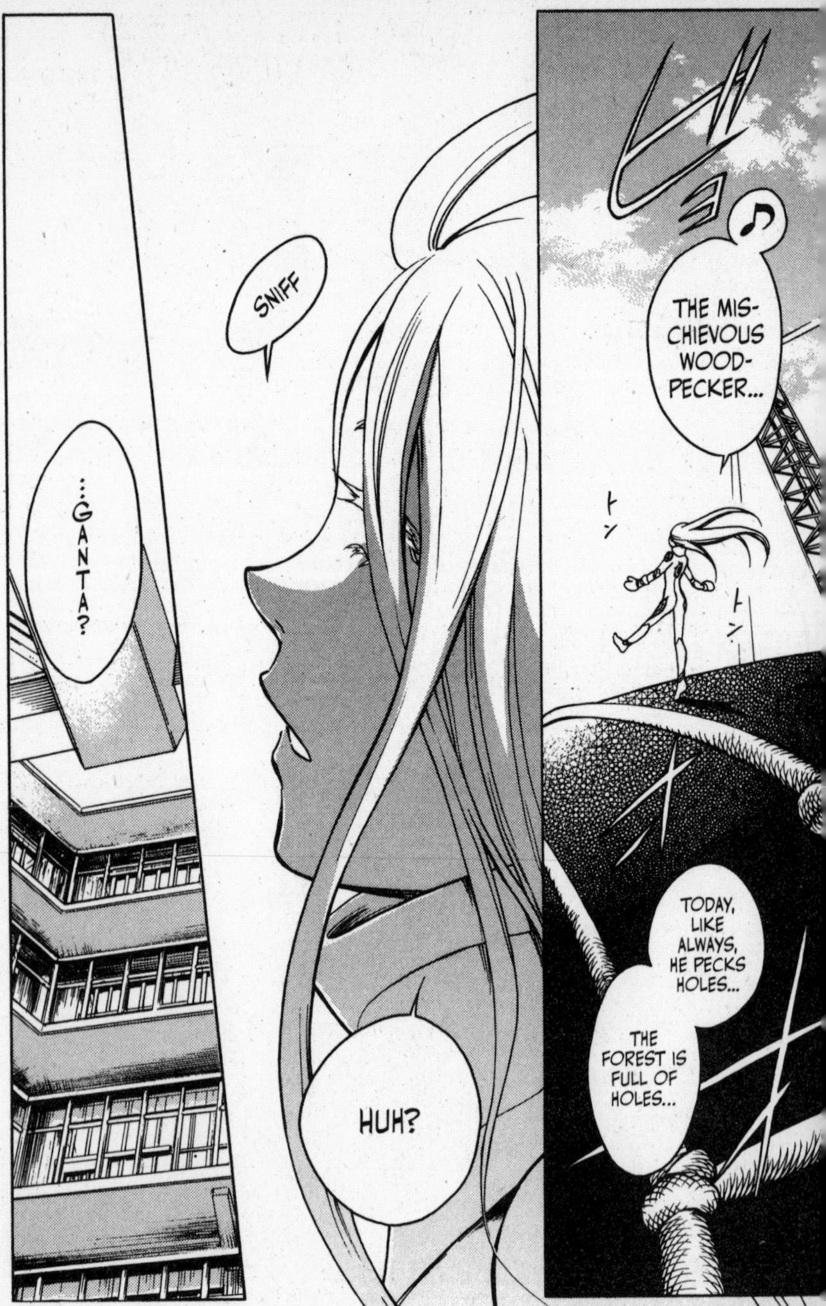
THE MIS-
CHIEVOUS
WOOD-
PECKER...
TODAY, LIKE ALWAYS, HE PECKS HOLES...
THE FOREST IS FULL OF HOLES...
SNIFF
HUH?
...GANTA?

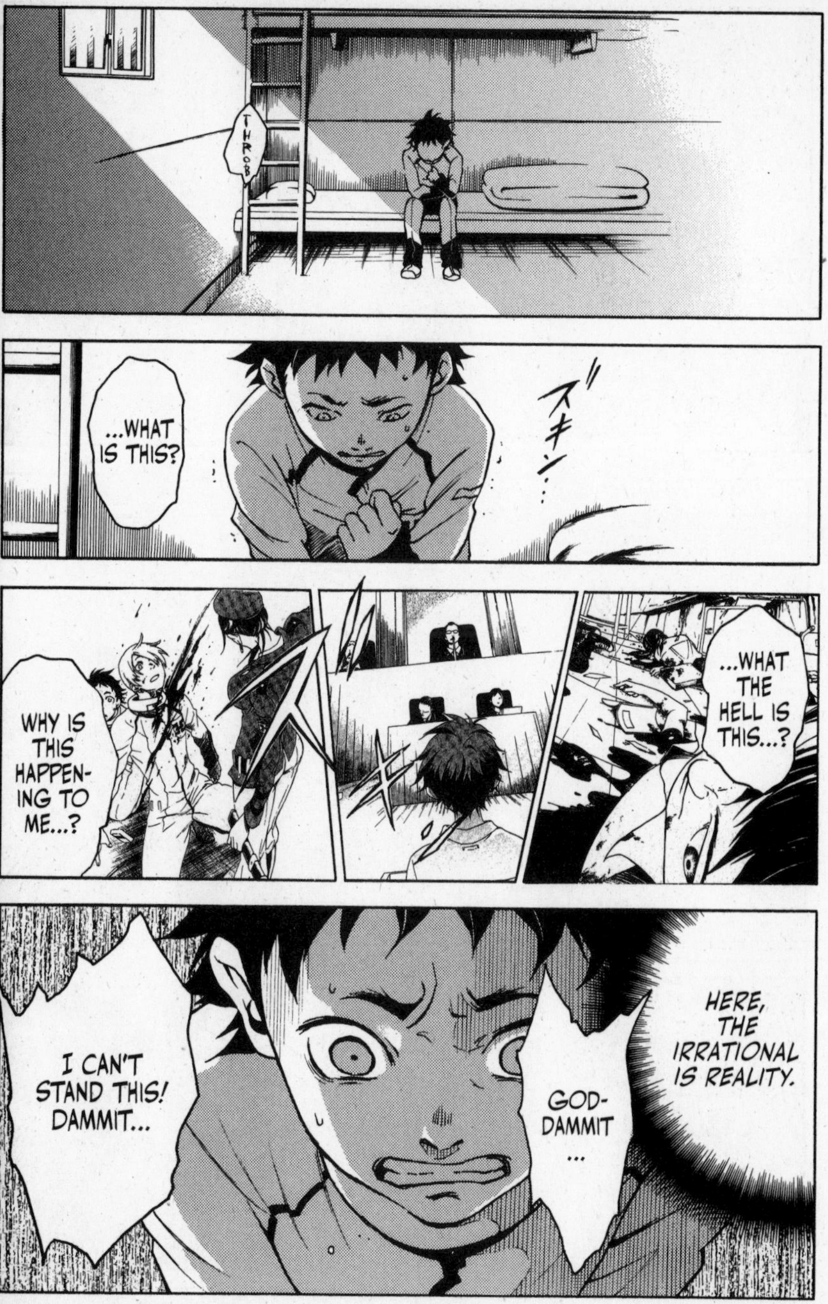
THROB
ズキン
...WHAT IS THIS?
...WHAT THE HELL IS THIS...?
WHY IS THIS HAPPENING TO ME...?
HERE, THE IRRATIONAL IS REALITY.
GOD-DAMMIT ...
I CAN'T STAND THIS! DAMMIT...

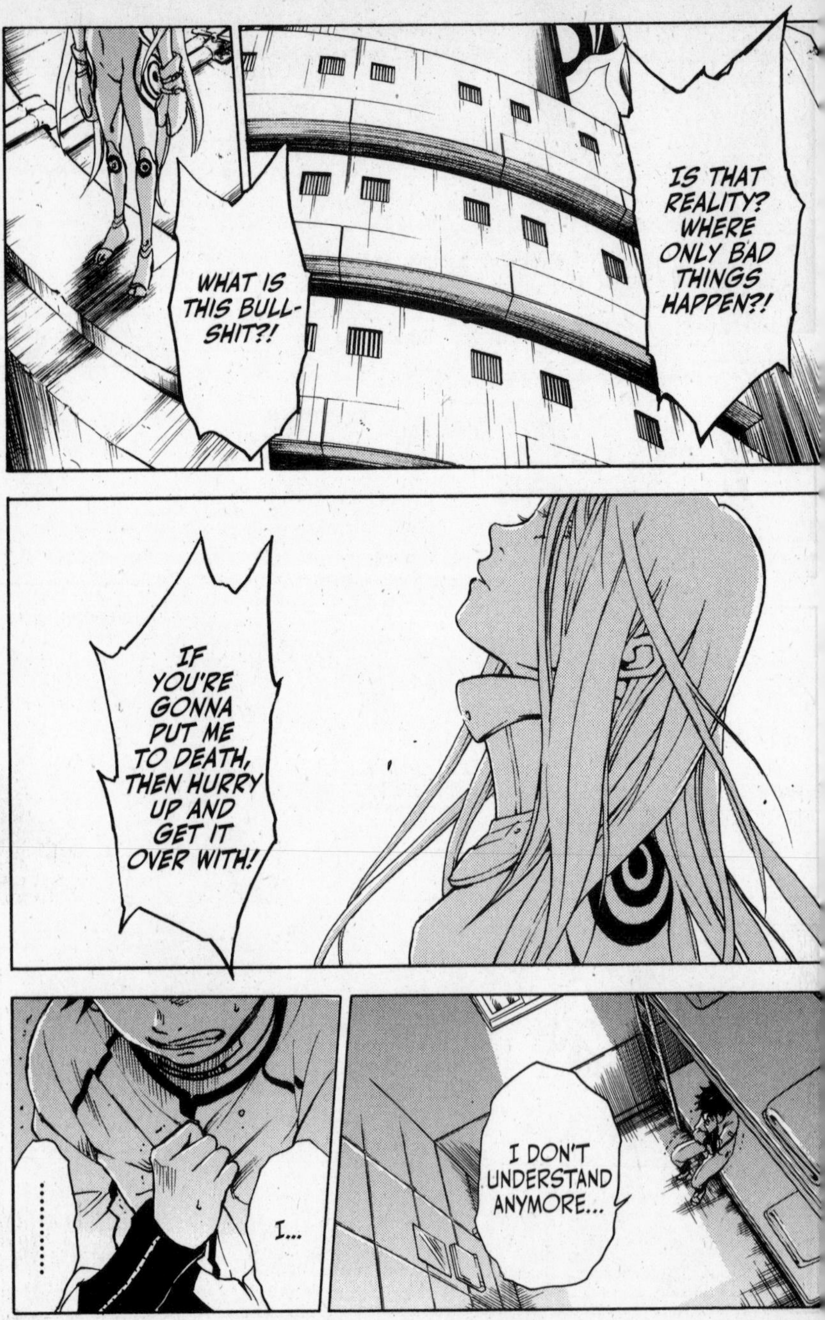
IS THAT REALITY? WHERE ONLY BAD THINGS HAPPEN?!
WHAT IS THIS BULL-SHIT?!
IF YOU'RE GONNA PUT ME TO DEATH, THEN HURRY UP AND GET IT OVER WITH!
I DON'T UNDERSTAND ANYMORE...
I...
....

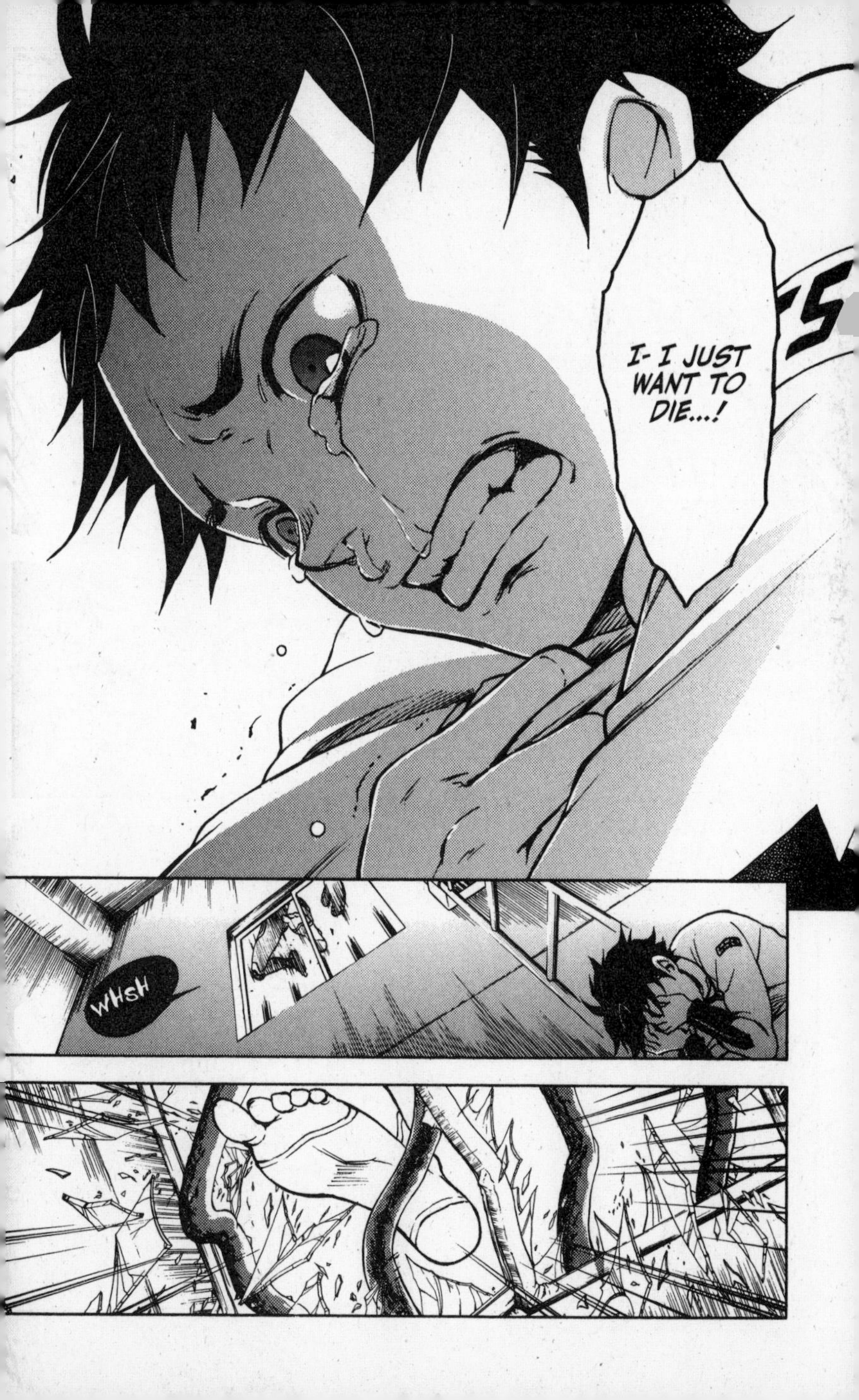
I- I JUST WANT TO DIE...!
WHSH

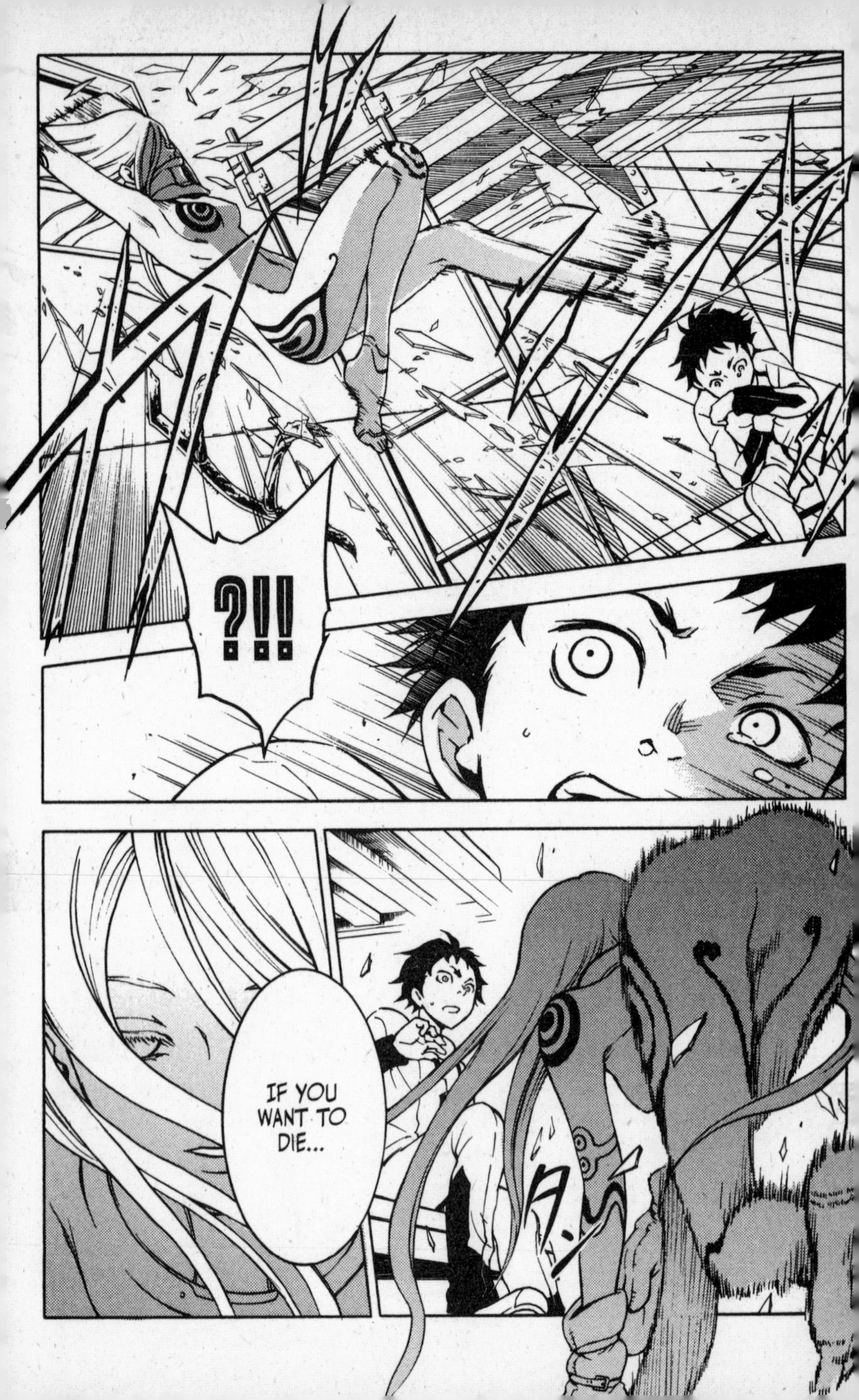
?!!
IF YOU WANT TO DIE...

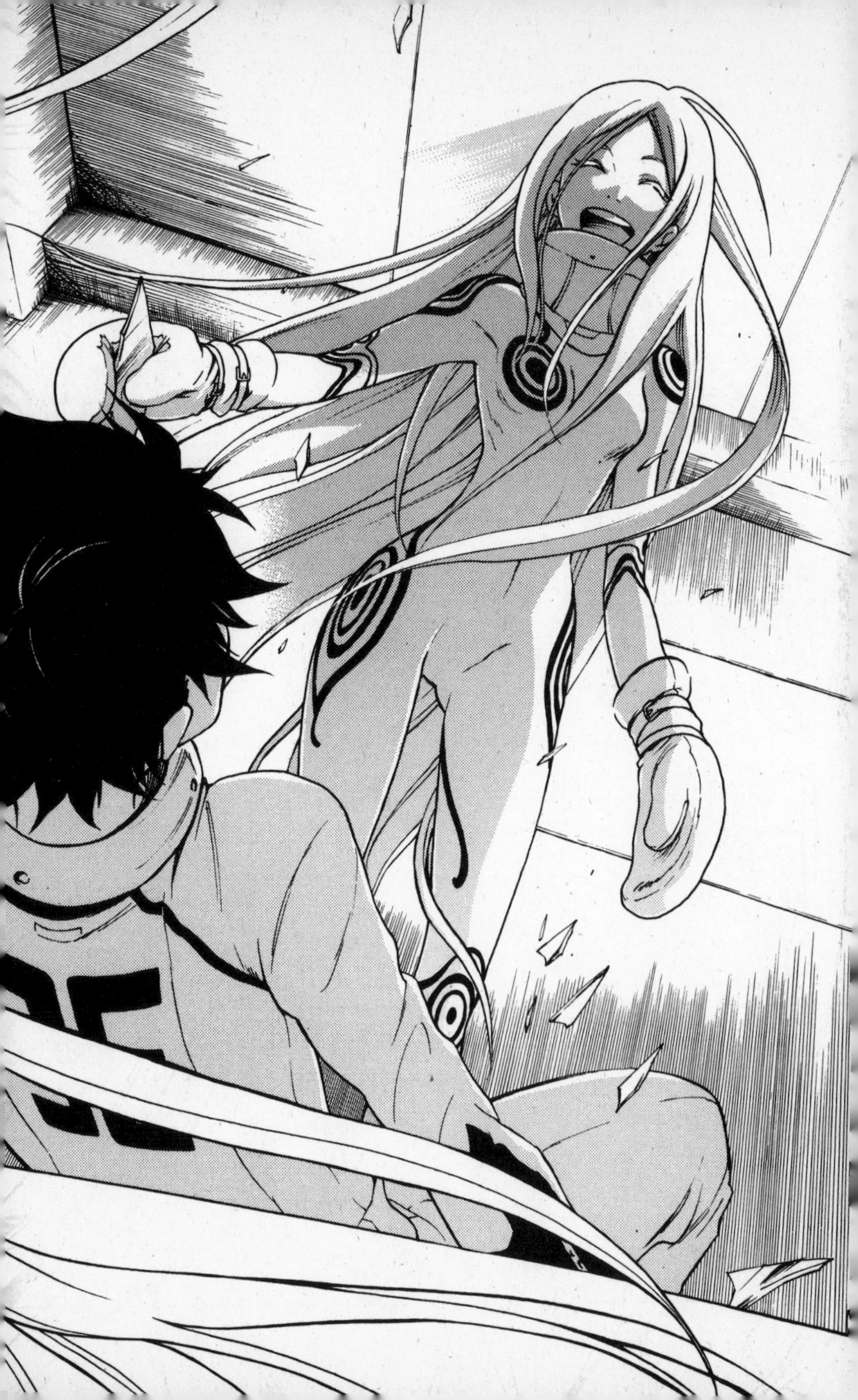

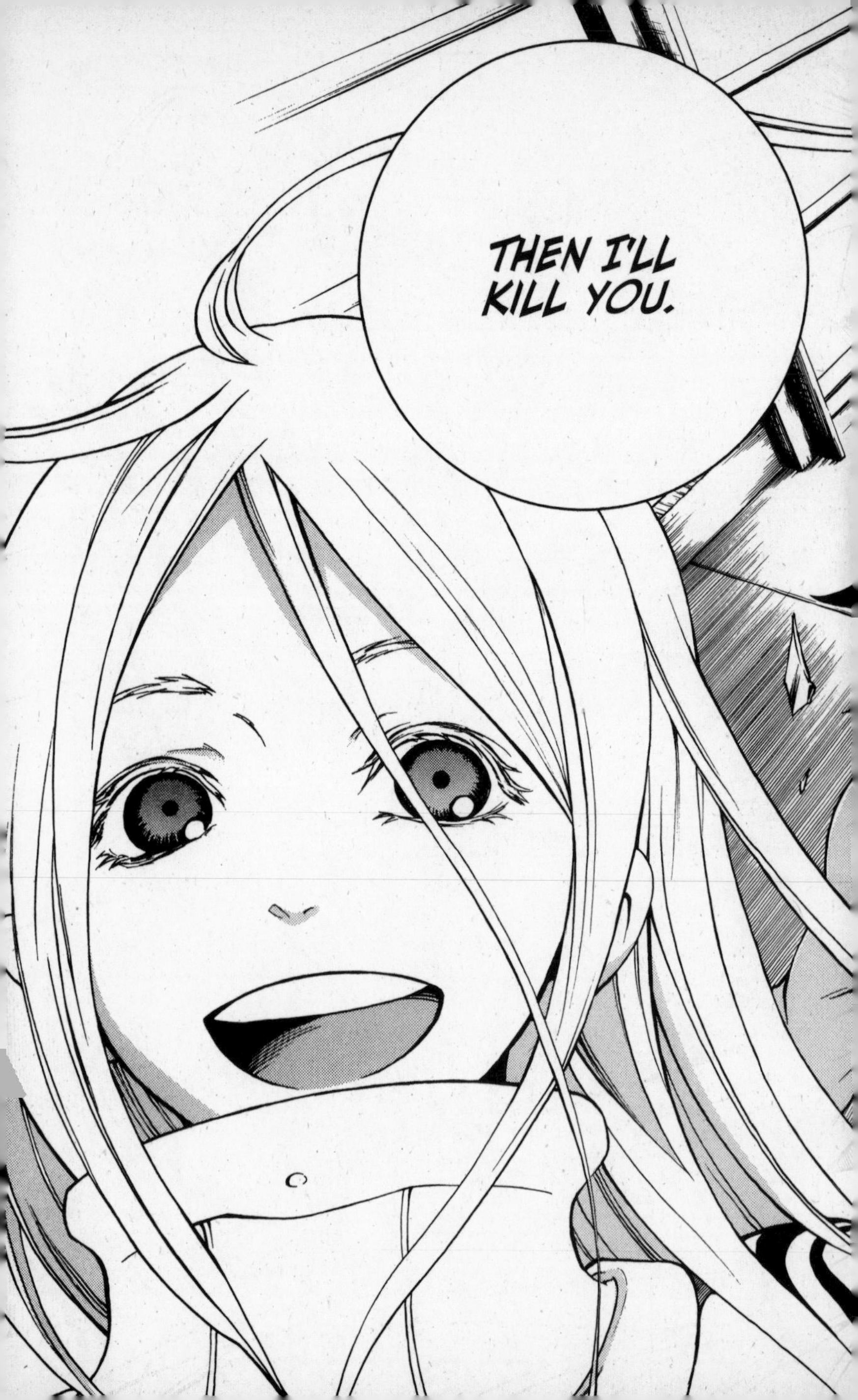
THEN I'LL KILL YOU.

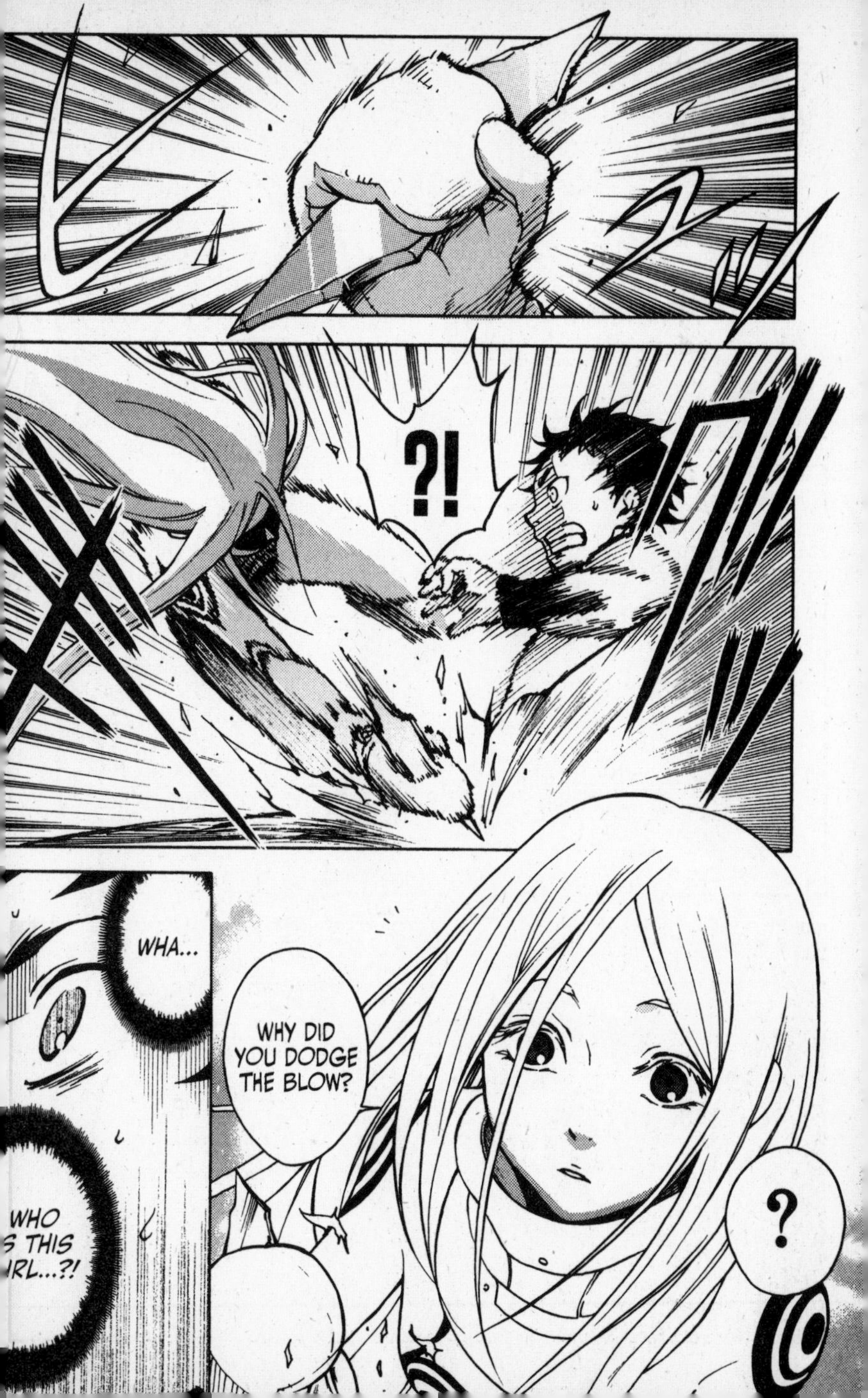
?!
WHY DID YOU DODGE THE BLOW?
?
WHA...
WHO S THIS IRL...?!

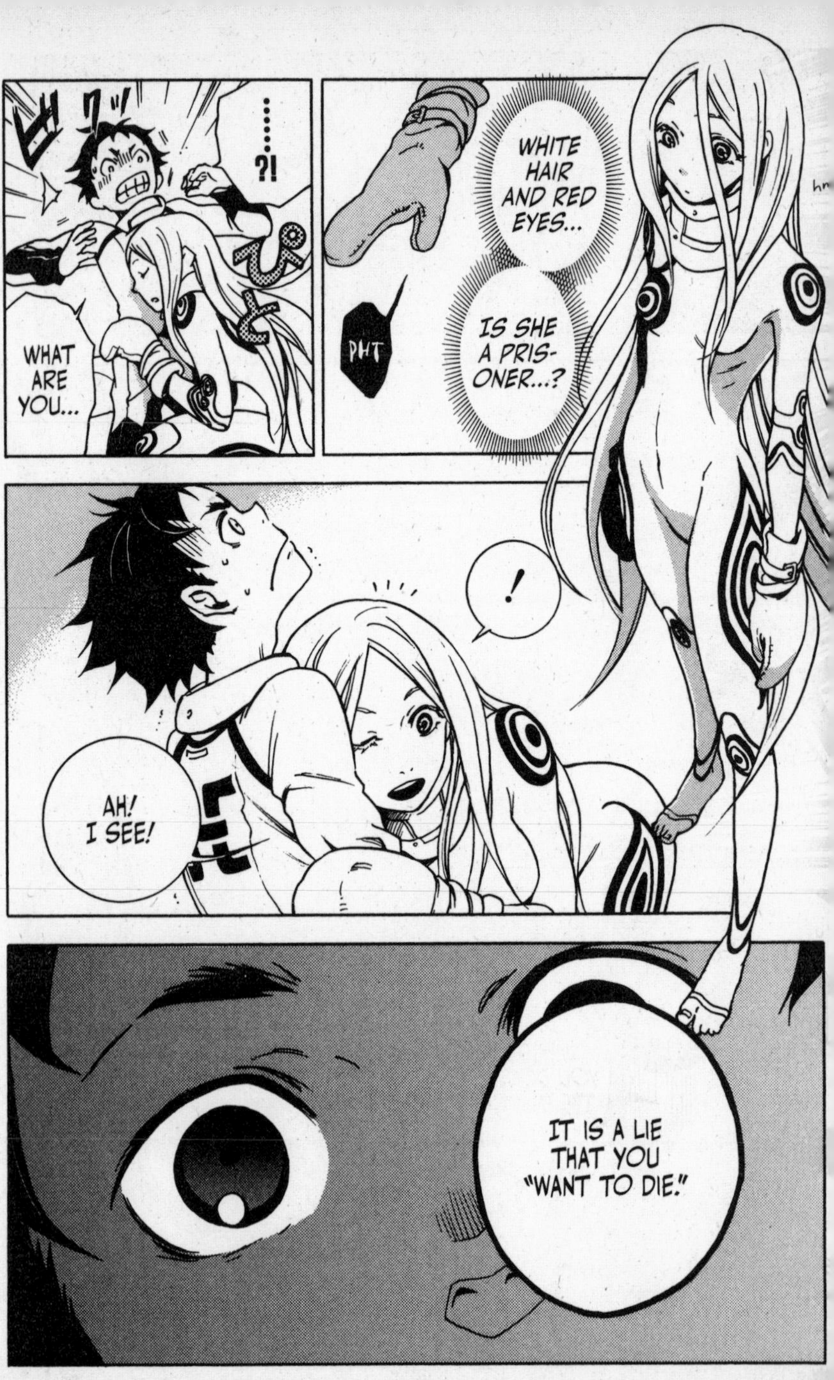
WHITE HAIR AND RED EYES...
IS SHE A PRISONER...?
PHT
......?!
WHAT ARE YOU...
!
AH! I SEE!
IT IS A LIE THAT YOU "WANT TO DIE."

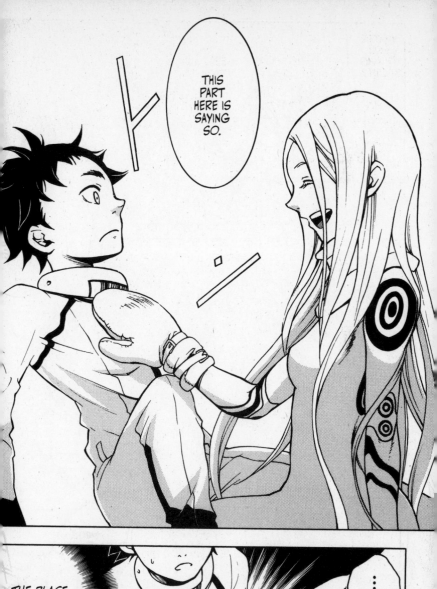

THIS PART HERE IS SAYING SO.

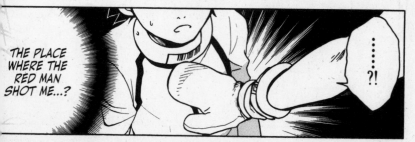

THE PLACE WHERE THE RED MAN SHOT ME...?

⁚⁚⁚⁚⁚
?!

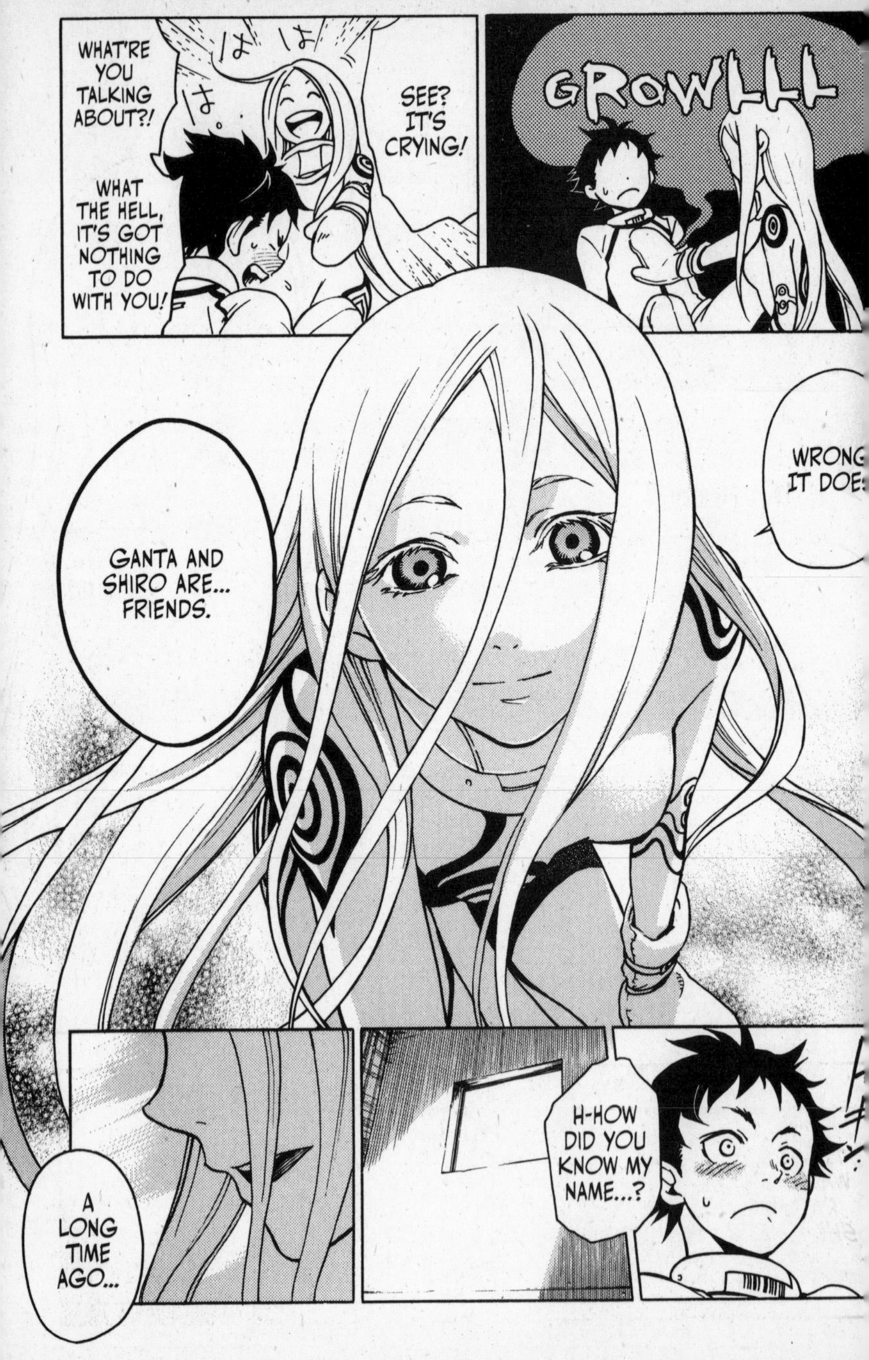
GROWLLL
SEE? IT'S CRYING!
はは
は。
WHAT'RE YOU TALKING ABOUT?!
WHAT THE HELL, IT'S GOT NOTHING TO DO WITH YOU!
WRONG IT DOE
GANTA AND SHIRO ARE... FRIENDS.
H-HOW DID YOU KNOW MY NAME...?
A LONG TIME AGO...

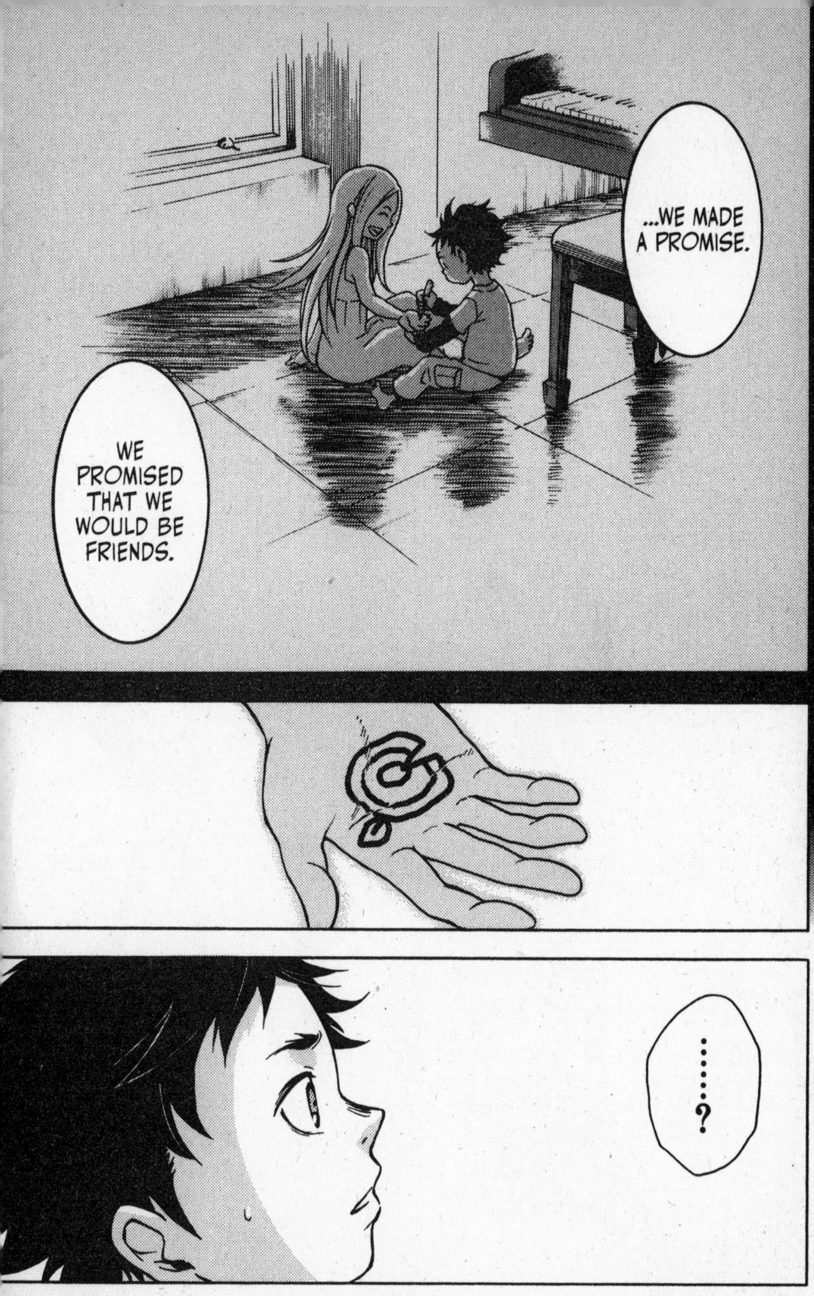
...WE MADE A PROMISE.
WE PROMISED THAT WE WOULD BE FRIENDS.
......?

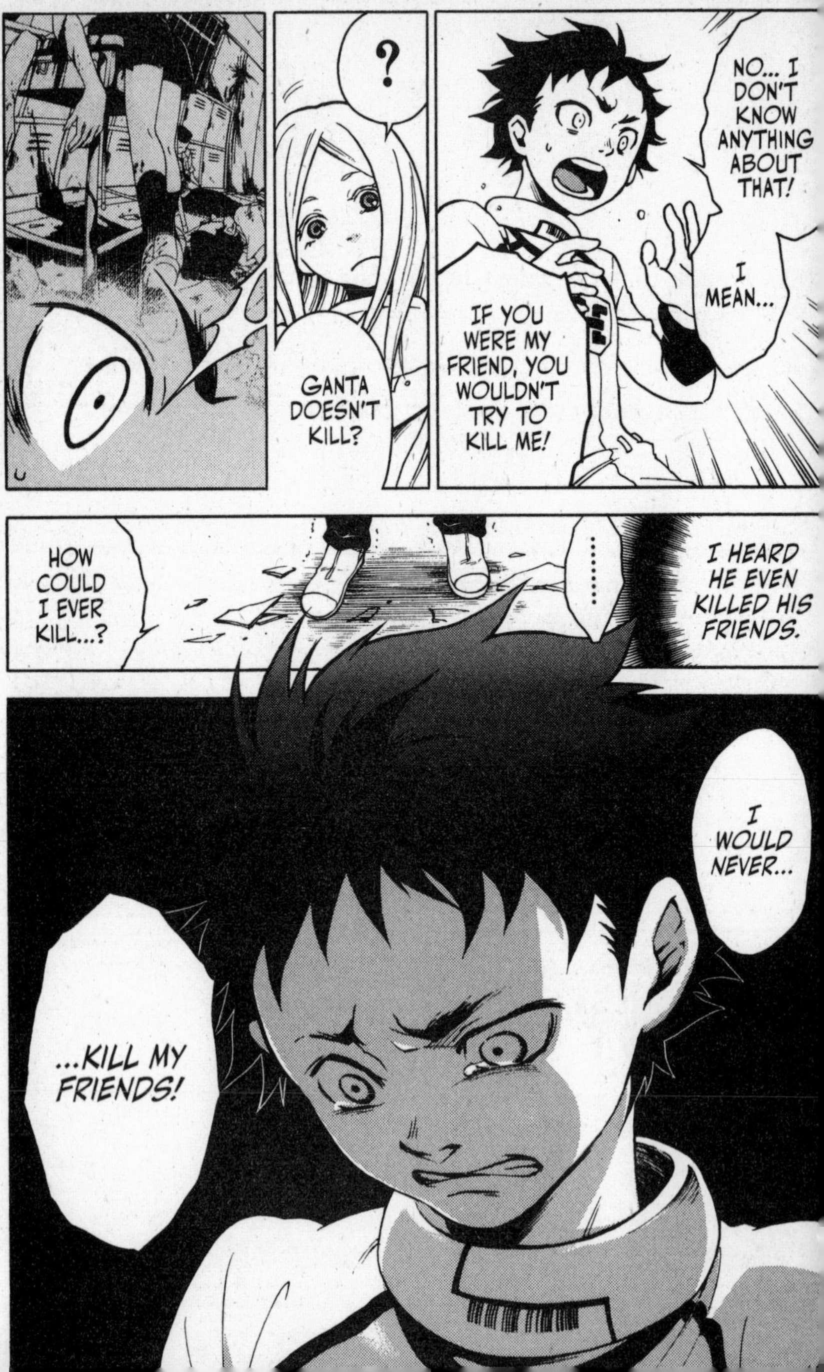
NO... I DON'T KNOW ANYTHING ABOUT THAT!
I MEAN...
IF YOU WERE MY FRIEND, YOU WOULDN'T TRY TO KILL ME!
?
GANTA DOESN'T KILL?
I HEARD HE EVEN KILLED HIS FRIENDS.
......
HOW COULD I EVER KILL...?
I WOULD NEVER...
...KILL MY FRIENDS!

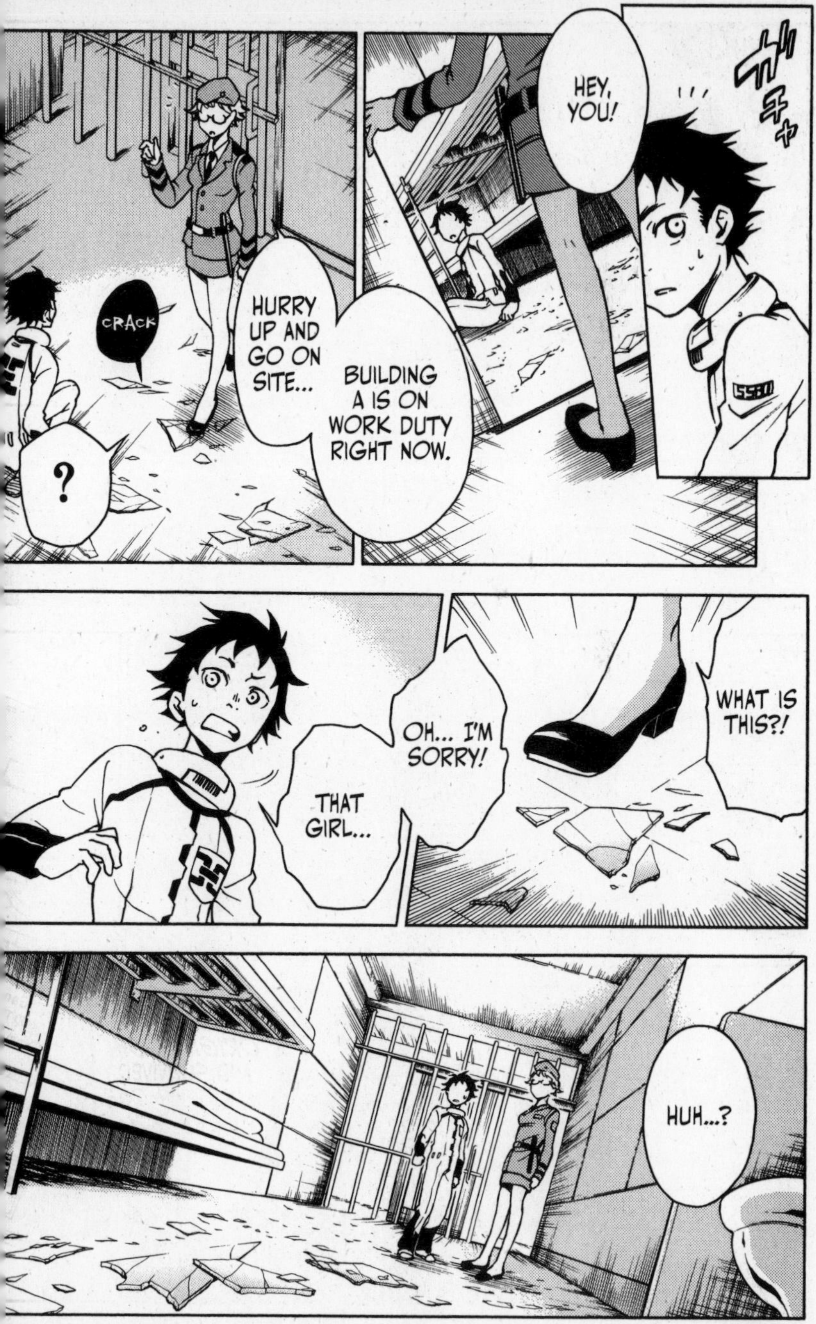
ガチャ
HEY, YOU!
BUILDING A IS ON WORK DUTY RIGHT NOW.
HURRY UP AND GO ON SITE...
CRACK
?
WHAT IS THIS?!
OH... I'M SORRY!
THAT GIRL...
HUH...?

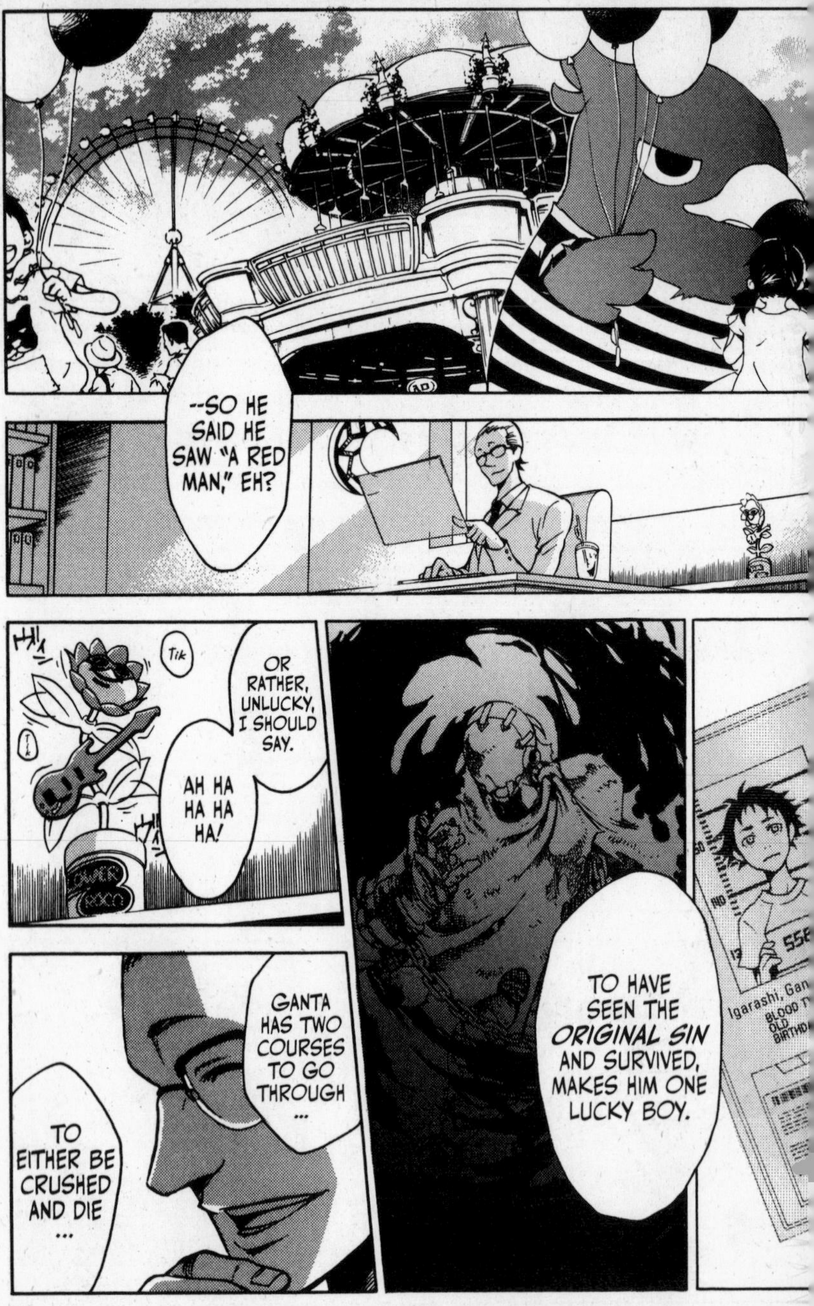
--SO HE SAID HE SAW "A RED MAN," EH?
TO HAVE SEEN THE *ORIGINAL SIN* AND SURVIVED, MAKES HIM ONE LUCKY BOY.
OR RATHER, UNLUCKY, I SHOULD SAY.
Tik
Tik
AH HA HA HA HA!
GANTA HAS TWO COURSES TO GO THROUGH ...
TO EITHER BE CRUSHED AND DIE ...

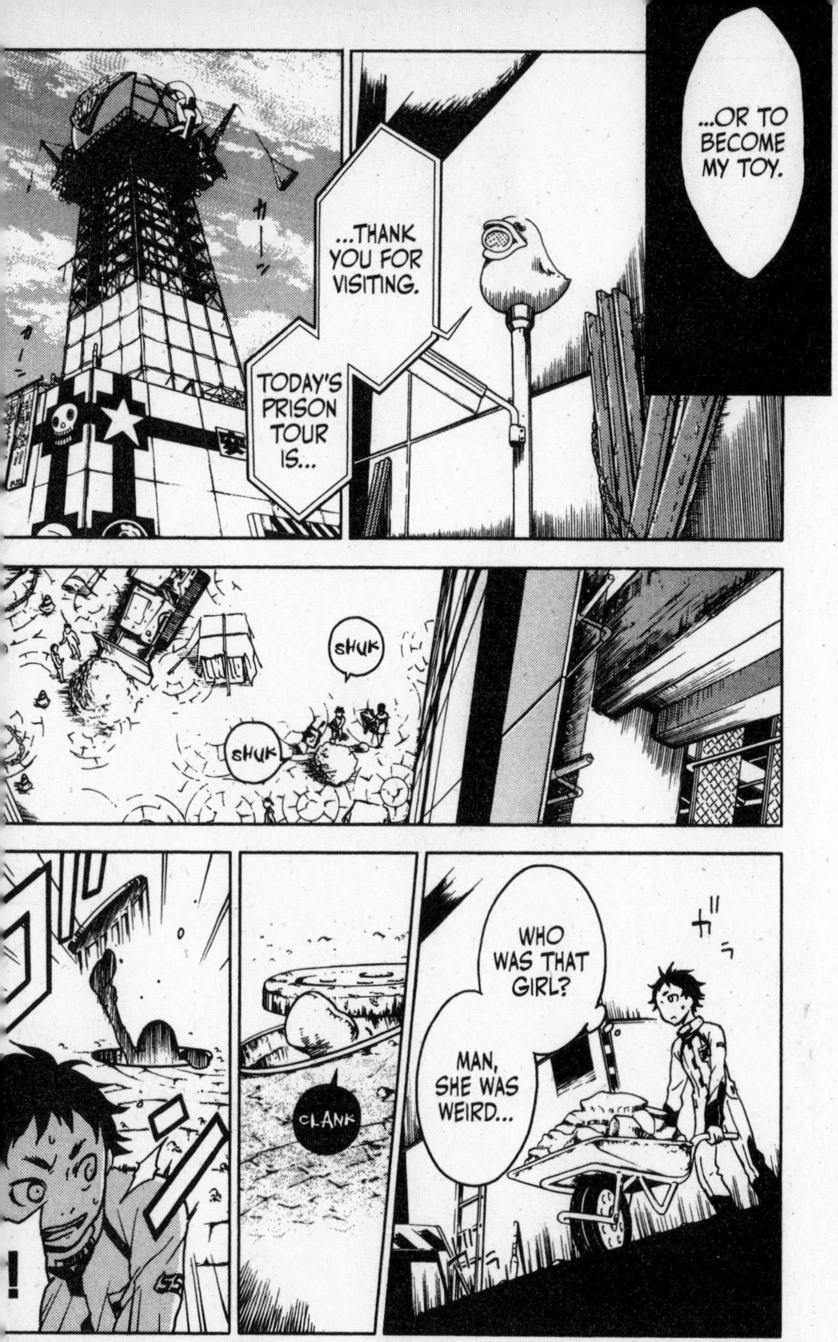
...OR TO BECOME MY TOY.
...THANK YOU FOR VISITING.
TODAY'S PRISON TOUR IS...
SHUK
SHUK
WHO WAS THAT GIRL?
MAN, SHE WAS WEIRD...
CLANK
!

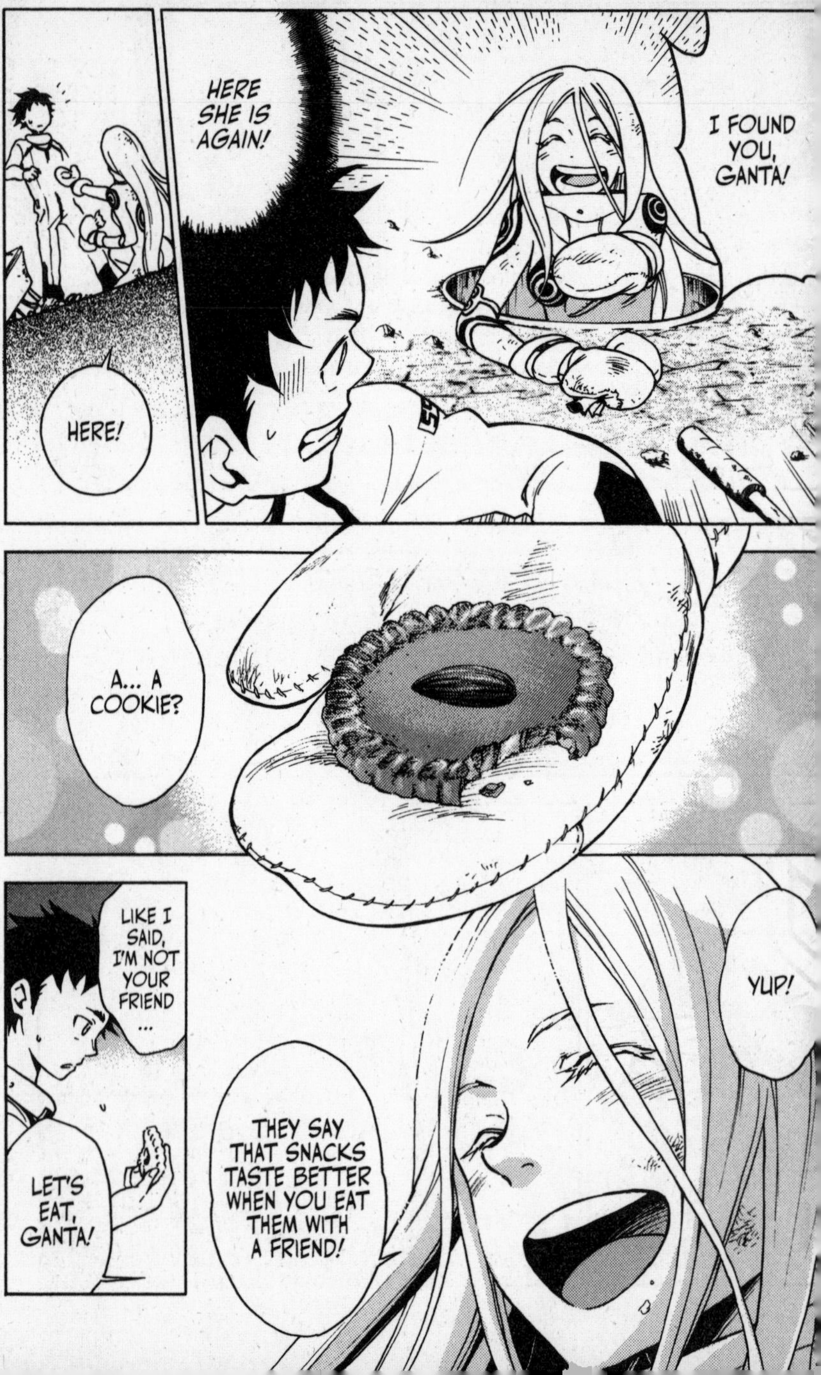
I FOUND YOU, GANTA!
HERE SHE IS AGAIN!
HERE!
A... A COOKIE?
YUP!
THEY SAY THAT SNACKS TASTE BETTER WHEN YOU EAT THEM WITH A FRIEND!
LIKE I SAID, I'M NOT YOUR FRIEND...
LET'S EAT, GANTA!

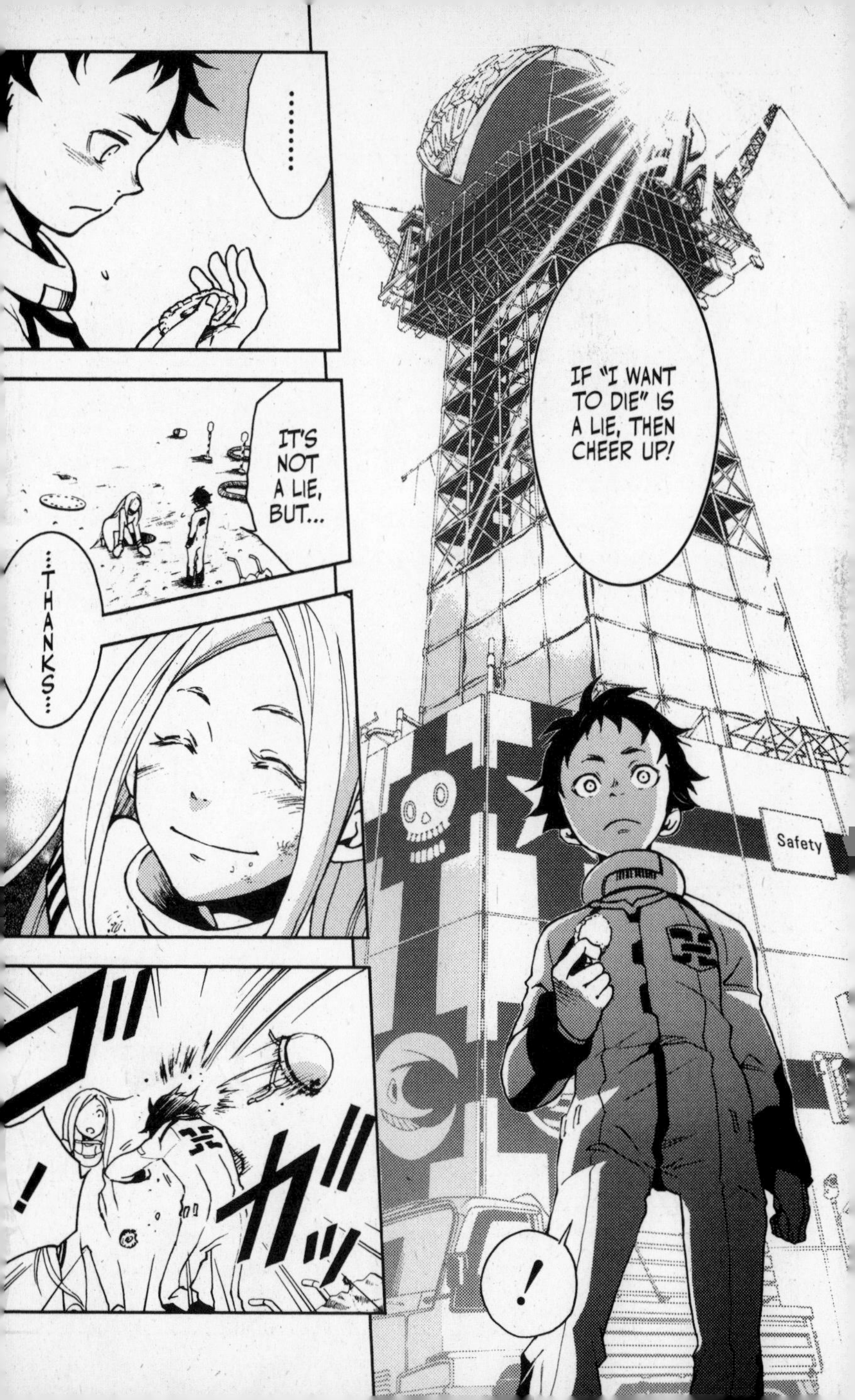
IF "I WANT TO DIE" IS A LIE, THEN CHEER UP!
Safety
!
......
IT'S NOT A LIE, BUT...
...THANKS...
ゴ
ガッ
!

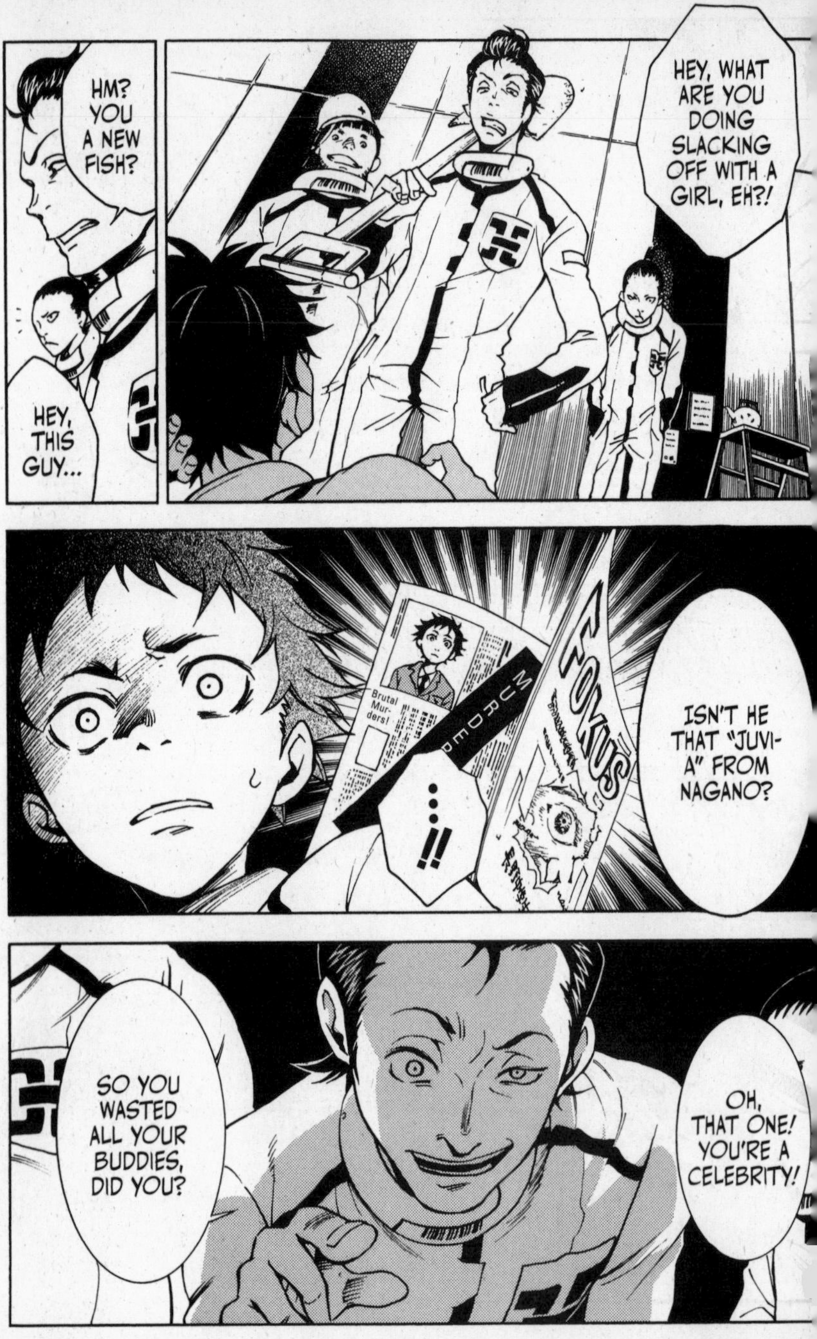
HEY, WHAT ARE YOU DOING SLACKING OFF WITH A GIRL, EH?!
HM? YOU A NEW FISH?
HEY, THIS GUY...
ISN'T HE THAT "JUVI-A" FROM NAGANO?
FOKUS
MURDER
Brutal Murders!
...!!
OH, THAT ONE! YOU'RE A CELEBRITY!
SO YOU WASTED ALL YOUR BUDDIES, DID YOU?

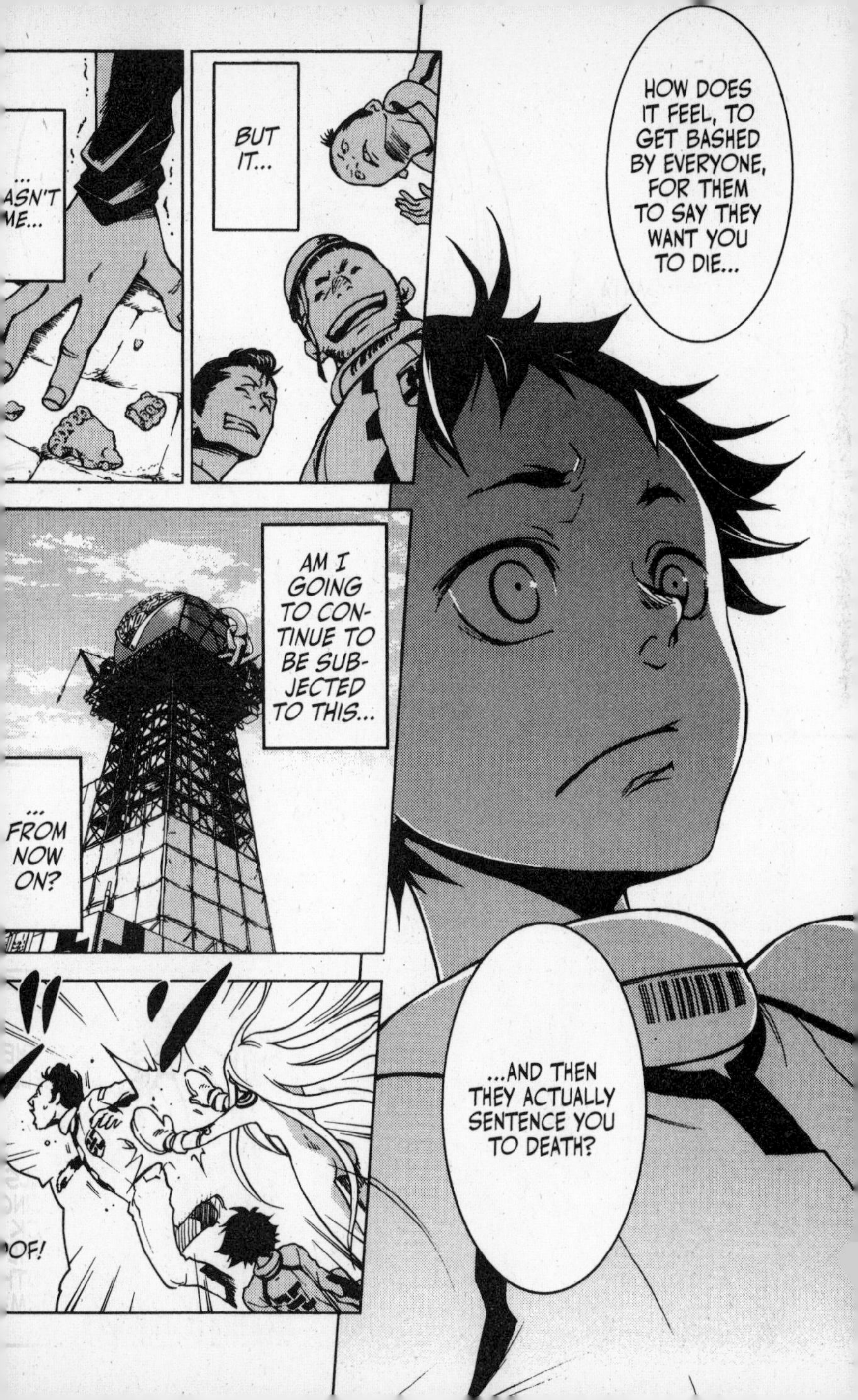
HOW DOES IT FEEL, TO GET BASHED BY EVERYONE, FOR THEM TO SAY THEY WANT YOU TO DIE...
...AND THEN THEY ACTUALLY SENTENCE YOU TO DEATH?
BUT IT...
...ASN'T ME...
AM I GOING TO CONTINUE TO BE SUBJECTED TO THIS...
...FROM NOW ON?
!!
OF!

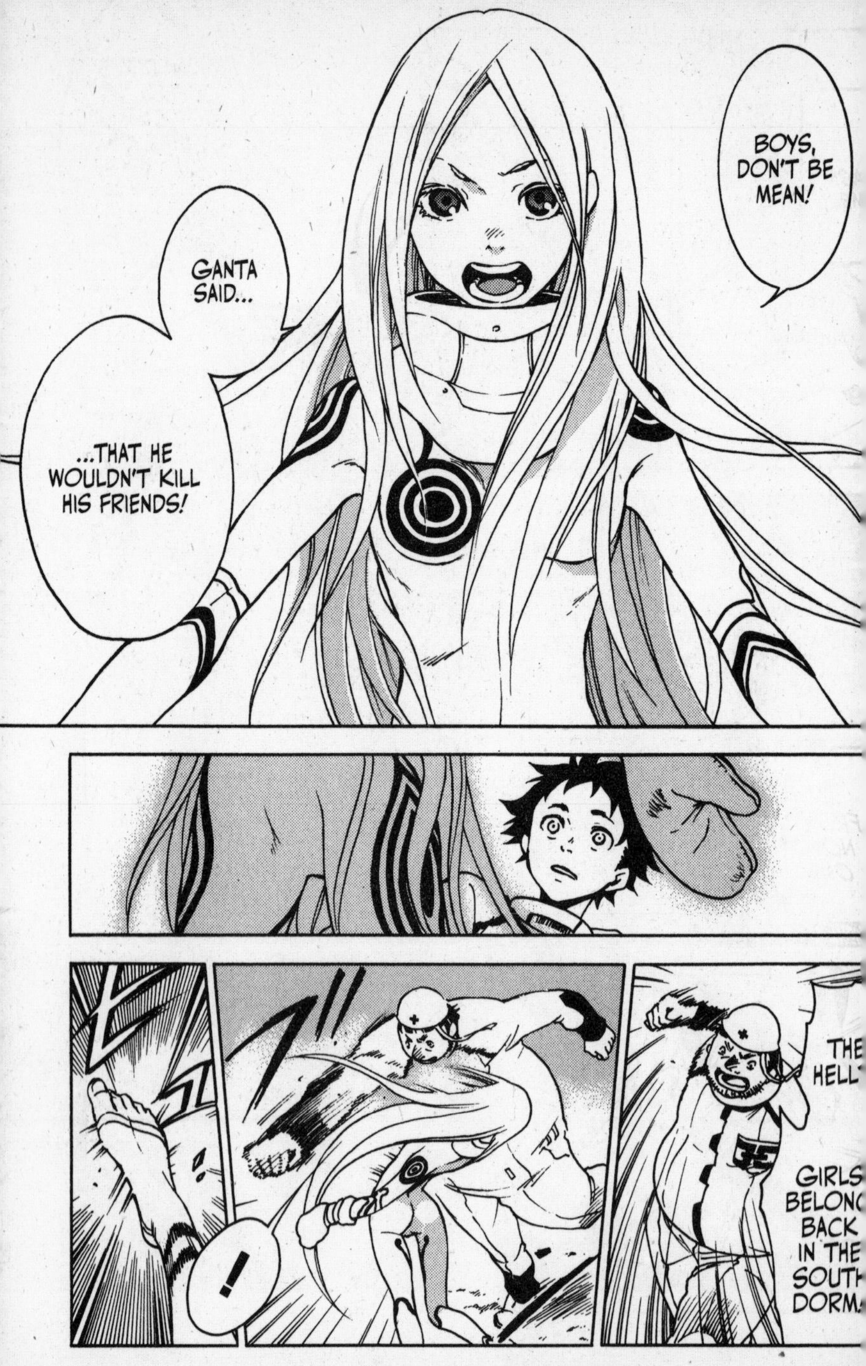
BOYS, DON'T BE MEAN!
GANTA SAID...
...THAT HE WOULDN'T KILL HIS FRIENDS!
THE HELL
GIRLS BELONG BACK IN THE SOUTH DORM.
!

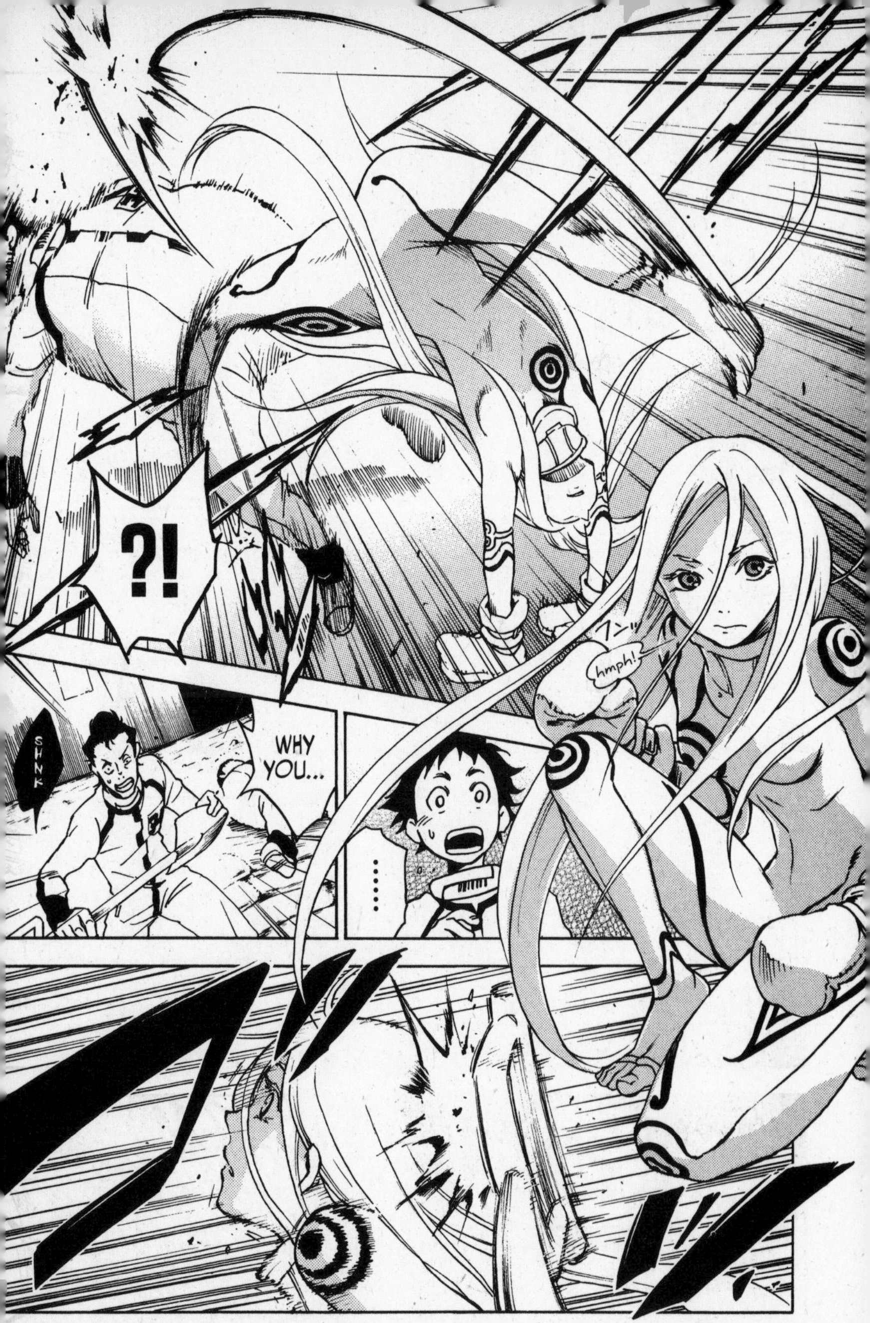
?!
フン
hmph!
......
WHY YOU...
SHNK

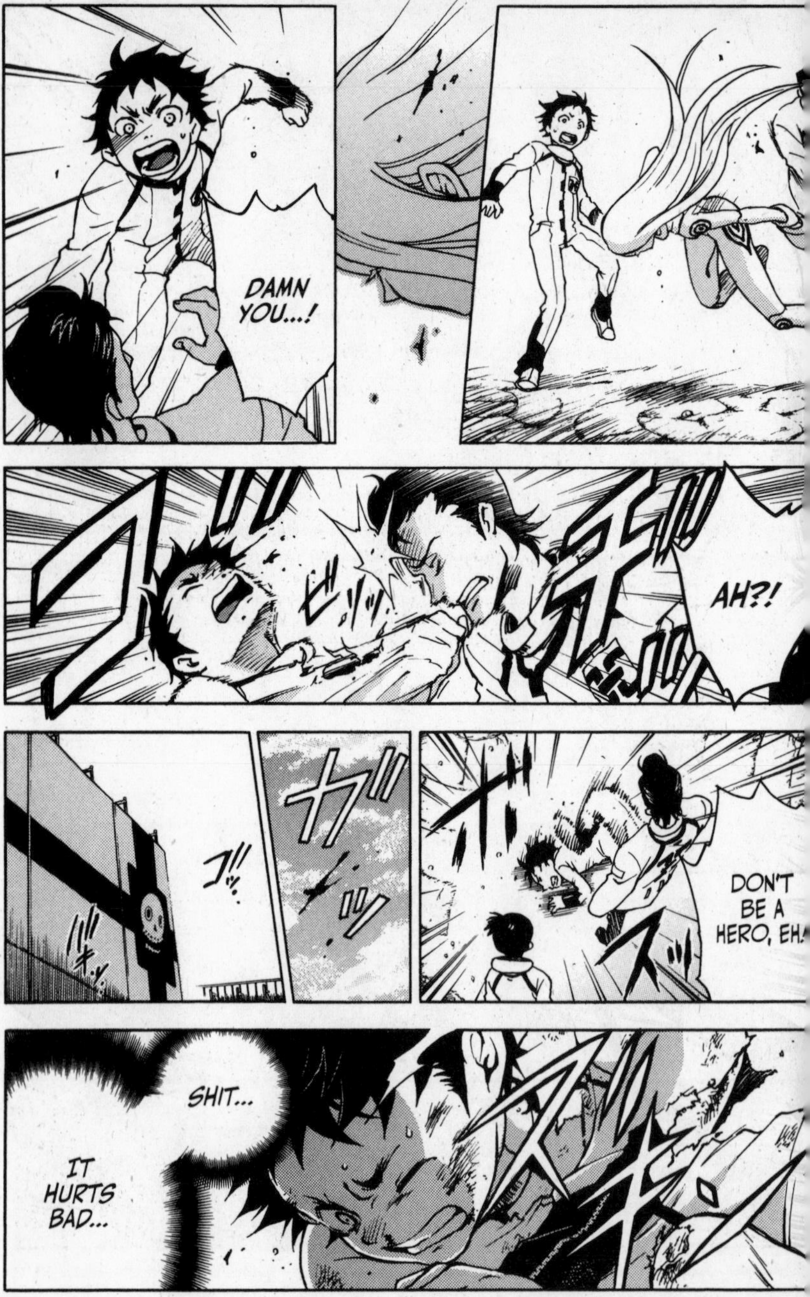
DAMN YOU...!
AH?!
DON'T BE A HERO, EH
SHIT...
IT HURTS BAD...

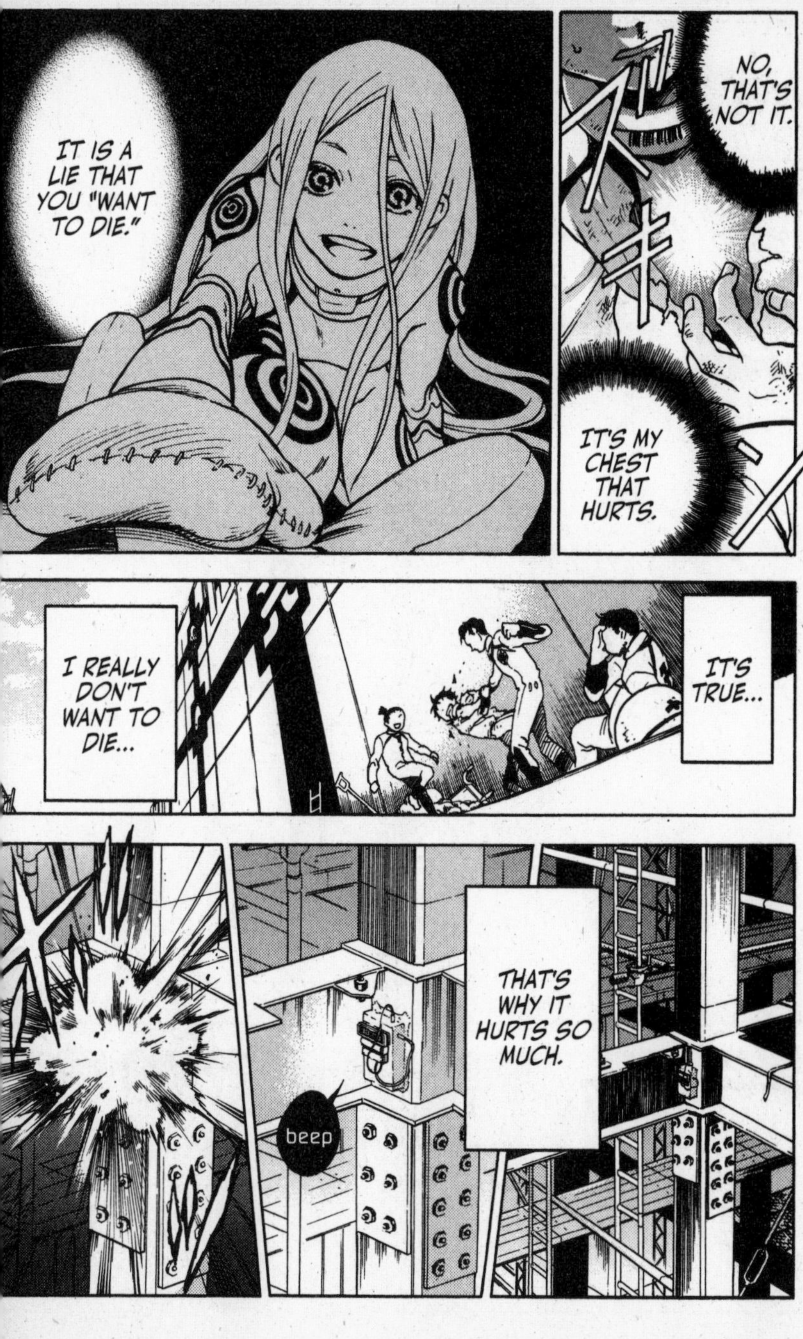
NO, THAT'S NOT IT.
IT'S MY CHEST THAT HURTS.
IT IS A LIE THAT YOU "WANT TO DIE."
IT'S TRUE...
I REALLY DON'T WANT TO DIE...
THAT'S WHY IT HURTS SO MUCH.
beep

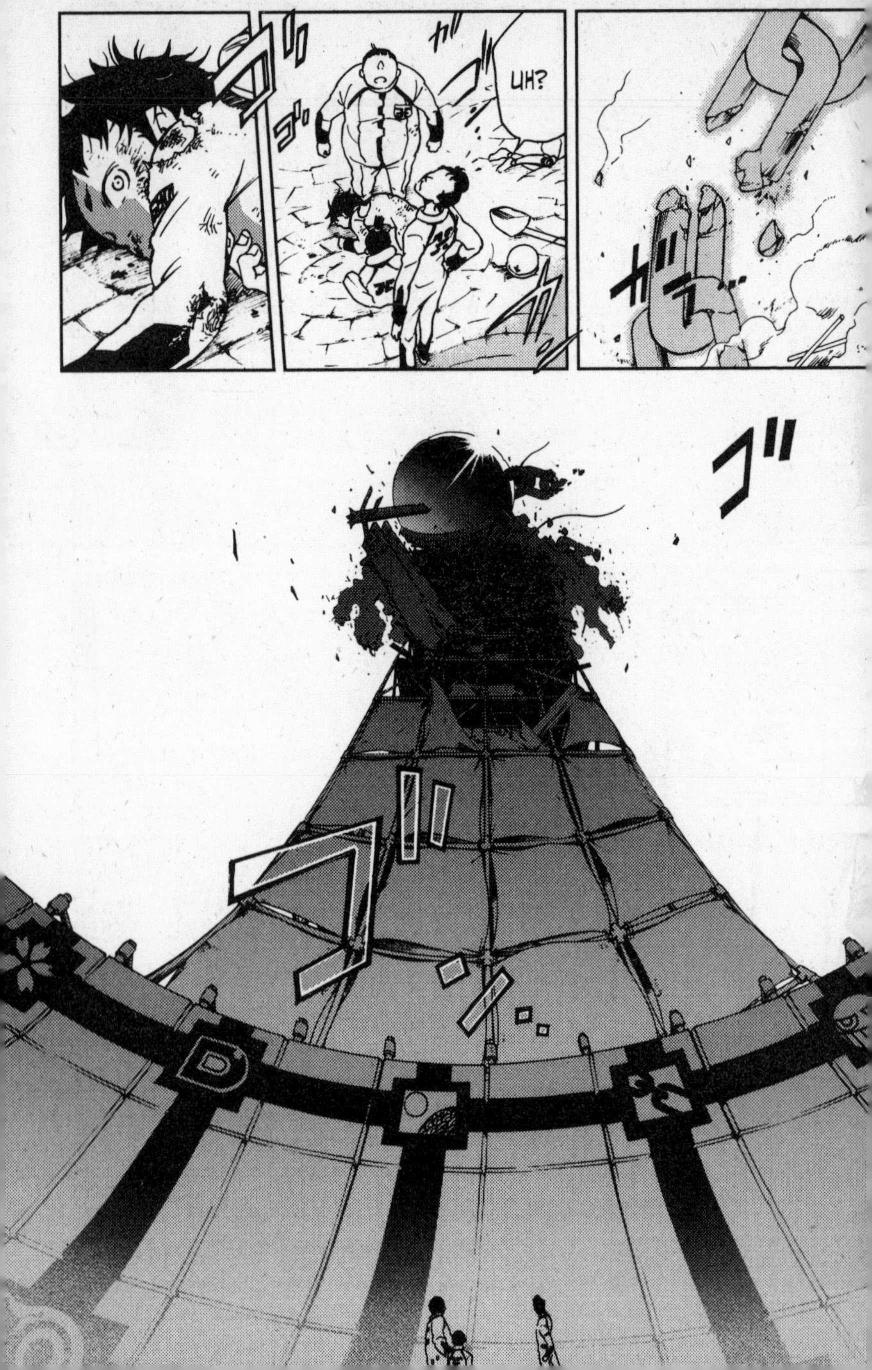
UH?

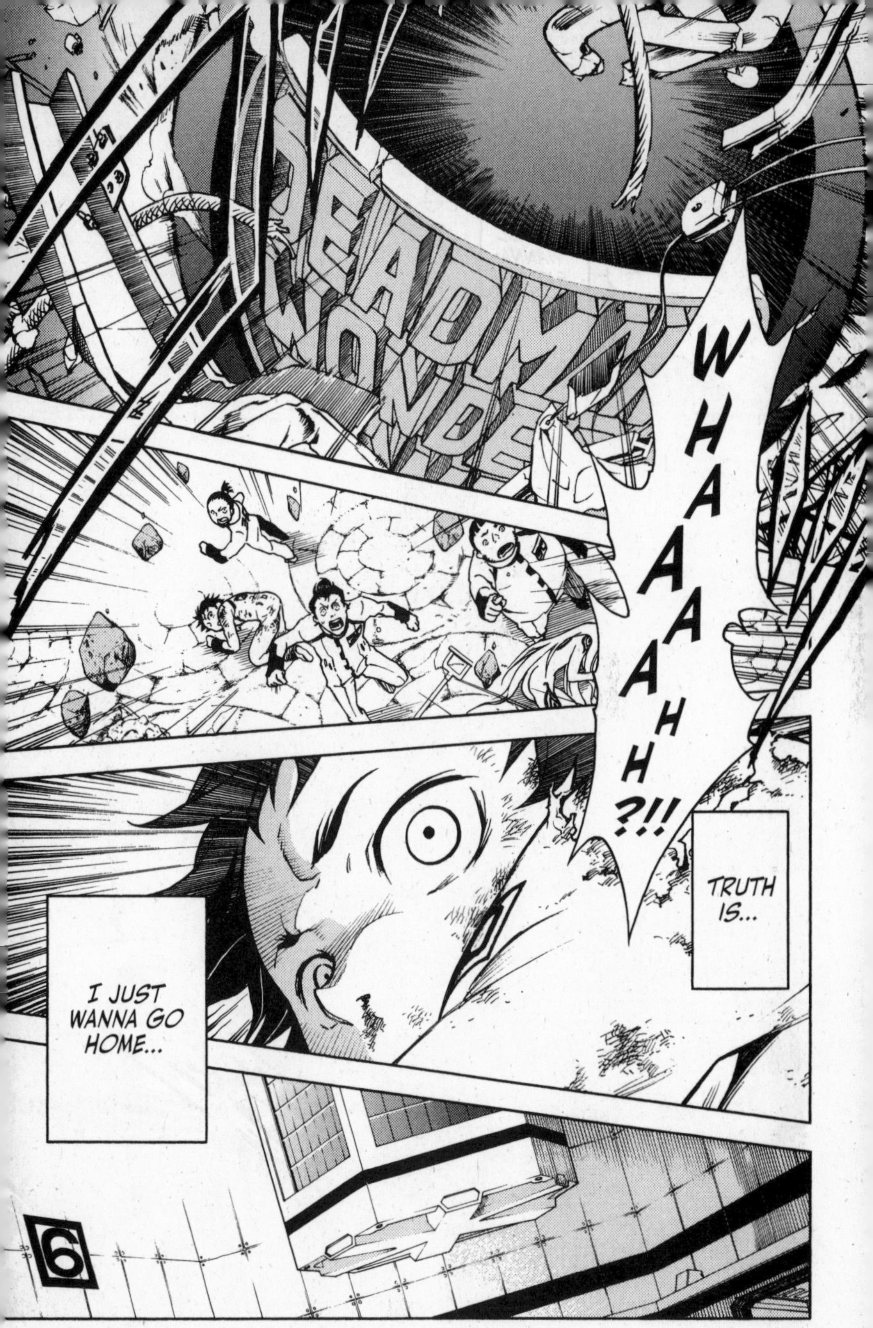
WHAAAAAHH?!!
TRUTH IS...
I JUST WANNA GO HOME...

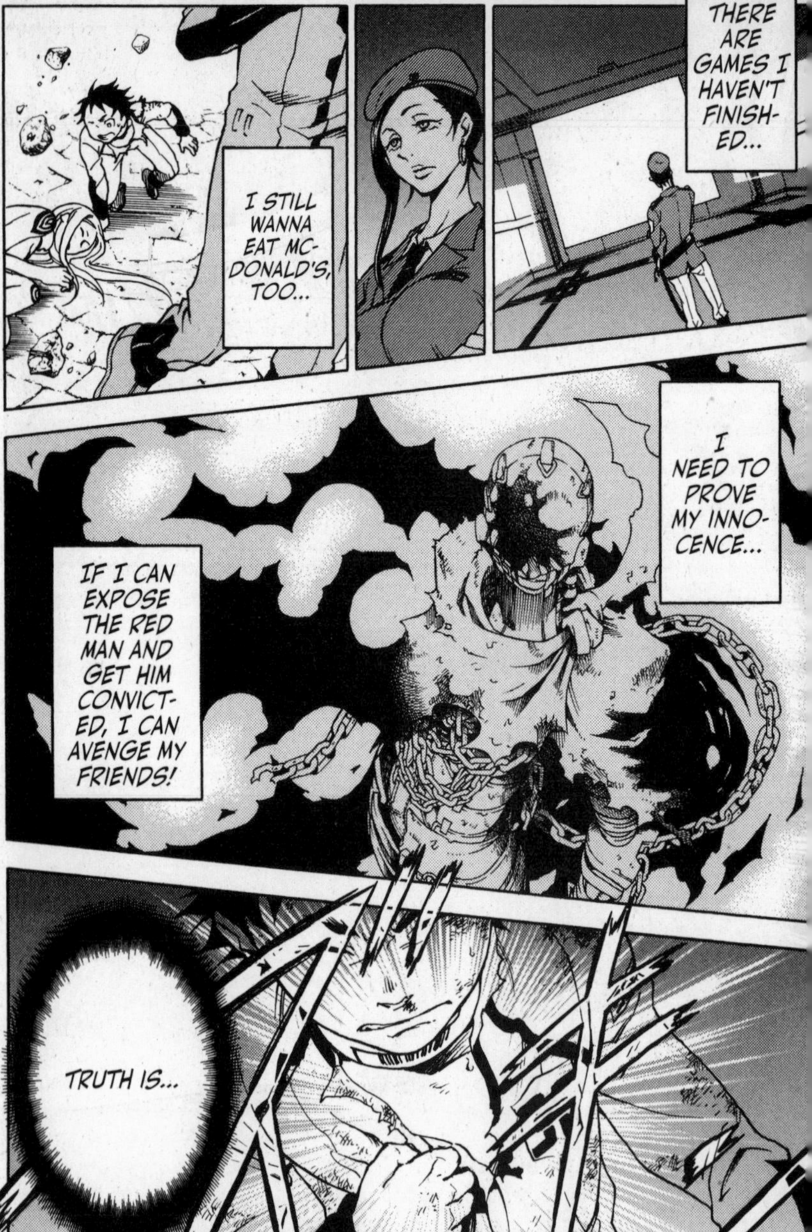
THERE ARE GAMES I HAVEN'T FINISHED...
I STILL WANNA EAT MC-DONALD'S, TOO...
I NEED TO PROVE MY INNOCENCE...
IF I CAN EXPOSE THE RED MAN AND GET HIM CONVICTED, I CAN AVENGE MY FRIENDS!
TRUTH IS...

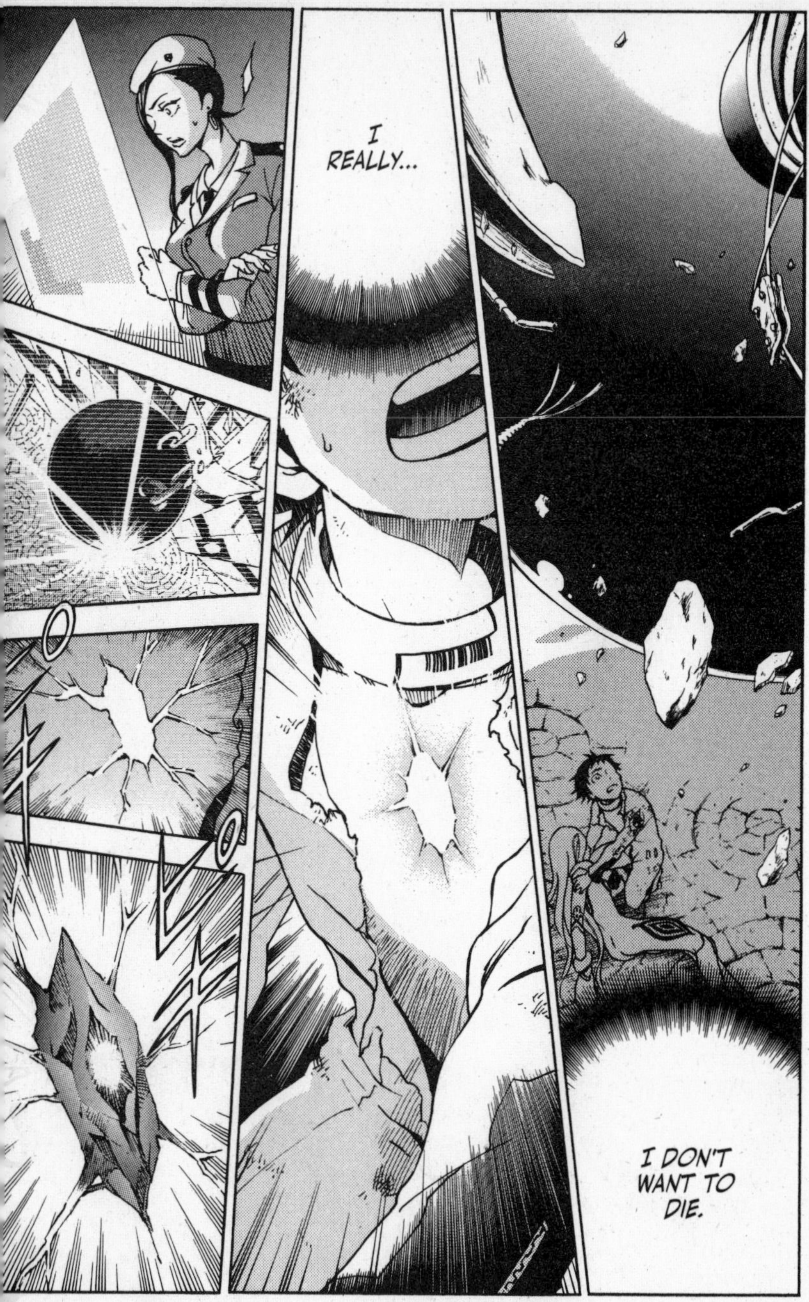
I DON'T WANT TO DIE.
I REALLY...

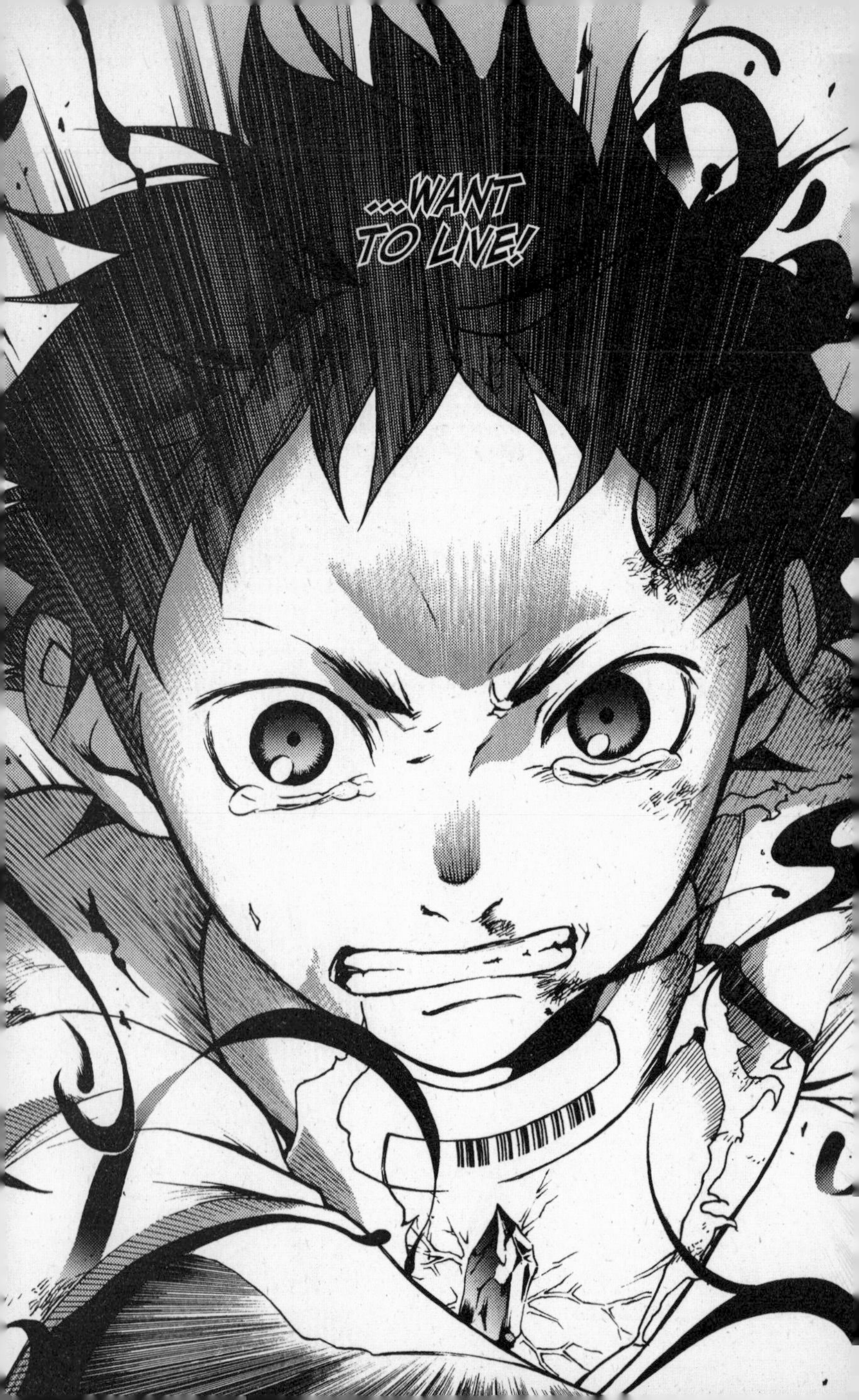
...WANT TO LIVE!

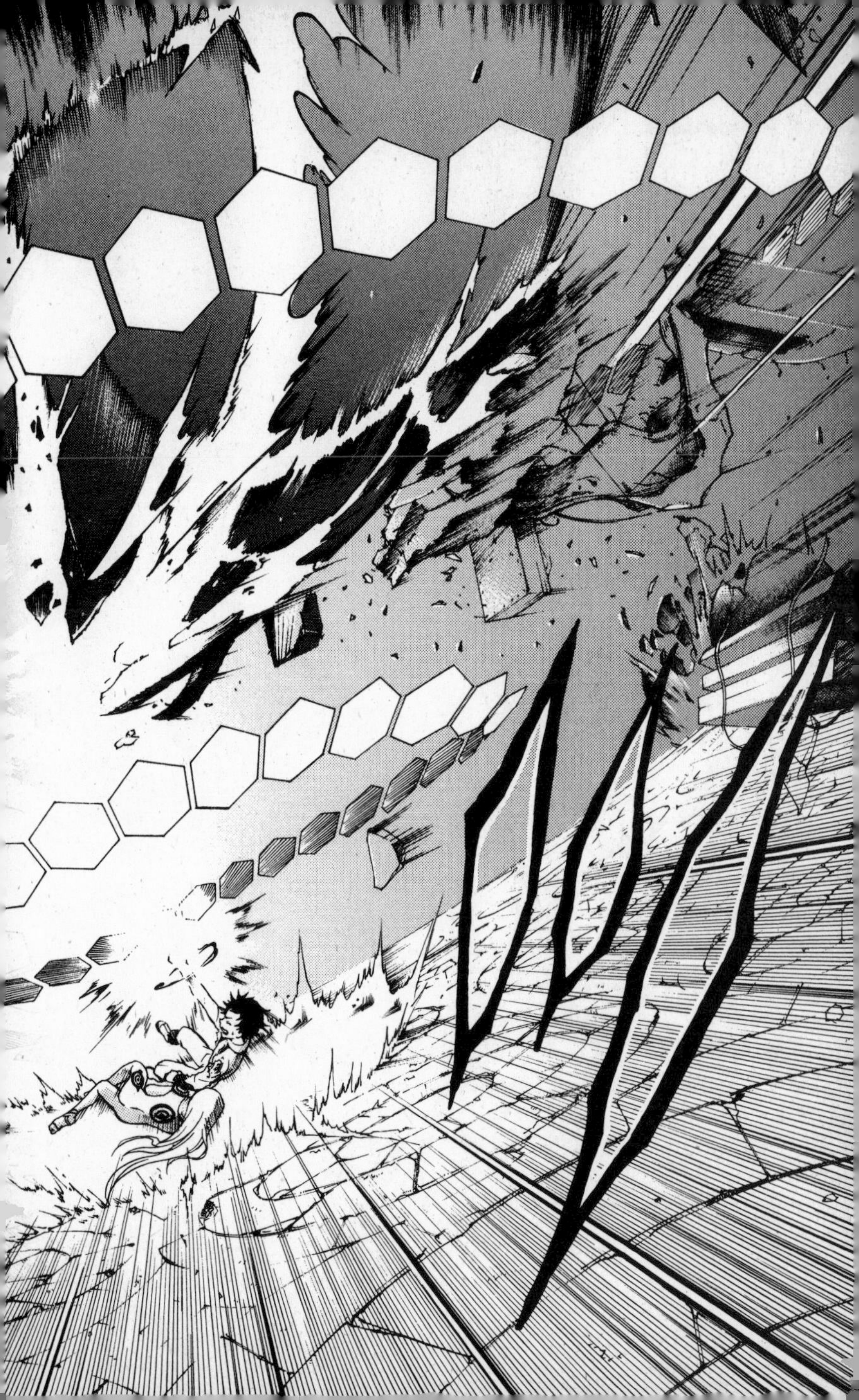

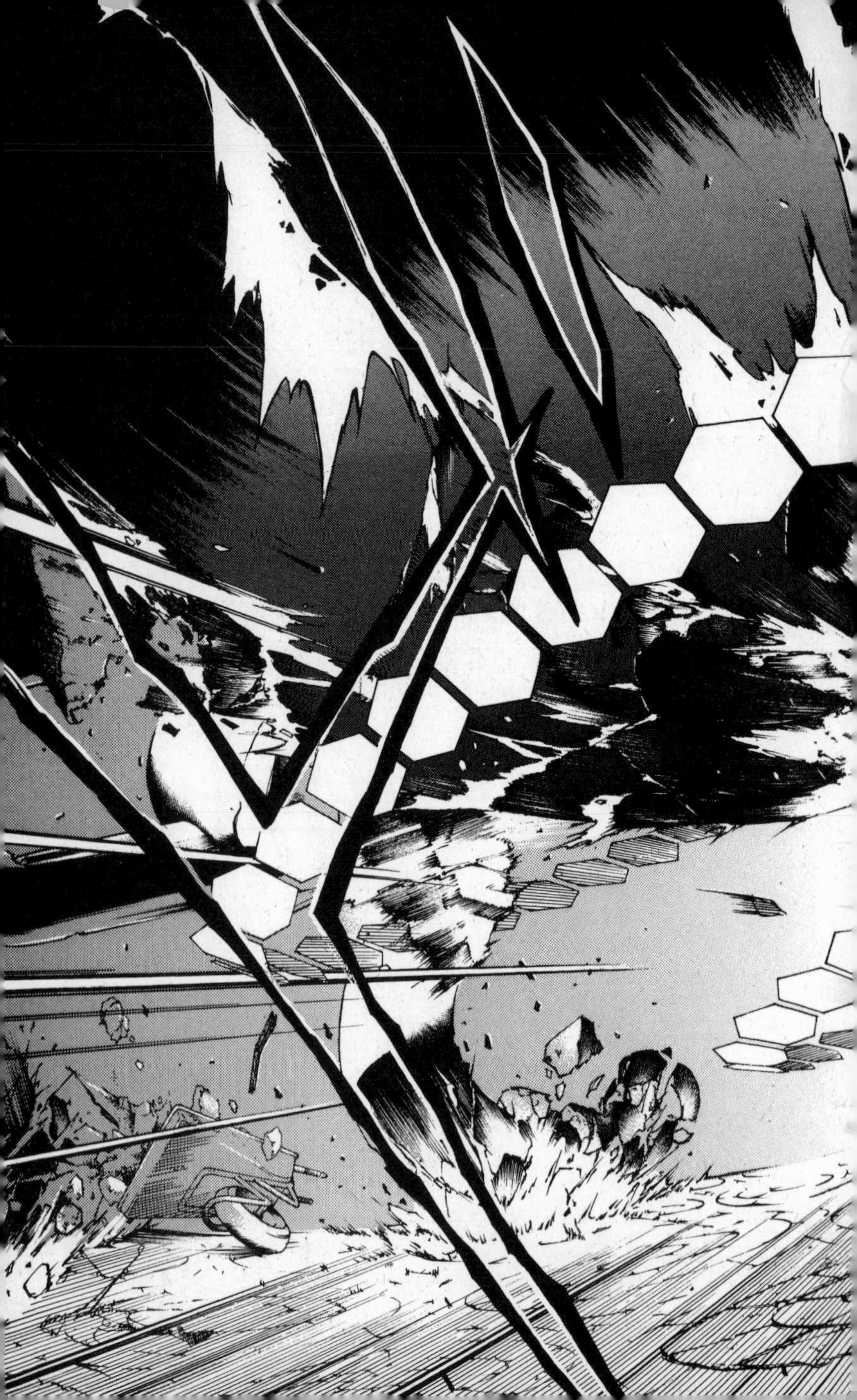

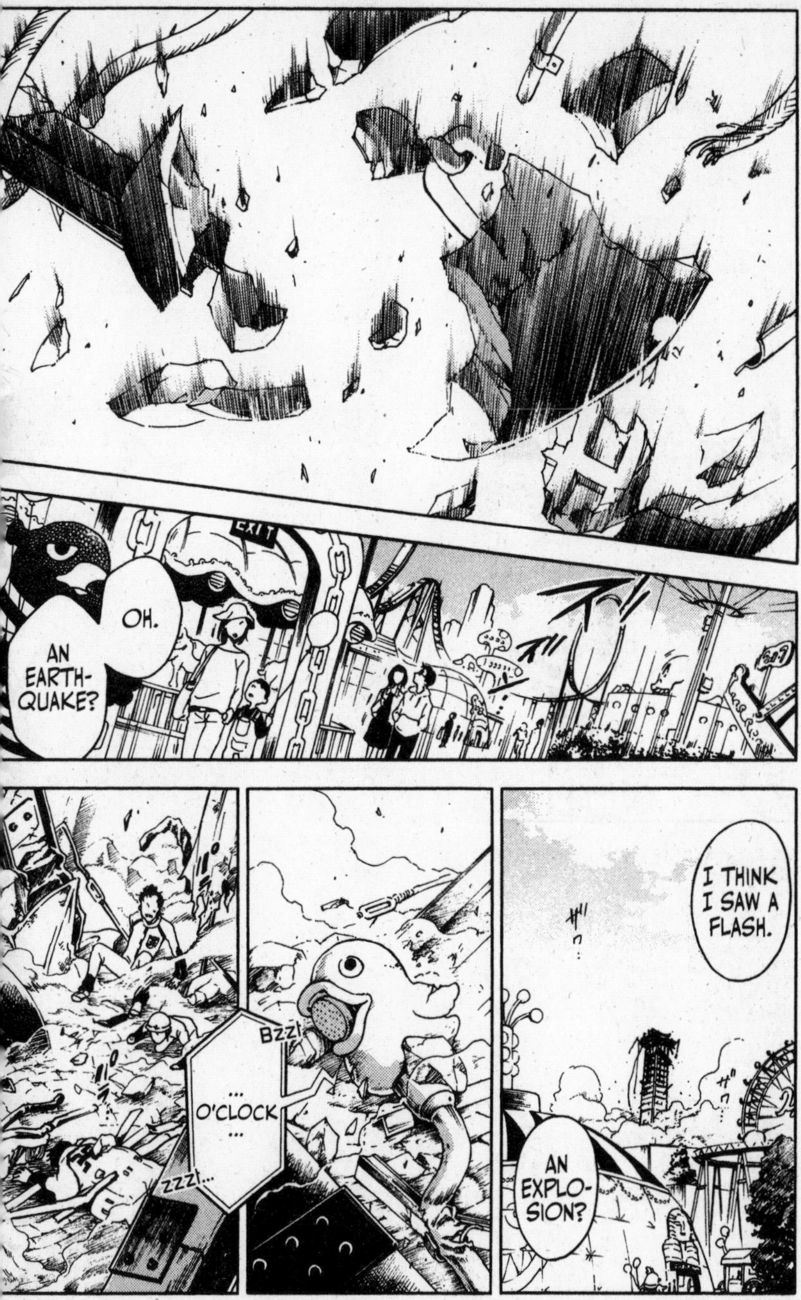
OH.
AN EARTH-QUAKE?
I THINK I SAW A FLASH.
AN EXPLOSION?
Bzzt
... O'CLOCK ...
zzzt...

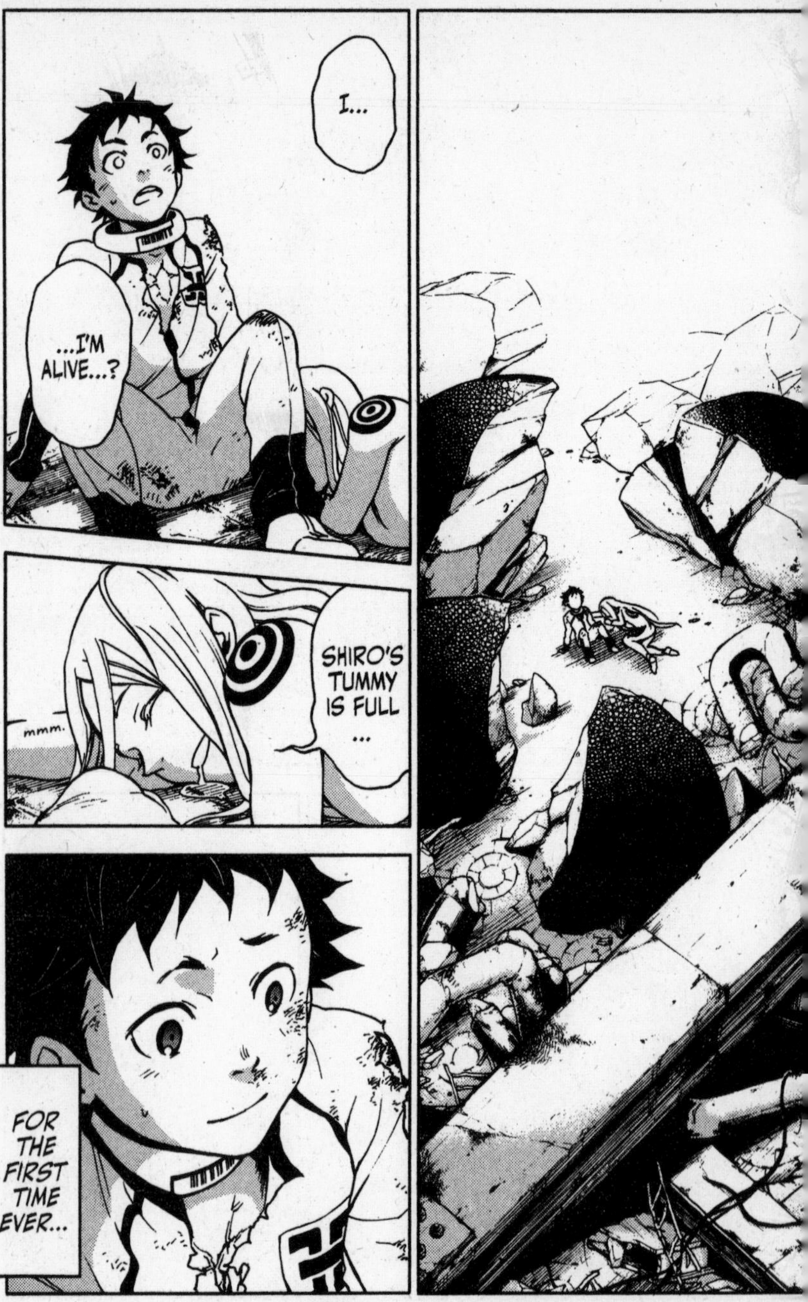
I...
...I'M ALIVE...?
SHIRO'S TUMMY IS FULL ...
mmm.
FOR THE FIRST TIME EVER...

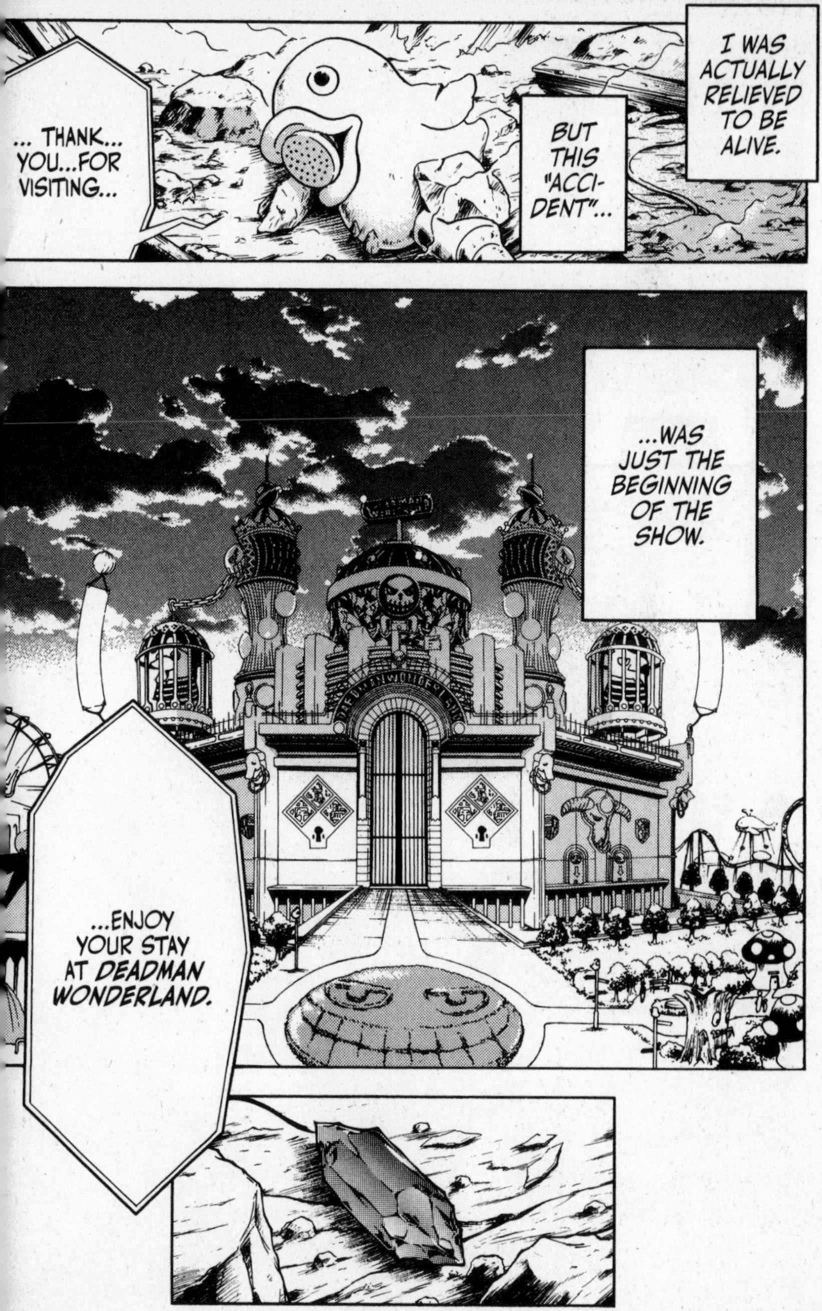
I WAS ACTUALLY RELIEVED TO BE ALIVE.
BUT THIS "ACCIDENT"...
... THANK... YOU...FOR VISITING...
...WAS JUST THE BEGINNING OF THE SHOW.
...ENJOY YOUR STAY AT *DEADMAN WONDERLAND.*

DEADMAN WONDERLAND

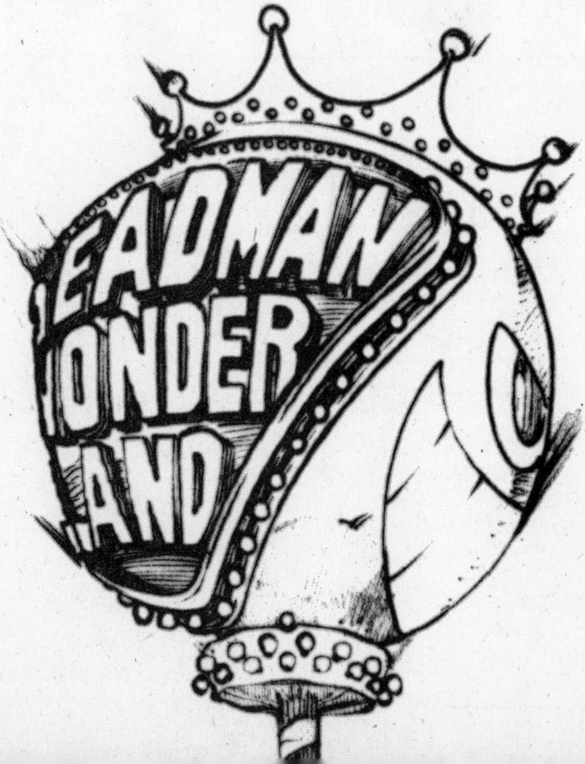
EADMAN
ONDER
AND

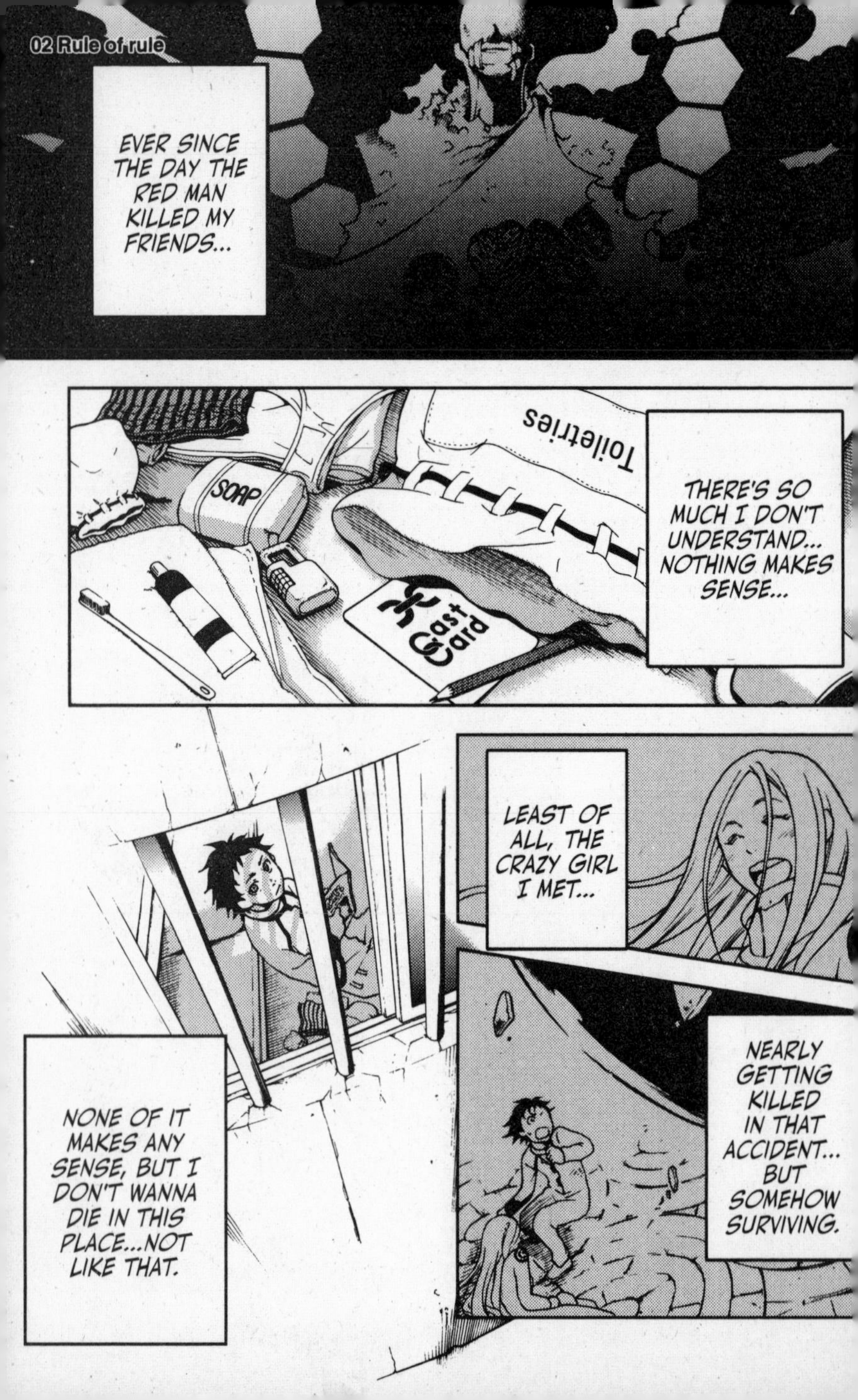
EVER SINCE THE DAY THE RED MAN KILLED MY FRIENDS...
Toiletries
SOAP
Cast Card
THERE'S SO MUCH I DON'T UNDERSTAND... NOTHING MAKES SENSE...
LEAST OF ALL, THE CRAZY GIRL I MET...
NEARLY GETTING KILLED IN THAT ACCIDENT... BUT SOMEHOW SURVIVING.
NONE OF IT MAKES ANY SENSE, BUT I DON'T WANNA DIE IN THIS PLACE...NOT LIKE THAT.

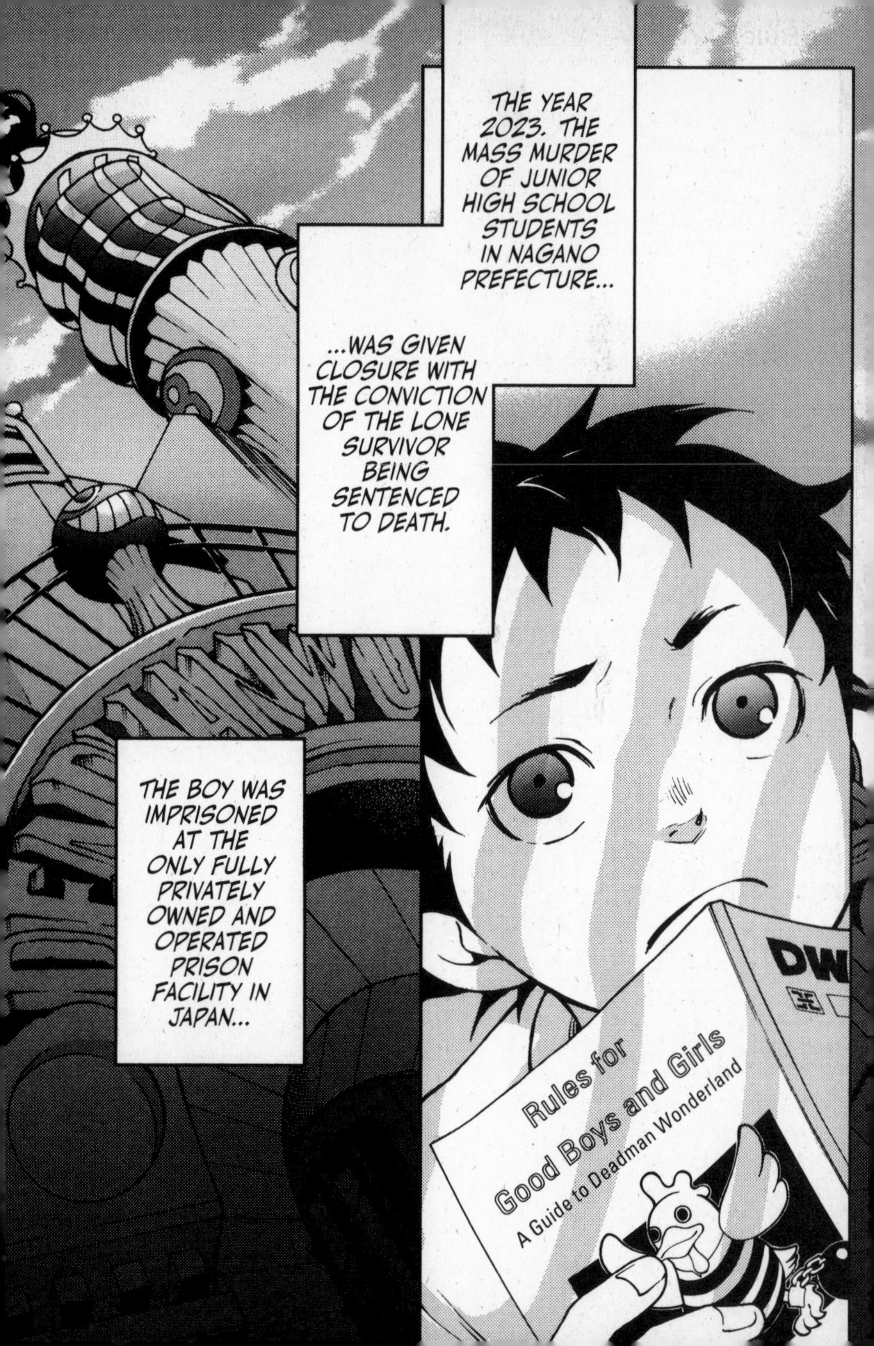
THE YEAR 2023. THE MASS MURDER OF JUNIOR HIGH SCHOOL STUDENTS IN NAGANO PREFECTURE...
...WAS GIVEN CLOSURE WITH THE CONVICTION OF THE LONE SURVIVOR BEING SENTENCED TO DEATH.
DW
Rules for Good Boys and Girls
A Guide to Deadman Wonderland
THE BOY WAS IMPRISONED AT THE ONLY FULLY PRIVATELY OWNED AND OPERATED PRISON FACILITY IN JAPAN...

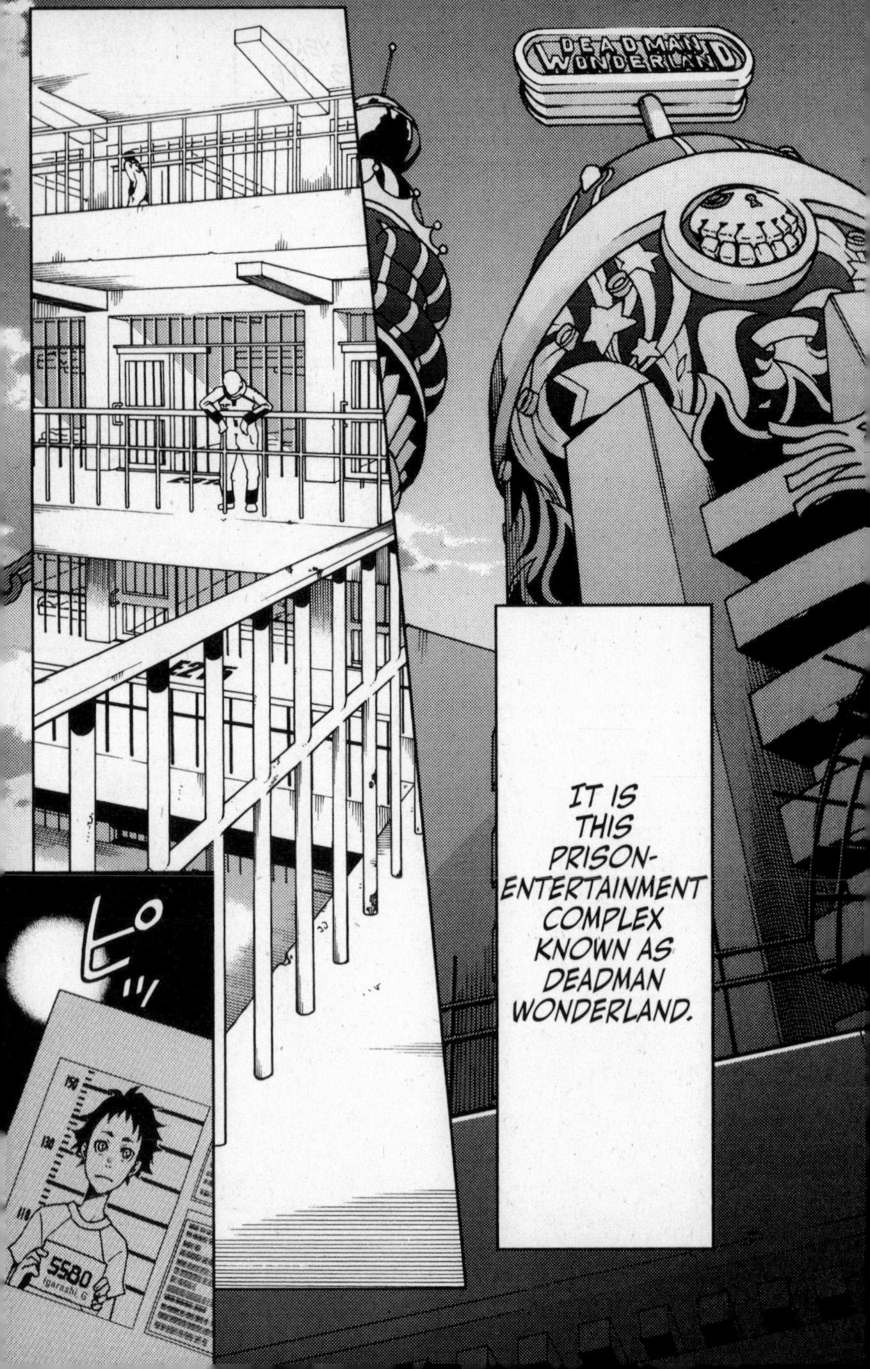
DEADMAN WONDERLAND
IT IS THIS PRISON-ENTERTAINMENT COMPLEX KNOWN AS DEADMAN WONDERLAND.
ピッ
5580
Igarashi, G

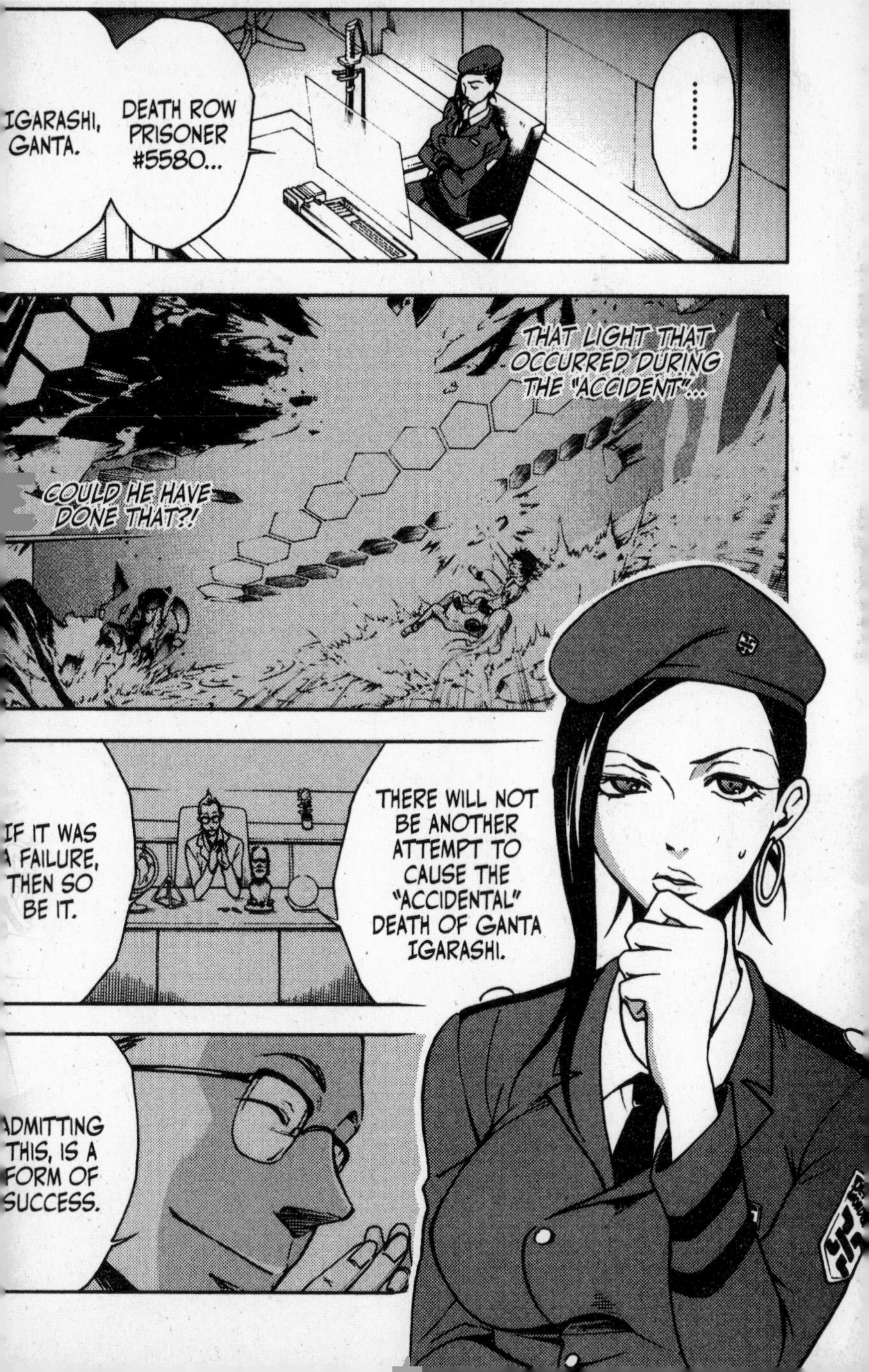
......
DEATH ROW PRISONER #5580...
IGARASHI, GANTA.
THAT LIGHT THAT OCCURRED DURING THE "ACCIDENT"...
COULD HE HAVE DONE THAT?!
THERE WILL NOT BE ANOTHER ATTEMPT TO CAUSE THE "ACCIDENTAL" DEATH OF GANTA IGARASHI.
IF IT WAS A FAILURE, THEN SO BE IT.
ADMITTING THIS, IS A FORM OF SUCCESS.

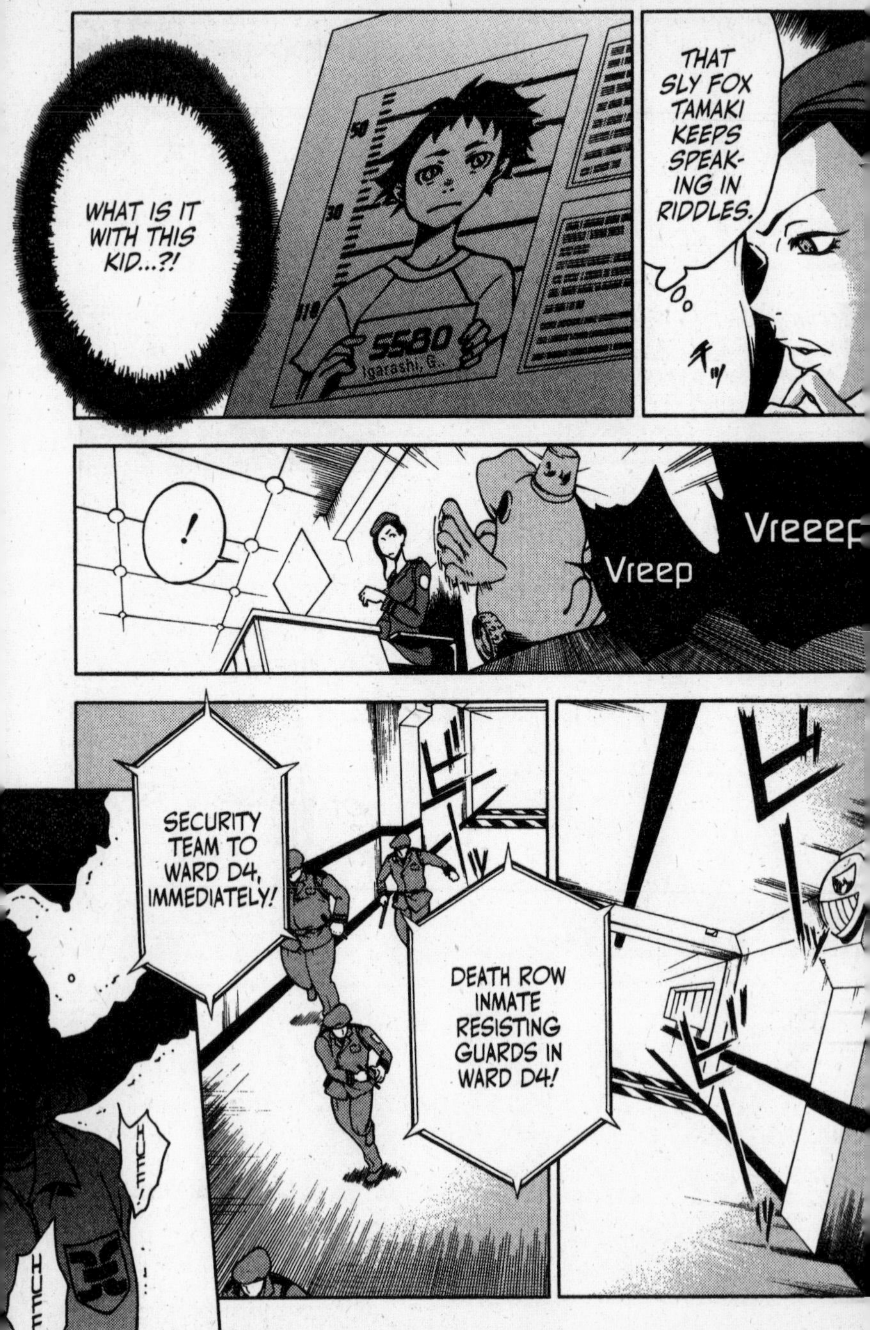
THAT SLY FOX TAMAKI KEEPS SPEAK-ING IN RIDDLES.
5580
Igarashi, G..
WHAT IS IT WITH THIS KID...?!
Vreeep
Vreep
!
SECURITY TEAM TO WARD D4, IMMEDIATELY!
DEATH ROW INMATE RESISTING GUARDS IN WARD D4!
HUFF!
HUFF!

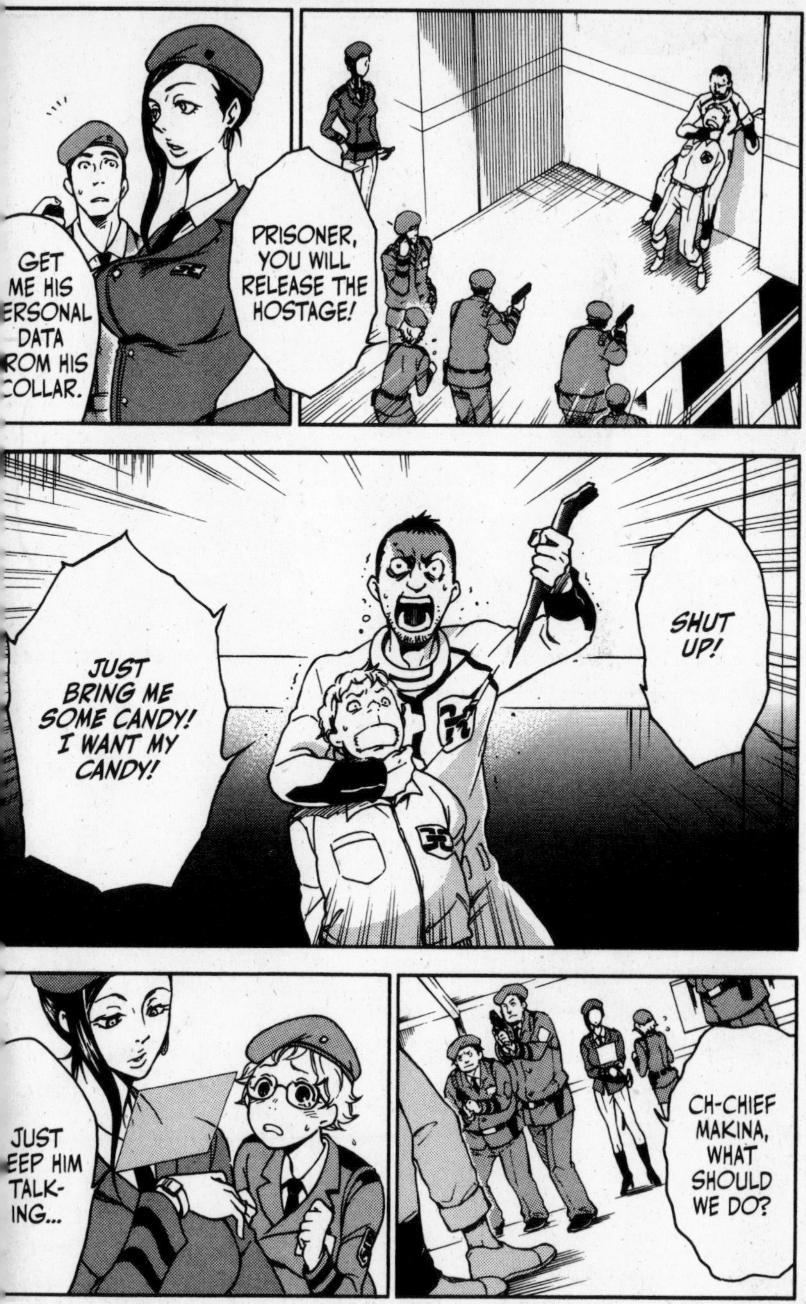
PRISONER, YOU WILL RELEASE THE HOSTAGE!
GET ME HIS ERSONAL DATA ROM HIS COLLAR.
SHUT UP!
JUST BRING ME SOME CANDY! I WANT MY CANDY!
CH-CHIEF MAKINA, WHAT SHOULD WE DO?
JUST EEP HIM TALK-ING...

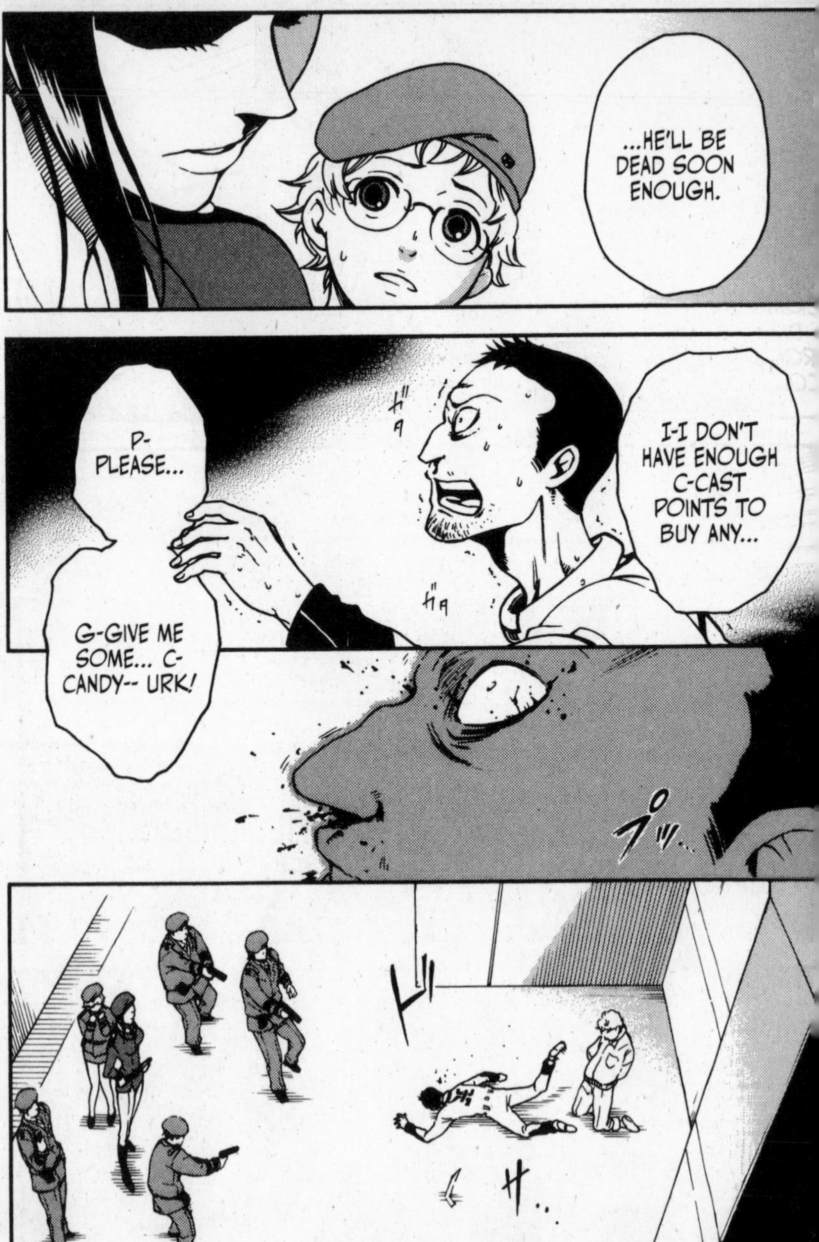
...HE'LL BE DEAD SOON ENOUGH.
I-I DON'T HAVE ENOUGH C-CAST POINTS TO BUY ANY...
P-PLEASE...
G-GIVE ME SOME... C-CANDY-- URK!

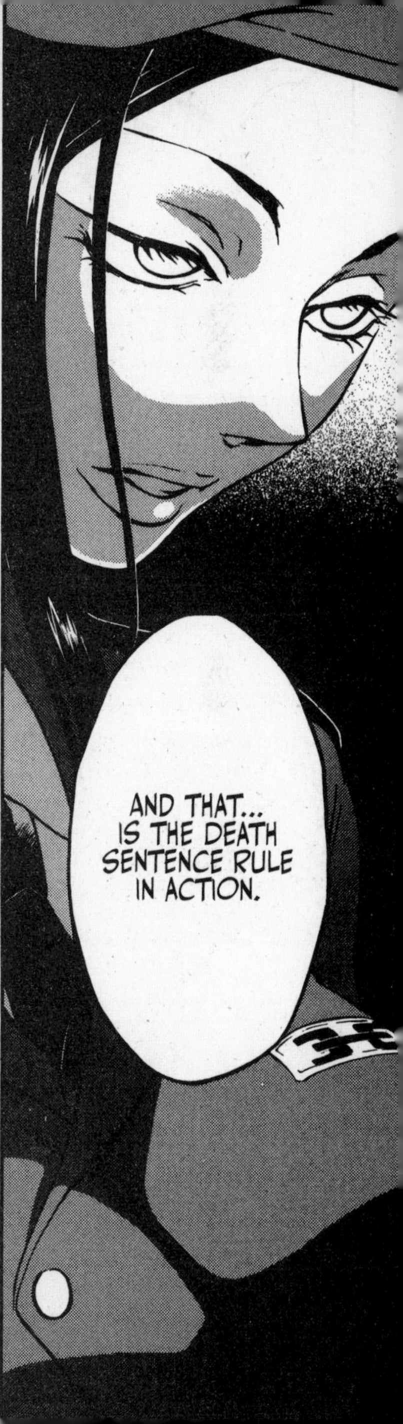
AND THAT... IS THE DEATH SENTENCE RULE IN ACTION.

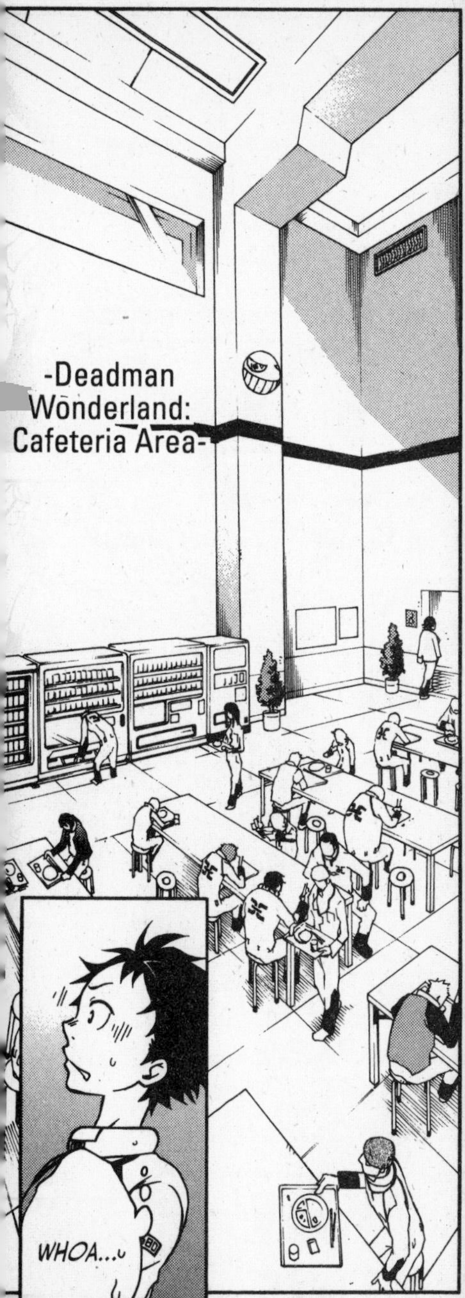
-Deadman Wonderland: Cafeteria Area-
WHOA...

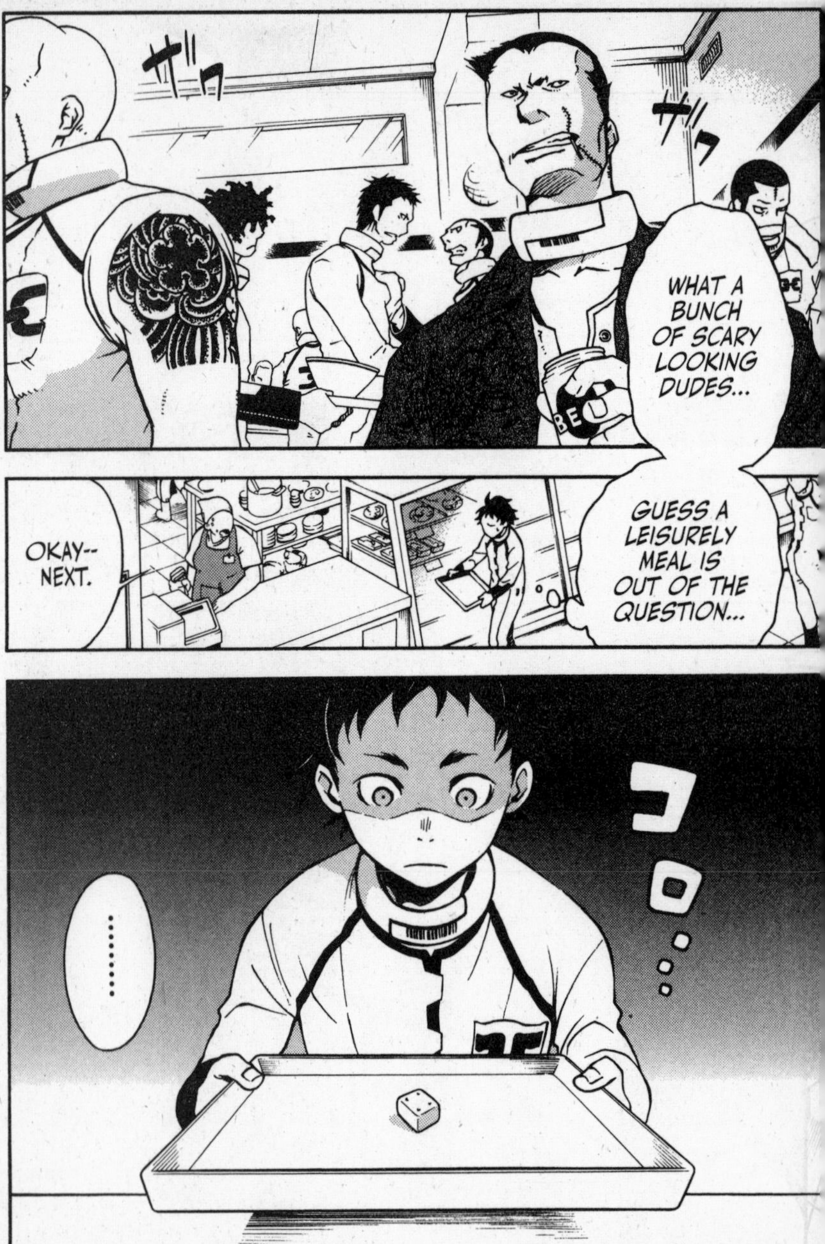
ザワ
ザワ
WHAT A BUNCH OF SCARY LOOKING DUDES...
GUESS A LEISURELY MEAL IS OUT OF THE QUESTION...
OKAY--NEXT.
コロ...
....

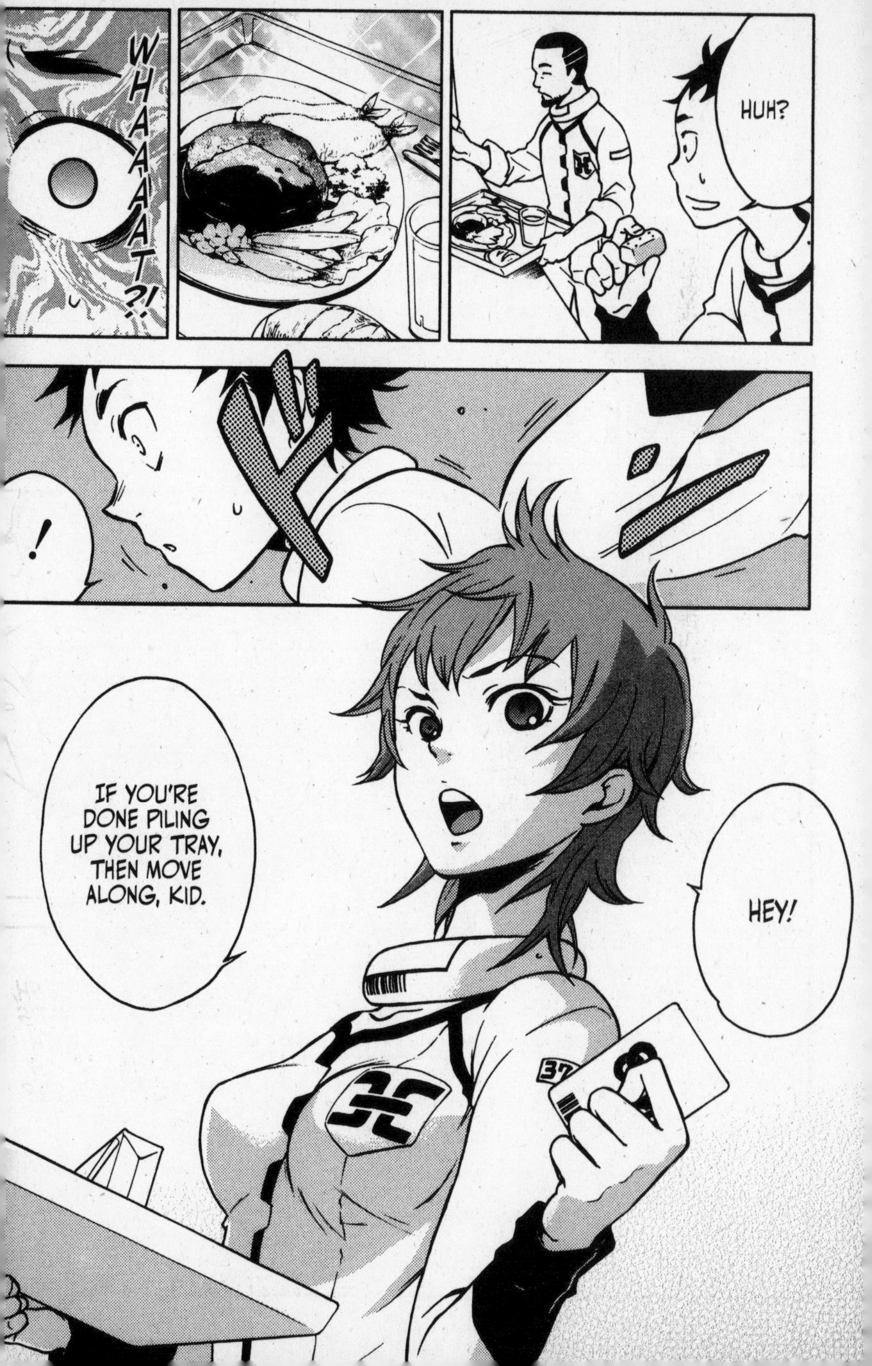
HUH?
WHAAAAAT?!
!
HEY!
IF YOU'RE DONE PILING UP YOUR TRAY, THEN MOVE ALONG, KID.

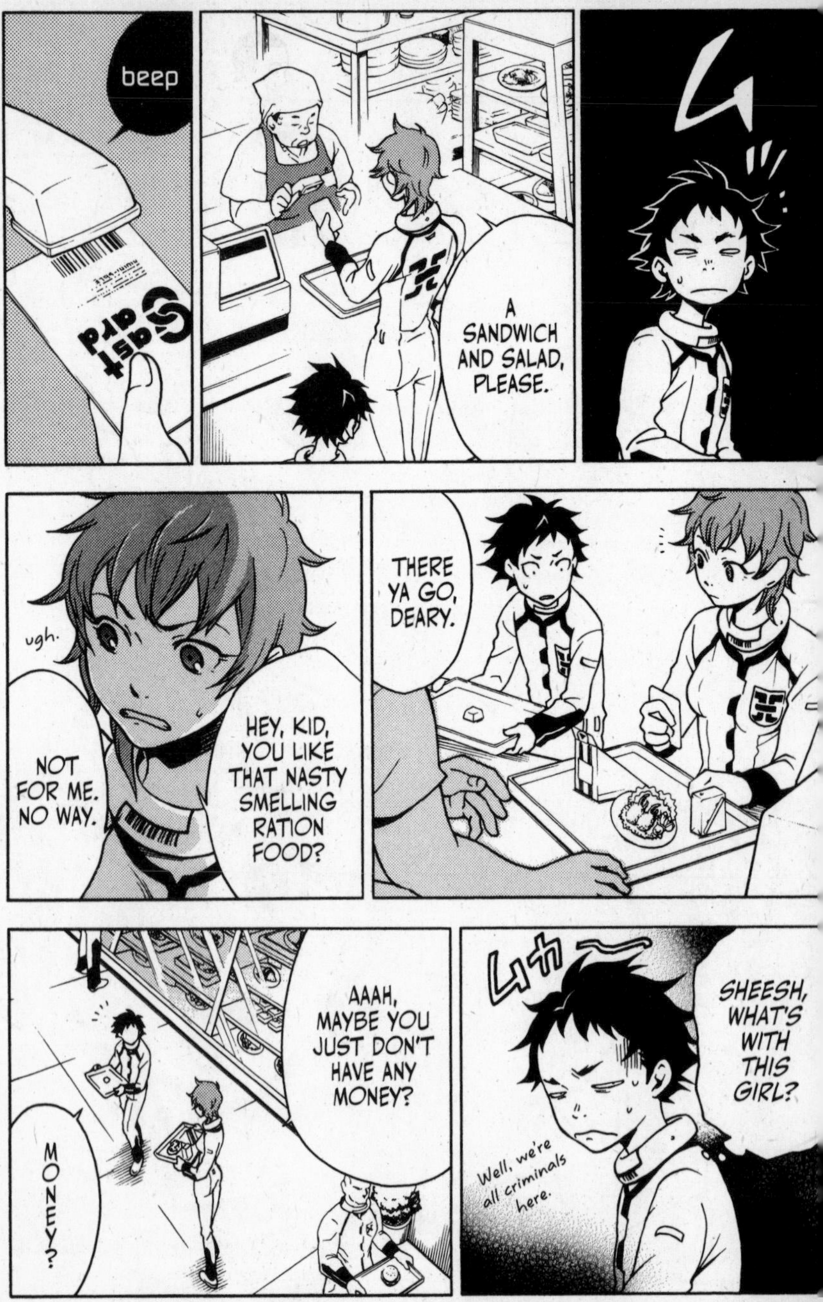
ム
A SANDWICH AND SALAD, PLEASE.
beep
Cast card
THERE YA GO, DEARY.
HEY, KID, YOU LIKE THAT NASTY SMELLING RATION FOOD?
NOT FOR ME. NO WAY.
ugh.
ムカ〜
SHEESH, WHAT'S WITH THIS GIRL?
Well, we're all criminals here.
AAAH, MAYBE YOU JUST DON'T HAVE ANY MONEY?
MONEY?

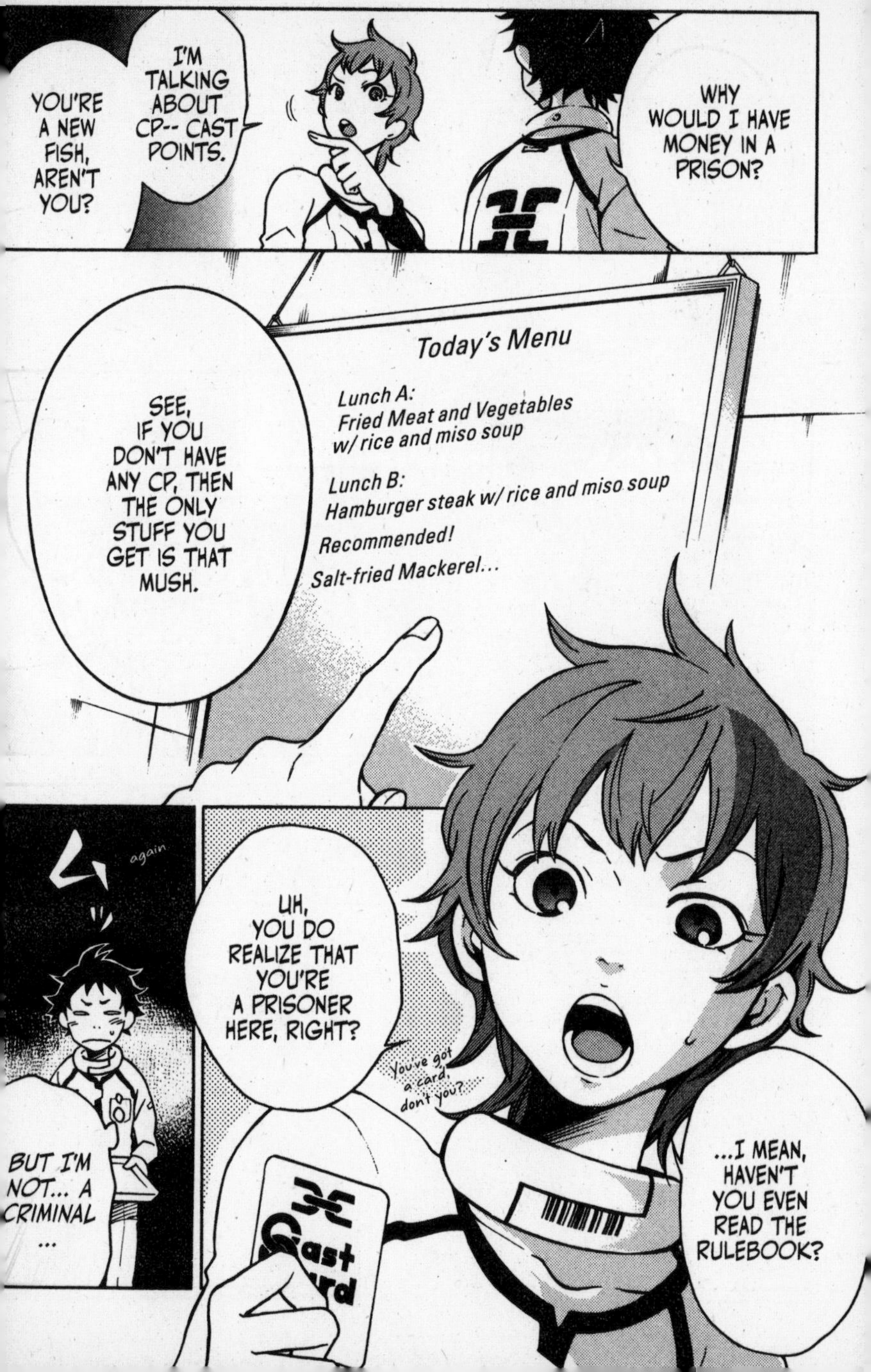
WHY WOULD I HAVE MONEY IN A PRISON?
I'M TALKING ABOUT CP-- CAST POINTS.
YOU'RE A NEW FISH, AREN'T YOU?
Today's Menu
Lunch A:
Fried Meat and Vegetables w/ rice and miso soup
Lunch B:
Hamburger steak w/ rice and miso soup
Recommended!
Salt-fried Mackerel...
SEE, IF YOU DON'T HAVE ANY CP, THEN THE ONLY STUFF YOU GET IS THAT MUSH.
UH, YOU DO REALIZE THAT YOU'RE A PRISONER HERE, RIGHT?
You've got a card, don't you?
...I MEAN, HAVEN'T YOU EVEN READ THE RULEBOOK?
Cast
ム
again
BUT I'M NOT... A CRIMINAL ...

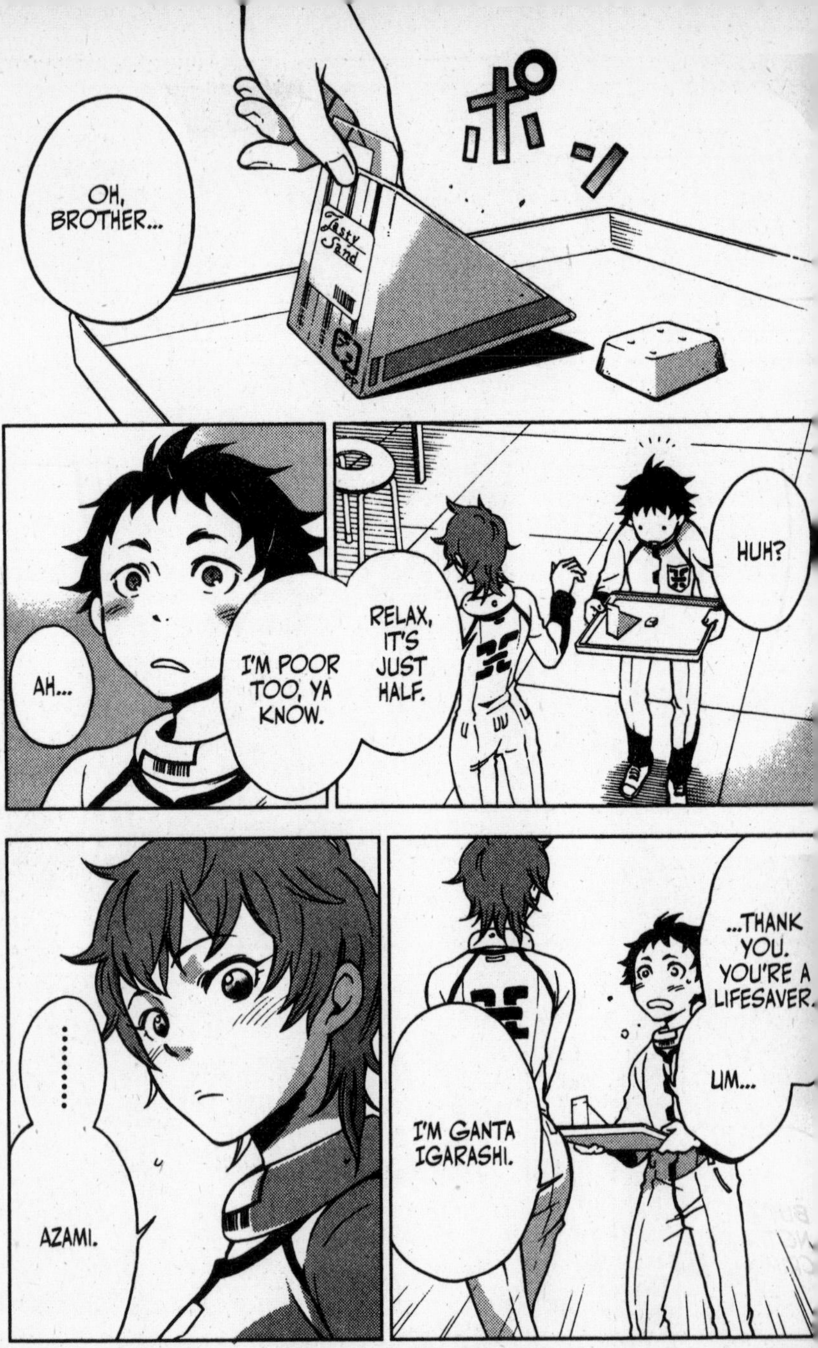
ポッ
OH, BROTHER...
Tasty Sand
HUH?
RELAX, IT'S JUST HALF.
I'M POOR TOO, YA KNOW.
AH...
...THANK YOU. YOU'RE A LIFESAVER.
UM...
I'M GANTA IGARASHI.
....
AZAMI.

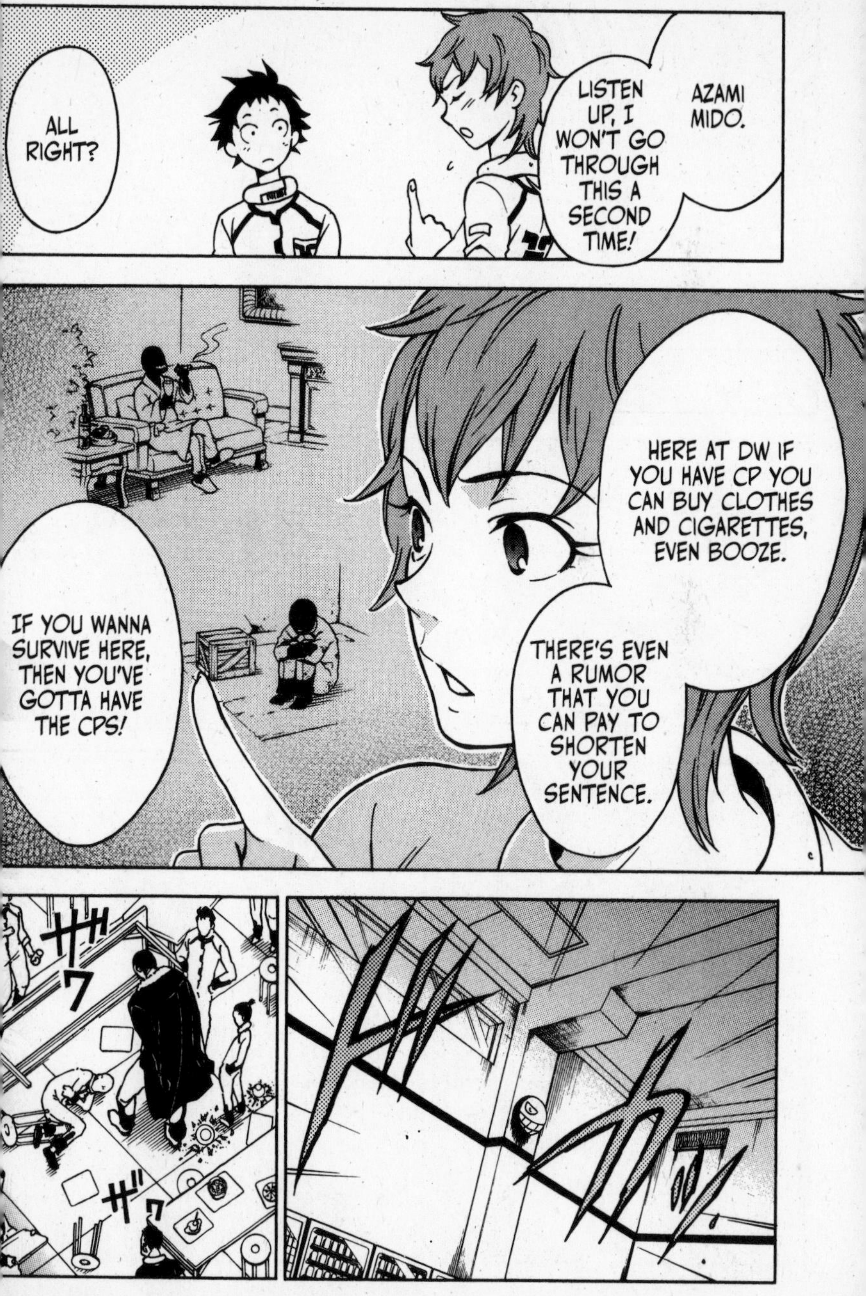
AZAMI MIDO.
LISTEN UP, I WON'T GO THROUGH THIS A SECOND TIME!
ALL RIGHT?
HERE AT DW IF YOU HAVE CP YOU CAN BUY CLOTHES AND CIGARETTES, EVEN BOOZE.
THERE'S EVEN A RUMOR THAT YOU CAN PAY TO SHORTEN YOUR SENTENCE.
IF YOU WANNA SURVIVE HERE, THEN YOU'VE GOTTA HAVE THE CPS!
ザワ
ザワ

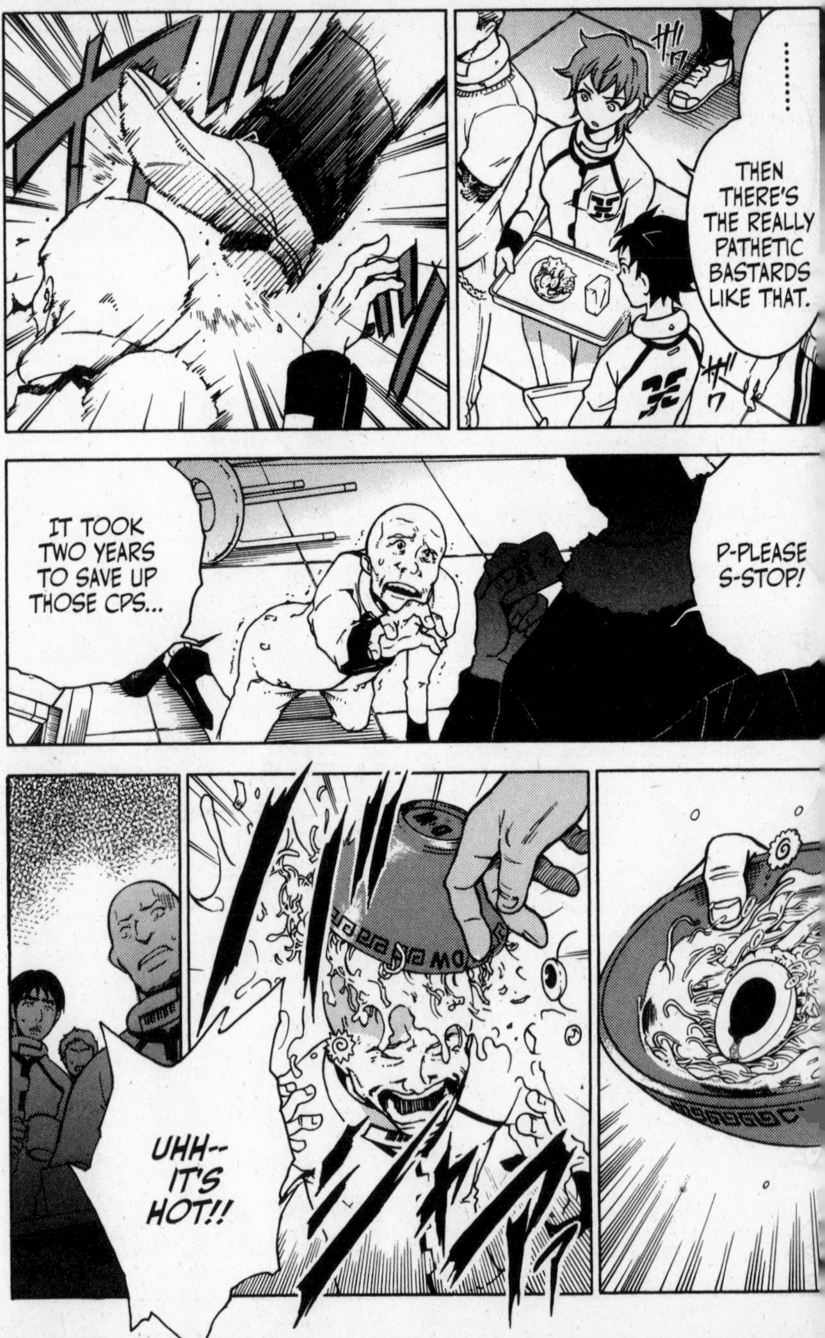
......
ザワ
THEN THERE'S THE REALLY PATHETIC BASTARDS LIKE THAT.
ザワ
P-PLEASE S-STOP!
IT TOOK TWO YEARS TO SAVE UP THOSE CPS...
UHH-- IT'S HOT!!

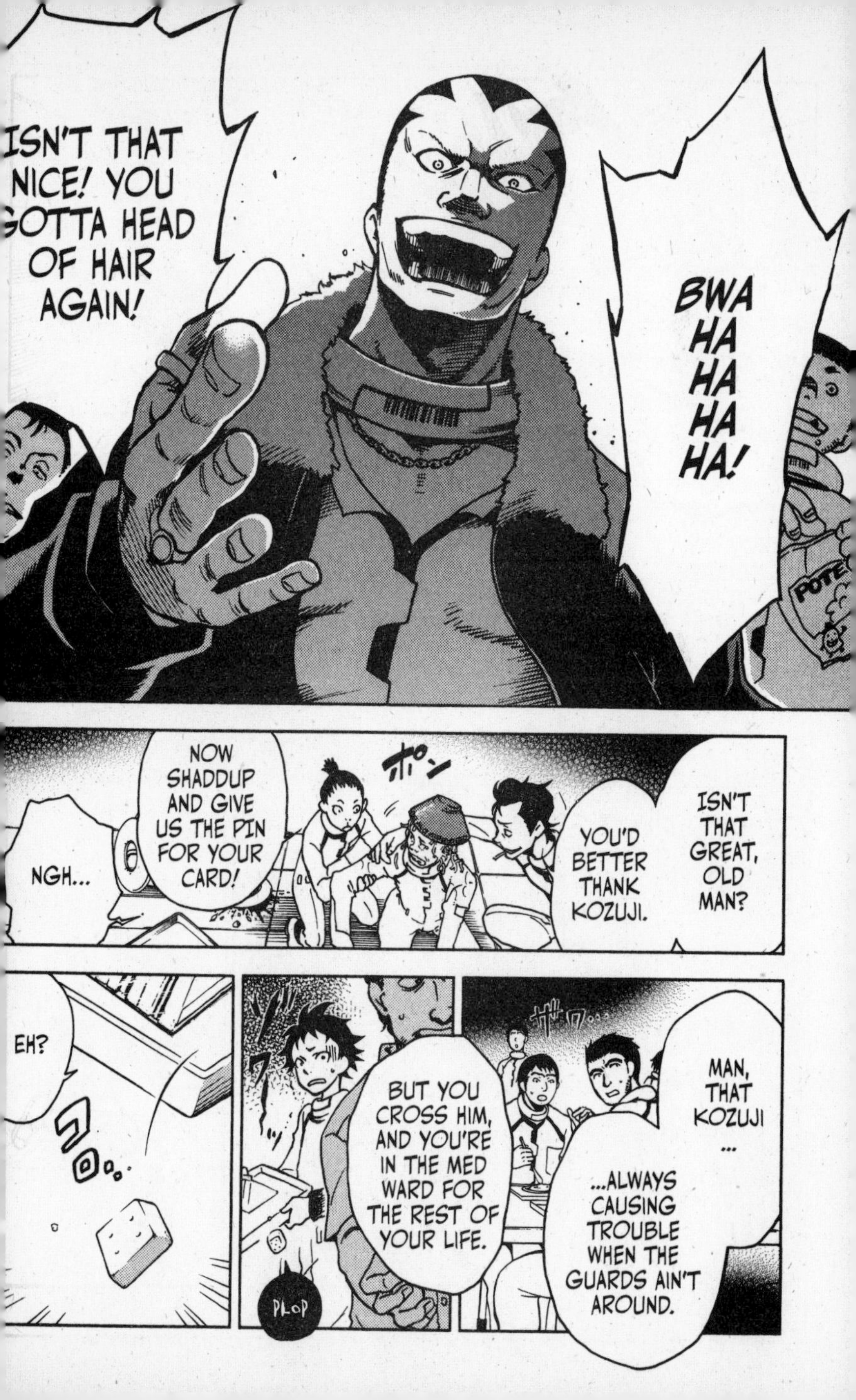
ISN'T THAT NICE! YOU GOTTA HEAD OF HAIR AGAIN!
BWA HA HA HA HA!
POTE
ISN'T THAT GREAT, OLD MAN?
YOU'D BETTER THANK KOZUJI.
ポン
NOW SHADDUP AND GIVE US THE PIN FOR YOUR CARD!
NGH...
MAN, THAT KOZUJI ...
...ALWAYS CAUSING TROUBLE WHEN THE GUARDS AIN'T AROUND.
ザワ...
BUT YOU CROSS HIM, AND YOU'RE IN THE MED WARD FOR THE REST OF YOUR LIFE.
PLOP
EH?
ゴロ...

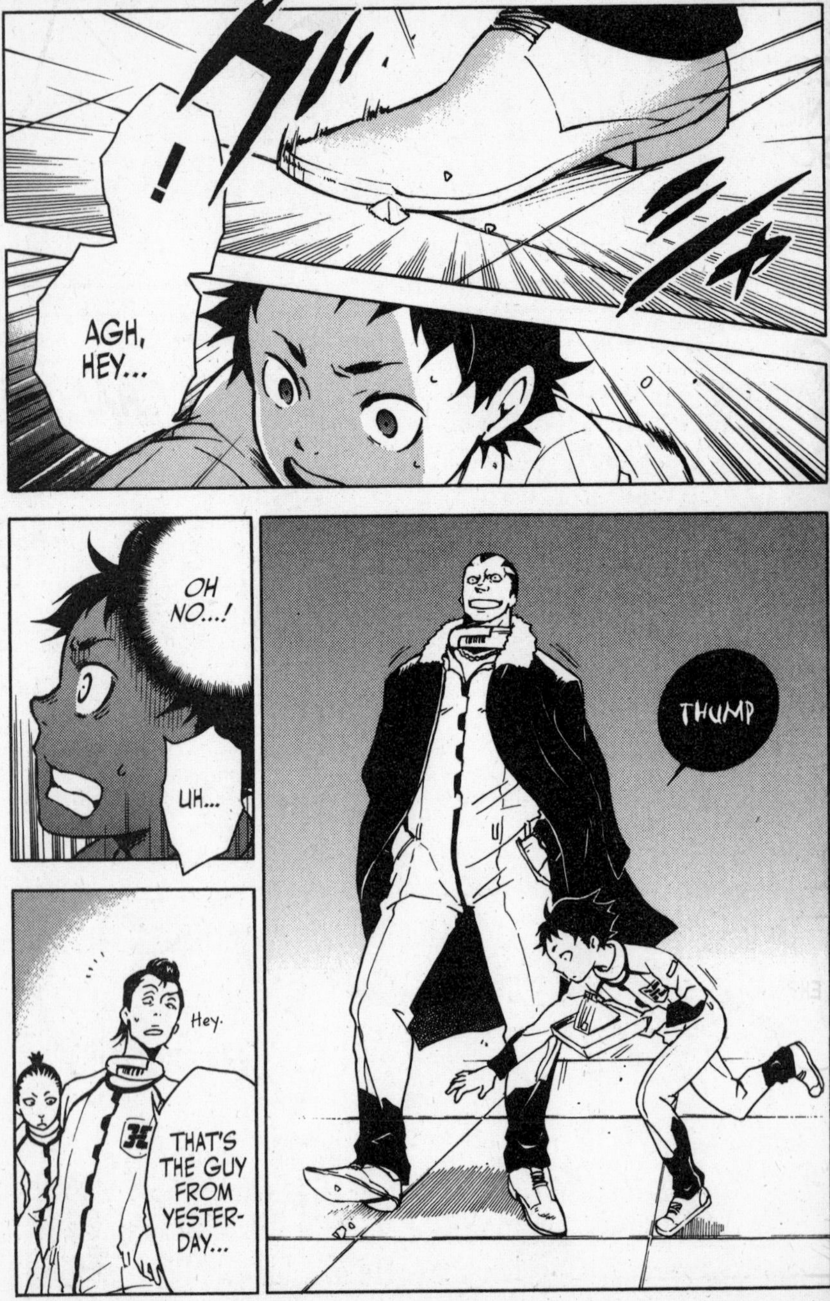
!
AGH, HEY...
THUMP
OH NO...!
UH...
Hey.
THAT'S THE GUY FROM YESTER-DAY...

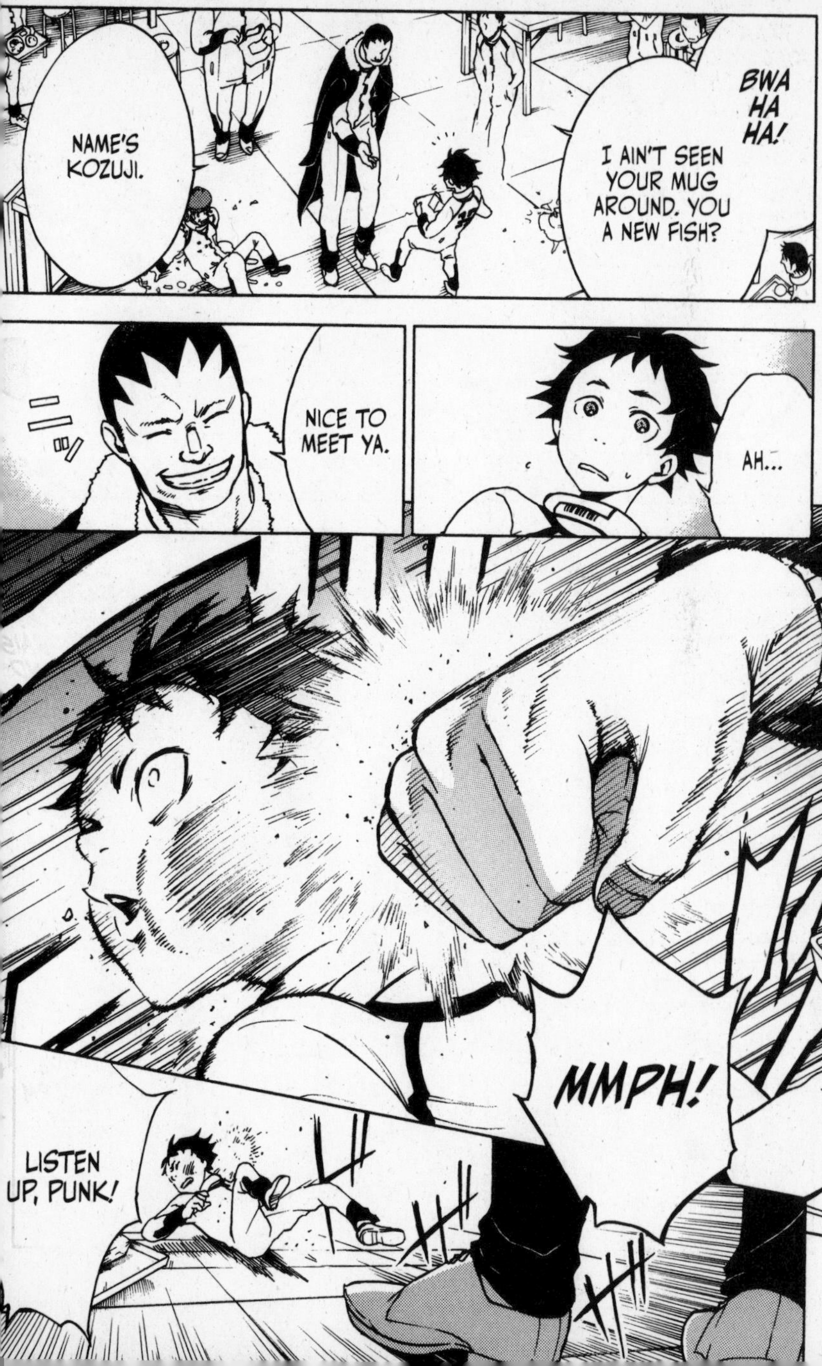
BWA HA HA!
I AIN'T SEEN YOUR MUG AROUND. YOU A NEW FISH?
NAME'S KOZUJI.
AH...
NICE TO MEET YA.
MMPH!
LISTEN UP, PUNK!

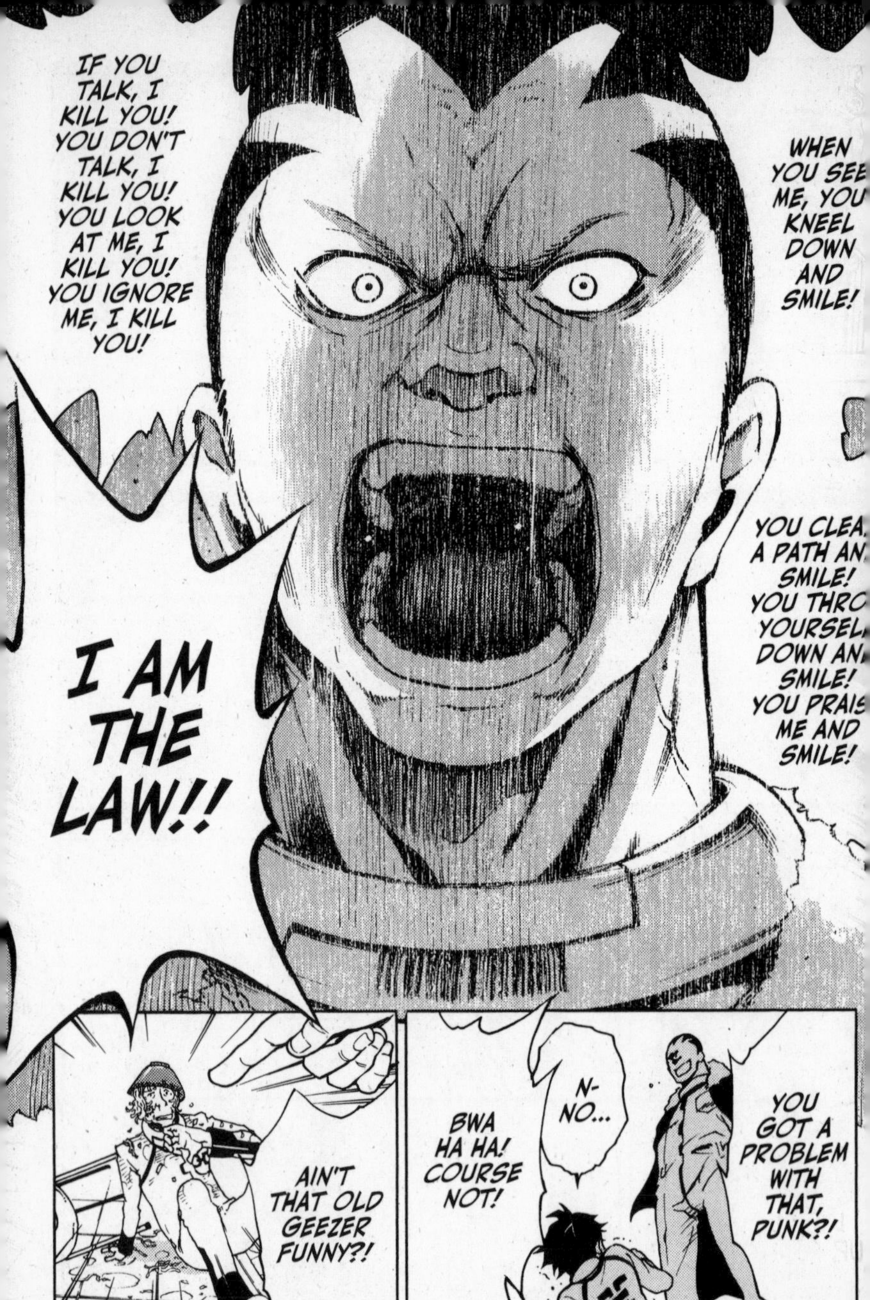
WHEN YOU SEE ME, YOU KNEEL DOWN AND SMILE!
YOU CLEA A PATH AN SMILE! YOU THRO YOURSEL DOWN AN SMILE! YOU PRAIS ME AND SMILE!
IF YOU TALK, I KILL YOU! YOU DON'T TALK, I KILL YOU! YOU LOOK AT ME, I KILL YOU! YOU IGNORE ME, I KILL YOU!
I AM THE LAW!!
YOU GOT A PROBLEM WITH THAT, PUNK?!
N-NO...
BWA HA HA! COURSE NOT!
AIN'T THAT OLD GEEZER FUNNY?!

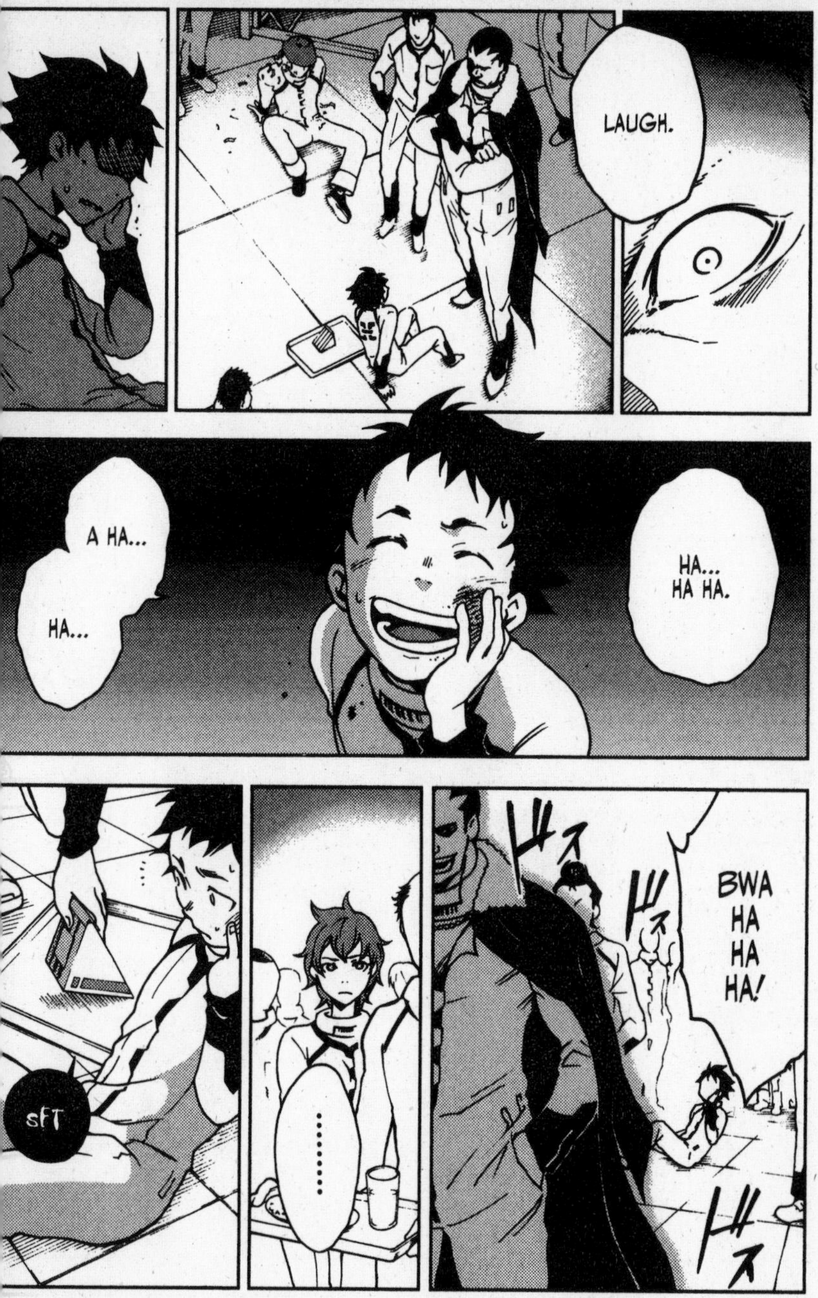
LAUGH.
HA... HA HA.
A HA...
HA...
BWA HA HA HA!
ドッス
ドッス
ドッス
......
...
sFT

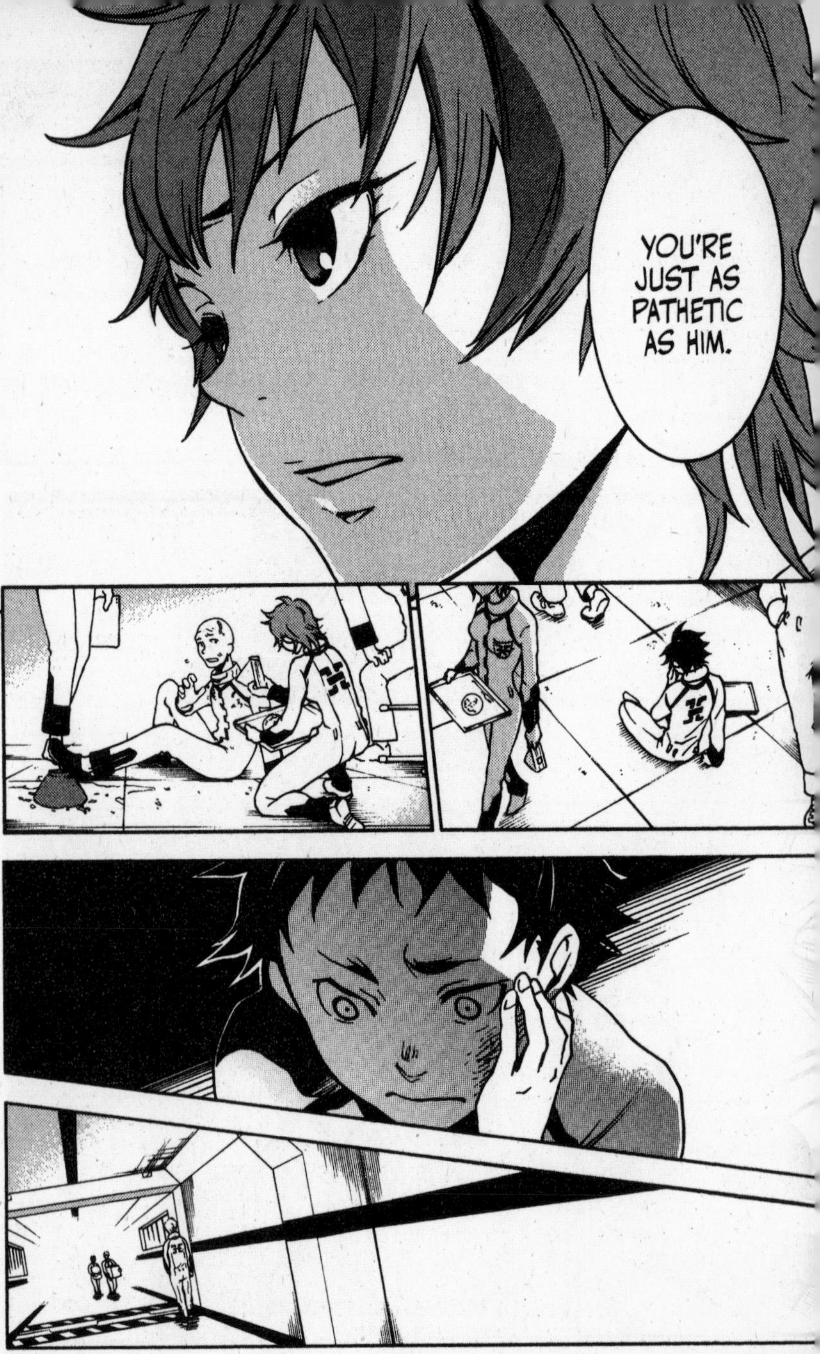
YOU'RE JUST AS PATHETIC AS HIM.

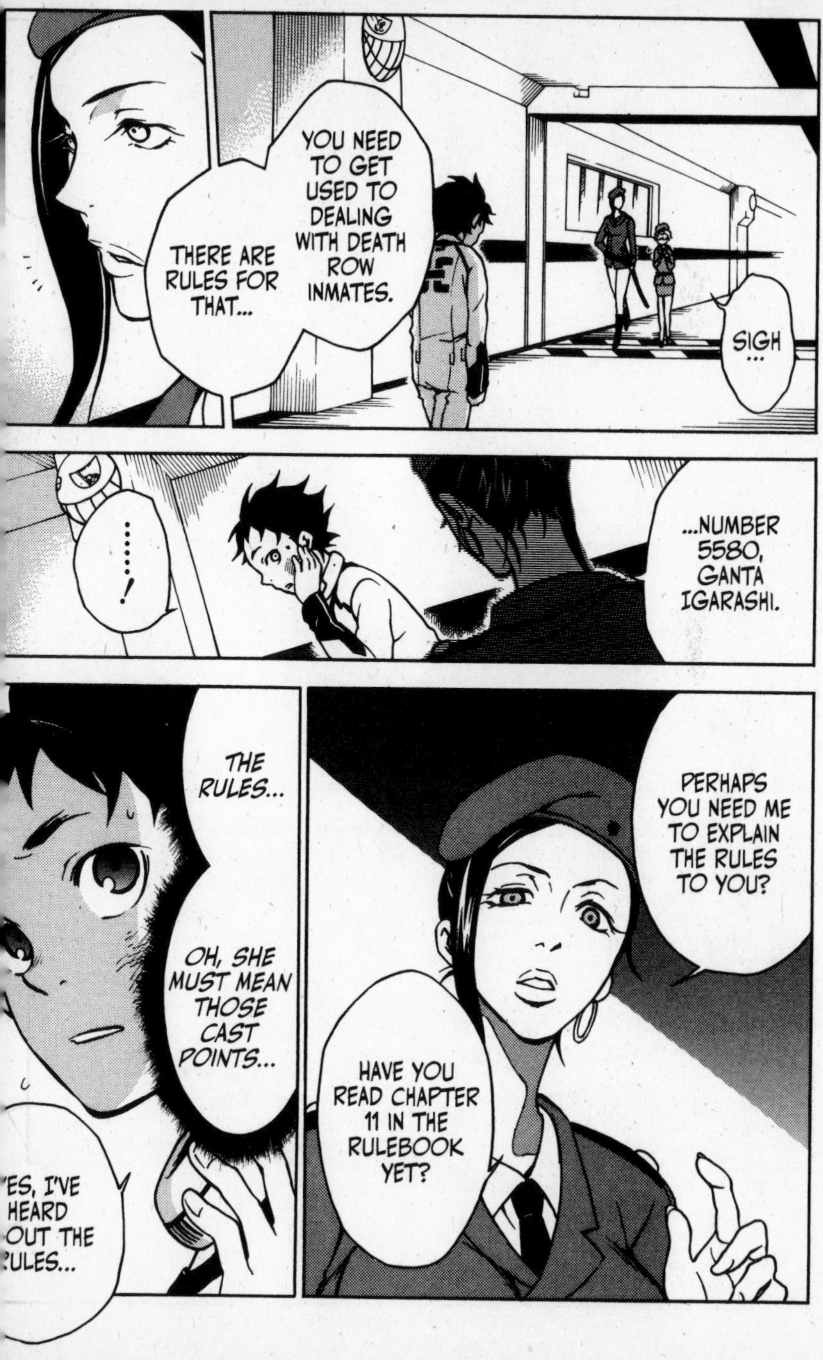
SIGH...
YOU NEED TO GET USED TO DEALING WITH DEATH ROW INMATES.
THERE ARE RULES FOR THAT...
...NUMBER 5580, GANTA IGARASHI.
......!
PERHAPS YOU NEED ME TO EXPLAIN THE RULES TO YOU?
HAVE YOU READ CHAPTER 11 IN THE RULEBOOK YET?
THE RULES...
OH, SHE MUST MEAN THOSE CAST POINTS...
ES, I'VE HEARD OUT THE ULES...

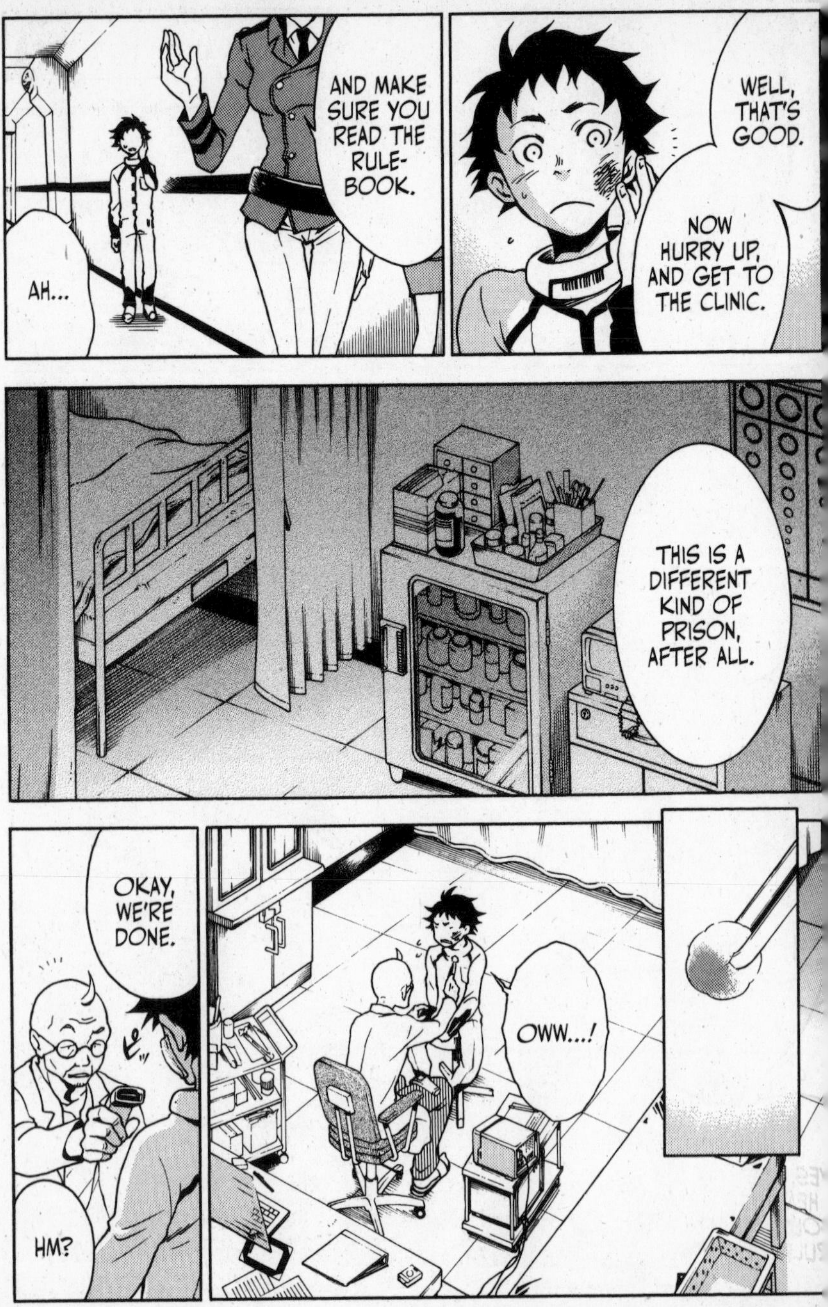
WELL, THAT'S GOOD.
NOW HURRY UP, AND GET TO THE CLINIC.
AND MAKE SURE YOU READ THE RULE-BOOK.
AH...
THIS IS A DIFFERENT KIND OF PRISON, AFTER ALL.
OWW...!
OKAY, WE'RE DONE.
HM?

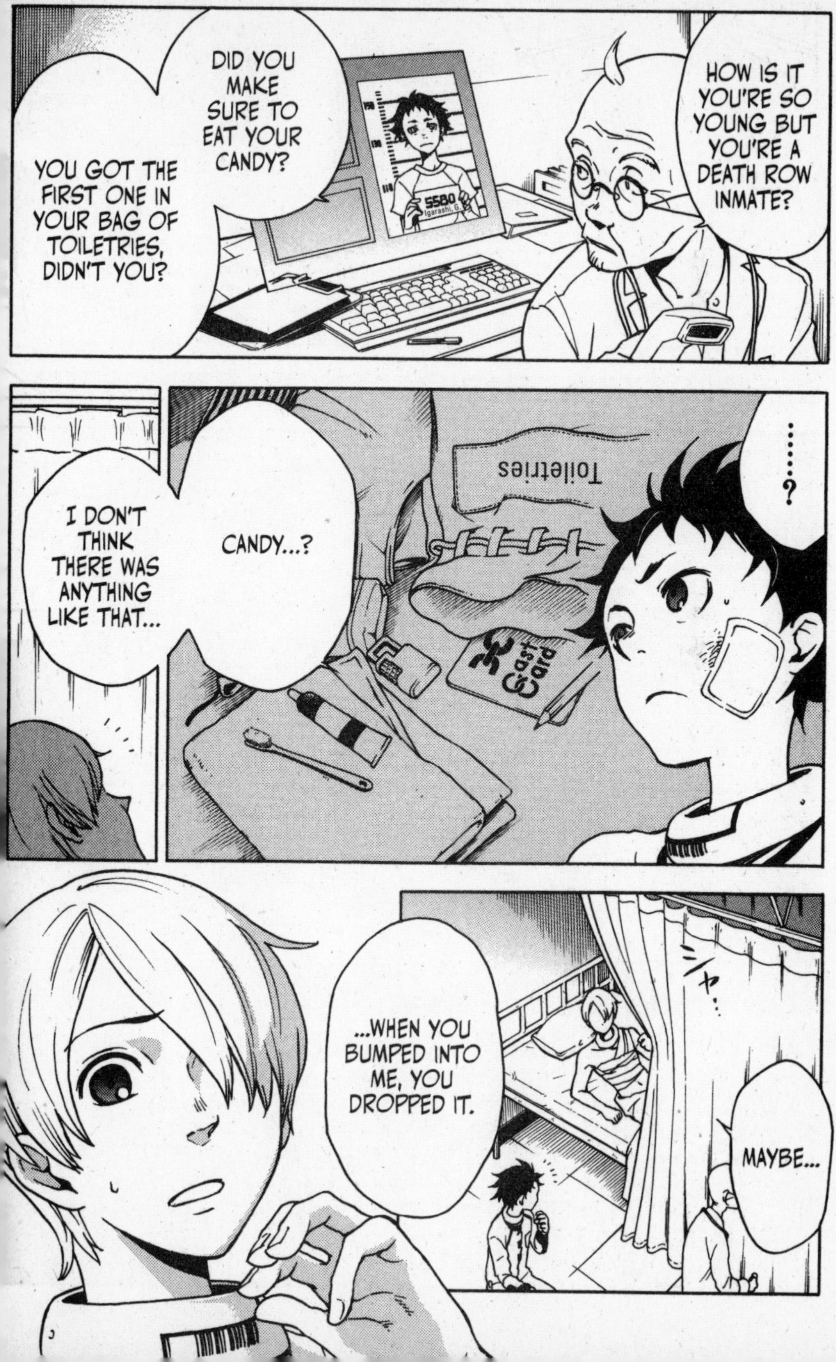
HOW IS IT YOU'RE SO YOUNG BUT YOU'RE A DEATH ROW INMATE?
DID YOU MAKE SURE TO EAT YOUR CANDY?
5580 Igarashi, G.
YOU GOT THE FIRST ONE IN YOUR BAG OF TOILETRIES, DIDN'T YOU?
......?
CANDY...?
I DON'T THINK THERE WAS ANYTHING LIKE THAT...
シャ...
MAYBE...
...WHEN YOU BUMPED INTO ME, YOU DROPPED IT.

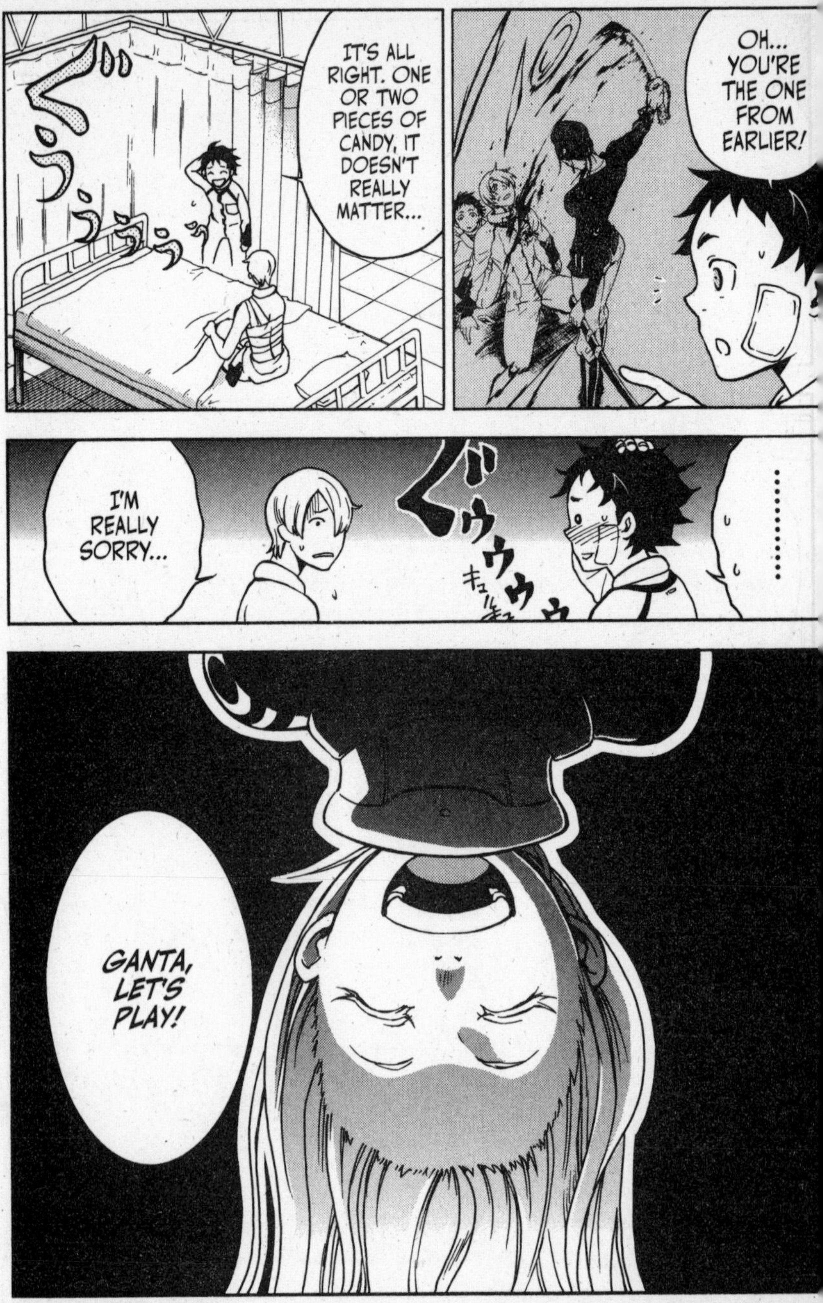
OH... YOU'RE THE ONE FROM EARLIER!
IT'S ALL RIGHT. ONE OR TWO PIECES OF CANDY, IT DOESN'T REALLY MATTER...
....
I'M REALLY SORRY...
GANTA, LET'S PLAY!

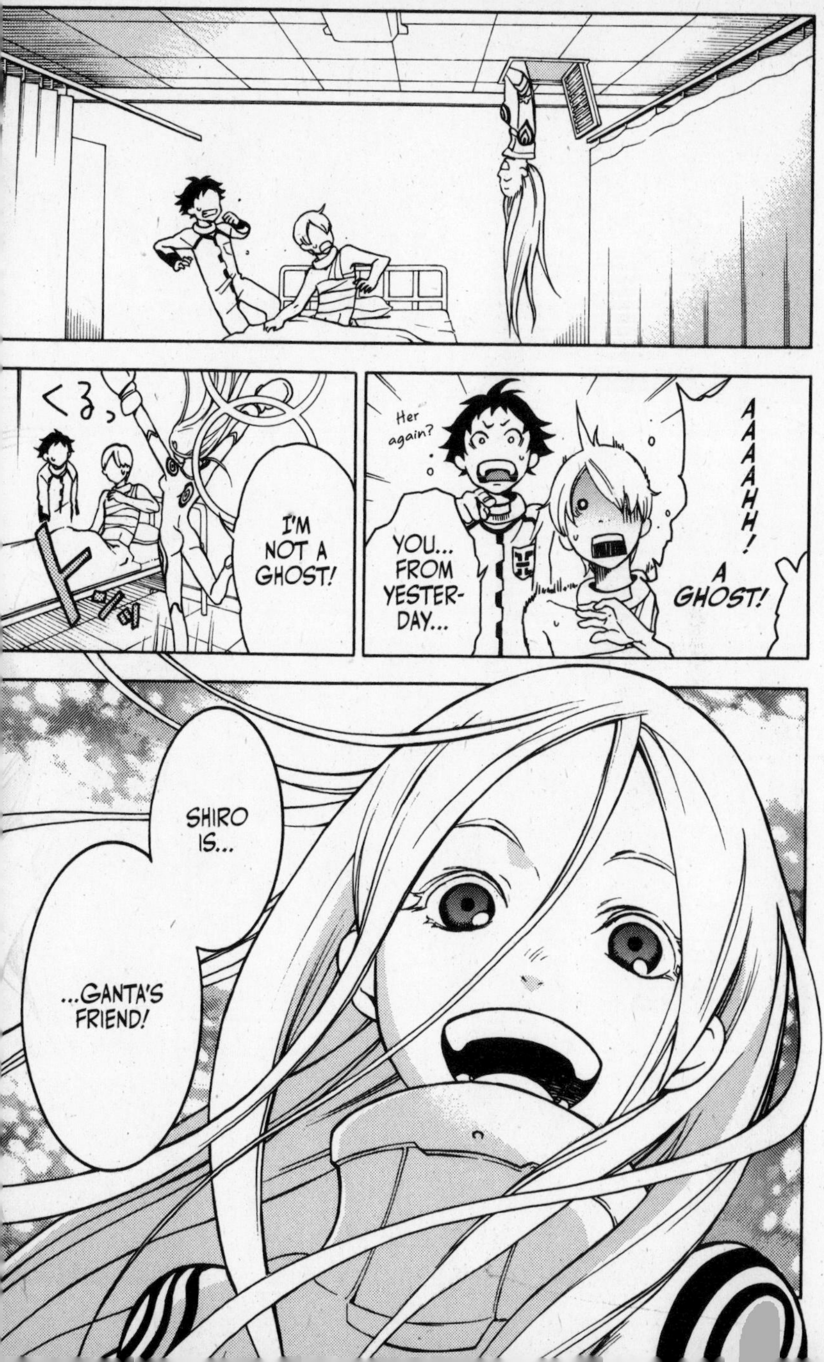
AAAAHH!
A GHOST!
Her again?
YOU... FROM YESTER-DAY...
くるっ
I'M NOT A GHOST!
SHIRO IS...
...GANTA'S FRIEND!

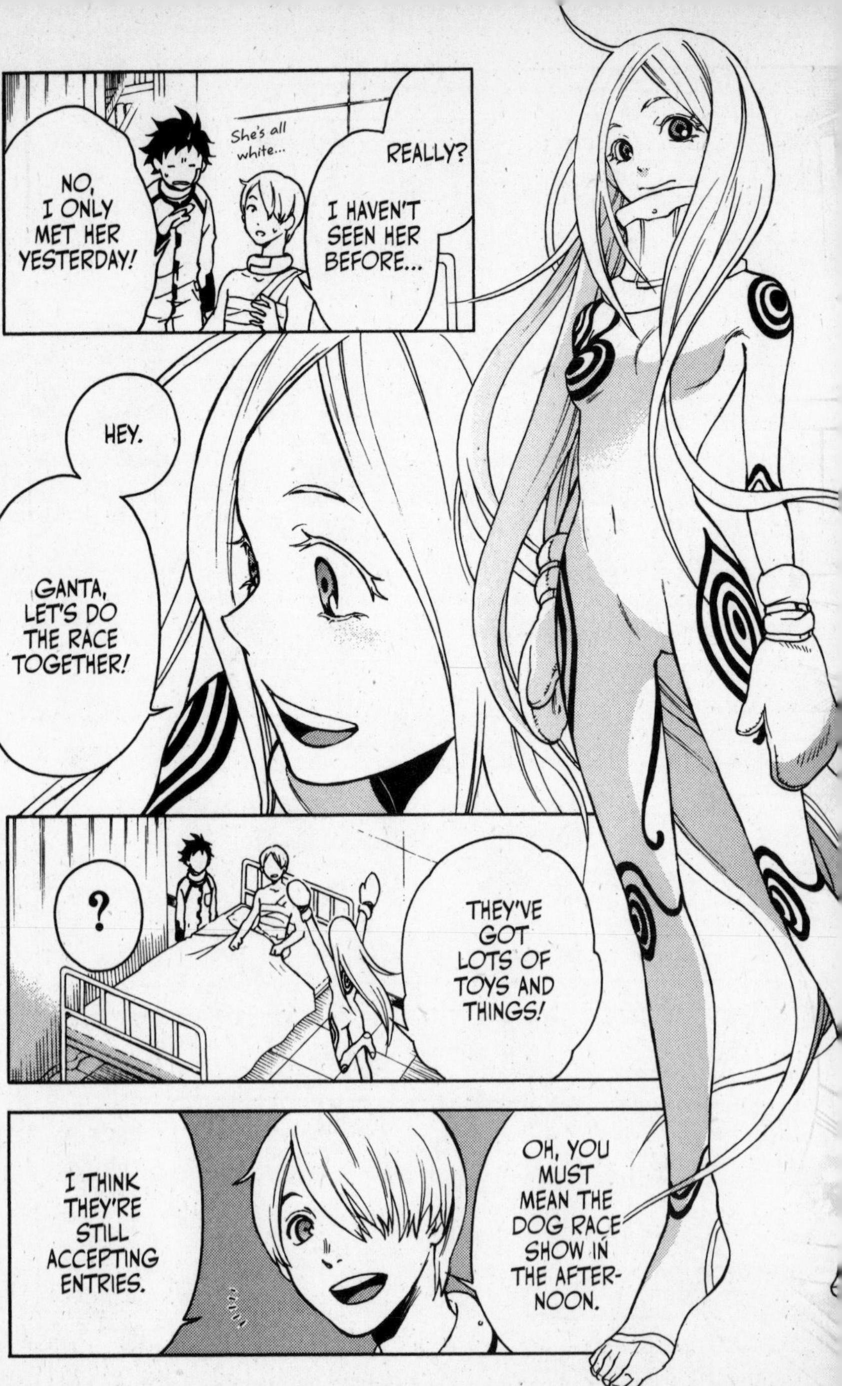
REALLY?
I HAVEN'T SEEN HER BEFORE...
She's all white...
NO, I ONLY MET HER YESTERDAY!
HEY.
GANTA, LET'S DO THE RACE TOGETHER!
THEY'VE GOT LOTS OF TOYS AND THINGS!
?
OH, YOU MUST MEAN THE DOG RACE SHOW IN THE AFTER-NOON.
I THINK THEY'RE STILL ACCEPTING ENTRIES.

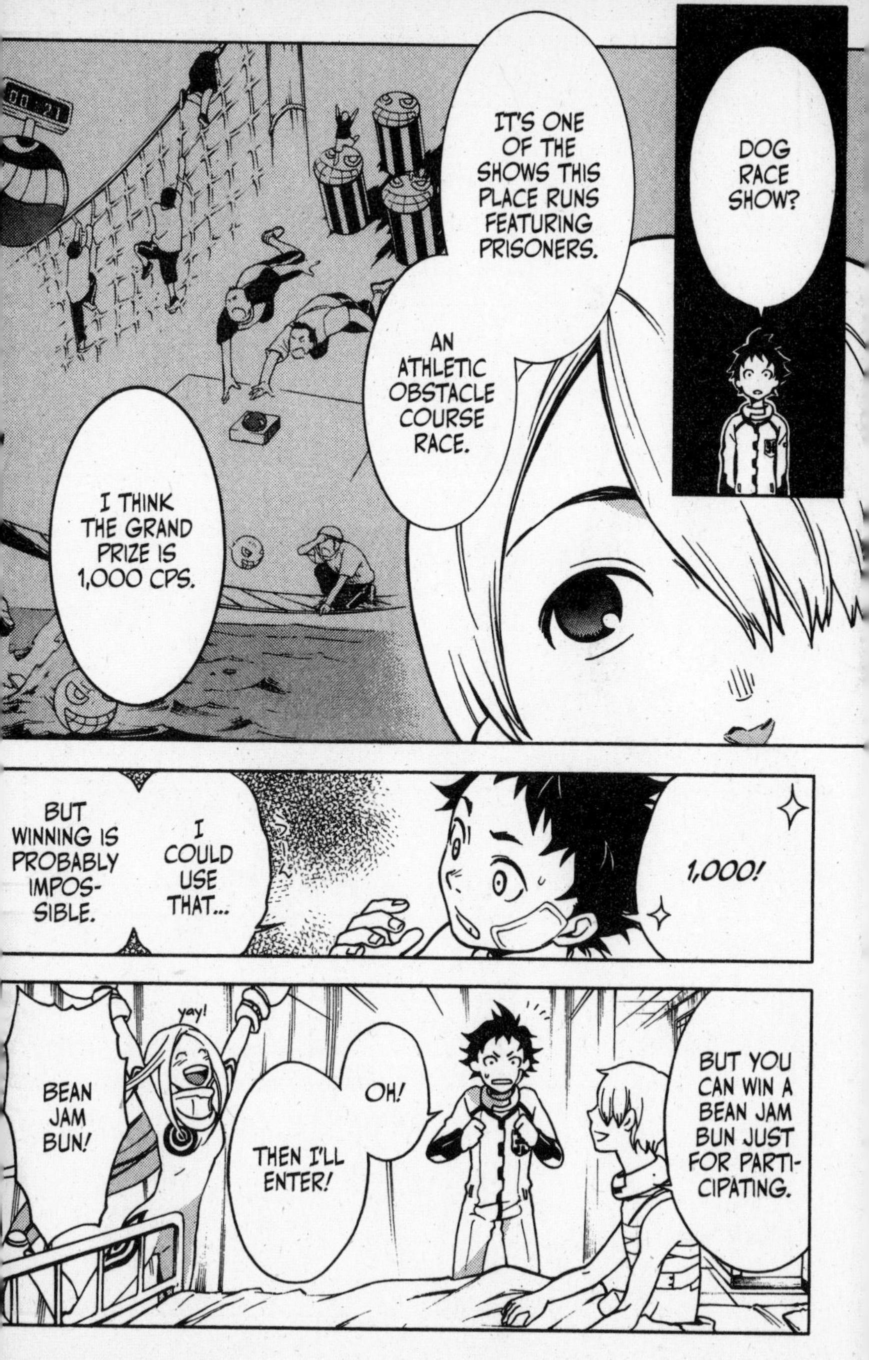
DOG RACE SHOW?
IT'S ONE OF THE SHOWS THIS PLACE RUNS FEATURING PRISONERS.
AN ATHLETIC OBSTACLE COURSE RACE.
I THINK THE GRAND PRIZE IS 1,000 CPS.
1,000!
I COULD USE THAT...
BUT WINNING IS PROBABLY IMPOS-SIBLE.
BUT YOU CAN WIN A BEAN JAM BUN JUST FOR PARTI-CIPATING.
OH!
THEN I'LL ENTER!
yay!
BEAN JAM BUN!

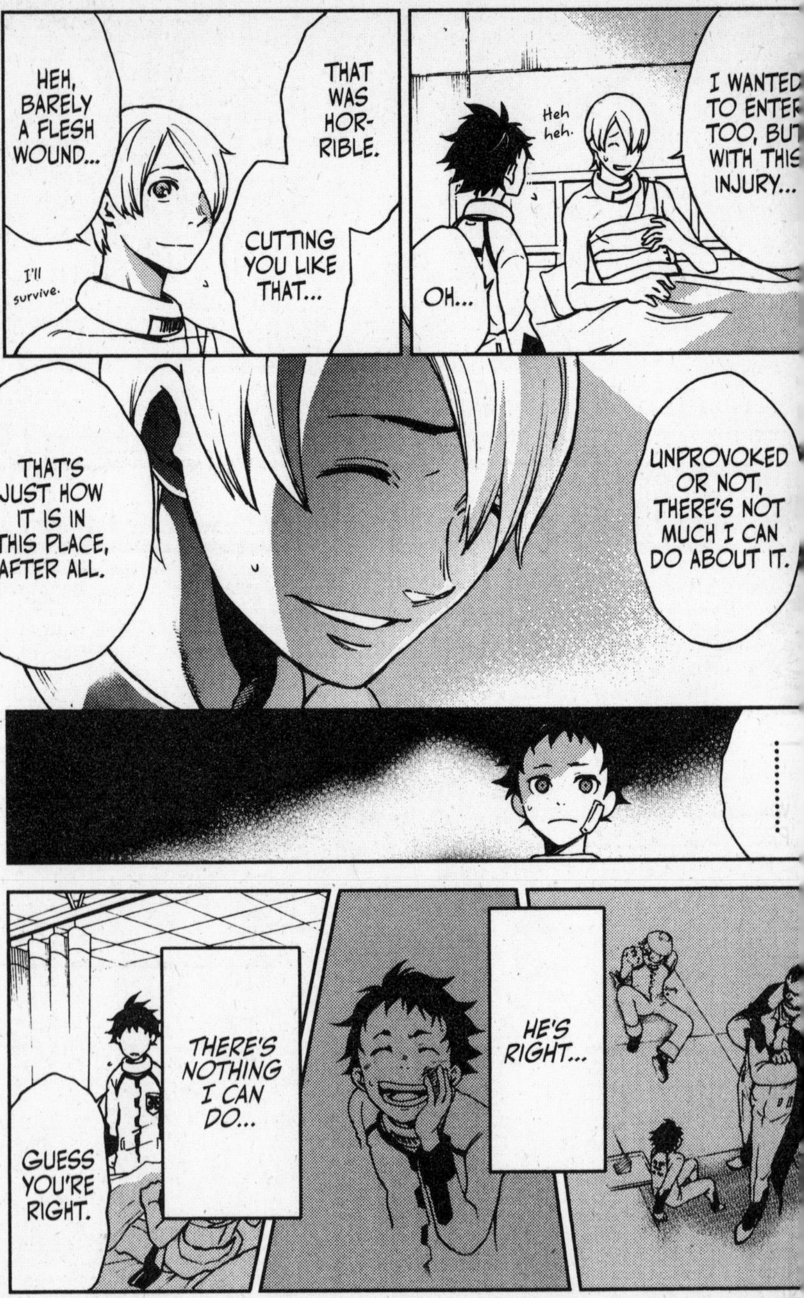
I WANTED TO ENTER TOO, BUT WITH THIS INJURY...
Heh heh.
OH...
THAT WAS HORRIBLE.
CUTTING YOU LIKE THAT...
HEH, BARELY A FLESH WOUND...
I'll survive.
UNPROVOKED OR NOT, THERE'S NOT MUCH I CAN DO ABOUT IT.
THAT'S JUST HOW IT IS IN THIS PLACE, AFTER ALL.
....
HE'S RIGHT...
THERE'S NOTHING I CAN DO...
GUESS YOU'RE RIGHT.

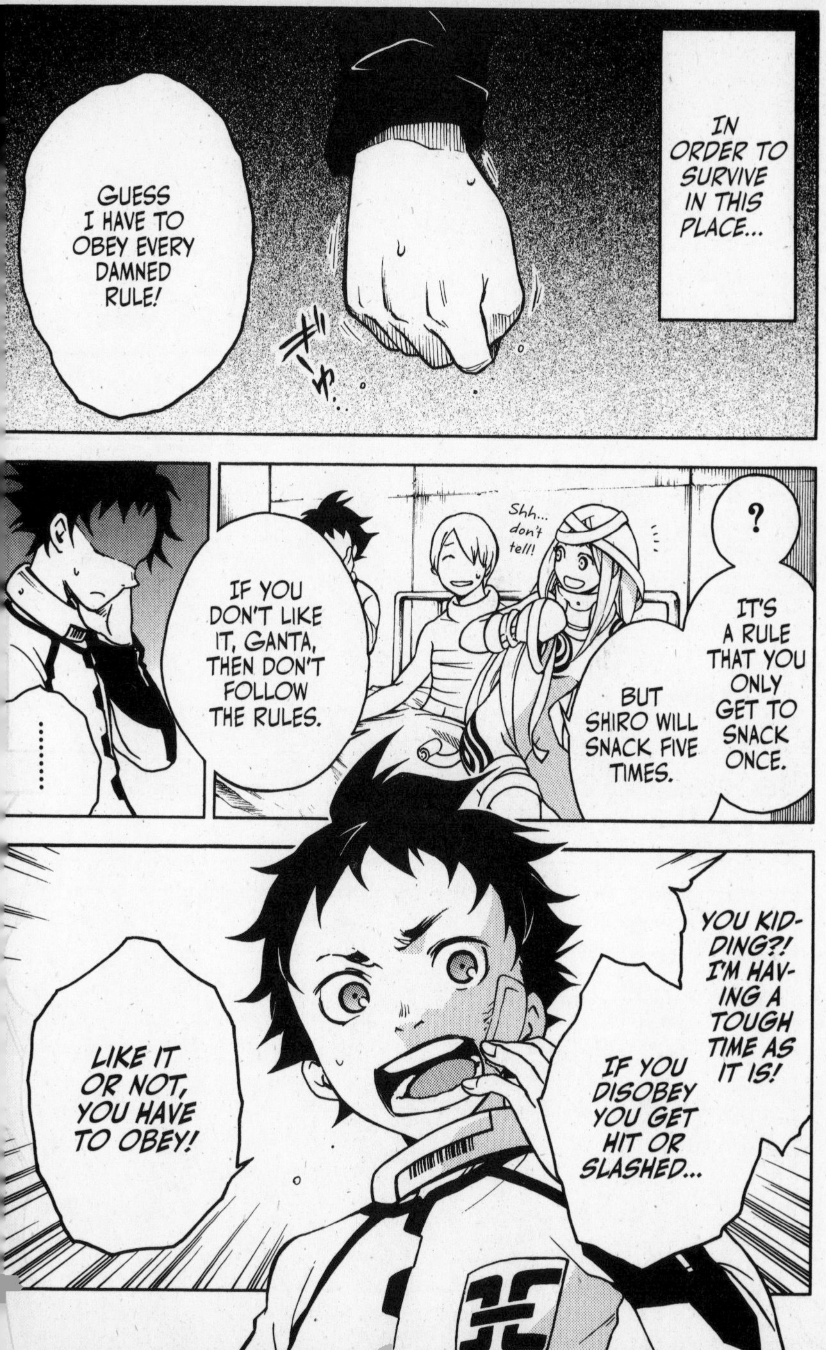
IN ORDER TO SURVIVE IN THIS PLACE...
GUESS I HAVE TO OBEY EVERY DAMNED RULE!
?
IT'S A RULE THAT YOU ONLY GET TO SNACK ONCE.
BUT SHIRO WILL SNACK FIVE TIMES.
Shh... don't tell!
IF YOU DON'T LIKE IT, GANTA, THEN DON'T FOLLOW THE RULES.
......
YOU KIDDING?! I'M HAVING A TOUGH TIME AS IT IS!
IF YOU DISOBEY YOU GET HIT OR SLASHED...
LIKE IT OR NOT, YOU HAVE TO OBEY!

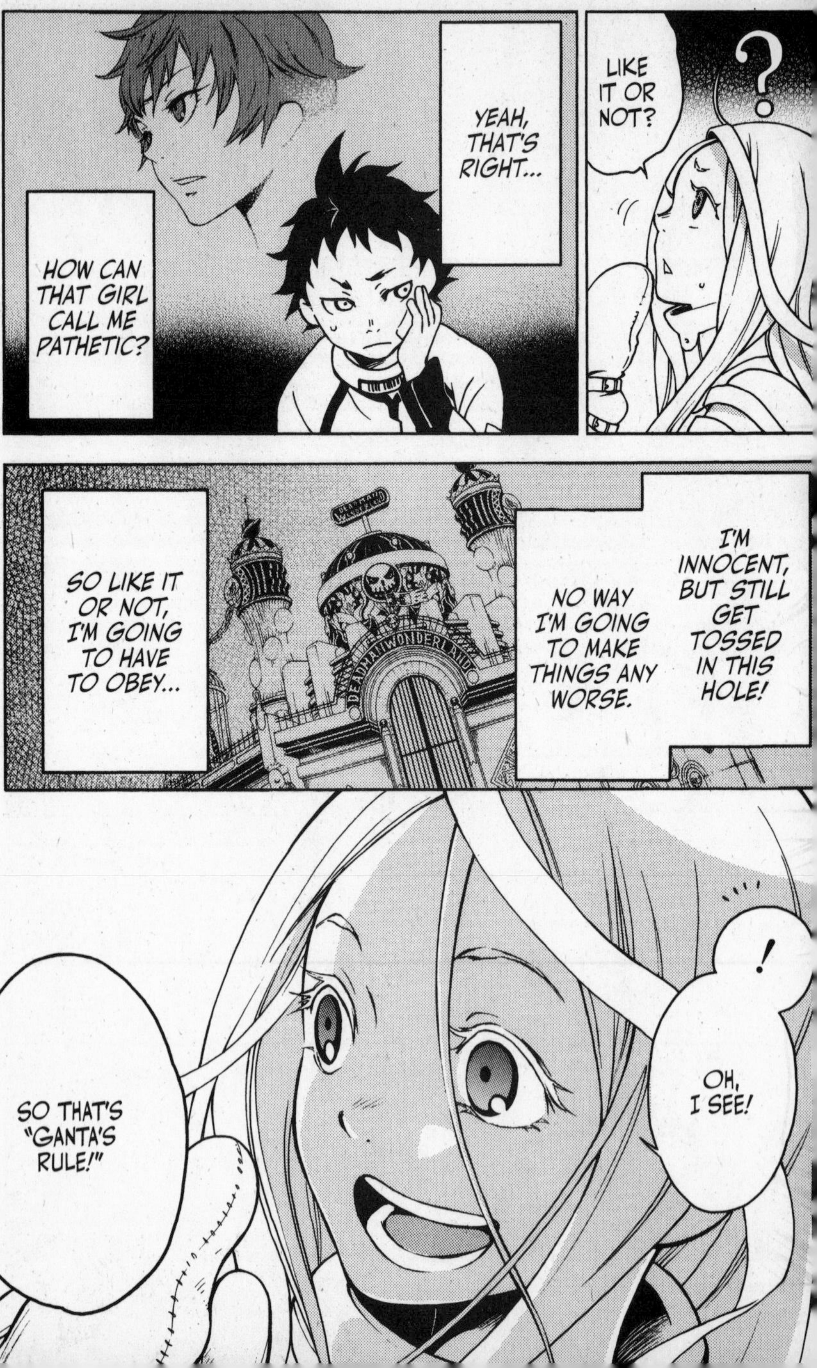
?
LIKE IT OR NOT?
YEAH, THAT'S RIGHT...
HOW CAN THAT GIRL CALL ME PATHETIC?
I'M INNOCENT, BUT STILL GET TOSSED IN THIS HOLE!
NO WAY I'M GOING TO MAKE THINGS ANY WORSE.
DEADMAN WONDERLAND
SO LIKE IT OR NOT, I'M GOING TO HAVE TO OBEY...
!
OH, I SEE!
SO THAT'S "GANTA'S RULE!"

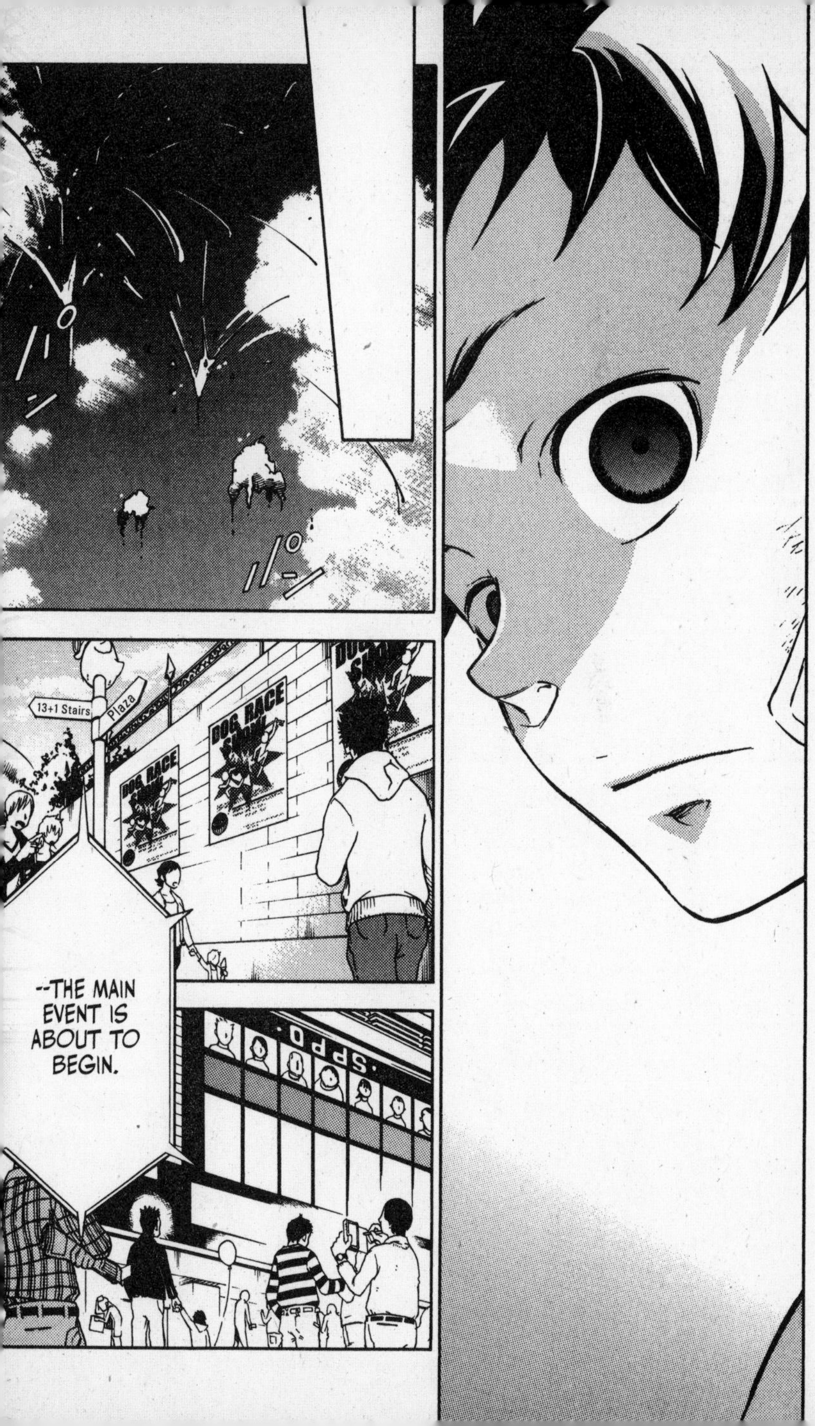
13+1 Stairs
Plaza
DOG RACE SHOW!
--THE MAIN EVENT IS ABOUT TO BEGIN.

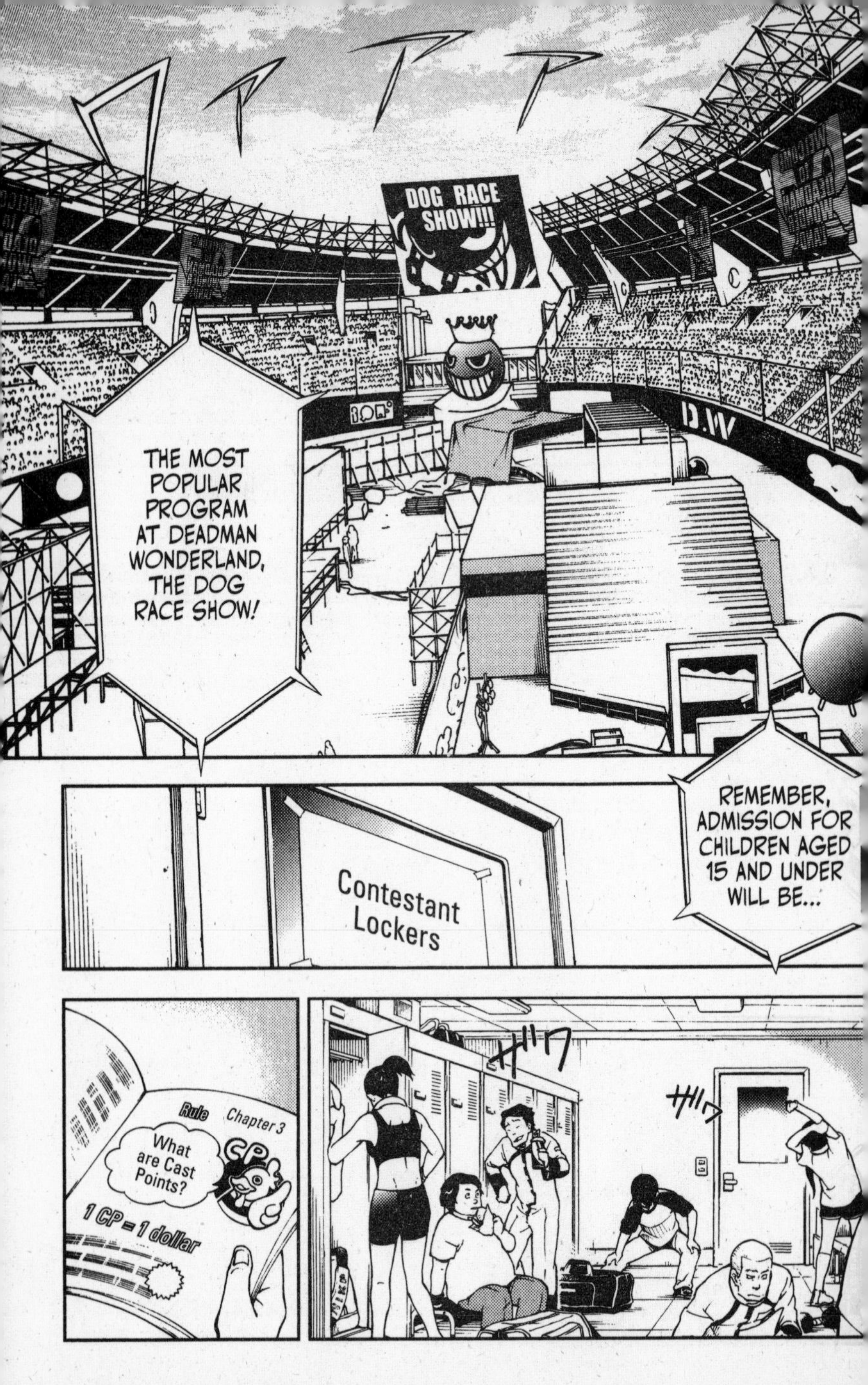
DOG RACE SHOW!!!
D.W
THE MOST POPULAR PROGRAM AT DEADMAN WONDERLAND, THE DOG RACE SHOW!
REMEMBER, ADMISSION FOR CHILDREN AGED 15 AND UNDER WILL BE...
Contestant Lockers
Rule Chapter 3
What are Cast Points?
1 CP = 1 dollar

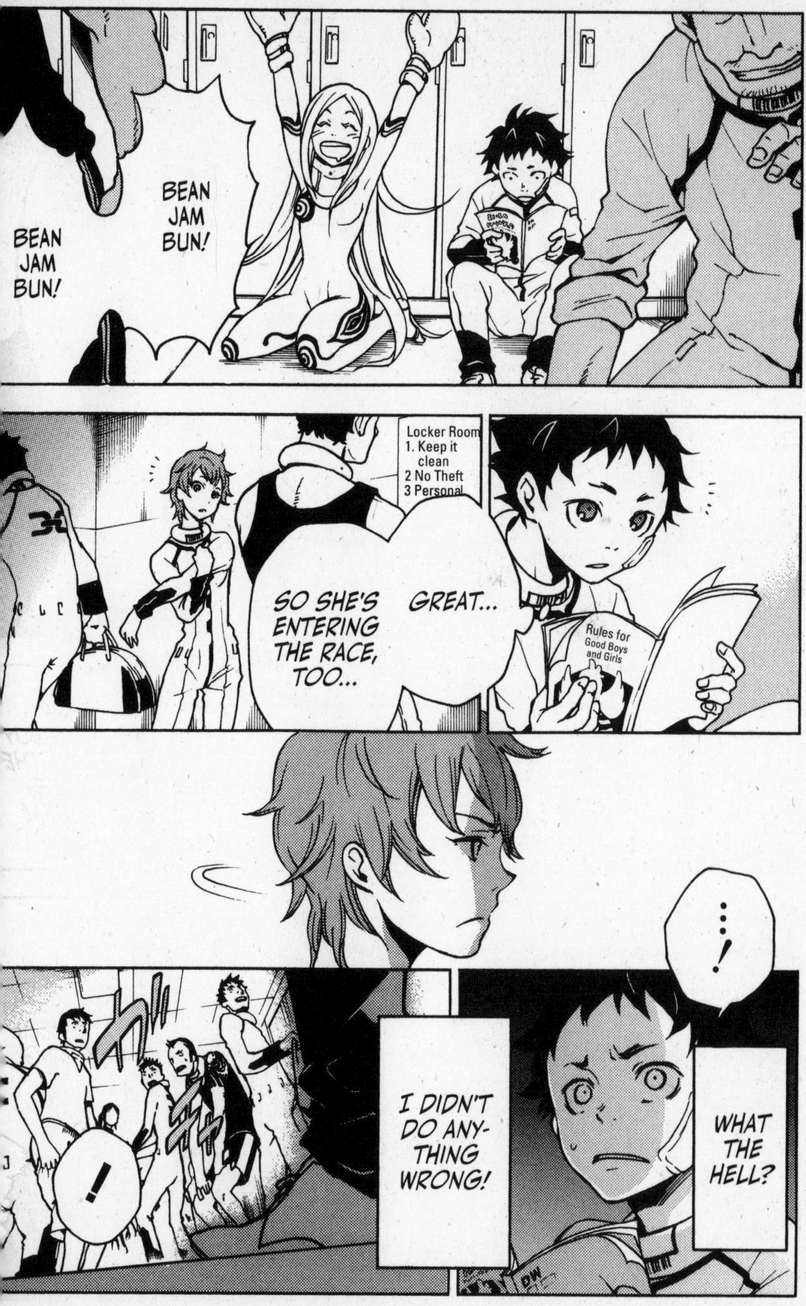
BEAN JAM BUN!
BEAN JAM BUN!
GREAT...
Rules for Good Boys and Girls
Locker Room
1. Keep it clean
2 No Theft
3 Personal
SO SHE'S ENTERING THE RACE, TOO...
...!
WHAT THE HELL?
I DIDN'T DO ANY-THING WRONG!
!

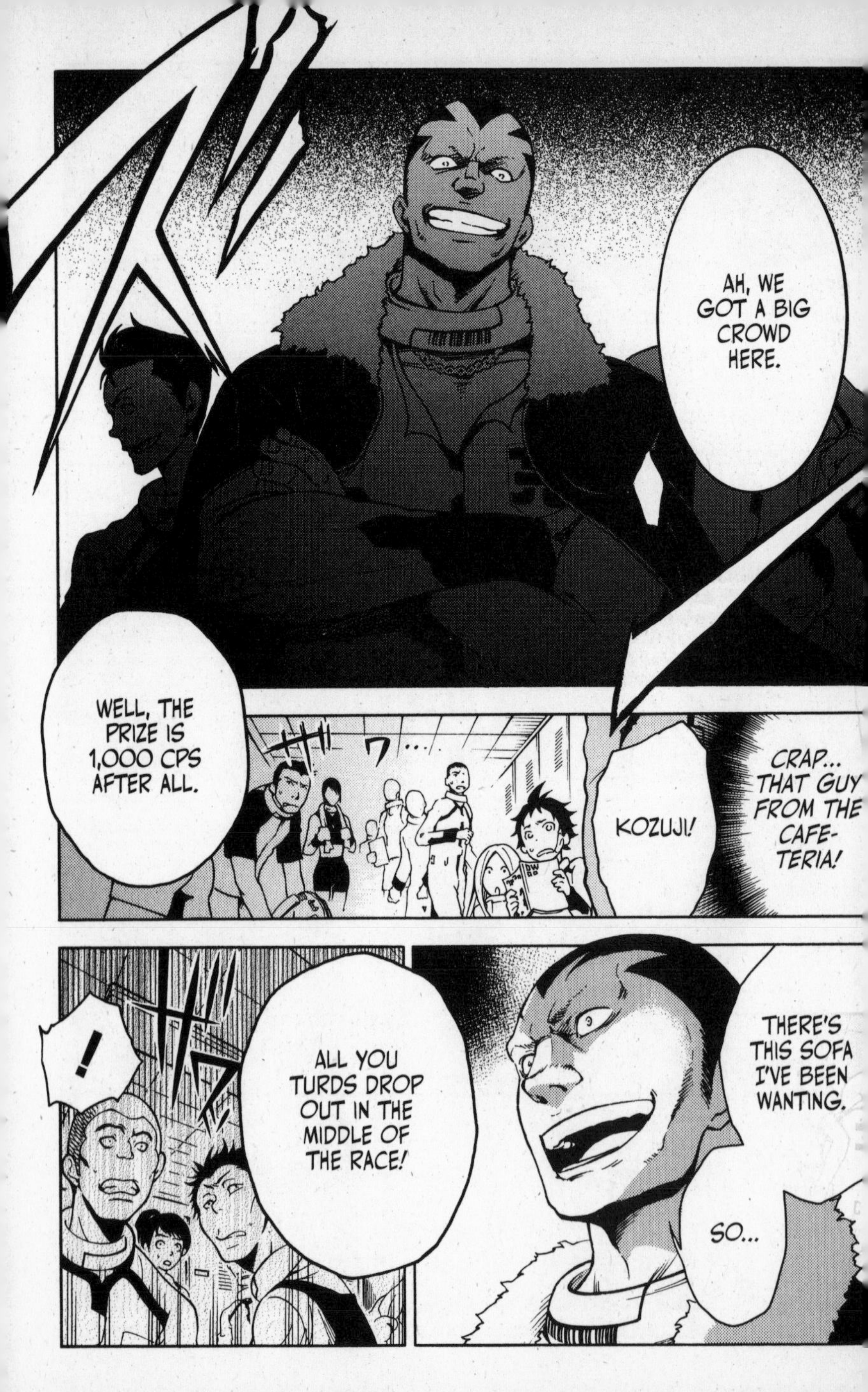
AH, WE GOT A BIG CROWD HERE.
CRAP... THAT GUY FROM THE CAFE-TERIA!
KOZUJI!
WELL, THE PRIZE IS 1,000 CPS AFTER ALL.
THERE'S THIS SOFA I'VE BEEN WANTING.
SO...
ALL YOU TURDS DROP OUT IN THE MIDDLE OF THE RACE!
!

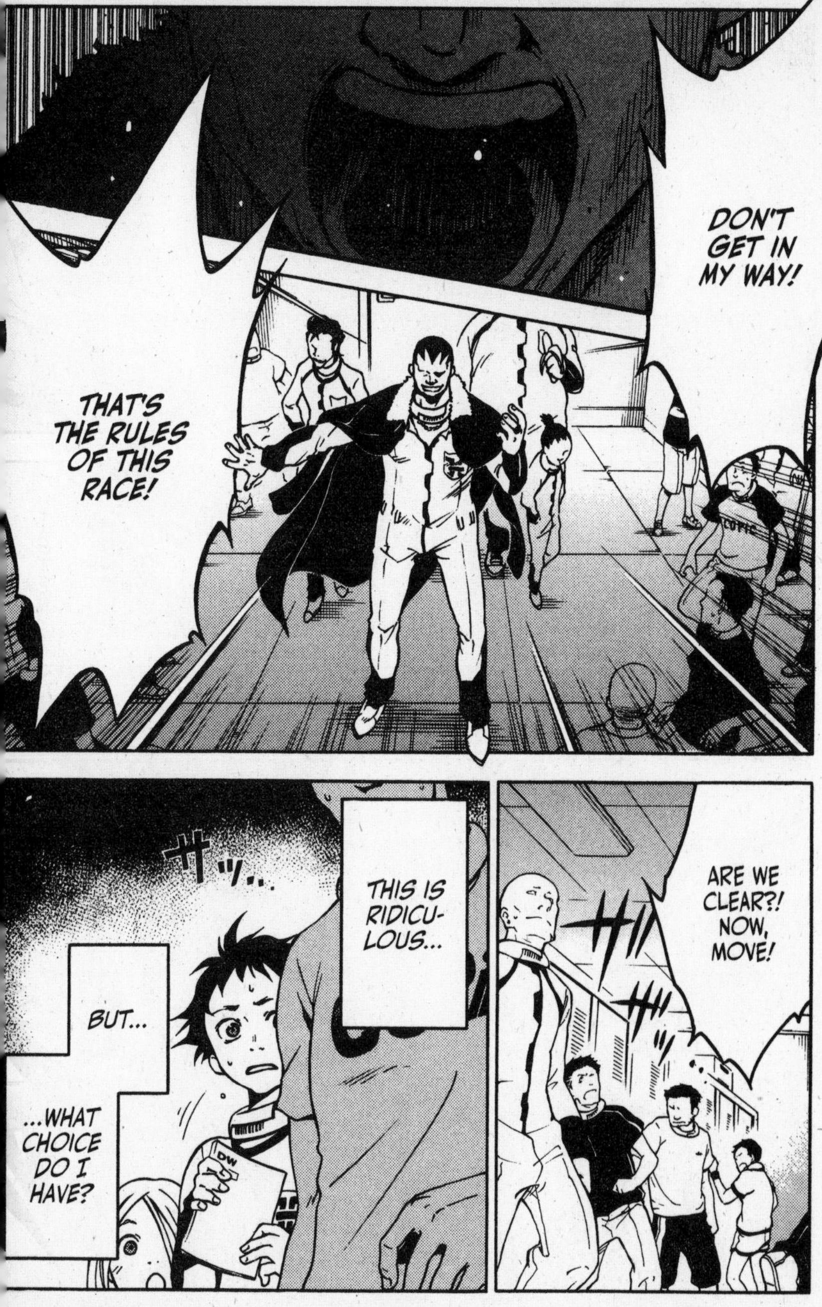
DON'T GET IN MY WAY!
THAT'S THE RULES OF THIS RACE!
ARE WE CLEAR?! NOW, MOVE!
ザッ...
THIS IS RIDICU-LOUS...
BUT...
...WHAT CHOICE DO I HAVE?

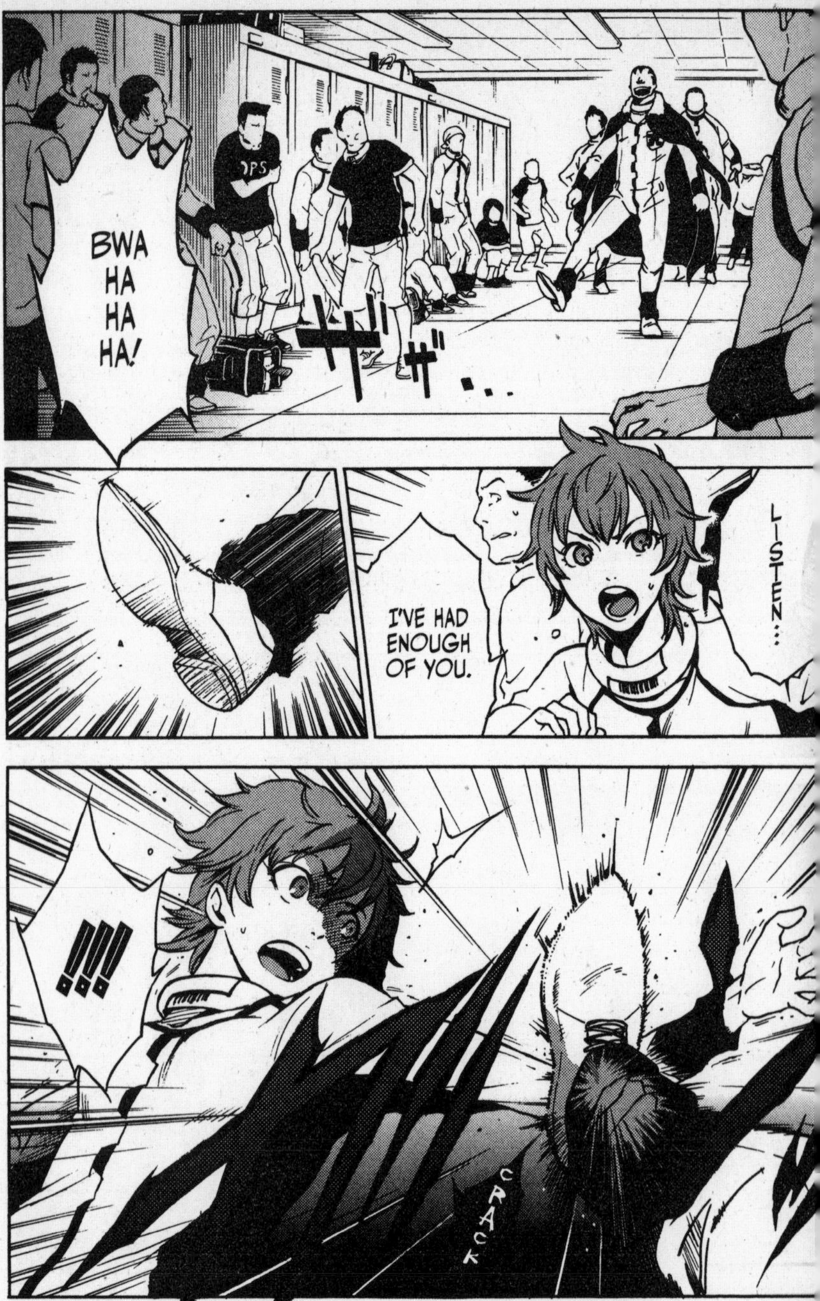
ザザ...
BWA HA HA HA!
LISTEN...
I'VE HAD ENOUGH OF YOU.
!!!
CRACK

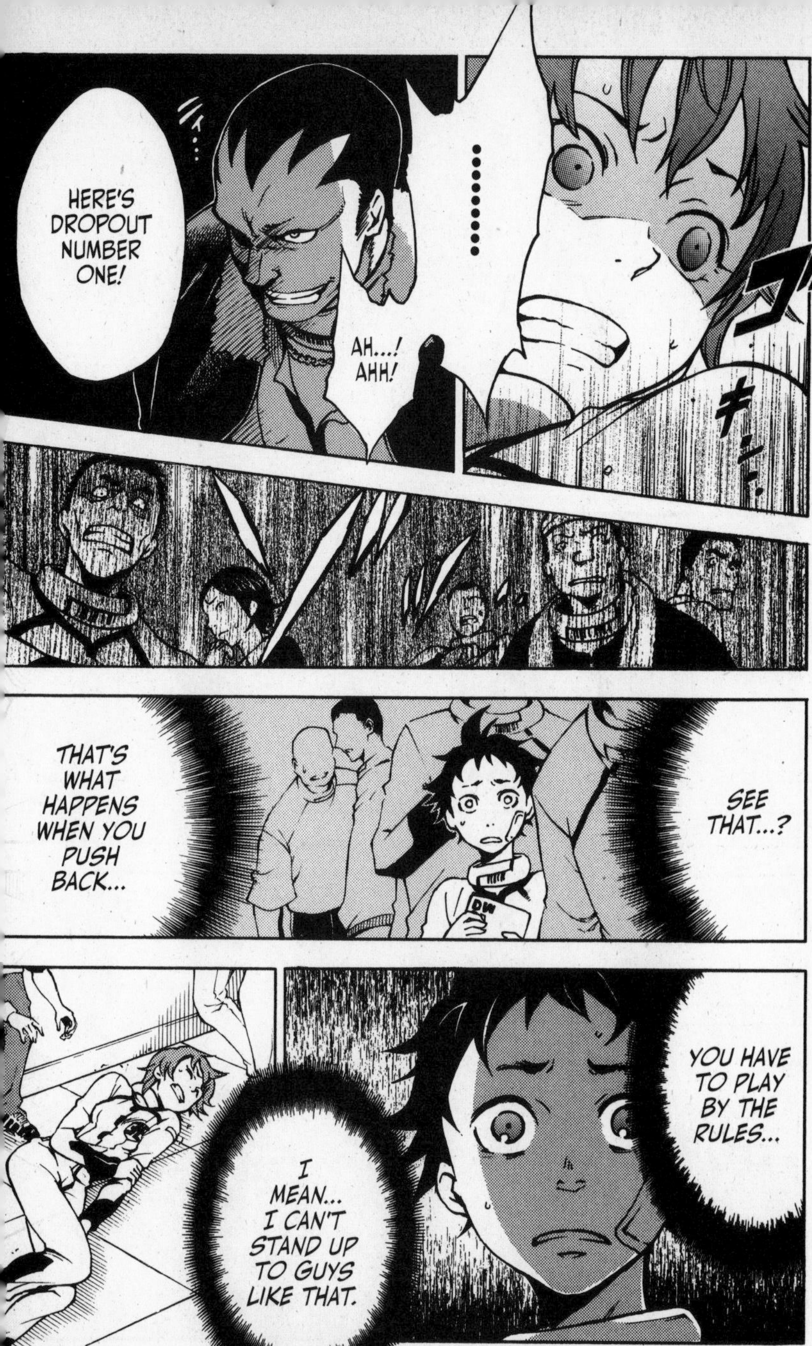
....
AH...! AHH!
HERE'S DROPOUT NUMBER ONE!
SEE THAT...?
THAT'S WHAT HAPPENS WHEN YOU PUSH BACK...
YOU HAVE TO PLAY BY THE RULES...
I MEAN... I CAN'T STAND UP TO GUYS LIKE THAT.

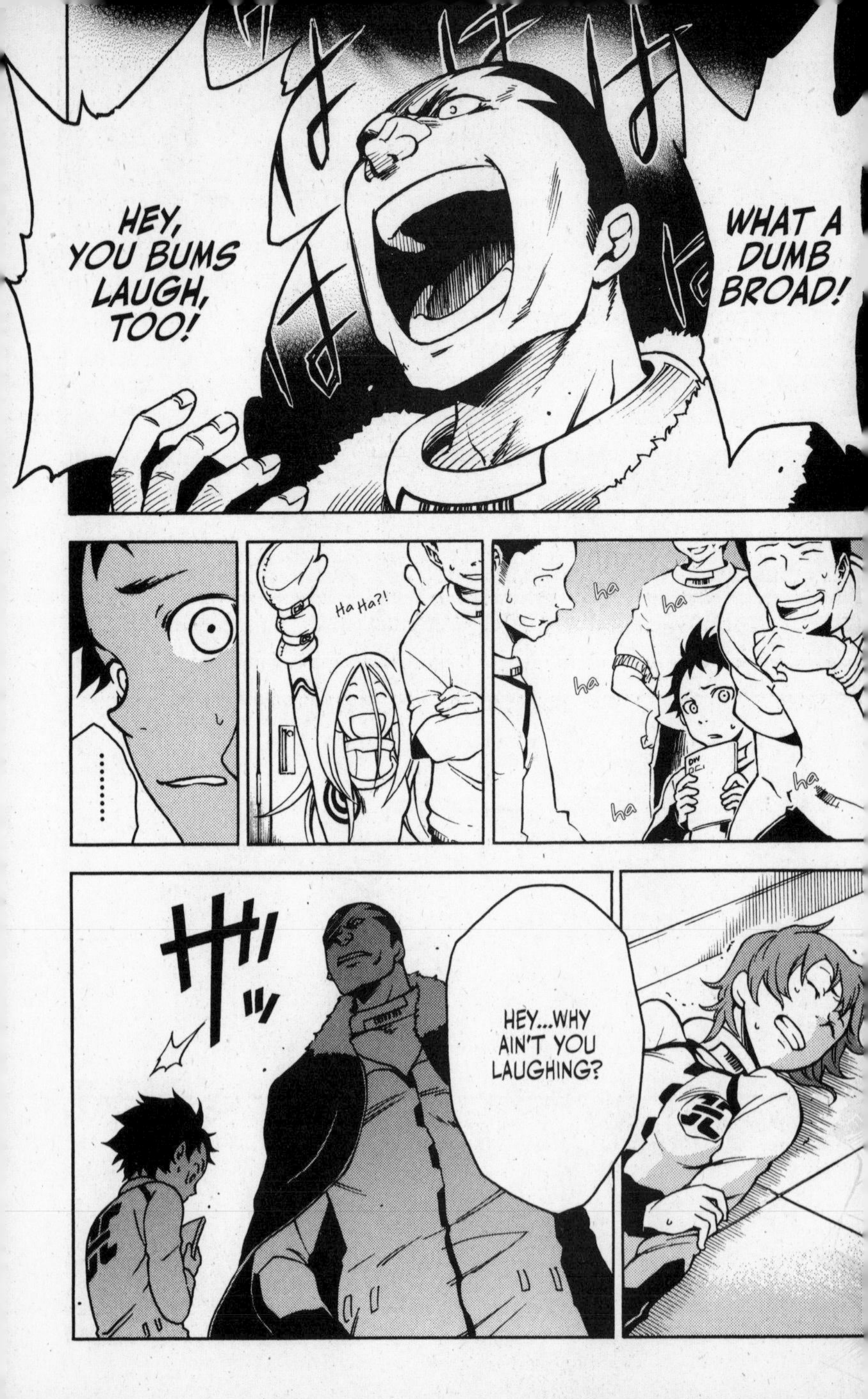

WHAT A DUMB BROAD!
HEY, YOU BUMS LAUGH, TOO!
ha
ha
ha
ha
ha
ha
Ha Ha?!
......
HEY...WHY AIN'T YOU LAUGHING?
ザッ

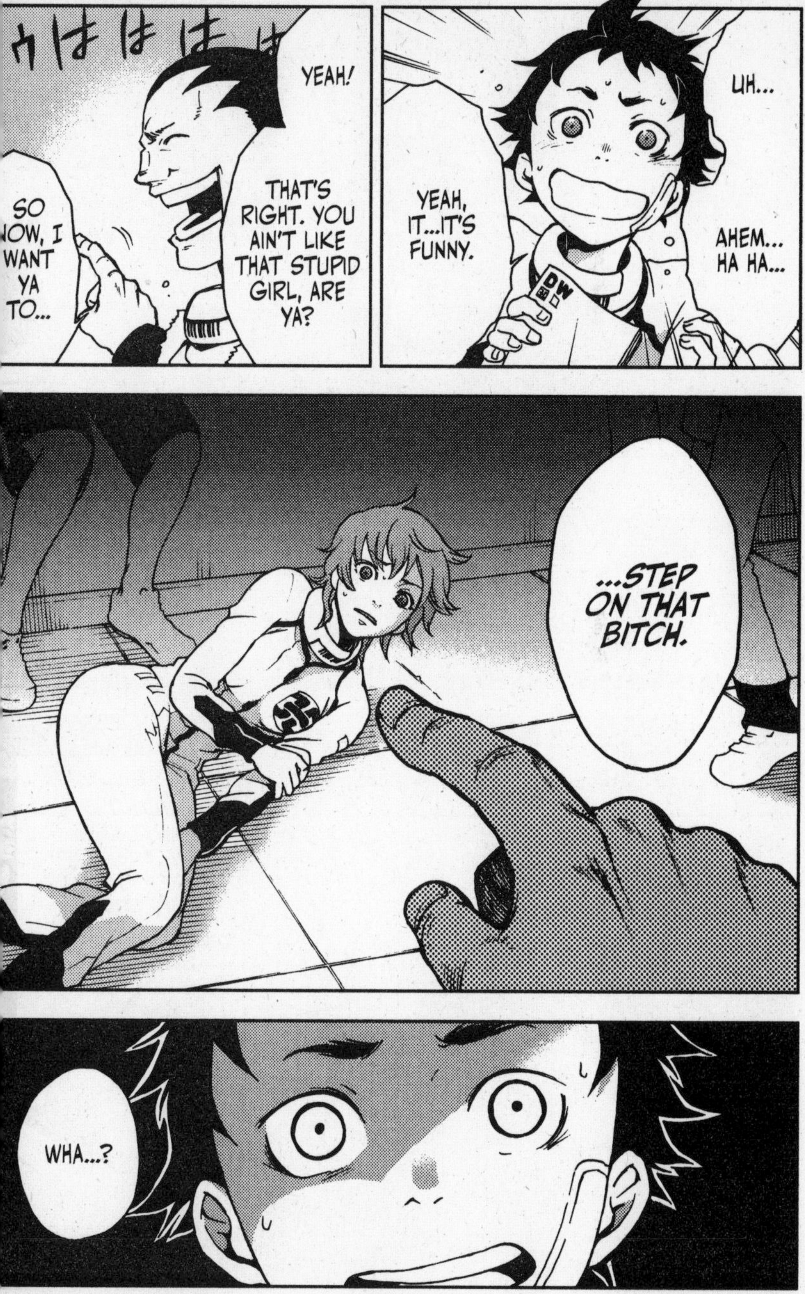
UH...
YEAH, IT...IT'S FUNNY.
AHEM... HA HA...
ウははは
YEAH!
THAT'S RIGHT. YOU AIN'T LIKE THAT STUPID GIRL, ARE YA?
SO NOW, I WANT YA TO...
...STEP ON THAT BITCH.
WHA...?

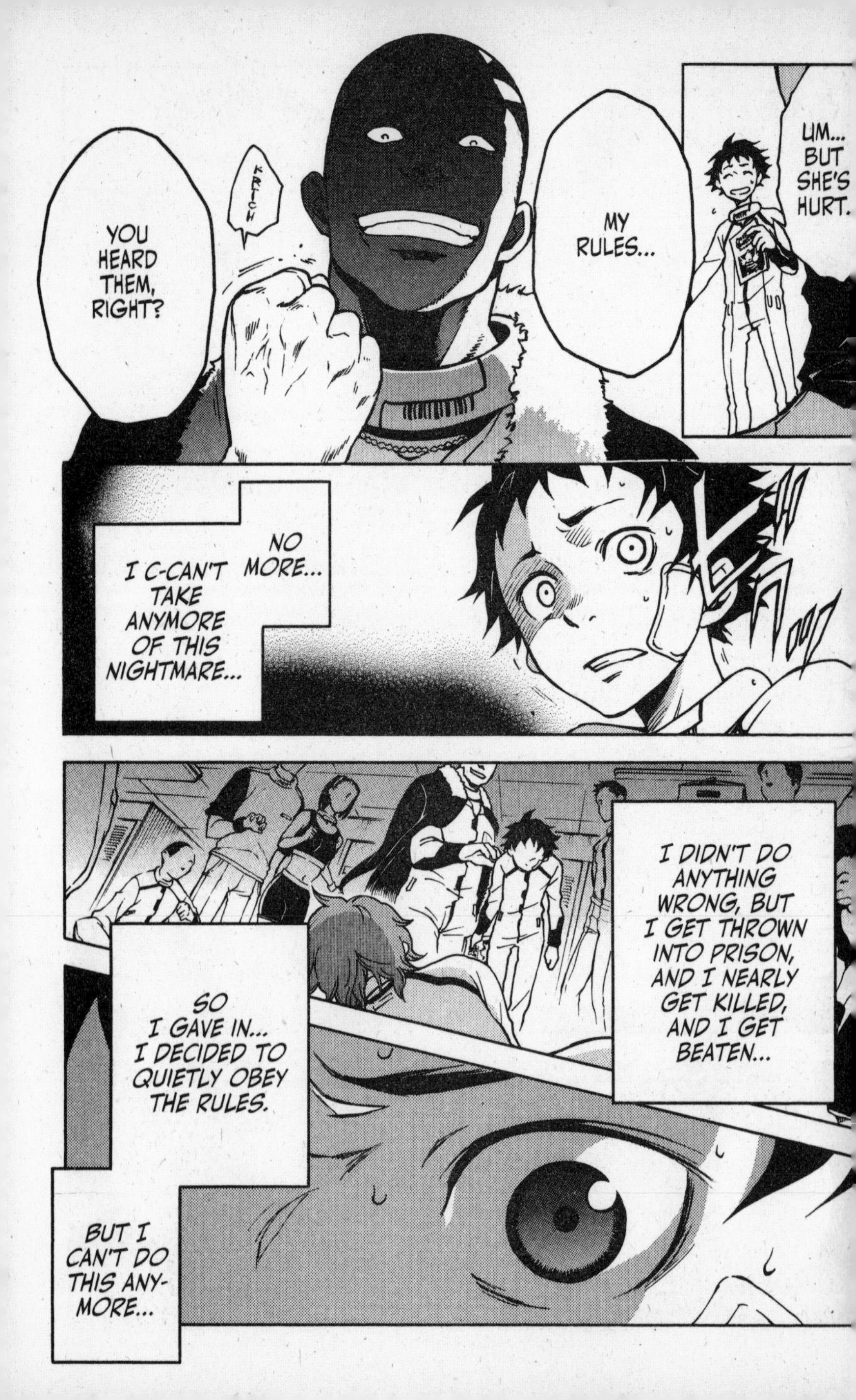
UM... BUT SHE'S HURT.
MY RULES...
KRICH
YOU HEARD THEM, RIGHT?
NO MORE...
I C-CAN'T TAKE ANYMORE OF THIS NIGHTMARE...
I DIDN'T DO ANYTHING WRONG, BUT I GET THROWN INTO PRISON, AND I NEARLY GET KILLED, AND I GET BEATEN...
SO I GAVE IN... I DECIDED TO QUIETLY OBEY THE RULES.
BUT I CAN'T DO THIS ANY-MORE...

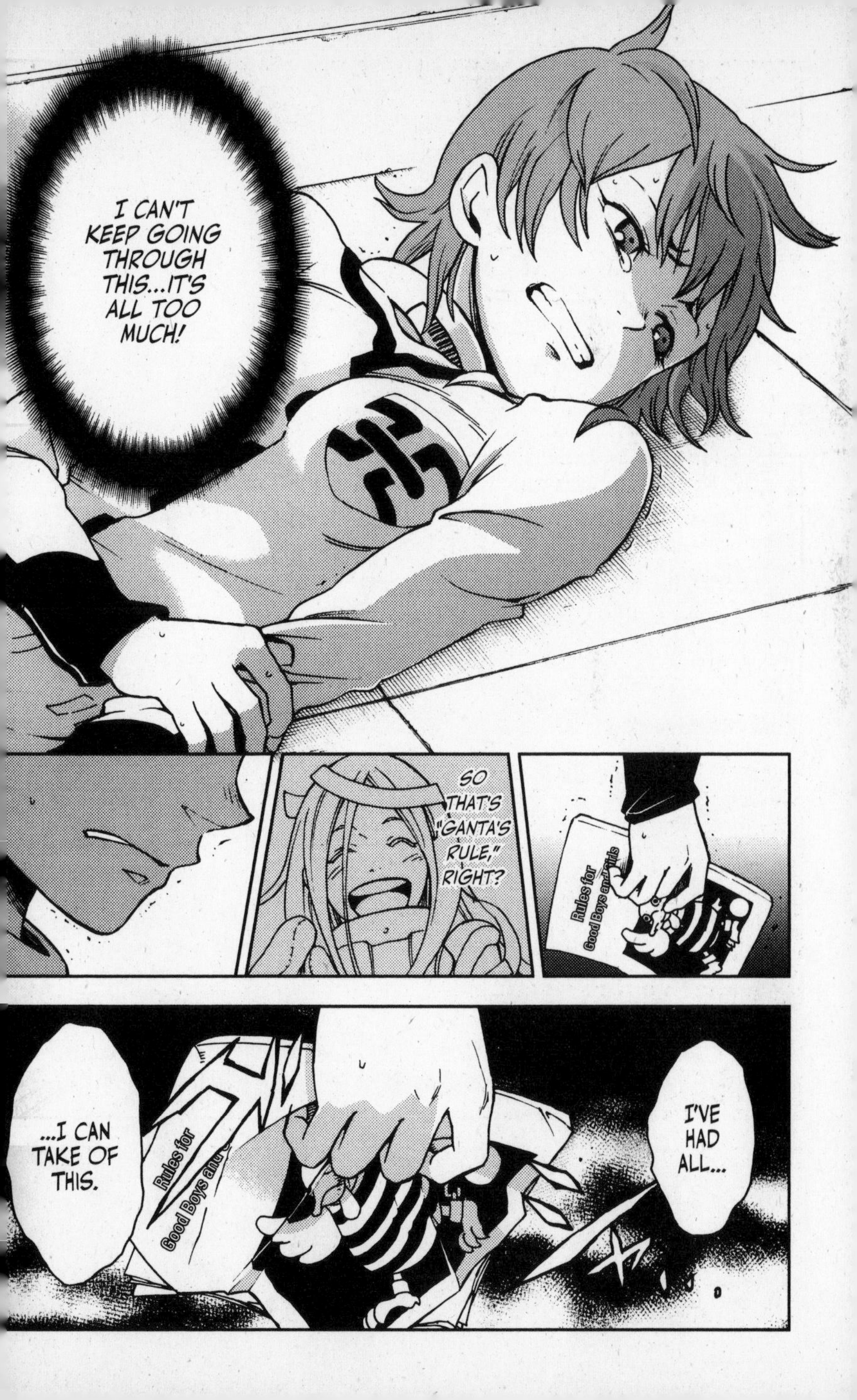
I CAN'T KEEP GOING THROUGH THIS...IT'S ALL TOO MUCH!
Rules for
Good Boys and
SO THAT'S "GANTA'S RULE," RIGHT?
I'VE HAD ALL...
...I CAN TAKE OF THIS.
Rules for
Good Boys and

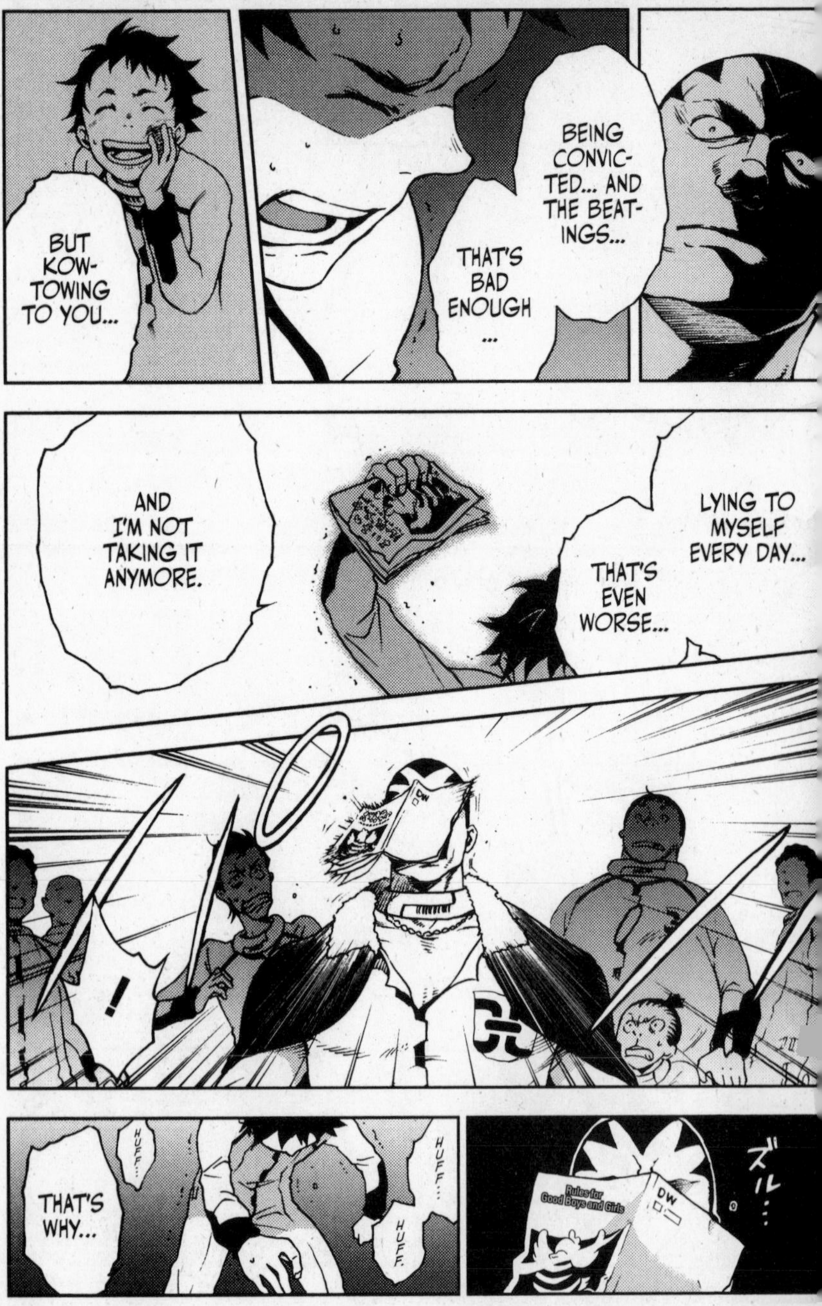
BEING CONVICTED... AND THE BEATINGS...
THAT'S BAD ENOUGH ...
BUT KOWTOWING TO YOU...
LYING TO MYSELF EVERY DAY...
THAT'S EVEN WORSE...
AND I'M NOT TAKING IT ANYMORE.
!
ズル…
Rules for Good Boys and Girls
DW
HUFF...
HUFF...
HUFF.
THAT'S WHY...

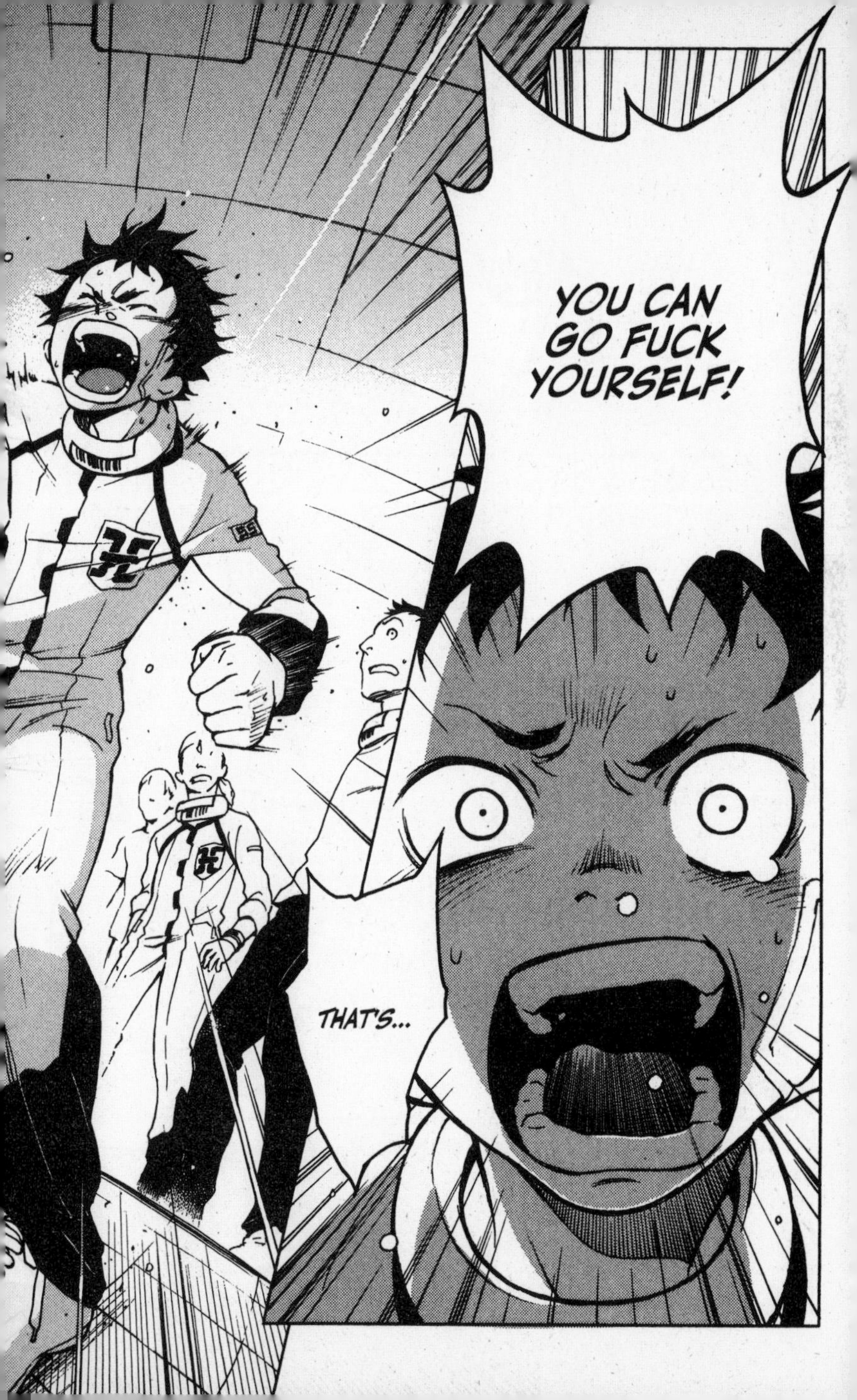
YOU CAN GO FUCK YOURSELF!
THAT'S...

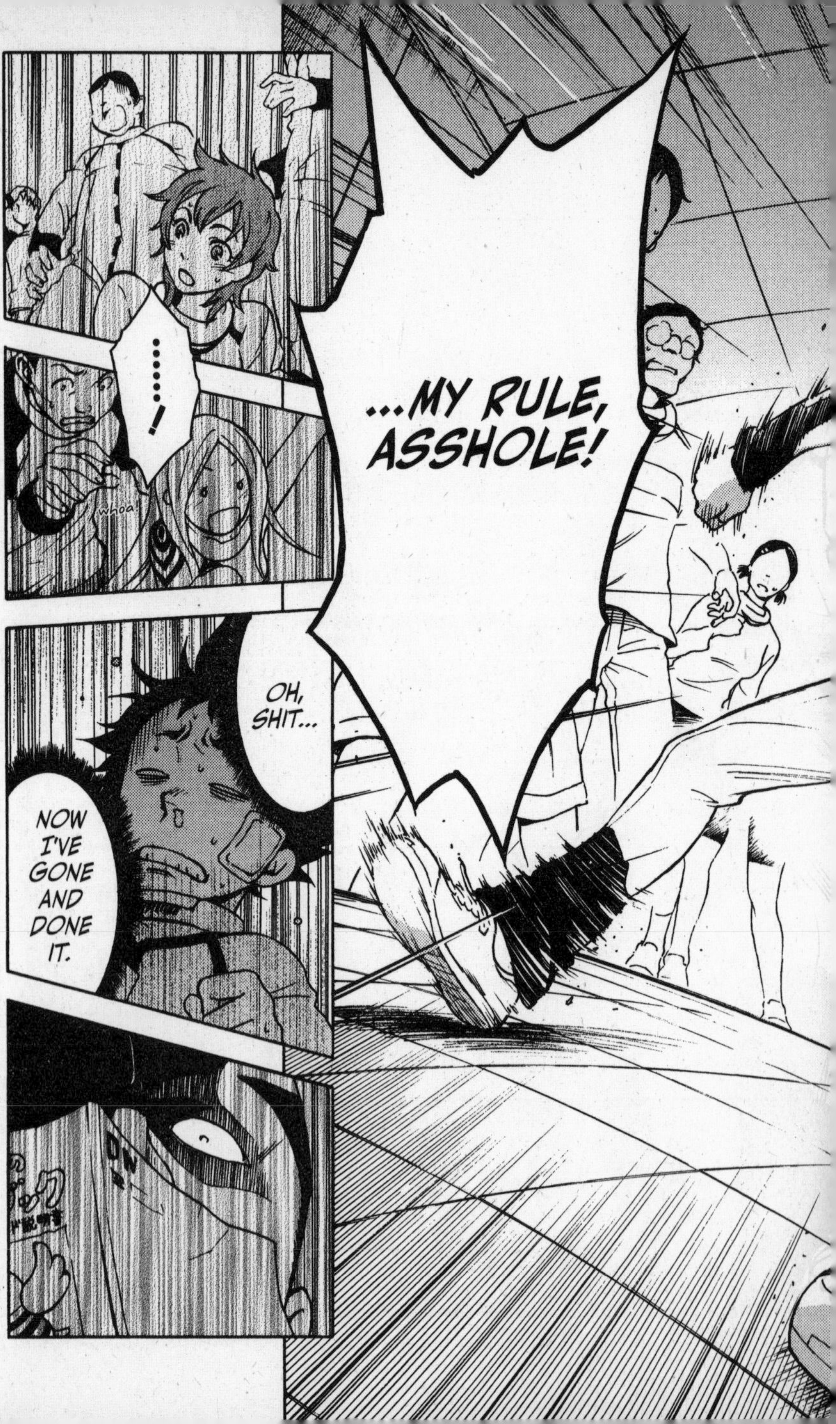
...MY RULE, ASSHOLE!
......!
whoa!
OH, SHIT...
NOW I'VE GONE AND DONE IT.

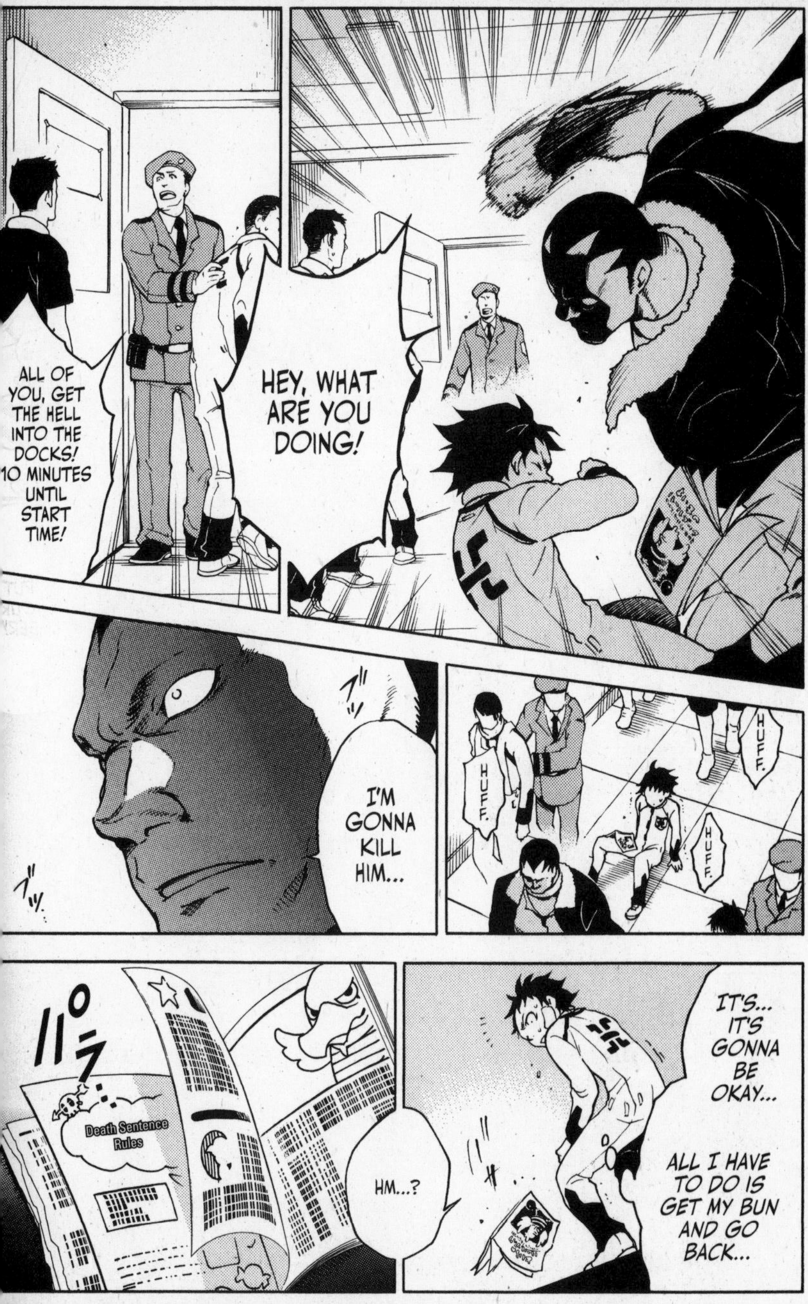
HEY, WHAT ARE YOU DOING!
ALL OF YOU, GET THE HELL INTO THE DOCKS! 10 MINUTES UNTIL START TIME!
HUFF.
HUFF.
HUFF.
I'M GONNA KILL HIM...
IT'S... IT'S GONNA BE OKAY...
ALL I HAVE TO DO IS GET MY BUN AND GO BACK...
HM...?
パラ
Death Sentence Rules

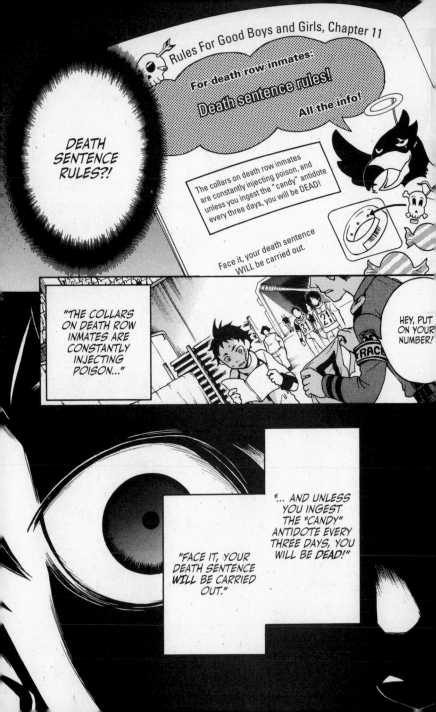

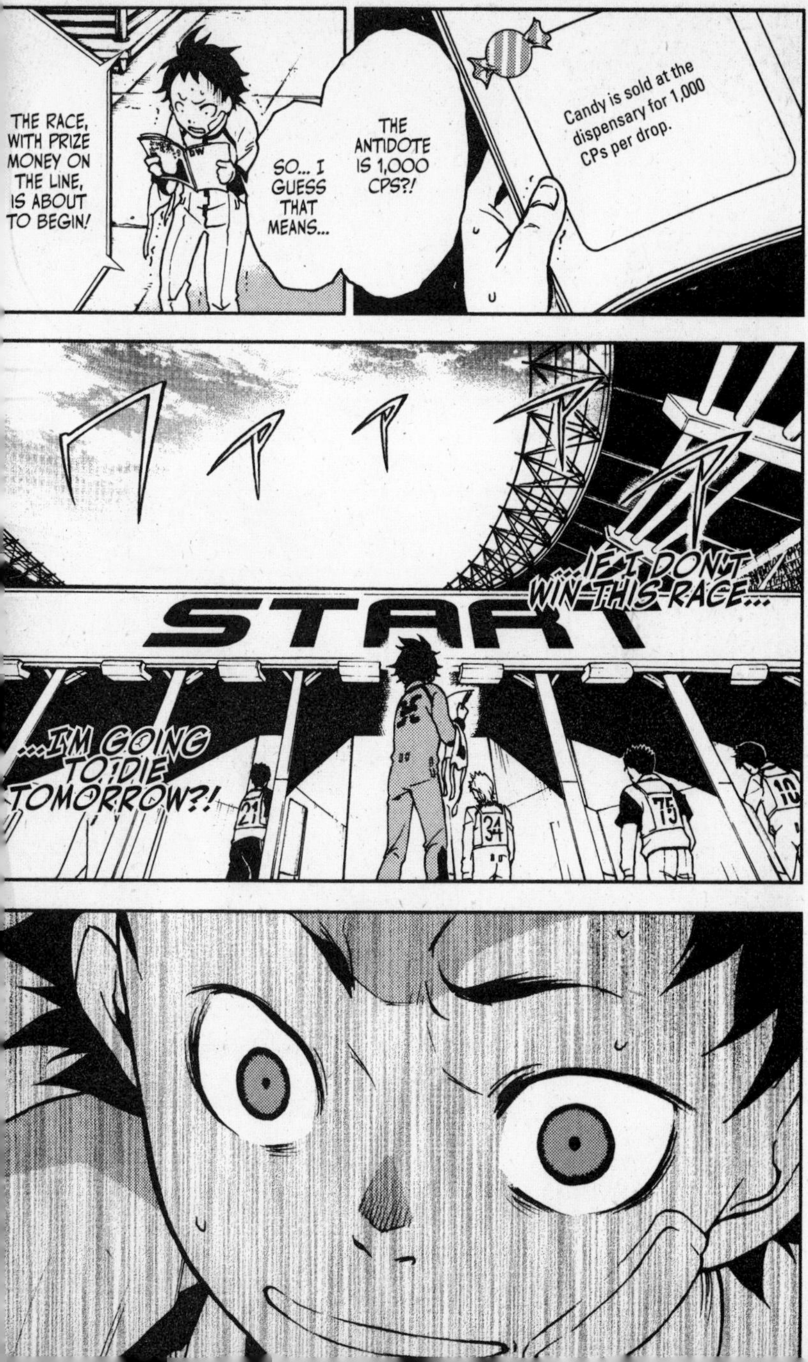
Candy is sold at the dispensary for 1,000 CPs per drop.
THE ANTIDOTE IS 1,000 CPS?!
SO... I GUESS THAT MEANS...
THE RACE, WITH PRIZE MONEY ON THE LINE, IS ABOUT TO BEGIN!
...IF I DON'T WIN THIS RACE...
START
...I'M GOING TO DIE TOMORROW?!

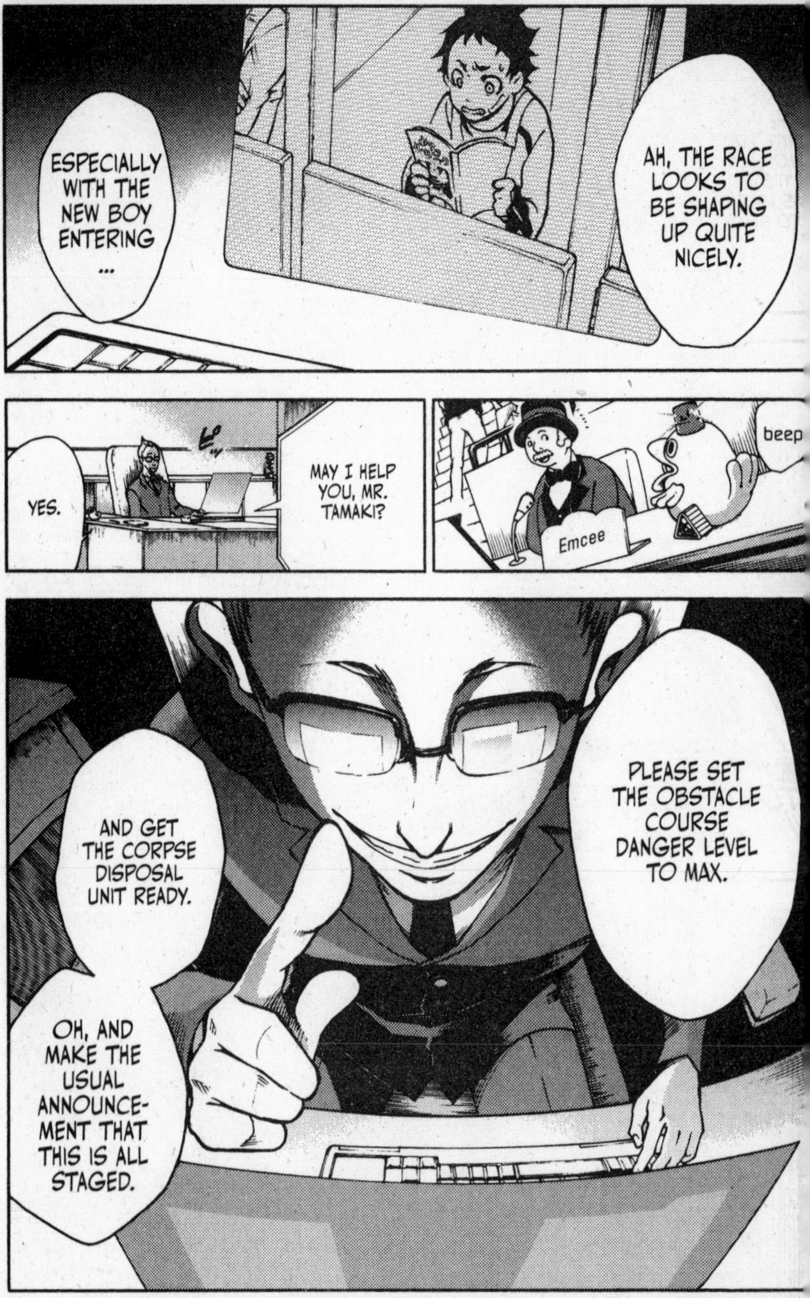
AH, THE RACE LOOKS TO BE SHAPING UP QUITE NICELY.
ESPECIALLY WITH THE NEW BOY ENTERING ...
beep
Emcee
MAY I HELP YOU, MR. TAMAKI?
YES.
PLEASE SET THE OBSTACLE COURSE DANGER LEVEL TO MAX.
AND GET THE CORPSE DISPOSAL UNIT READY.
OH, AND MAKE THE USUAL ANNOUNCEMENT-MENT THAT THIS IS ALL STAGED.

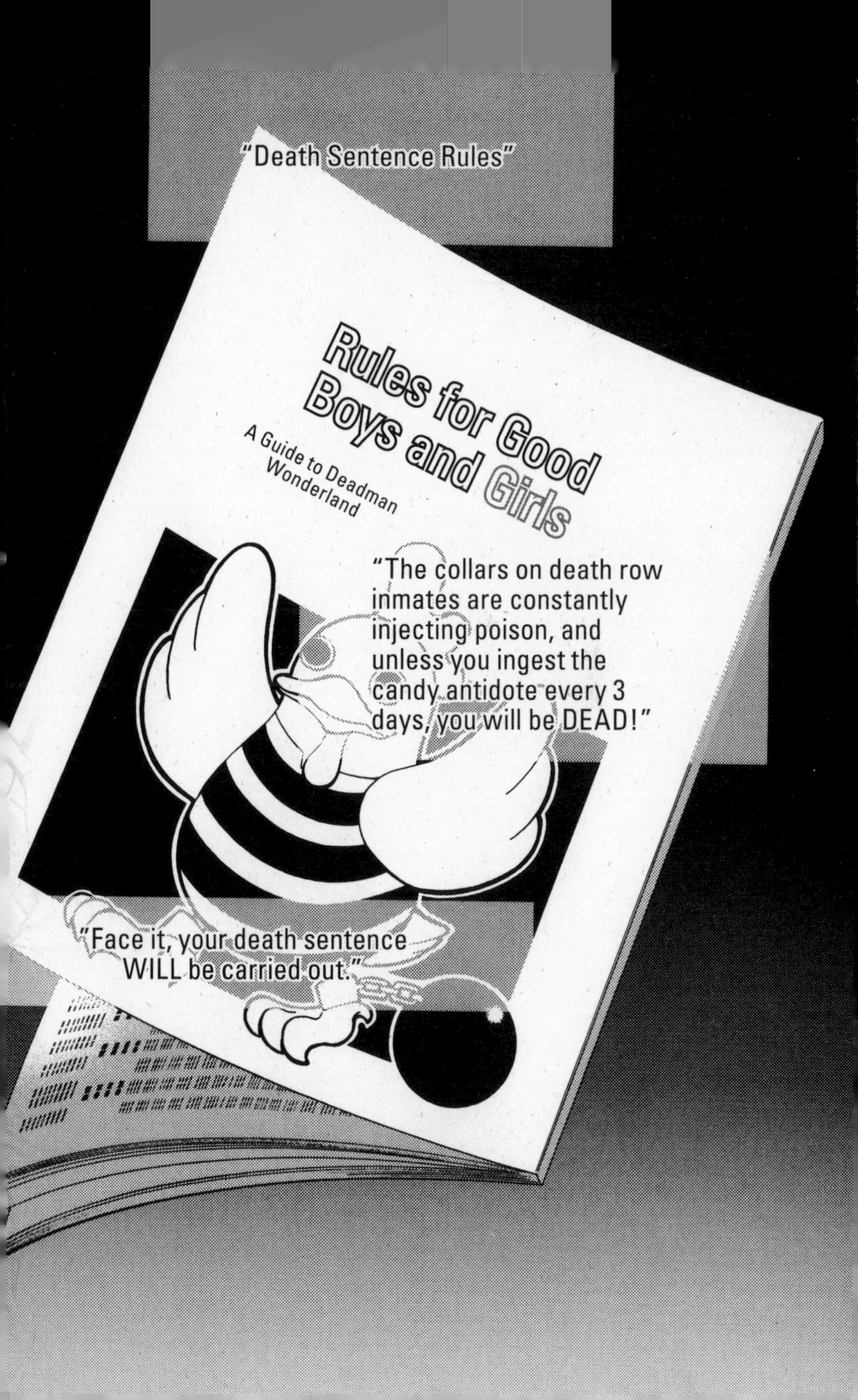
"Death Sentence Rules"
Rules for Good Boys and Girls
A Guide to Deadman Wonderland
"The collars on death row inmates are constantly injecting poison, and unless you ingest the candy antidote every 3 days, you will be DEAD!"
"Face it, your death sentence WILL be carried out."

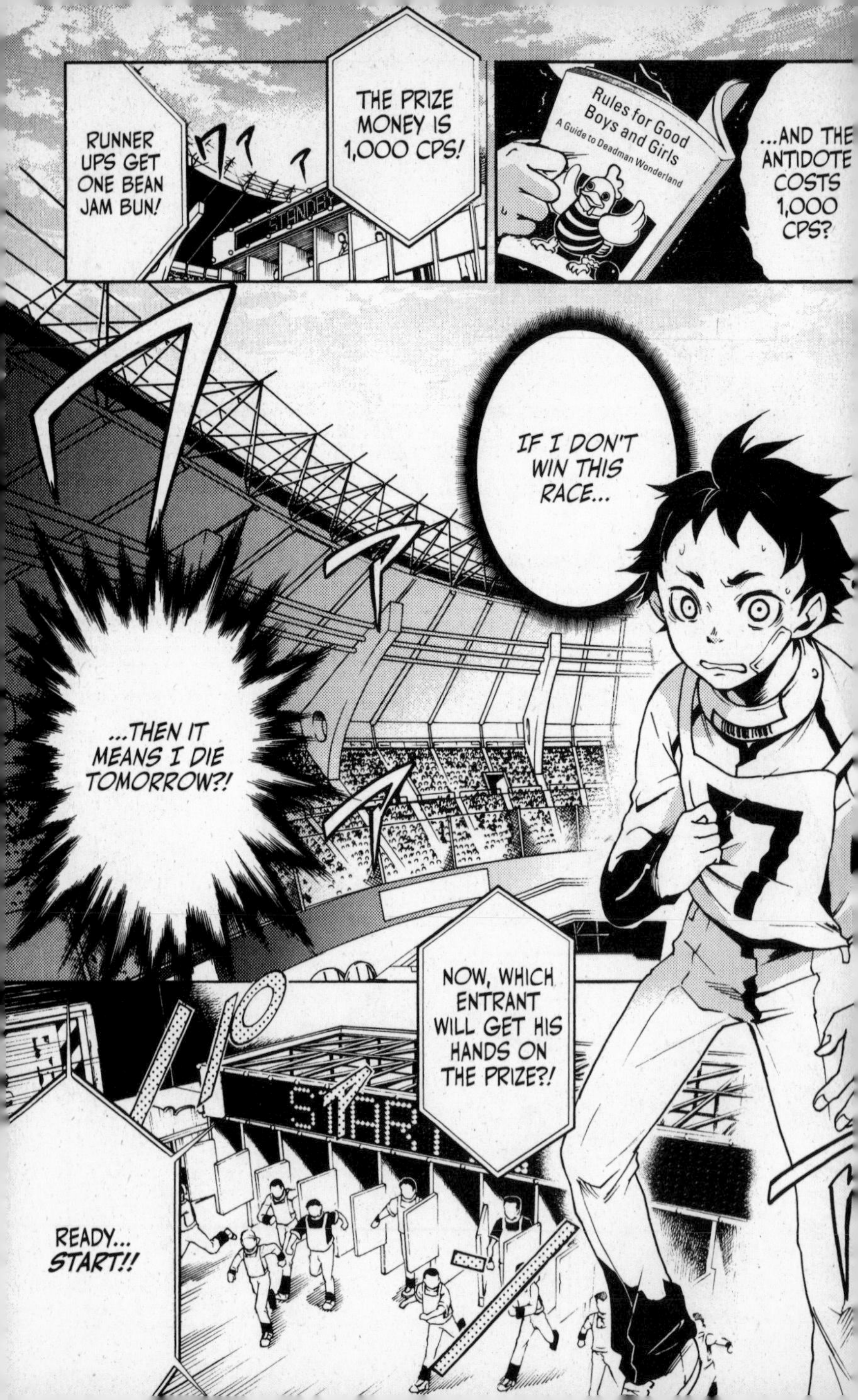
Rules for Good Boys and Girls
A Guide to Deadman Wonderland
...AND THE ANTIDOTE COSTS 1,000 CPS?
THE PRIZE MONEY IS 1,000 CPS!
RUNNER UPS GET ONE BEAN JAM BUN!
STANDBY
IF I DON'T WIN THIS RACE...
...THEN IT MEANS I DIE TOMORROW?!
NOW, WHICH ENTRANT WILL GET HIS HANDS ON THE PRIZE?!
START
READY... START!!

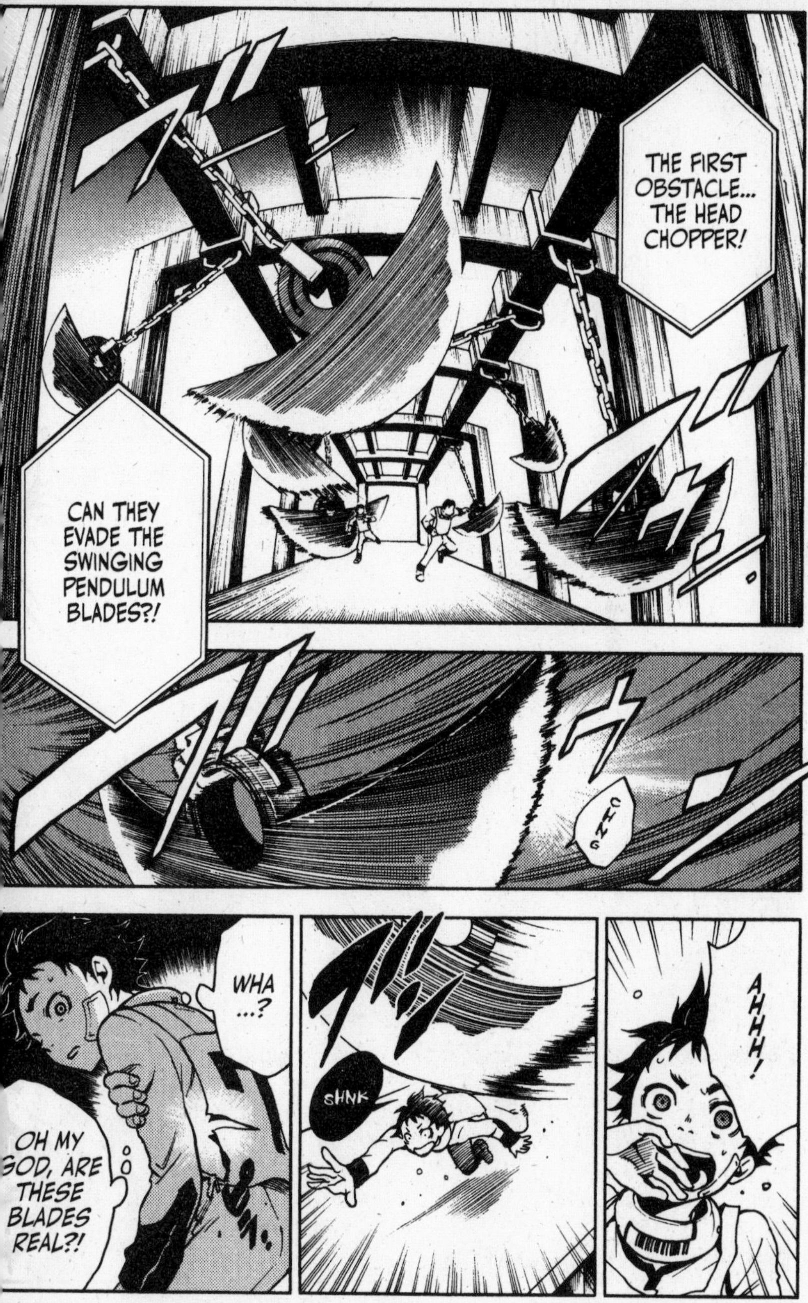
THE FIRST OBSTACLE... THE HEAD CHOPPER!
CAN THEY EVADE THE SWINGING PENDULUM BLADES?!
CHING
AHHHH!
SHNK
WHA ...?
OH MY GOD, ARE THESE BLADES REAL?!

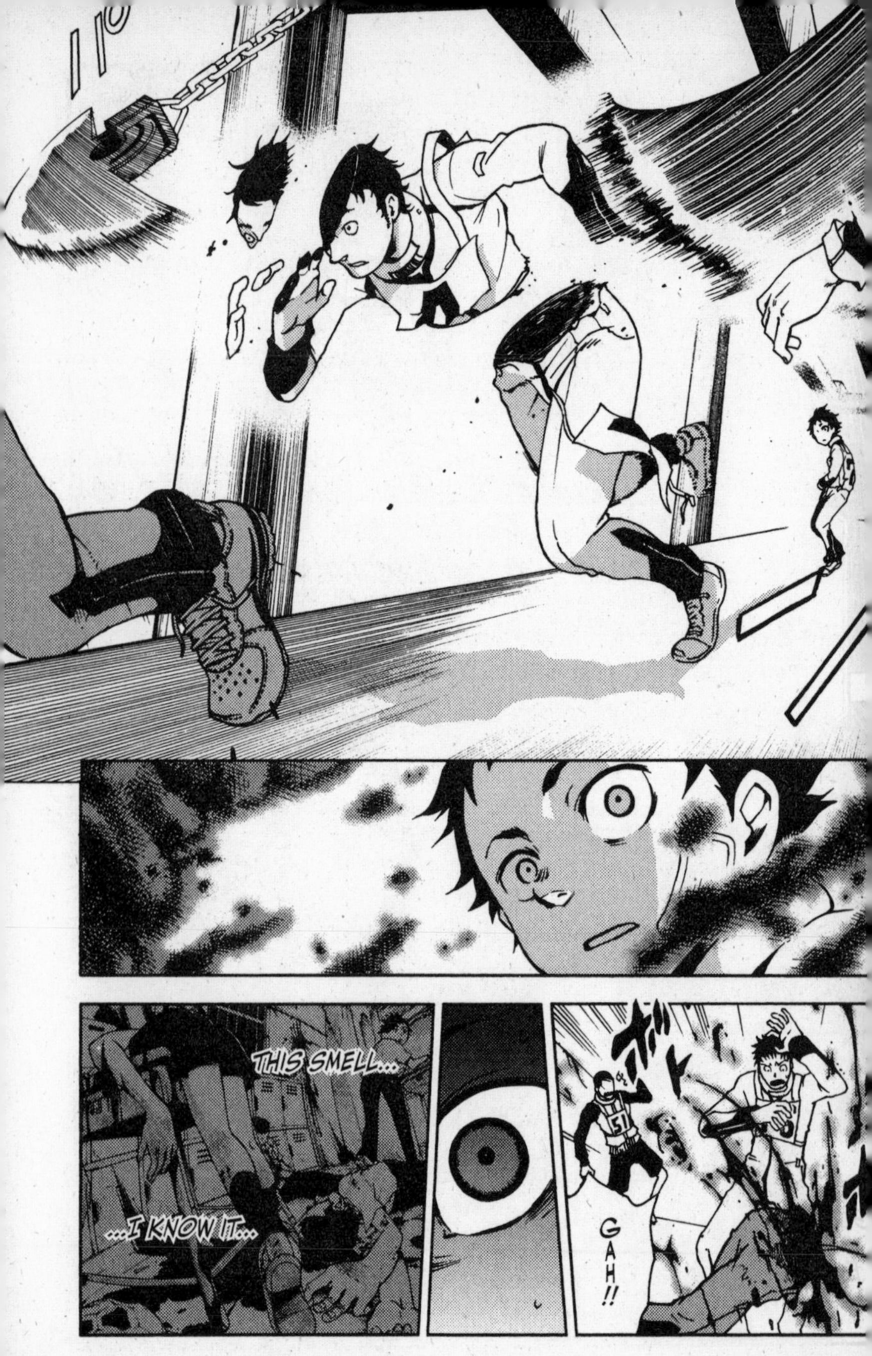
GAH!!
THIS SMELL...
...I KNOW IT...

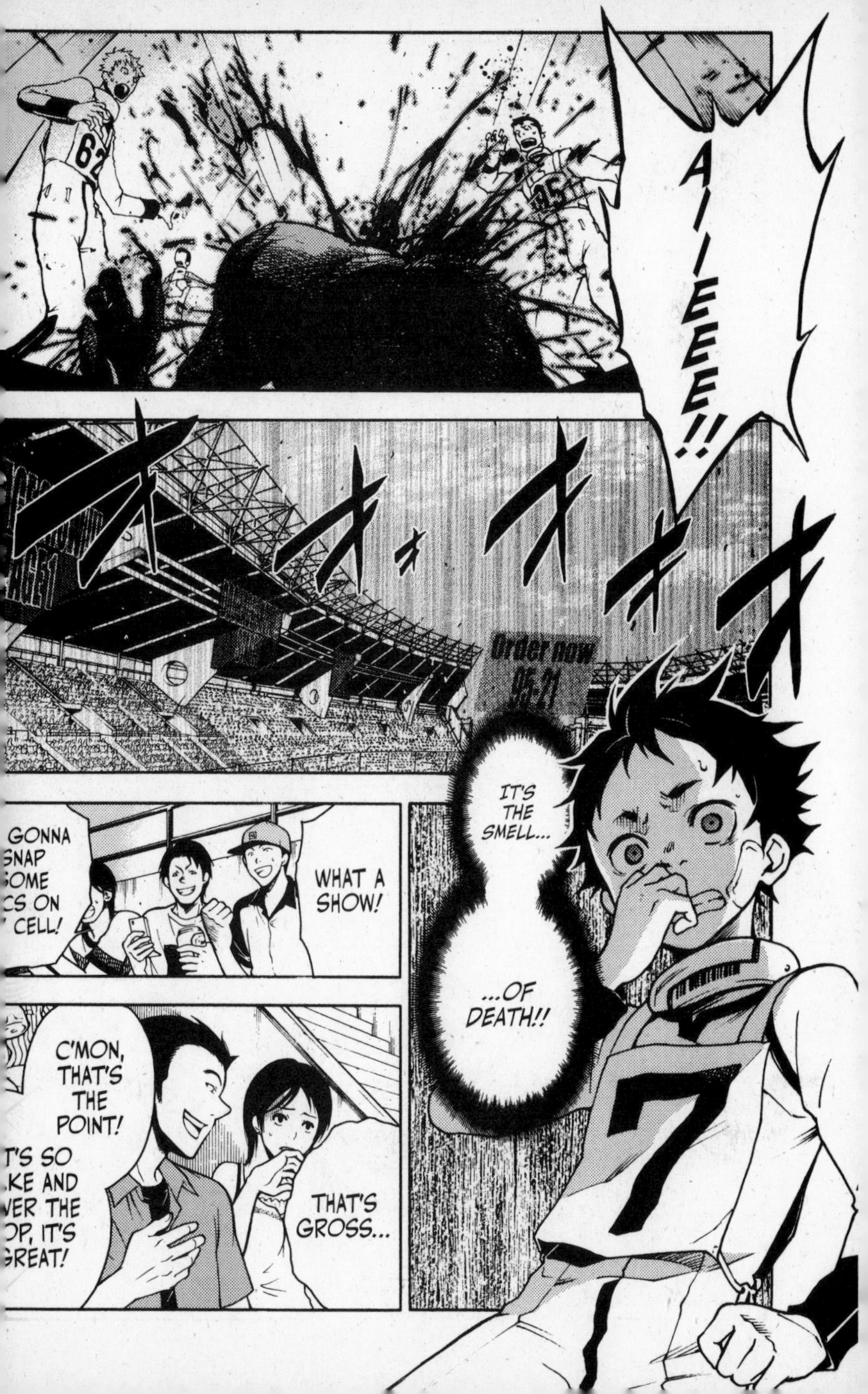
AIIEEEE!!
オオォオオオ
Order now 95-21
IT'S THE SMELL...
...OF DEATH!!
WHAT A SHOW!
GONNA SNAP SOME CS ON CELL!
THAT'S GROSS...
C'MON, THAT'S THE POINT!
T'S SO KE AND VER THE OP, IT'S GREAT!

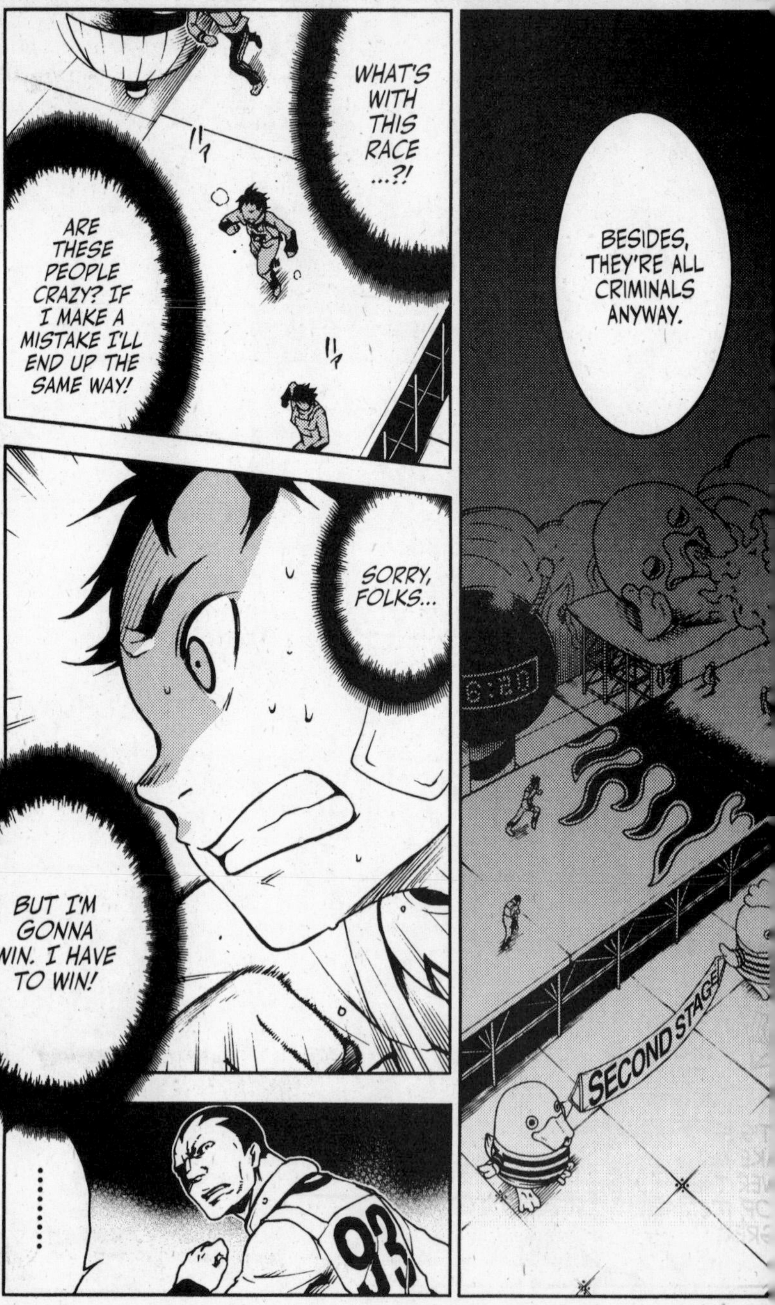
BESIDES, THEY'RE ALL CRIMINALS ANYWAY.
6:20
SECOND STAGE
WHAT'S WITH THIS RACE ...?!
ARE THESE PEOPLE CRAZY? IF I MAKE A MISTAKE I'LL END UP THE SAME WAY!
SORRY, FOLKS...
BUT I'M GONNA WIN. I HAVE TO WIN!
....

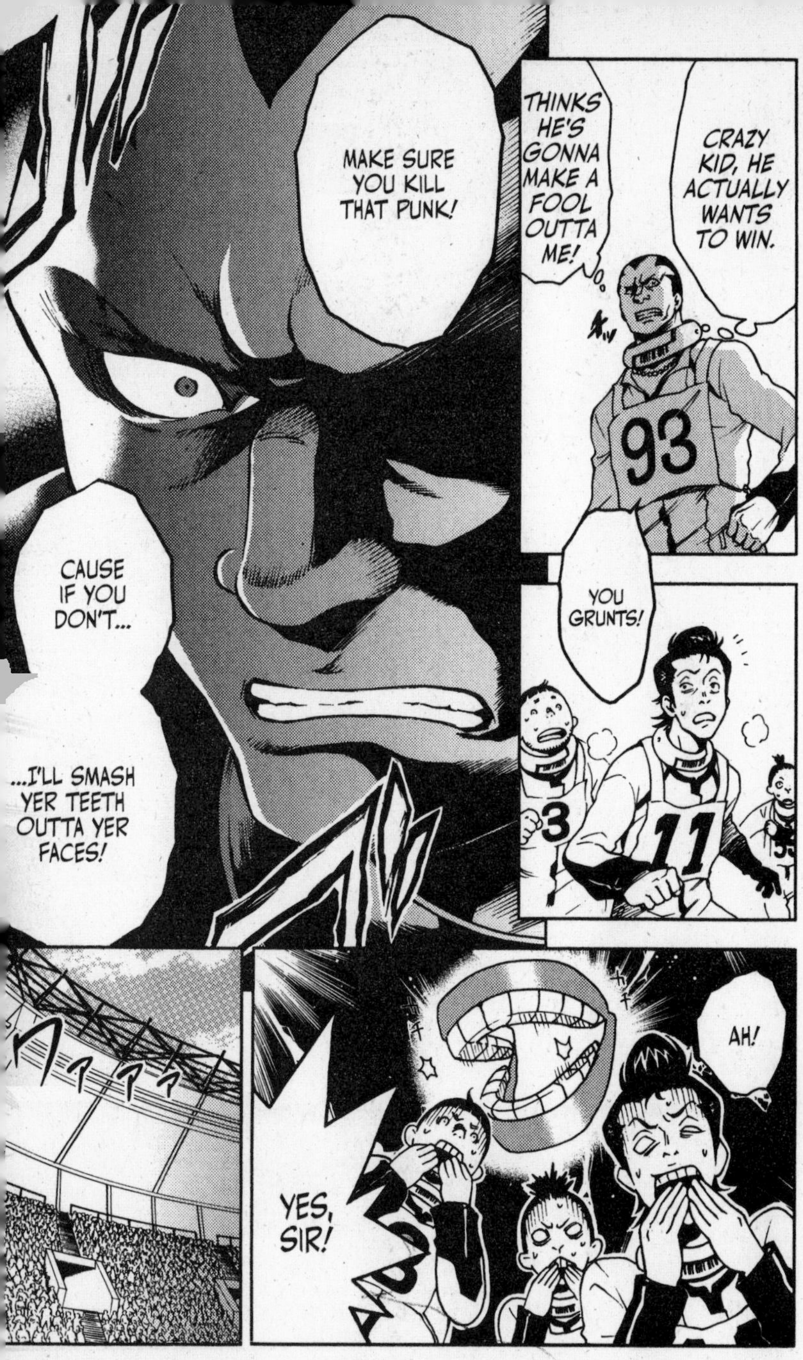
CRAZY KID, HE ACTUALLY WANTS TO WIN.
THINKS HE'S GONNA MAKE A FOOL OUTTA ME!
93
YOU GRUNTS!
11
3
MAKE SURE YOU KILL THAT PUNK!
CAUSE IF YOU DON'T...
...I'LL SMASH YER TEETH OUTTA YER FACES!
AH!
YES, SIR!

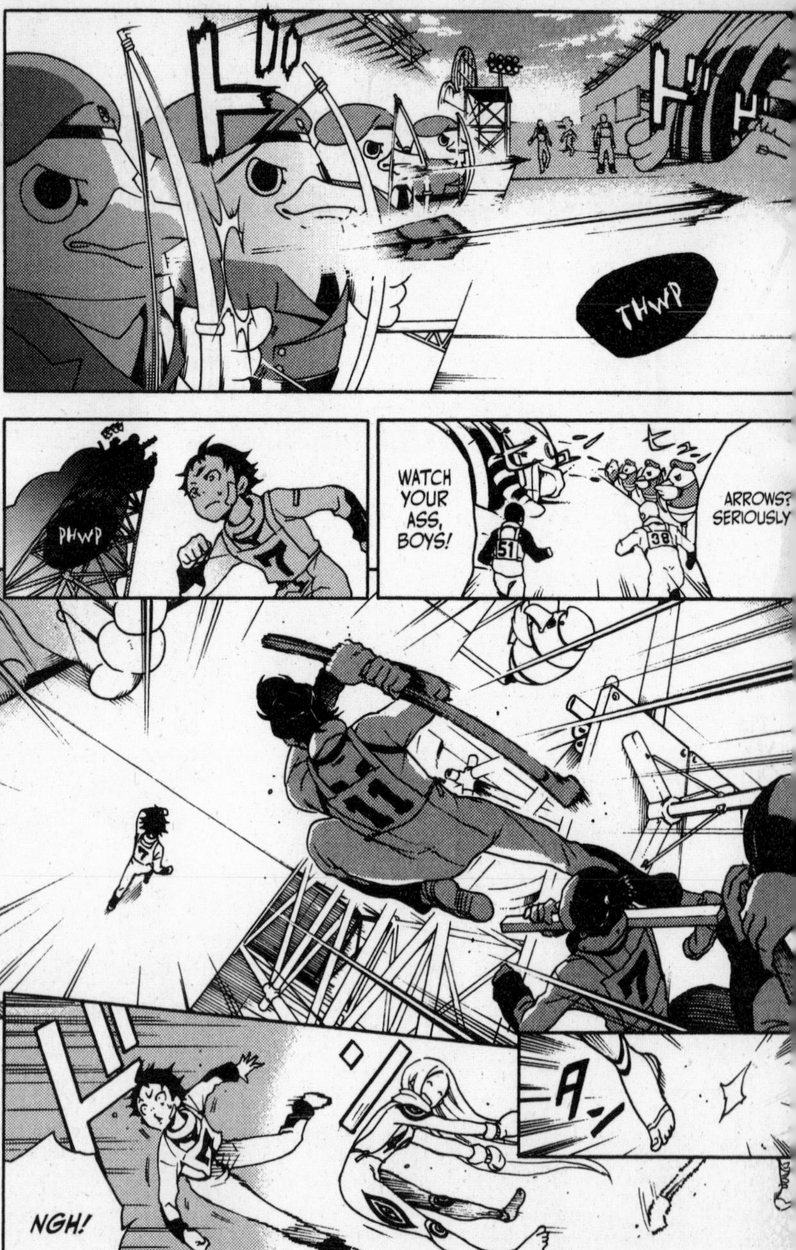
THWP
ARROWS? SERIOUSLY
WATCH YOUR ASS, BOYS!
PHWP
NGH!

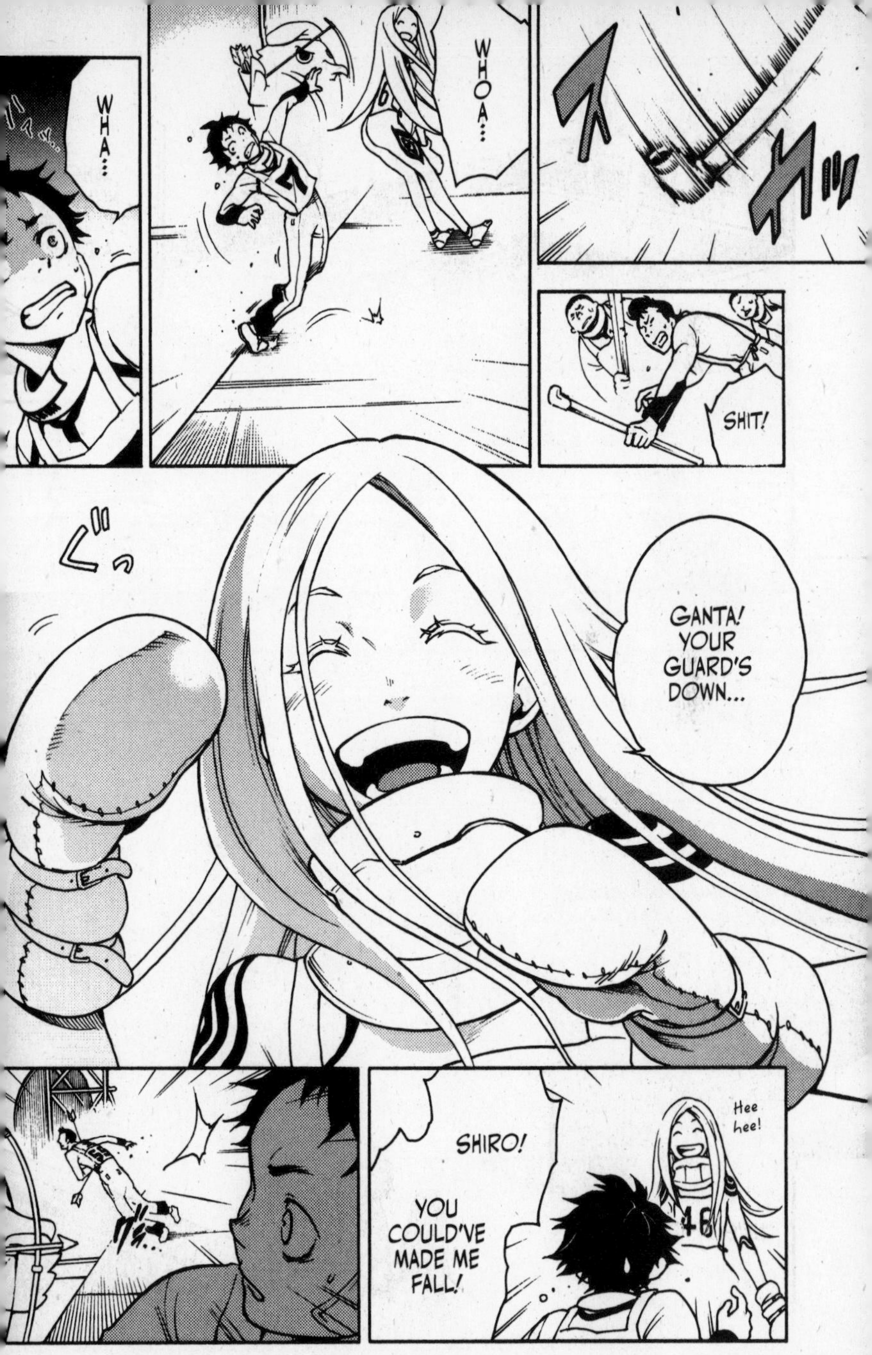
SHIT!
WHOA...
WHA...
GANTA! YOUR GUARD'S DOWN...
Hee hee!
SHIRO!
YOU COULD'VE MADE ME FALL!

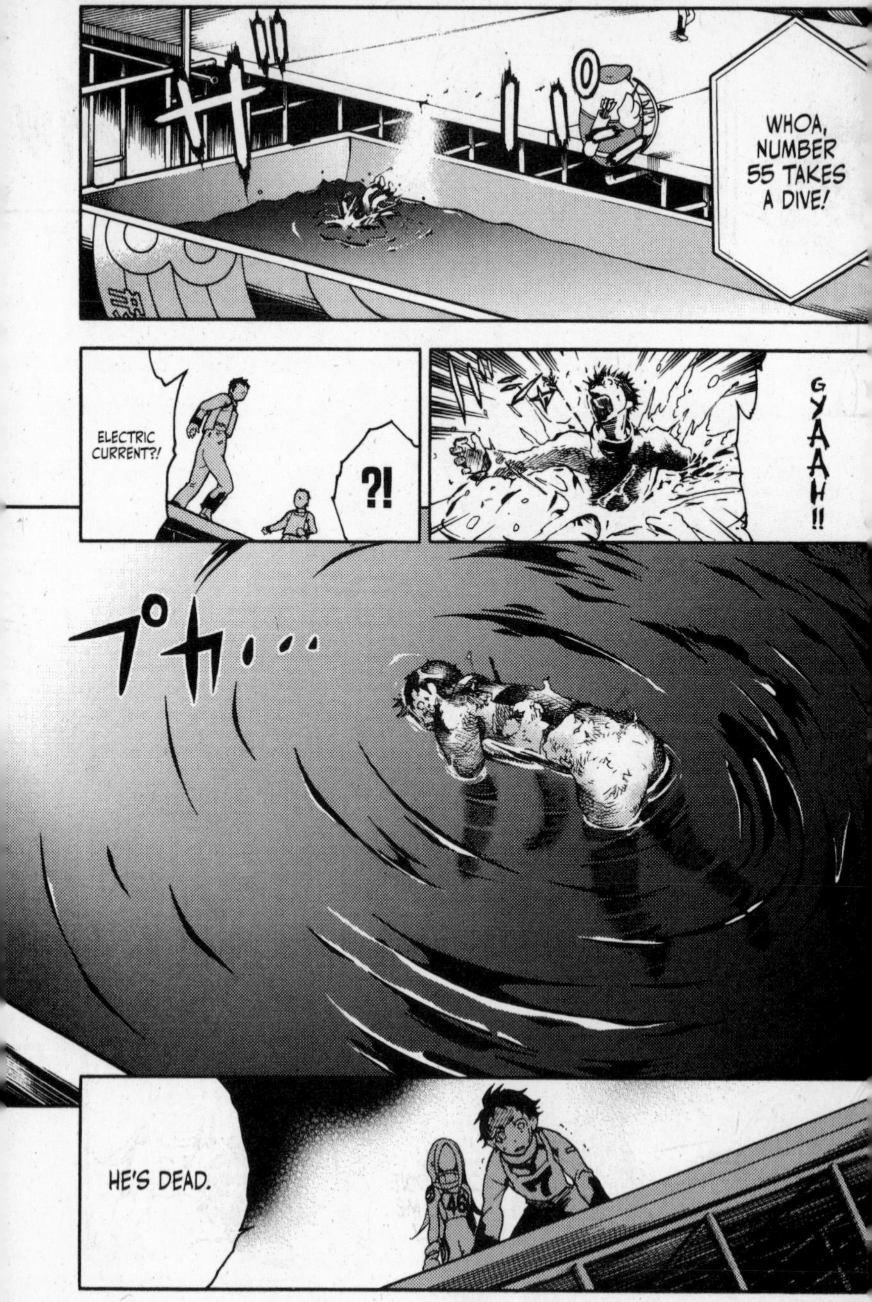
WHOA, NUMBER 55 TAKES A DIVE!
GYAAAH!!
?!
ELECTRIC CURRENT?!
プカ…
HE'S DEAD.

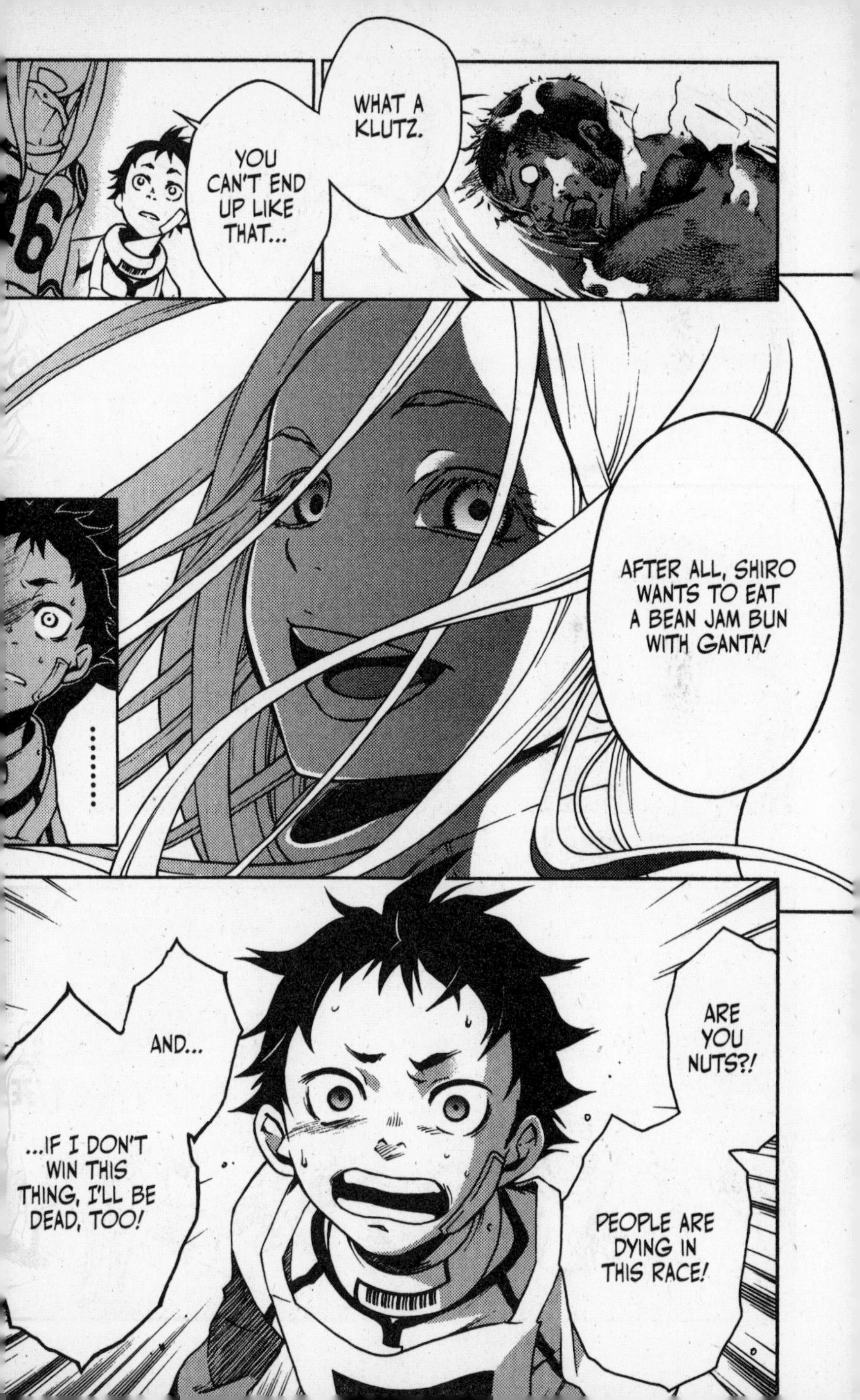

WHAT A KLUTZ.
YOU CAN'T END UP LIKE THAT...
AFTER ALL, SHIRO WANTS TO EAT A BEAN JAM BUN WITH GANTA!
......
ARE YOU NUTS?!
PEOPLE ARE DYING IN THIS RACE!
AND...
...IF I DON'T WIN THIS THING, I'LL BE DEAD, TOO!

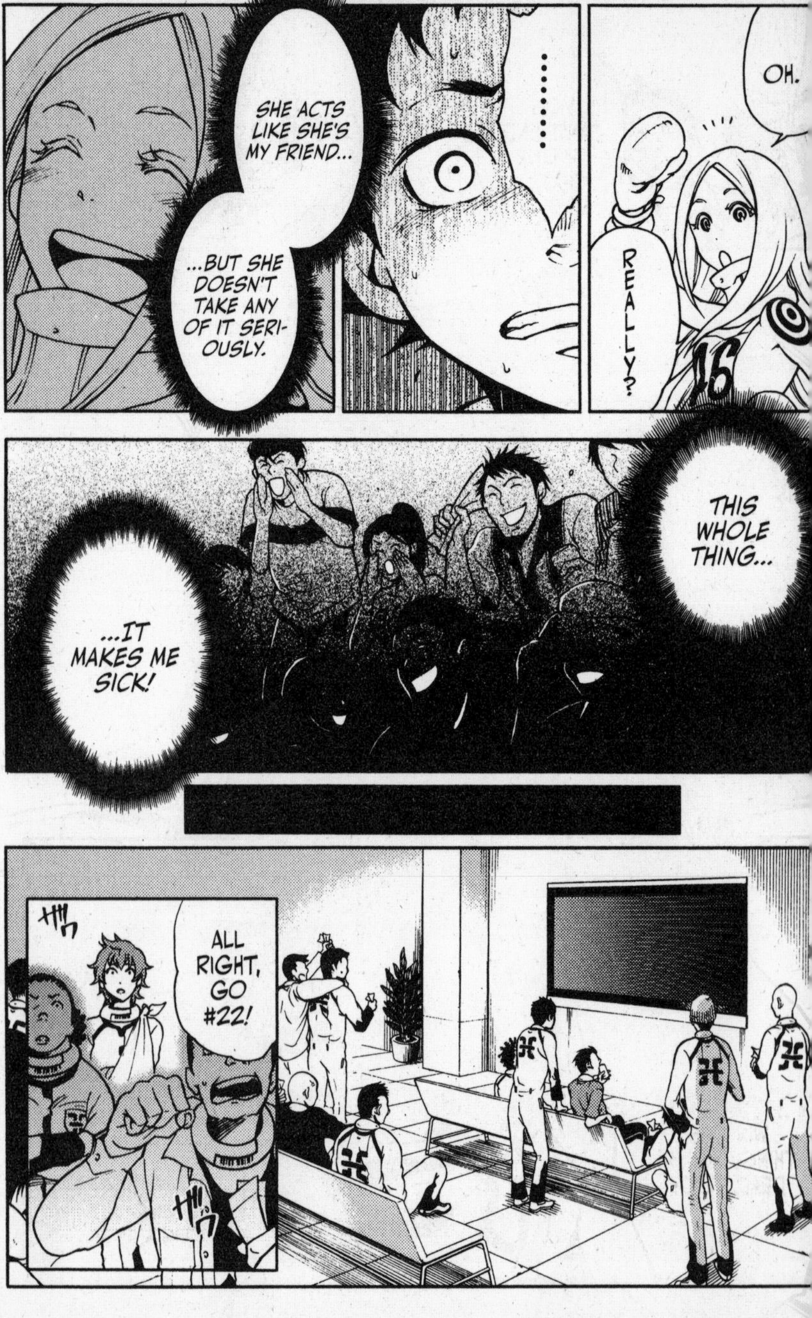
OH.
REALLY?
......
SHE ACTS LIKE SHE'S MY FRIEND...
...BUT SHE DOESN'T TAKE ANY OF IT SERIOUSLY.
THIS WHOLE THING...
...IT MAKES ME SICK!
ALL RIGHT, GO #22!

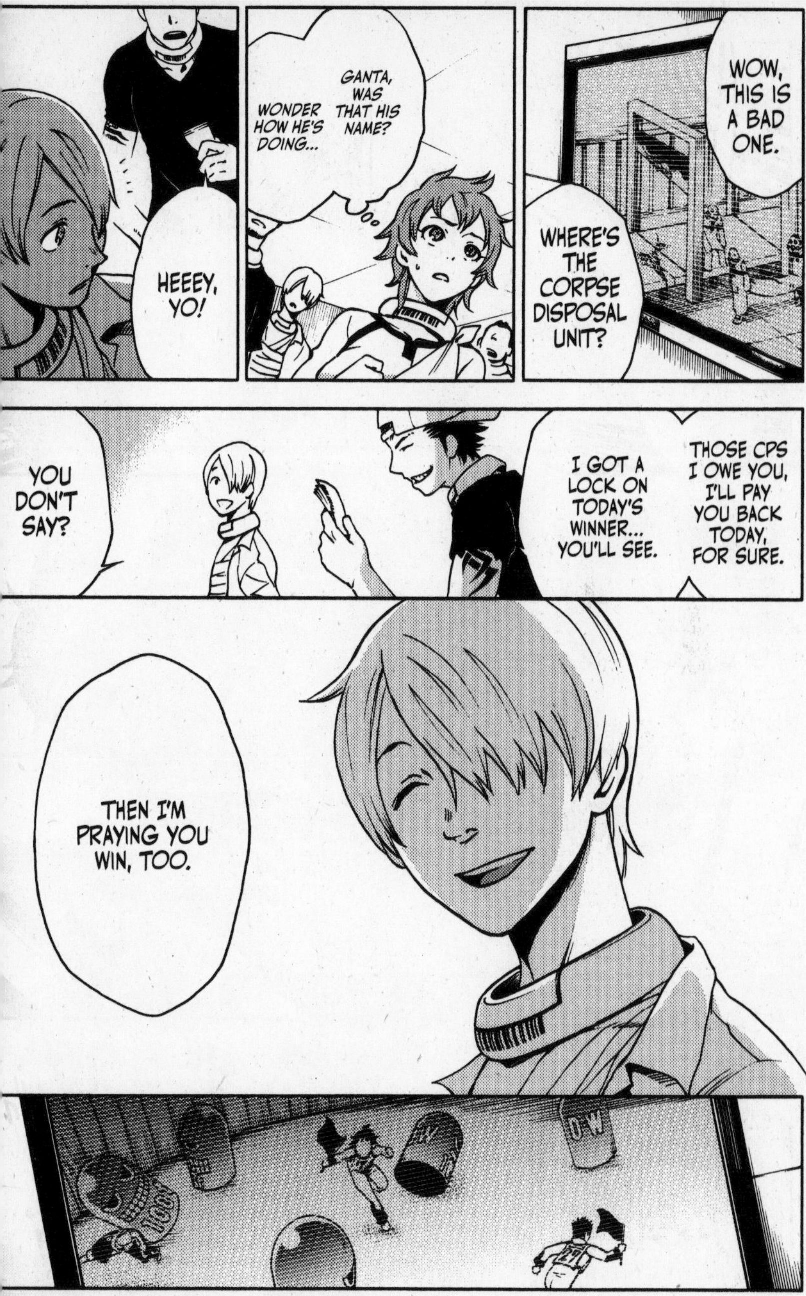
WOW, THIS IS A BAD ONE.
WHERE'S THE CORPSE DISPOSAL UNIT?
GANTA, WAS THAT HIS NAME?
WONDER HOW HE'S DOING...
HEEEY, YO!
THOSE CPS I OWE YOU, I'LL PAY YOU BACK TODAY, FOR SURE.
I GOT A LOCK ON TODAY'S WINNER... YOU'LL SEE.
YOU DON'T SAY?
THEN I'M PRAYING YOU WIN, TOO.

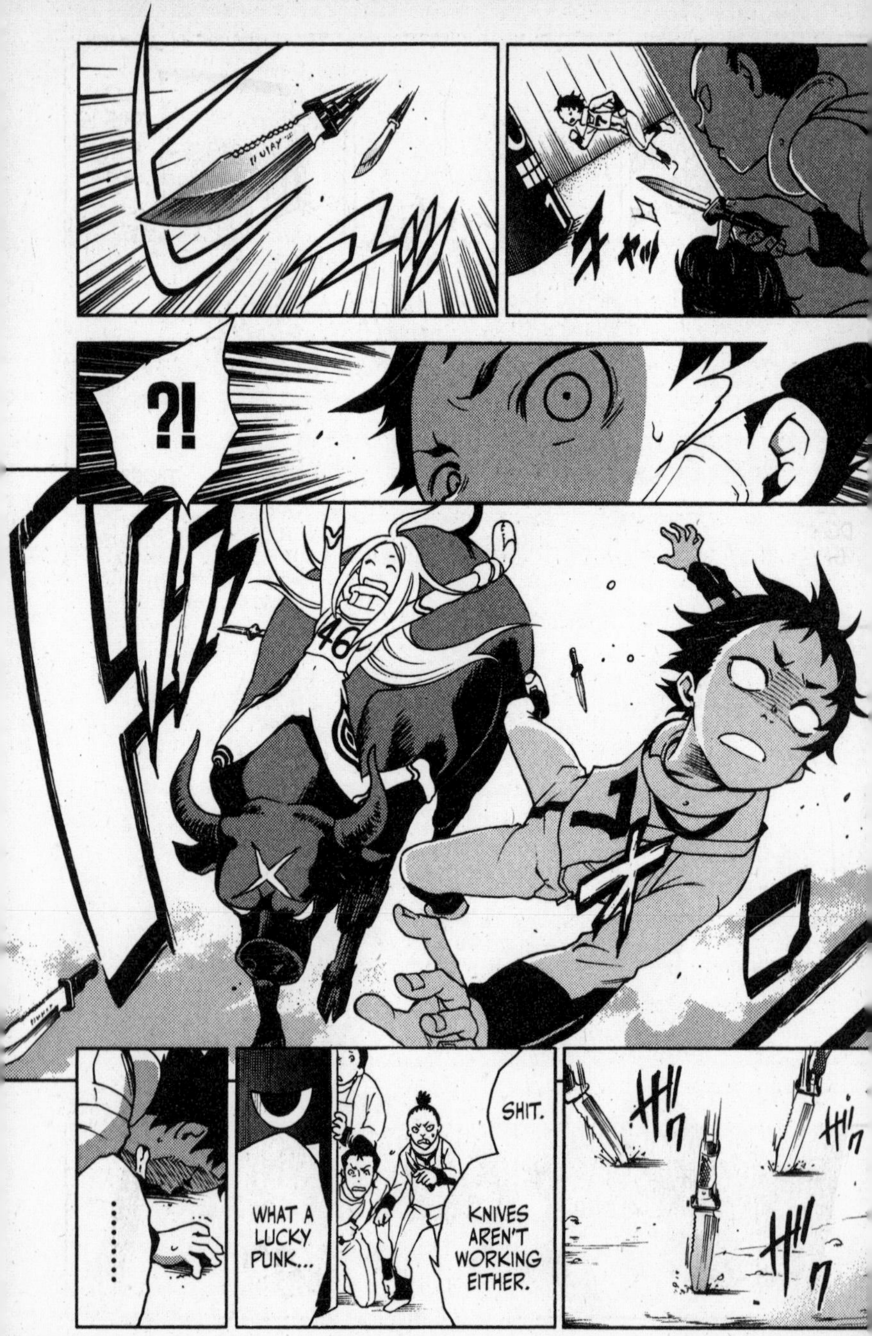
チャッ
?!
ザク
ザク
ザク
SHIT.
KNIVES AREN'T WORKING EITHER.
WHAT A LUCKY PUNK...
....

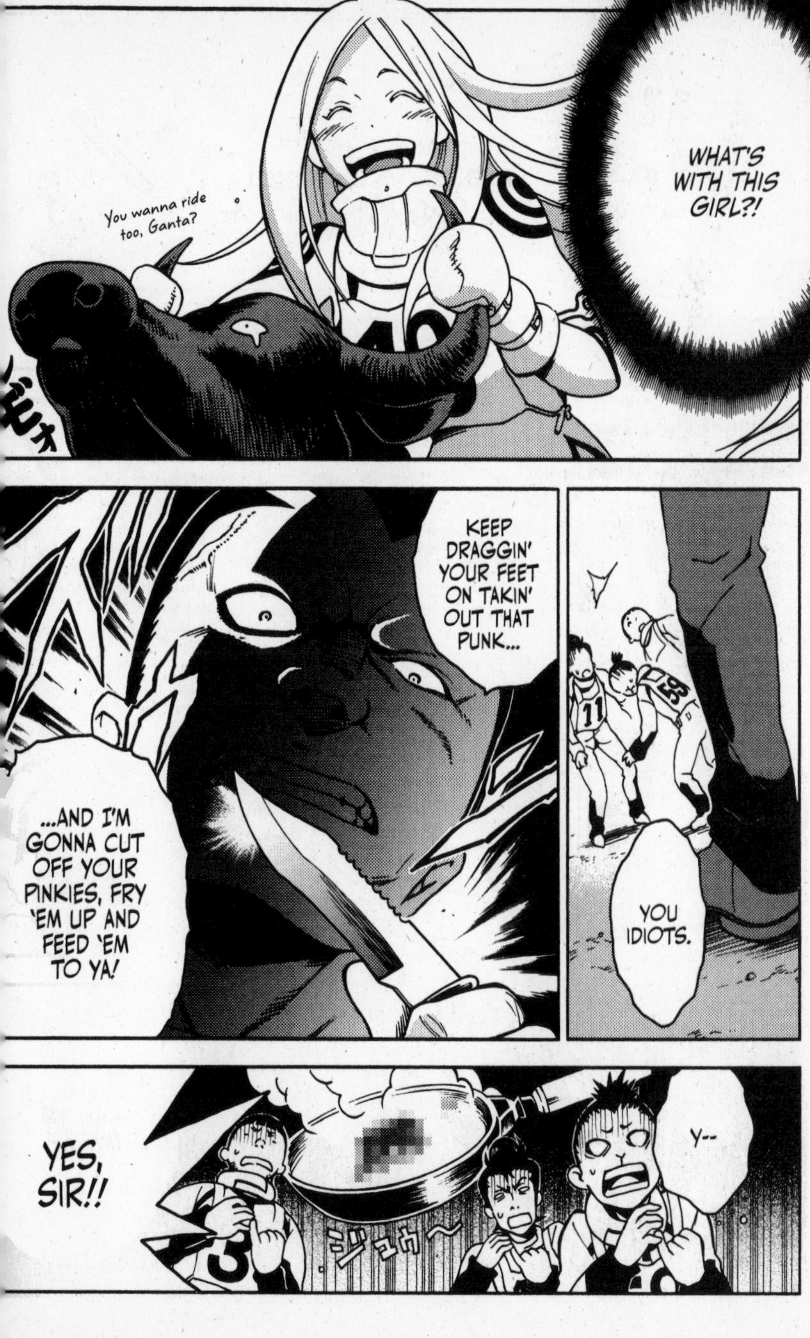
WHAT'S WITH THIS GIRL?!
You wanna ride too, Ganta?
YOU IDIOTS.
KEEP DRAGGIN' YOUR FEET ON TAKIN' OUT THAT PUNK...
...AND I'M GONNA CUT OFF YOUR PINKIES, FRY 'EM UP AND FEED 'EM TO YA!
Y--
YES, SIR!!
ジュウ〜

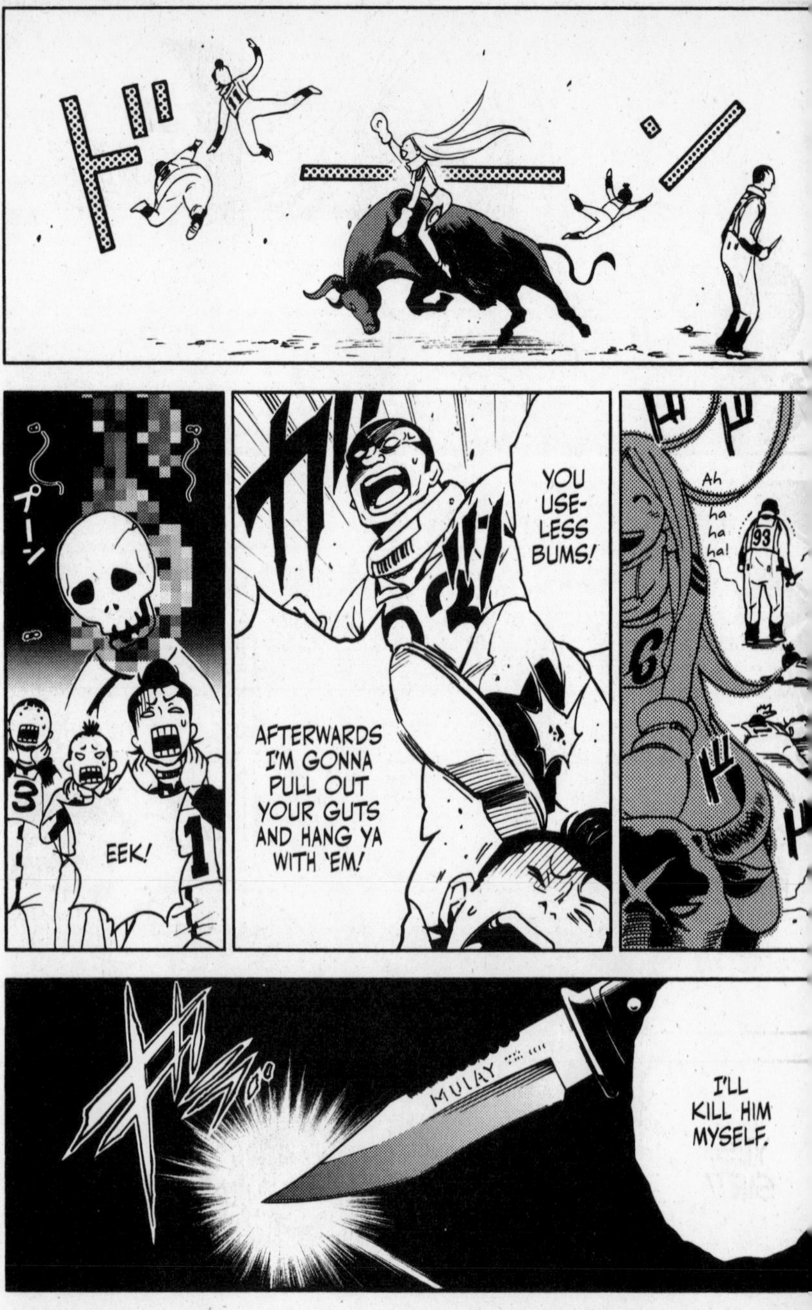
Ah ha ha ha!
YOU USE-LESS BUMS!
AFTERWARDS I'M GONNA PULL OUT YOUR GUTS AND HANG YA WITH 'EM!
EEK!
I'LL KILL HIM MYSELF.

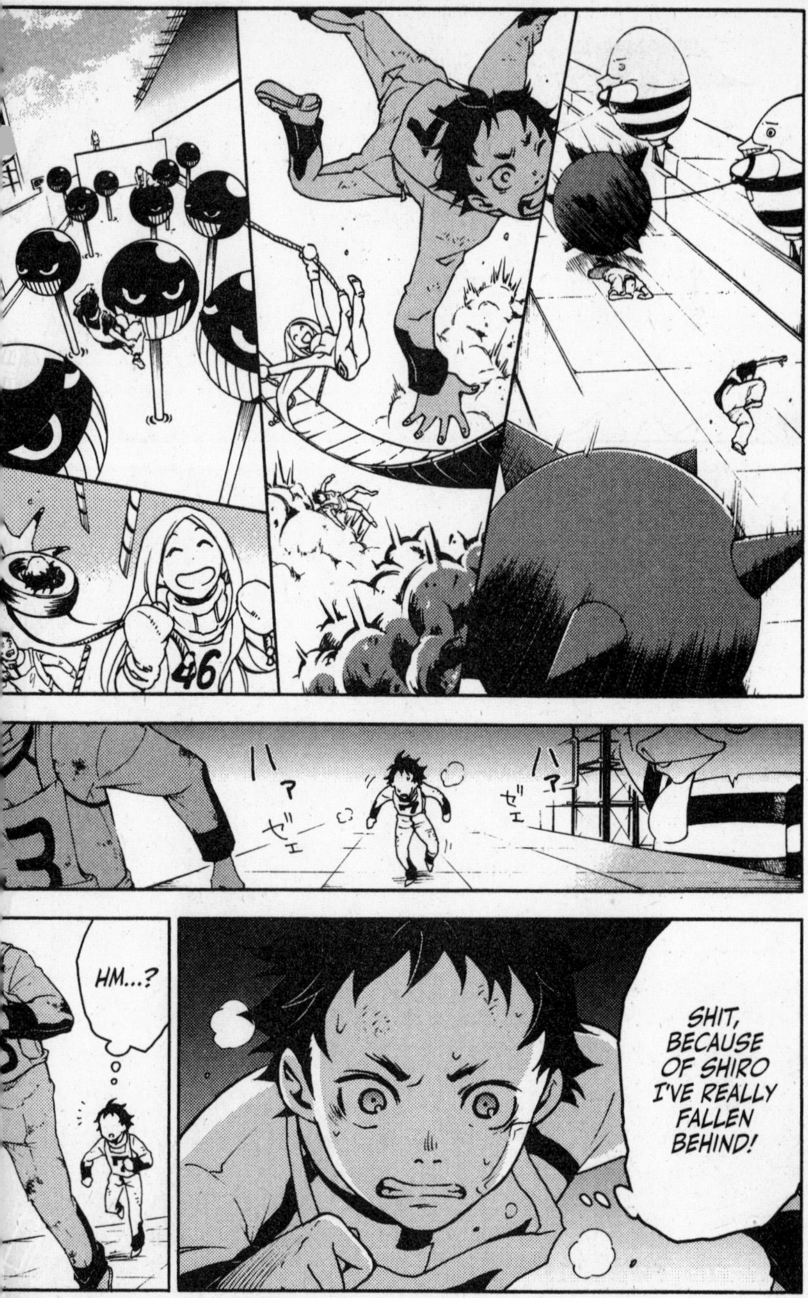
ハァ
ゼェ
ハァ
ゼェ
SHIT, BECAUSE OF SHIRO I'VE REALLY FALLEN BEHIND!
HM...?

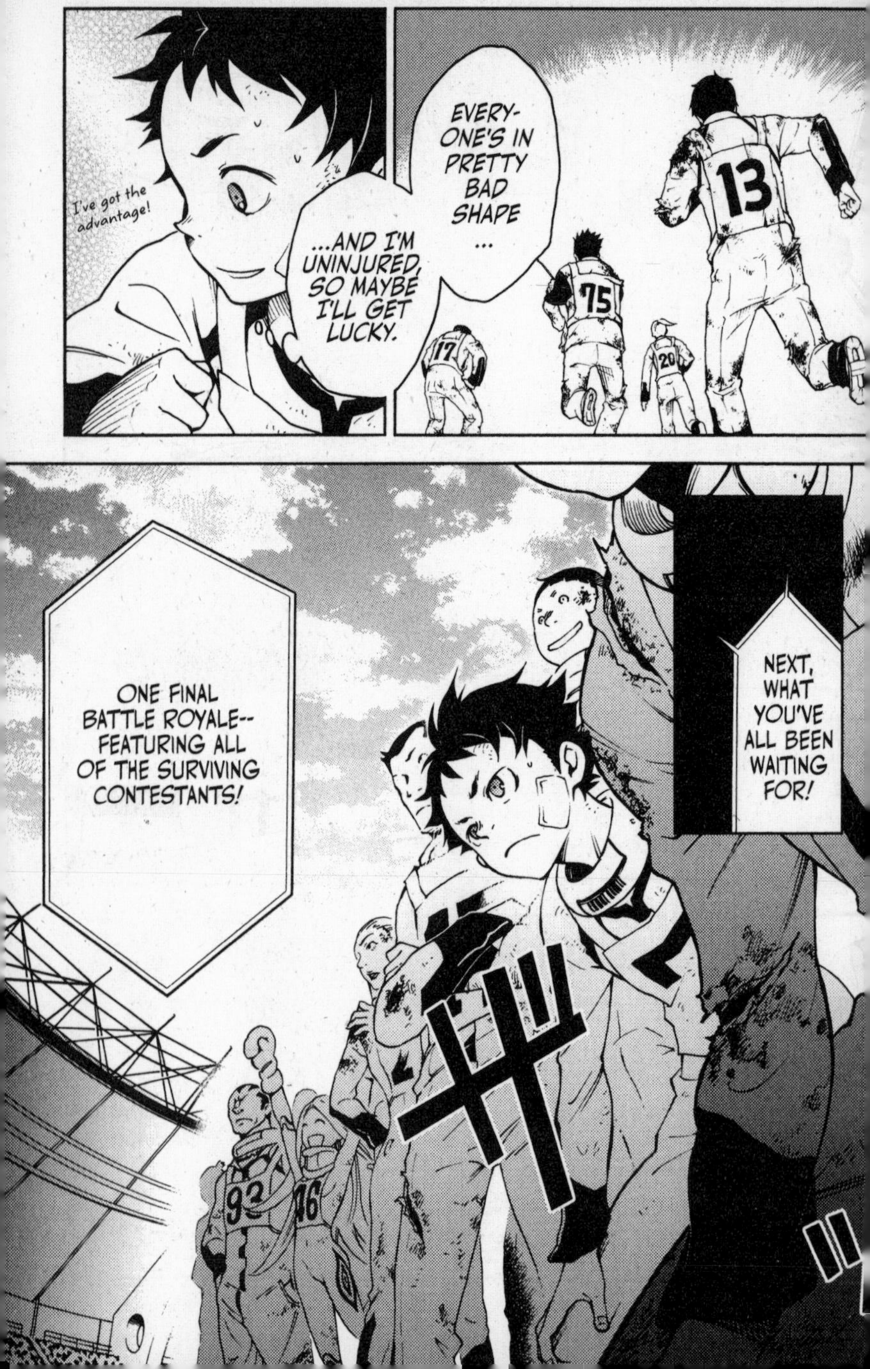
EVERY-ONE'S IN PRETTY BAD SHAPE ...
...AND I'M UNINJURED, SO MAYBE I'LL GET LUCKY.
I've got the advantage!
NEXT, WHAT YOU'VE ALL BEEN WAITING FOR!
ONE FINAL BATTLE ROYALE--FEATURING ALL OF THE SURVIVING CONTESTANTS!

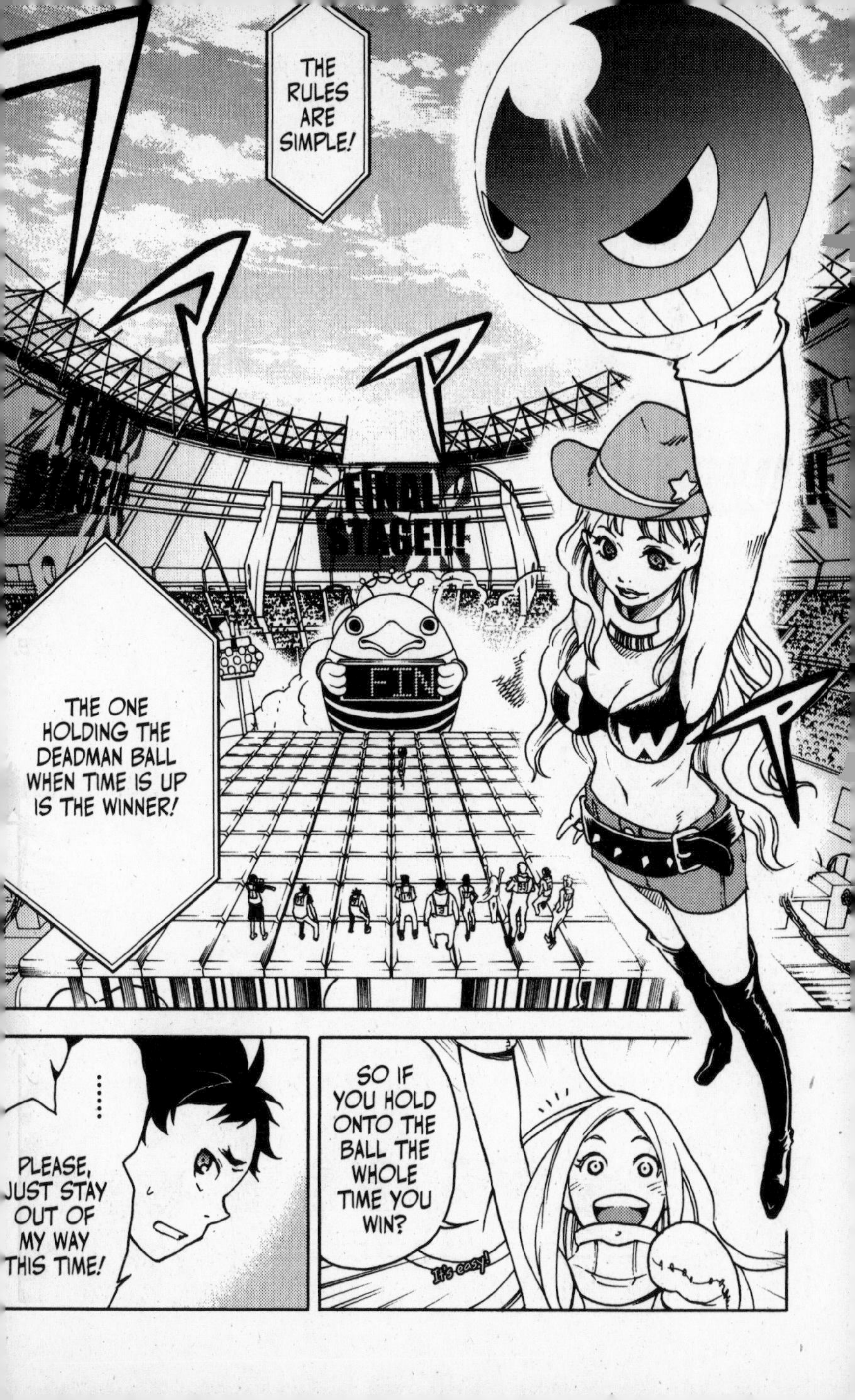
THE RULES ARE SIMPLE!
FINAL STAGE!!!
FINAL STAGE!!
THE ONE HOLDING THE DEADMAN BALL WHEN TIME IS UP IS THE WINNER!
FIN
SO IF YOU HOLD ONTO THE BALL THE WHOLE TIME YOU WIN?
It's easy!
......
PLEASE, JUST STAY OUT OF MY WAY THIS TIME!

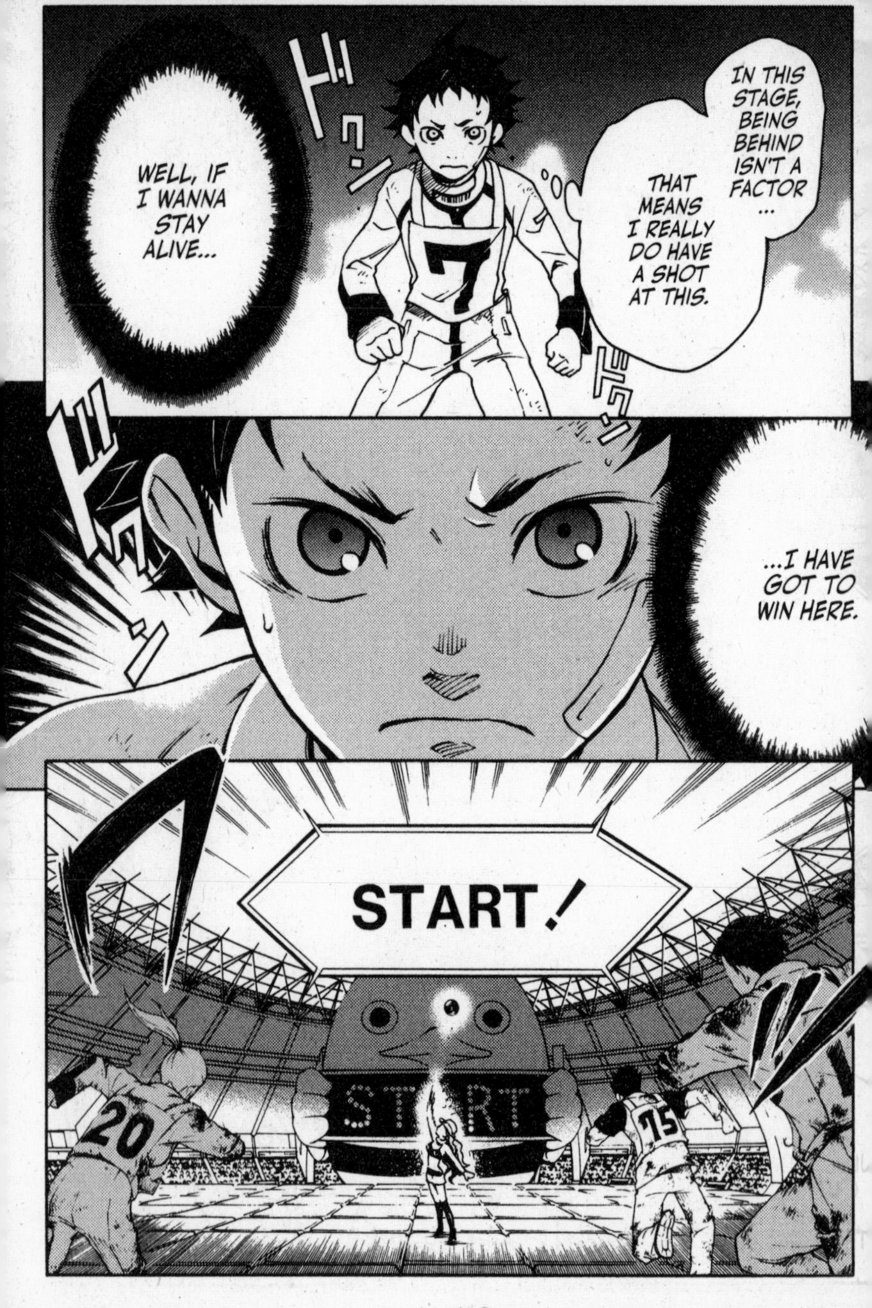

IN THIS STAGE, BEING BEHIND ISN'T A FACTOR...
THAT MEANS I REALLY DO HAVE A SHOT AT THIS.
WELL, IF I WANNA STAY ALIVE...
...I HAVE GOT TO WIN HERE.
START!
START

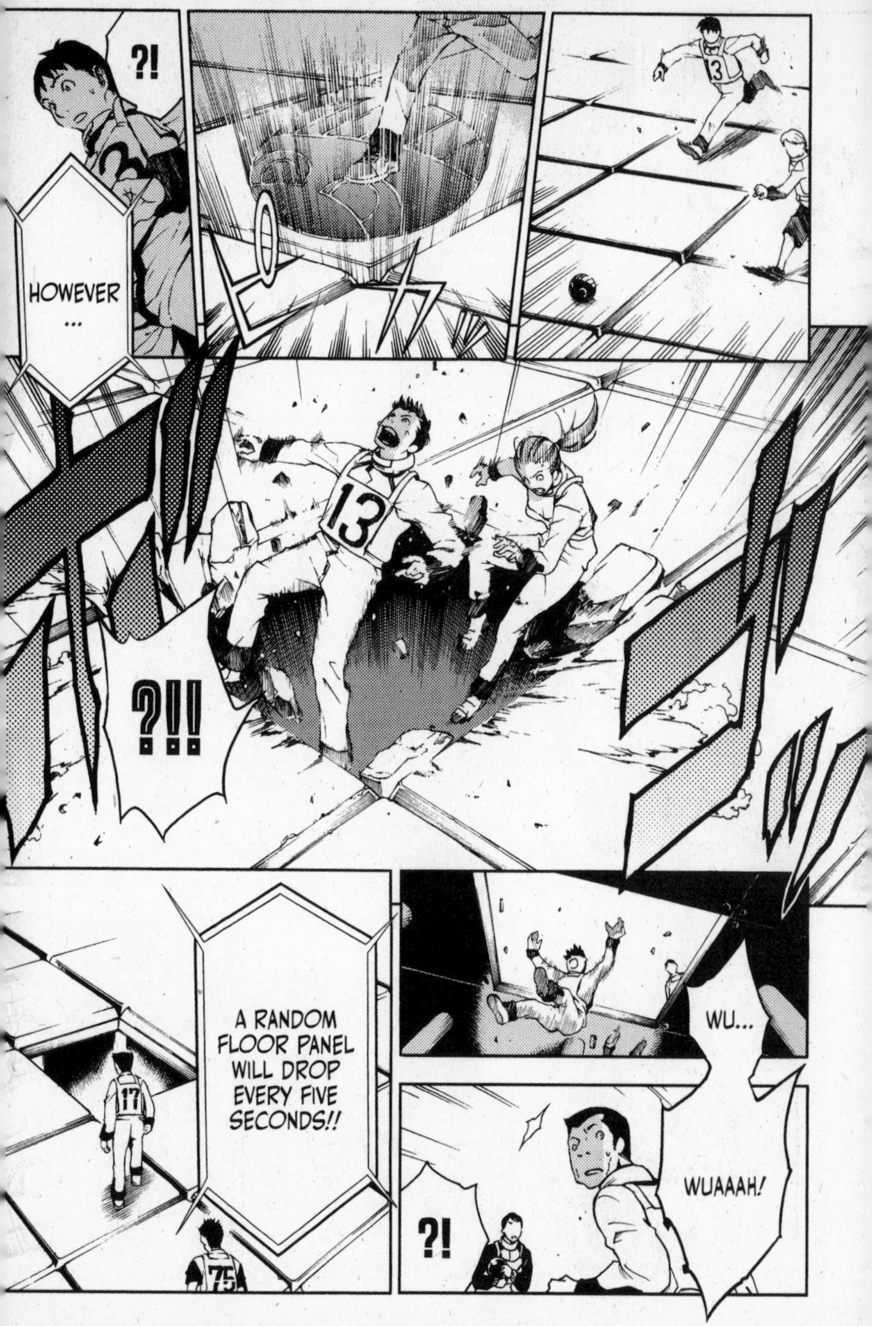
?!
HOWEVER ...
?!!
WU...
WUAAAH!
?!
A RANDOM FLOOR PANEL WILL DROP EVERY FIVE SECONDS!!

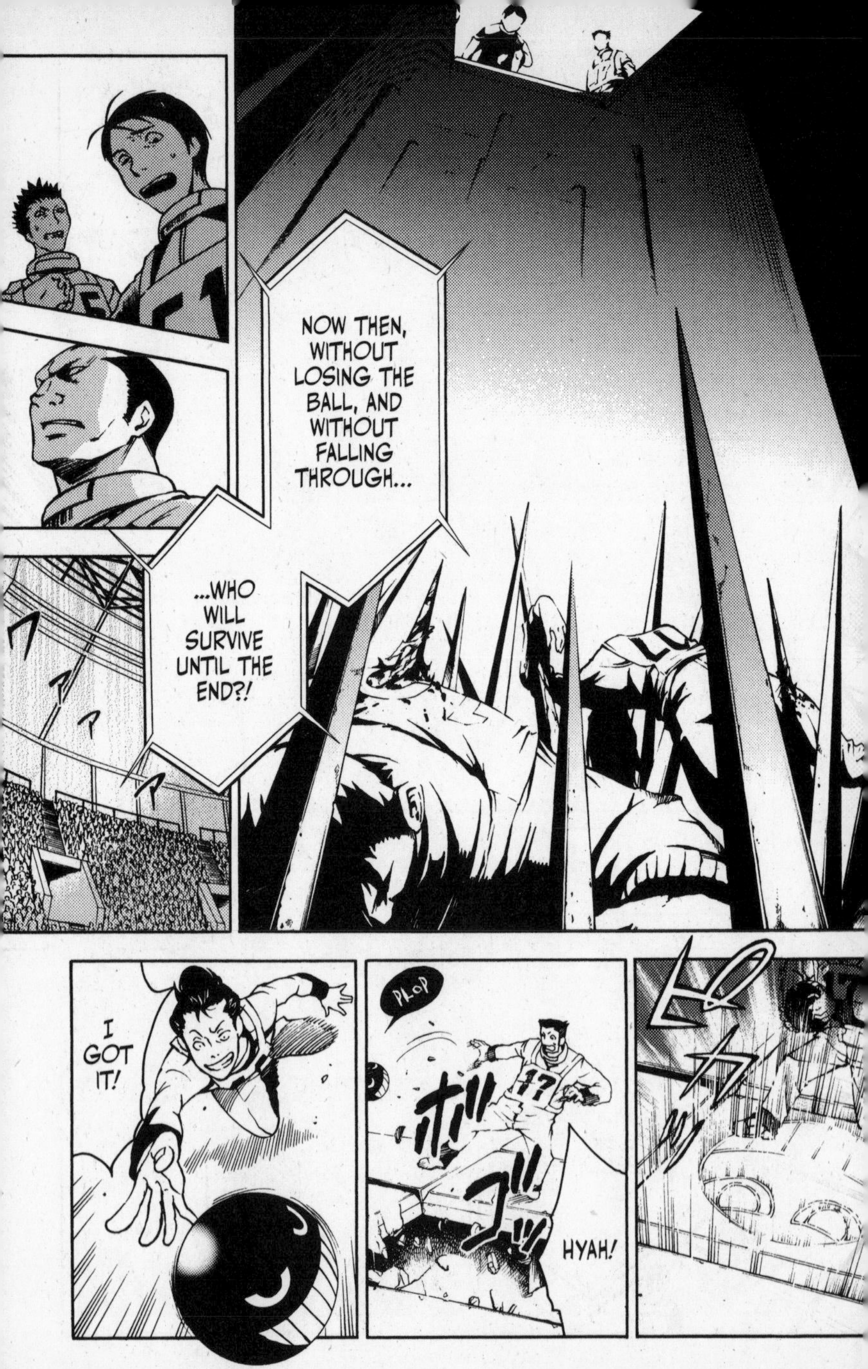
NOW THEN, WITHOUT LOSING THE BALL, AND WITHOUT FALLING THROUGH...
...WHO WILL SURVIVE UNTIL THE END?!
PLOP
HYAH!
I GOT IT!

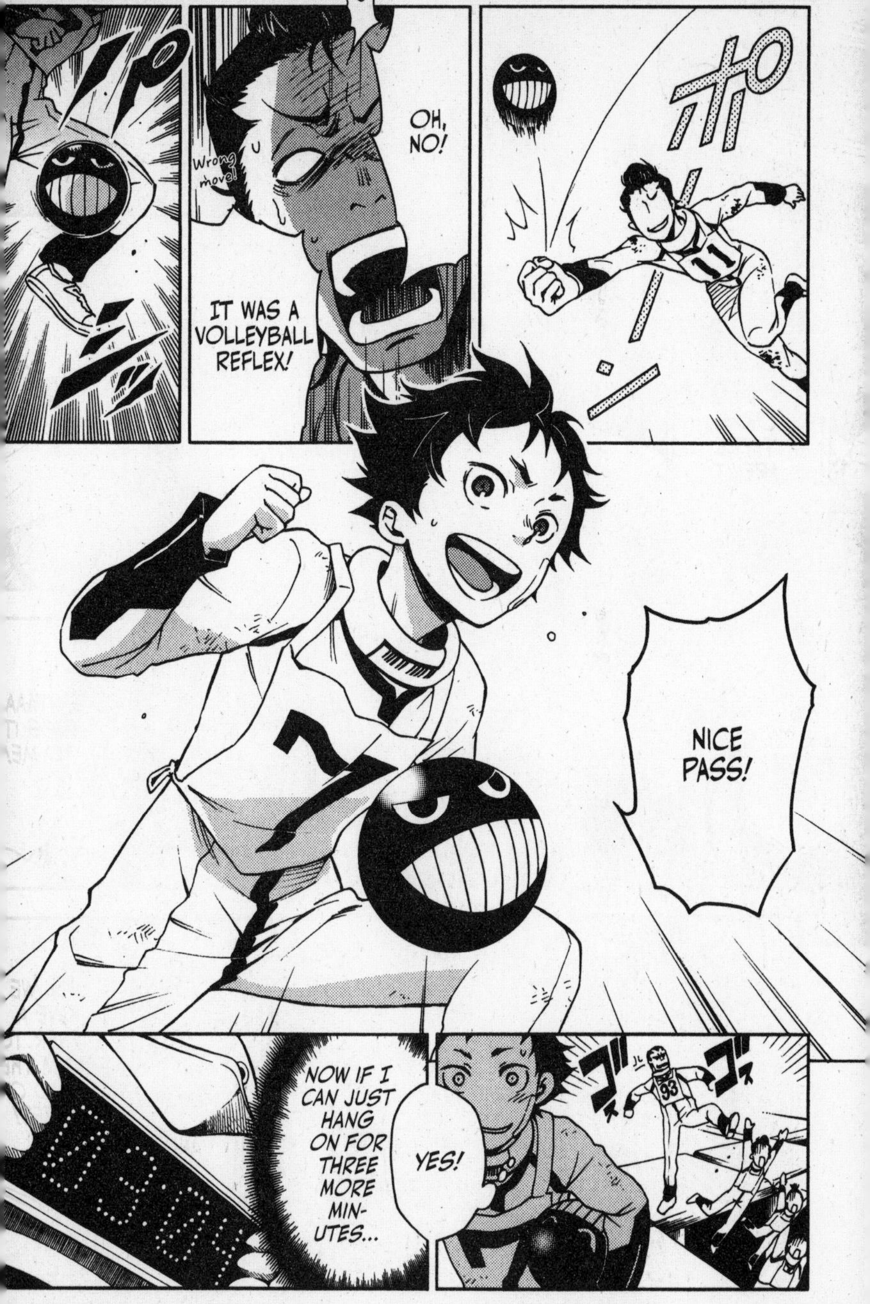
OH, NO!
Wrong move!
IT WAS A VOLLEYBALL REFLEX!
NICE PASS!
YES!
NOW IF I CAN JUST HANG ON FOR THREE MORE MIN-UTES...

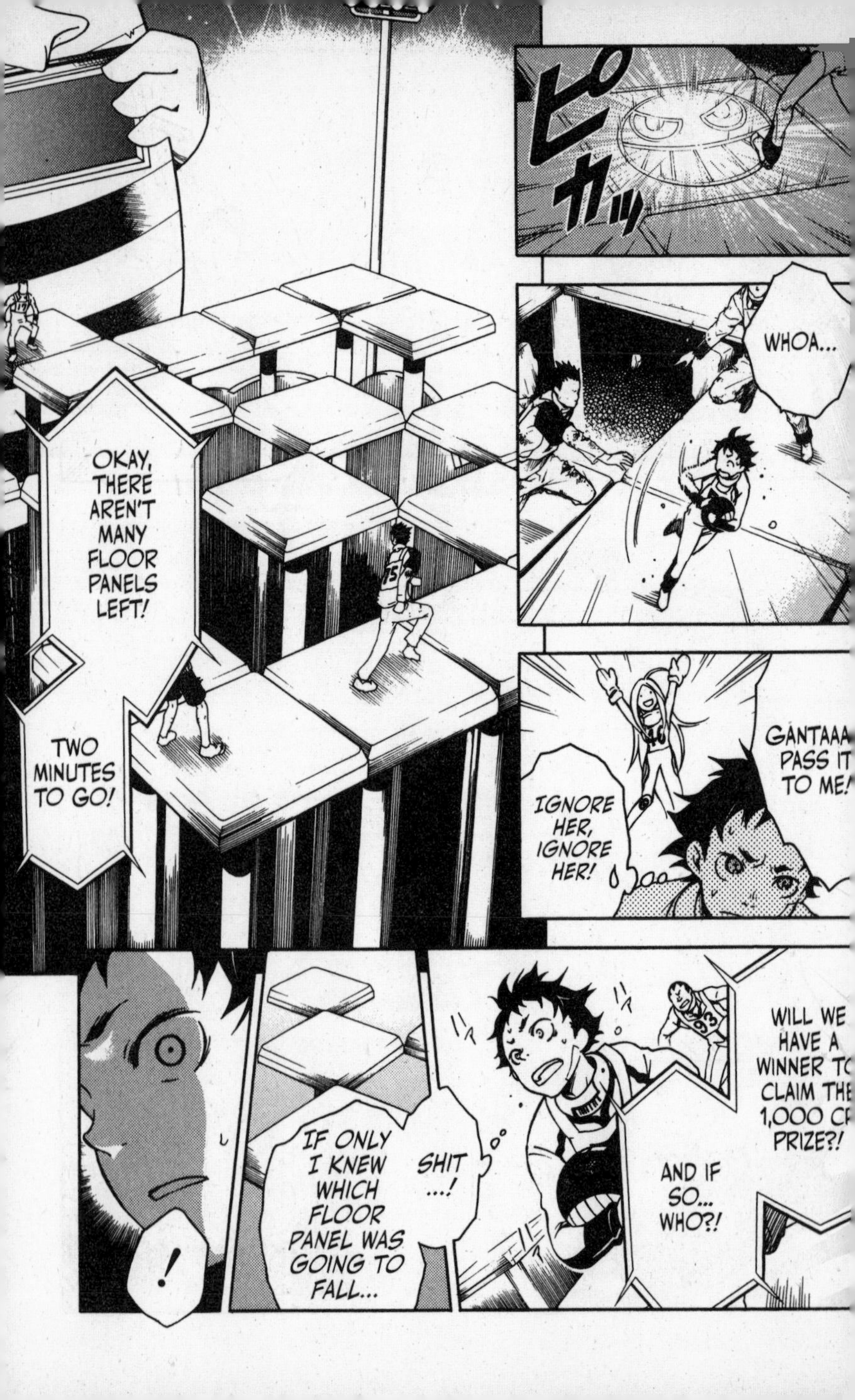

ピカッ
WHOA...
GANTAAA PASS IT TO ME!
IGNORE HER, IGNORE HER!
OKAY, THERE AREN'T MANY FLOOR PANELS LEFT!
TWO MINUTES TO GO!
WILL WE HAVE A WINNER TO CLAIM THE 1,000 CP PRIZE?!
AND IF SO... WHO?!
SHIT ...!
IF ONLY I KNEW WHICH FLOOR PANEL WAS GOING TO FALL...
!

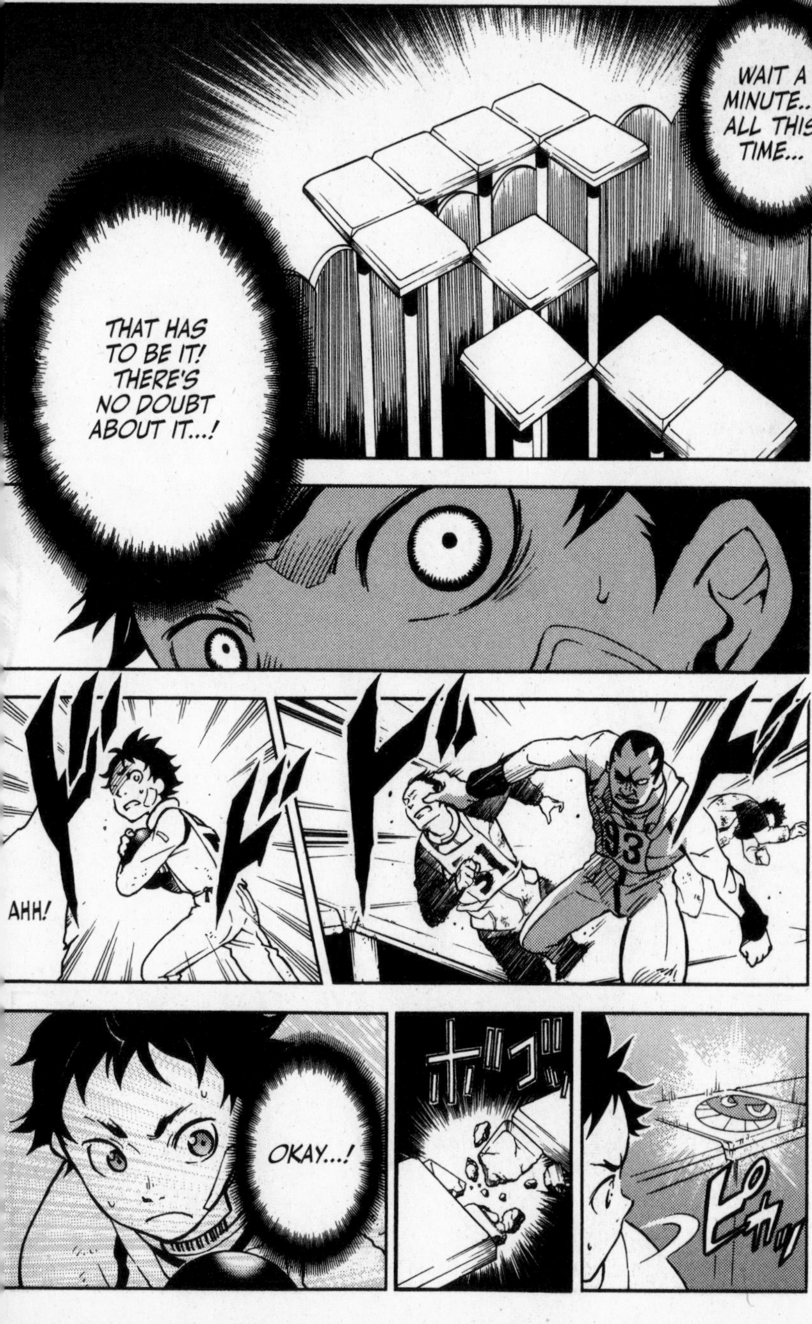
WAIT A MINUTE... ALL THIS TIME...
THAT HAS TO BE IT! THERE'S NO DOUBT ABOUT IT...!
AHH!
ピカッ
ボゴッ
OKAY...!

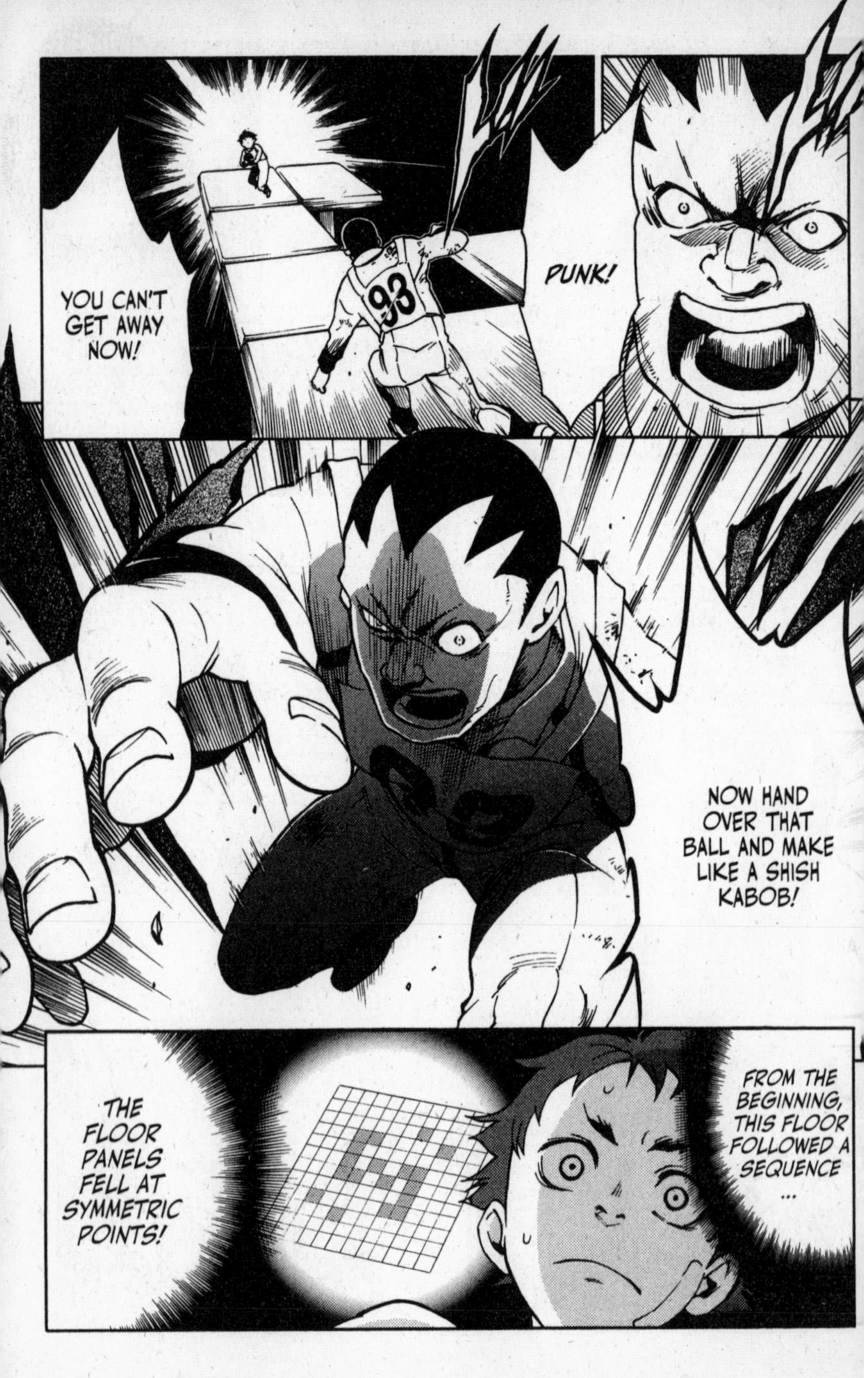
PUNK!
YOU CAN'T GET AWAY NOW!
NOW HAND OVER THAT BALL AND MAKE LIKE A SHISH KABOB!
FROM THE BEGINNING, THIS FLOOR FOLLOWED A SEQUENCE ...
THE FLOOR PANELS FELL AT SYMMETRIC POINTS!

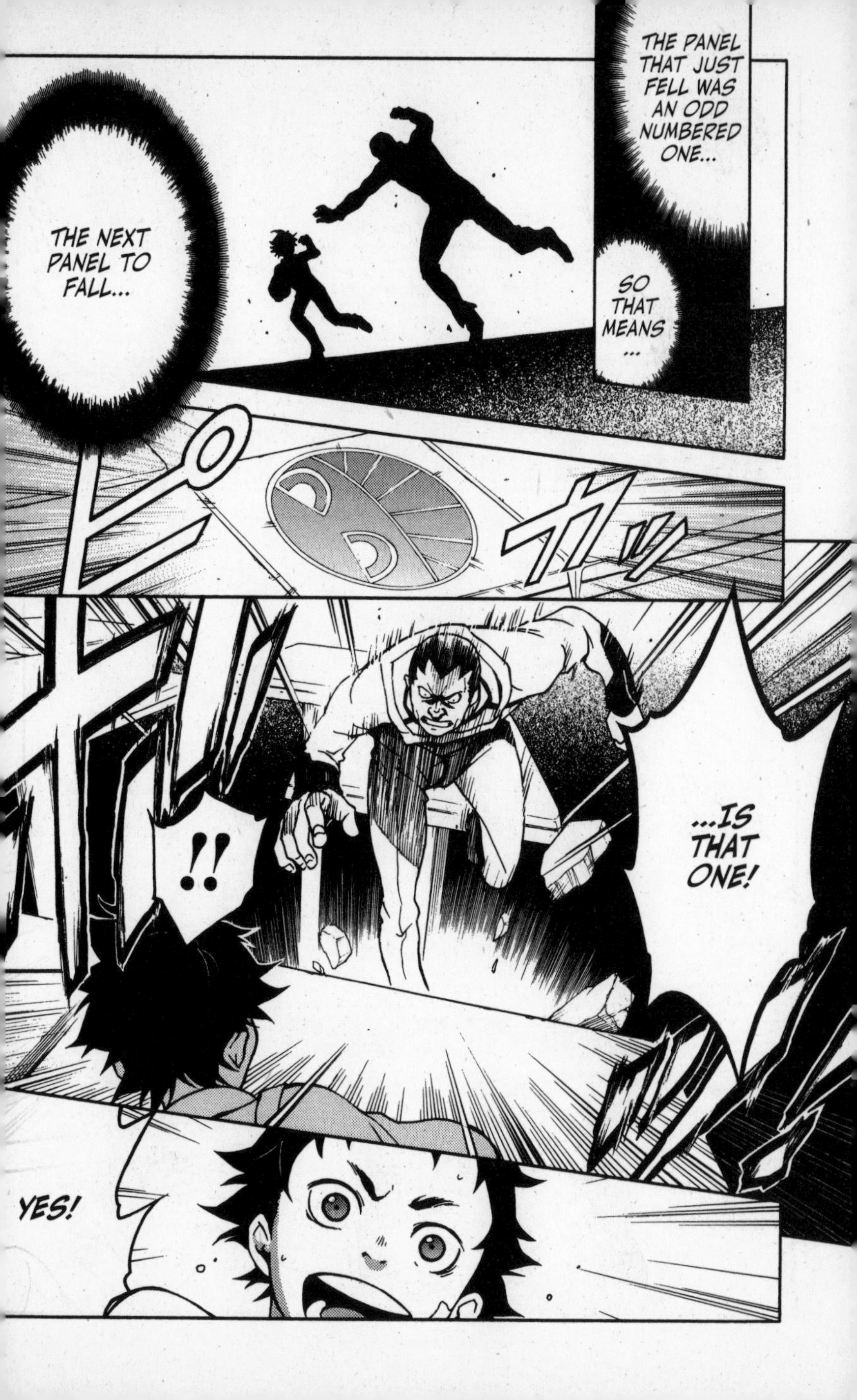
THE PANEL THAT JUST FELL WAS AN ODD NUMBERED ONE...
SO THAT MEANS ...
THE NEXT PANEL TO FALL...
ガッ
...IS THAT ONE!
!!
YES!

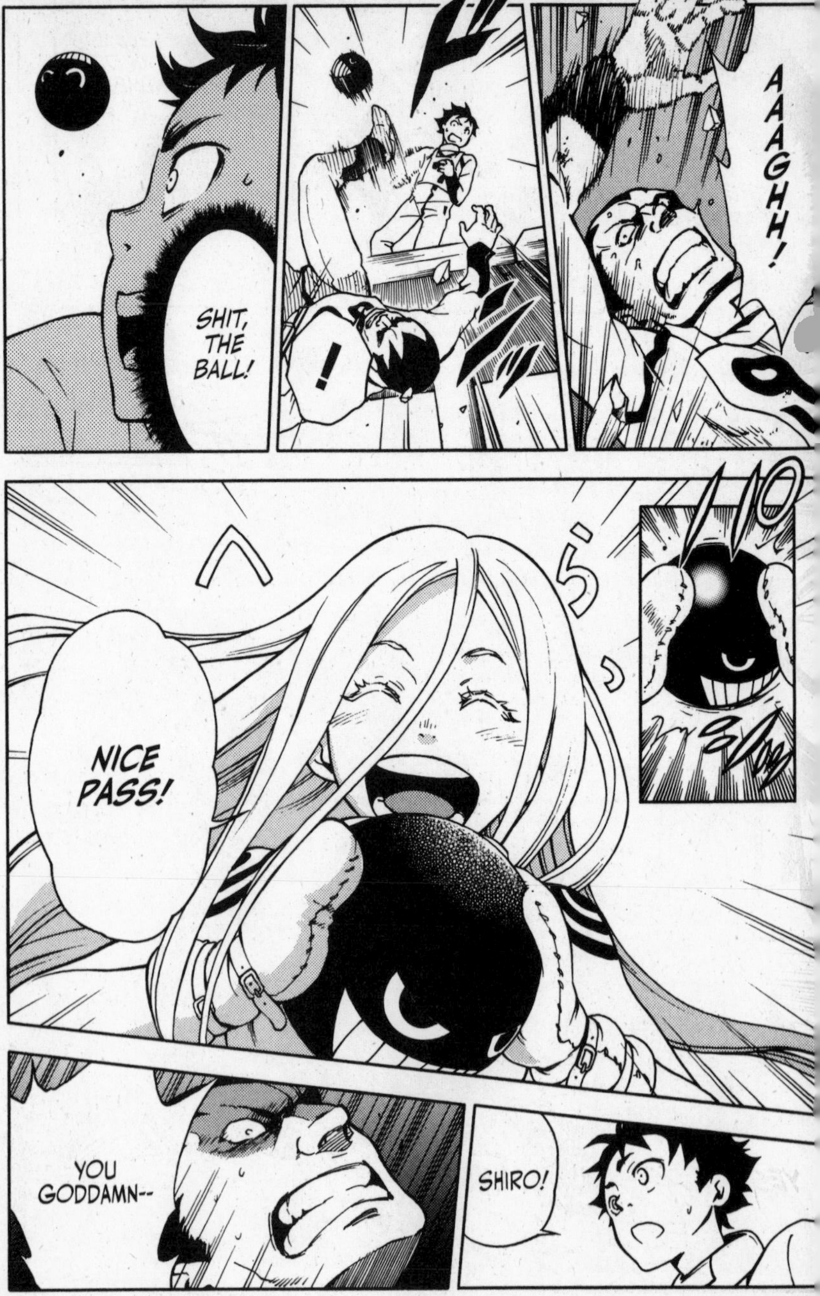
AAAGHH!
!
SHIT, THE BALL!
NICE PASS!
SHIRO!
YOU GODDAMN--

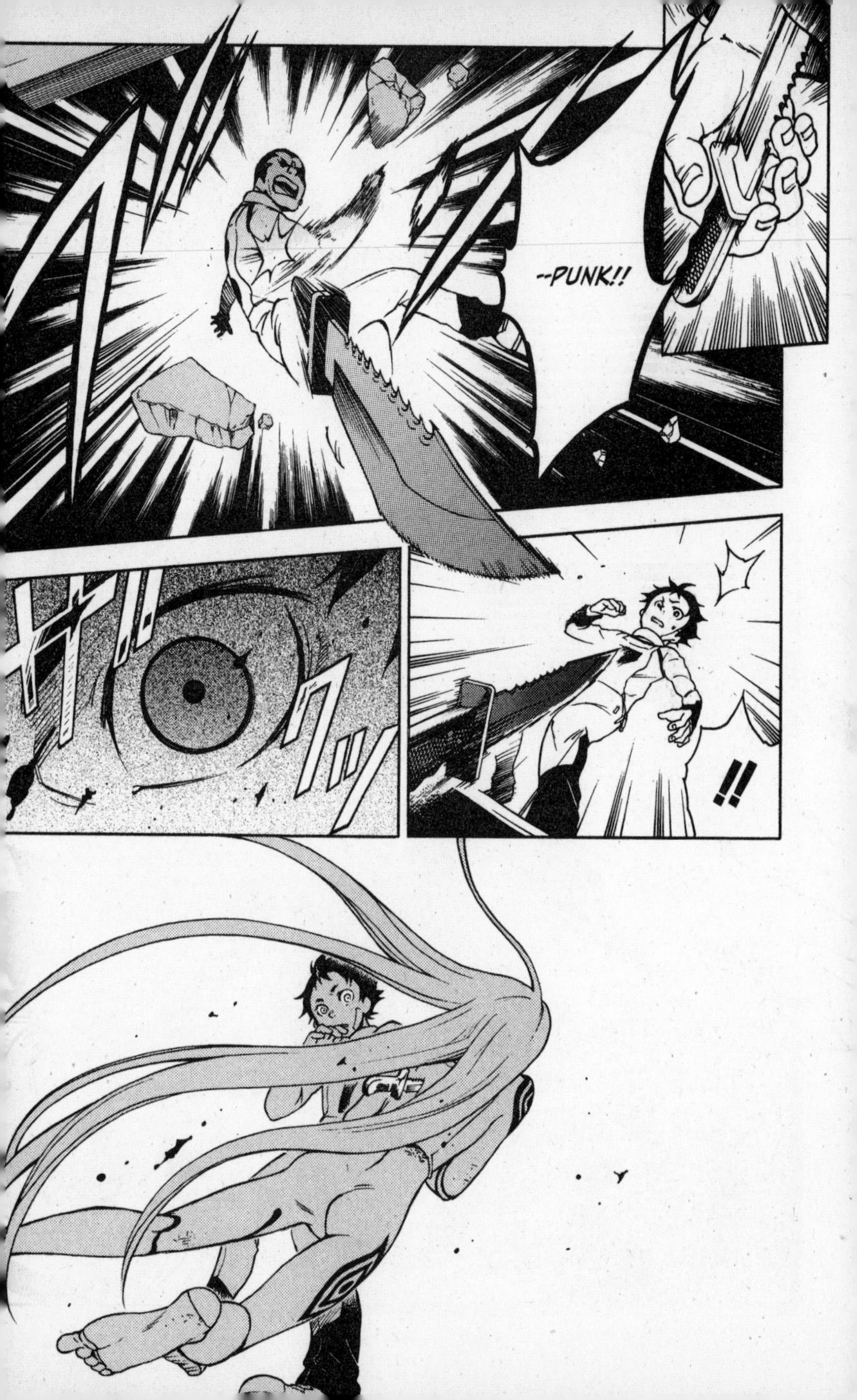
--PUNK!!
!!

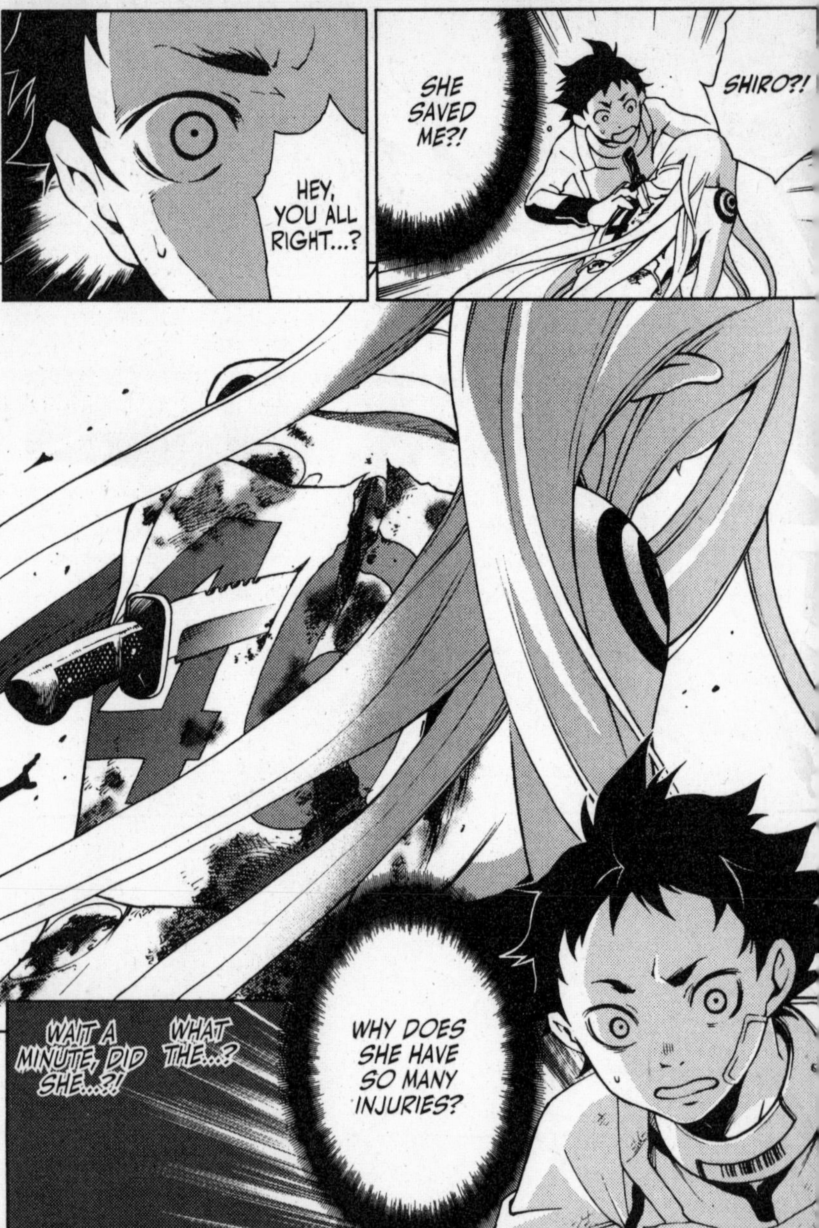
SHIRO?!
SHE SAVED ME?!
HEY, YOU ALL RIGHT...?
WHY DOES SHE HAVE SO MANY INJURIES?
WHAT THE...?
WAIT A MINUTE, DID SHE...?!

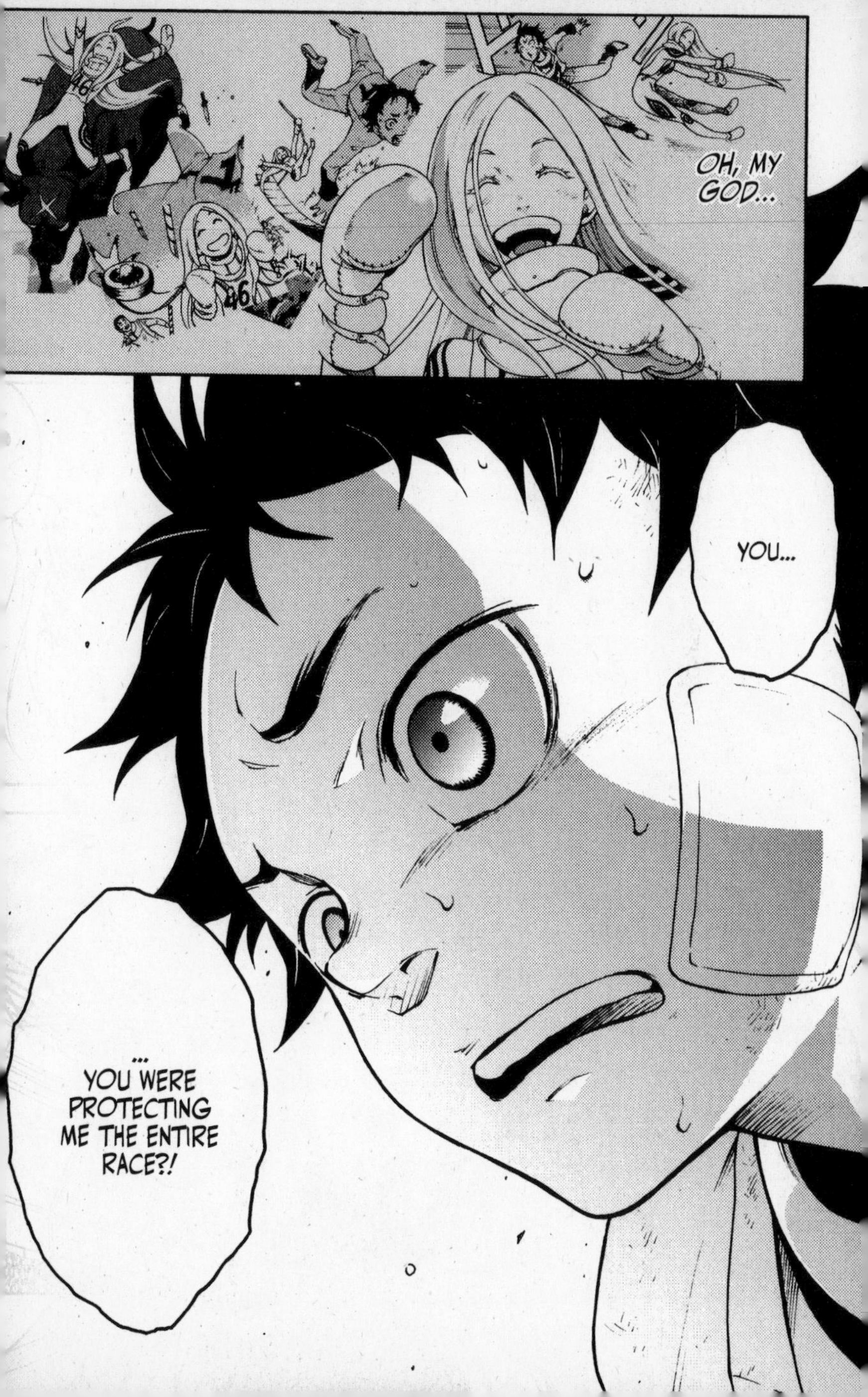
OH, MY GOD...
YOU...
...YOU WERE PROTECTING ME THE ENTIRE RACE?!

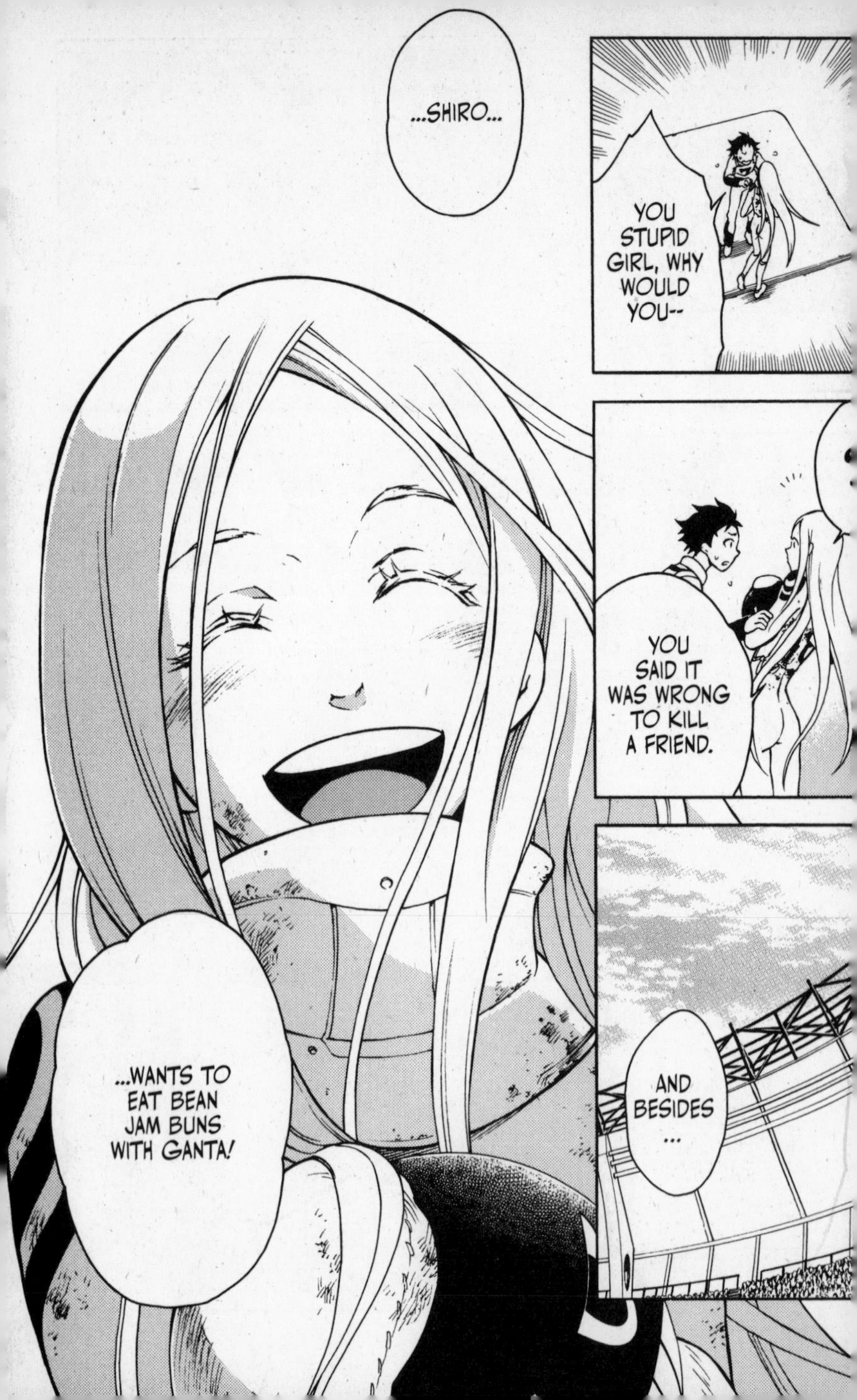
YOU STUPID GIRL, WHY WOULD YOU--
YOU SAID IT WAS WRONG TO KILL A FRIEND.
AND BESIDES ...
...SHIRO...
...WANTS TO EAT BEAN JAM BUNS WITH GANTA!

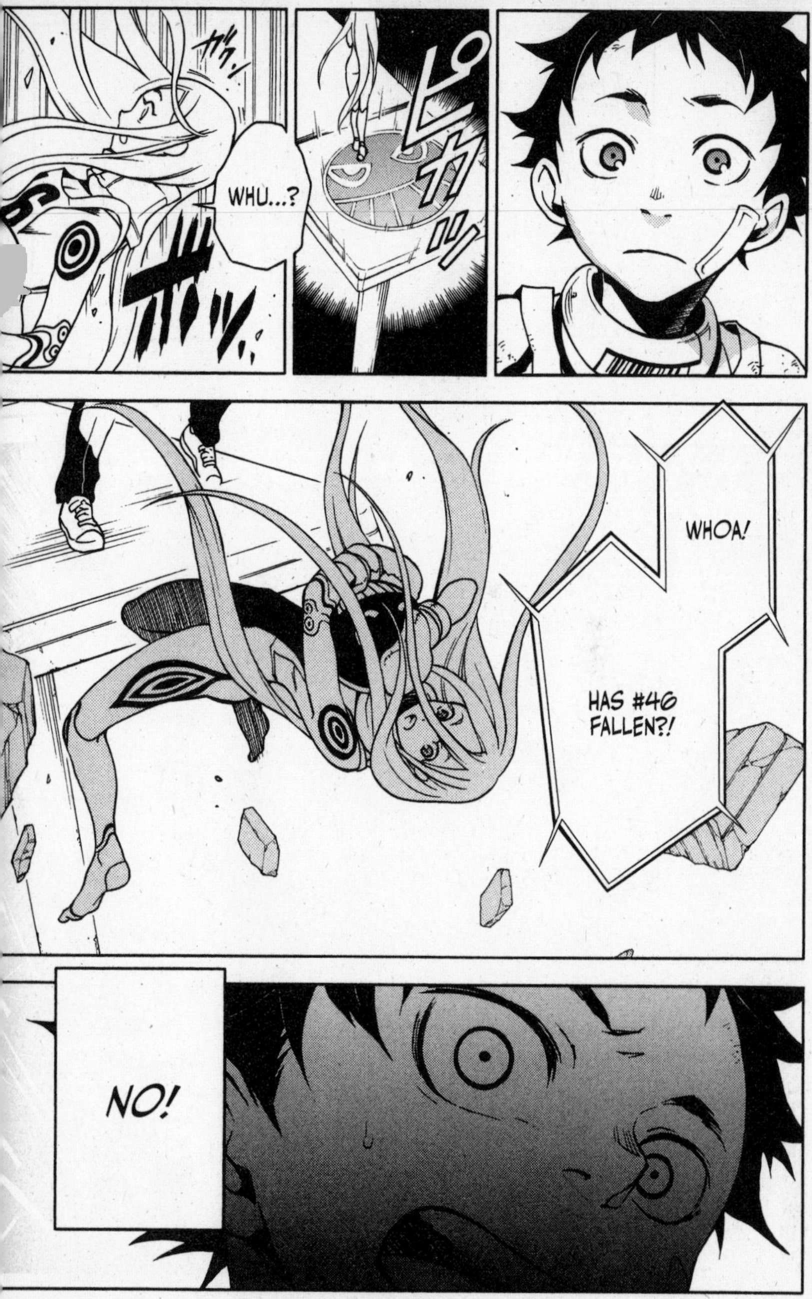
WHU...?
WHOA!
HAS #46
FALLEN?!
NO!

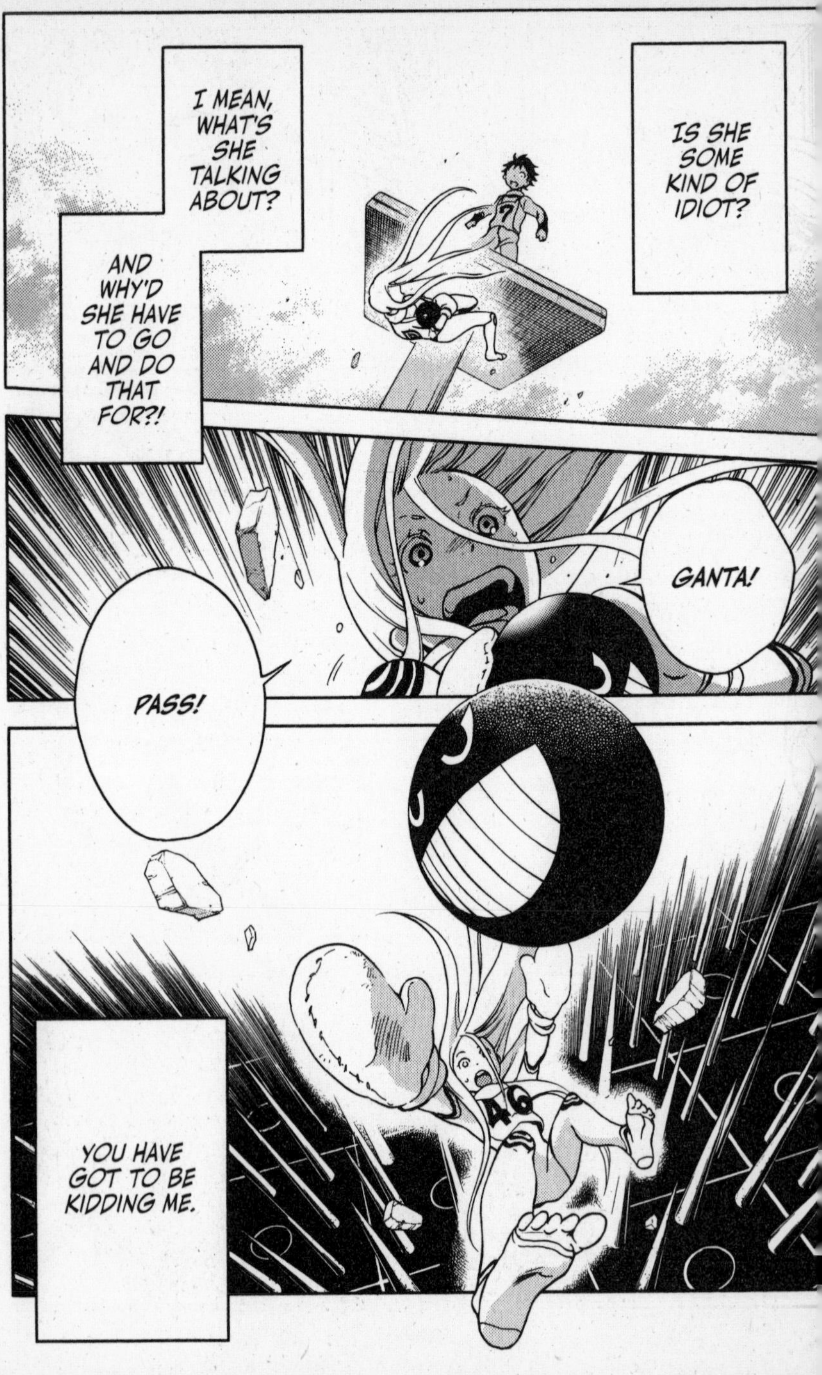

IS SHE SOME KIND OF IDIOT?
I MEAN, WHAT'S SHE TALKING ABOUT?
AND WHY'D SHE HAVE TO GO AND DO THAT FOR?!
GANTA!
PASS!
YOU HAVE GOT TO BE KIDDING ME.

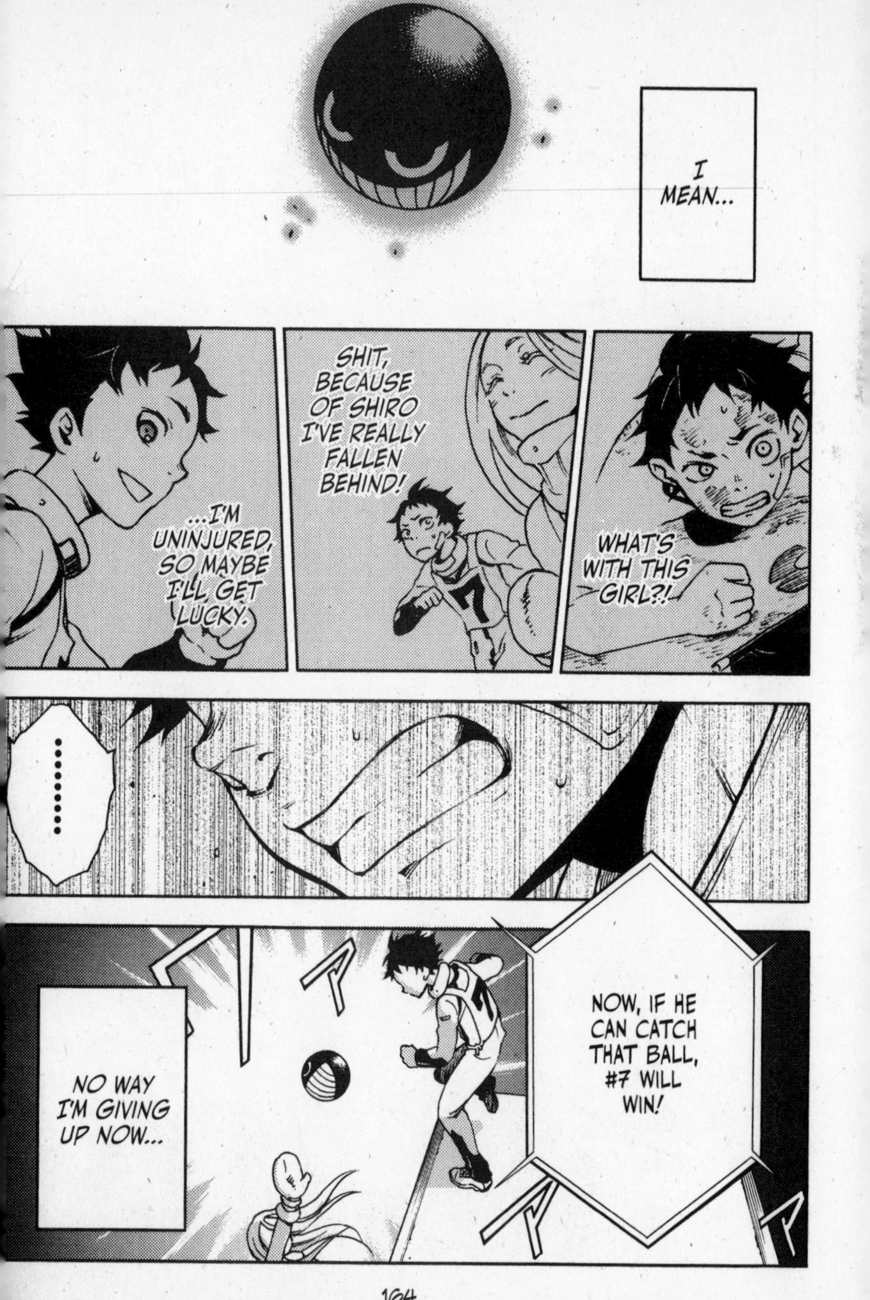
I MEAN...
WHAT'S WITH THIS GIRL?!
SHIT, BECAUSE OF SHIRO I'VE REALLY FALLEN BEHIND!
...I'M UNINJURED, SO MAYBE I'LL GET LUCKY.
....
NOW, IF HE CAN CATCH THAT BALL, #7 WILL WIN!
NO WAY I'M GIVING UP NOW...

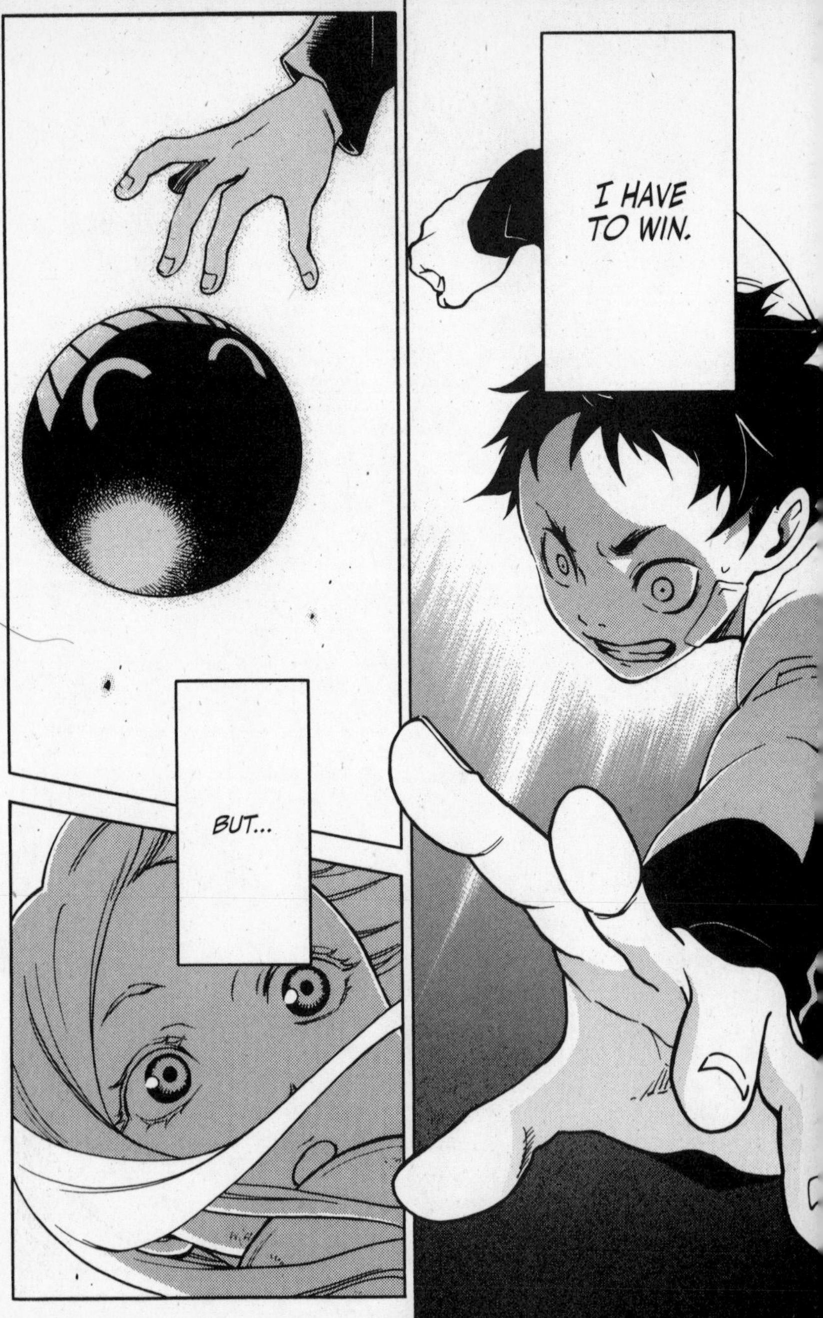
I HAVE TO WIN.
BUT...

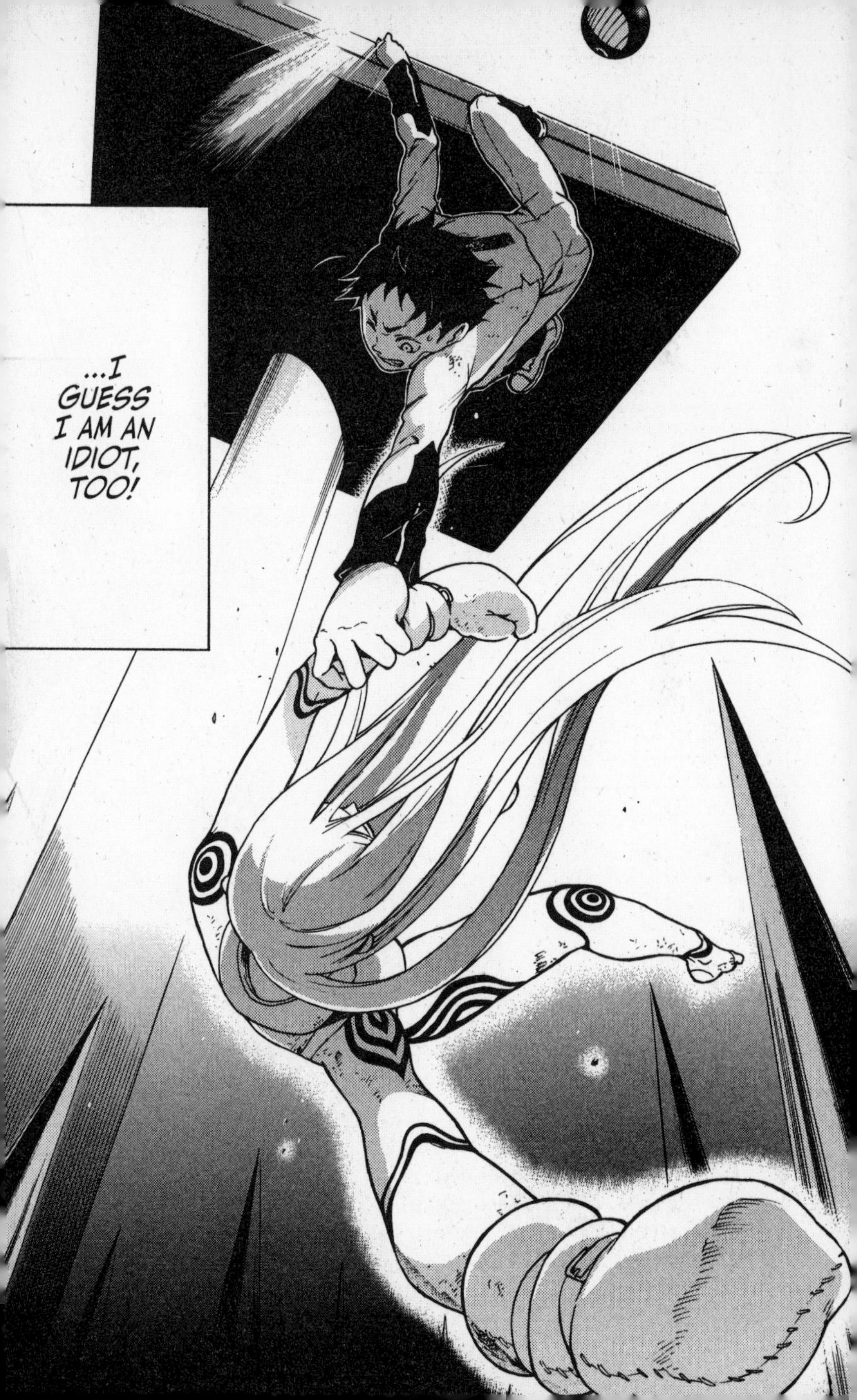
...I GUESS I AM AN IDIOT, TOO!

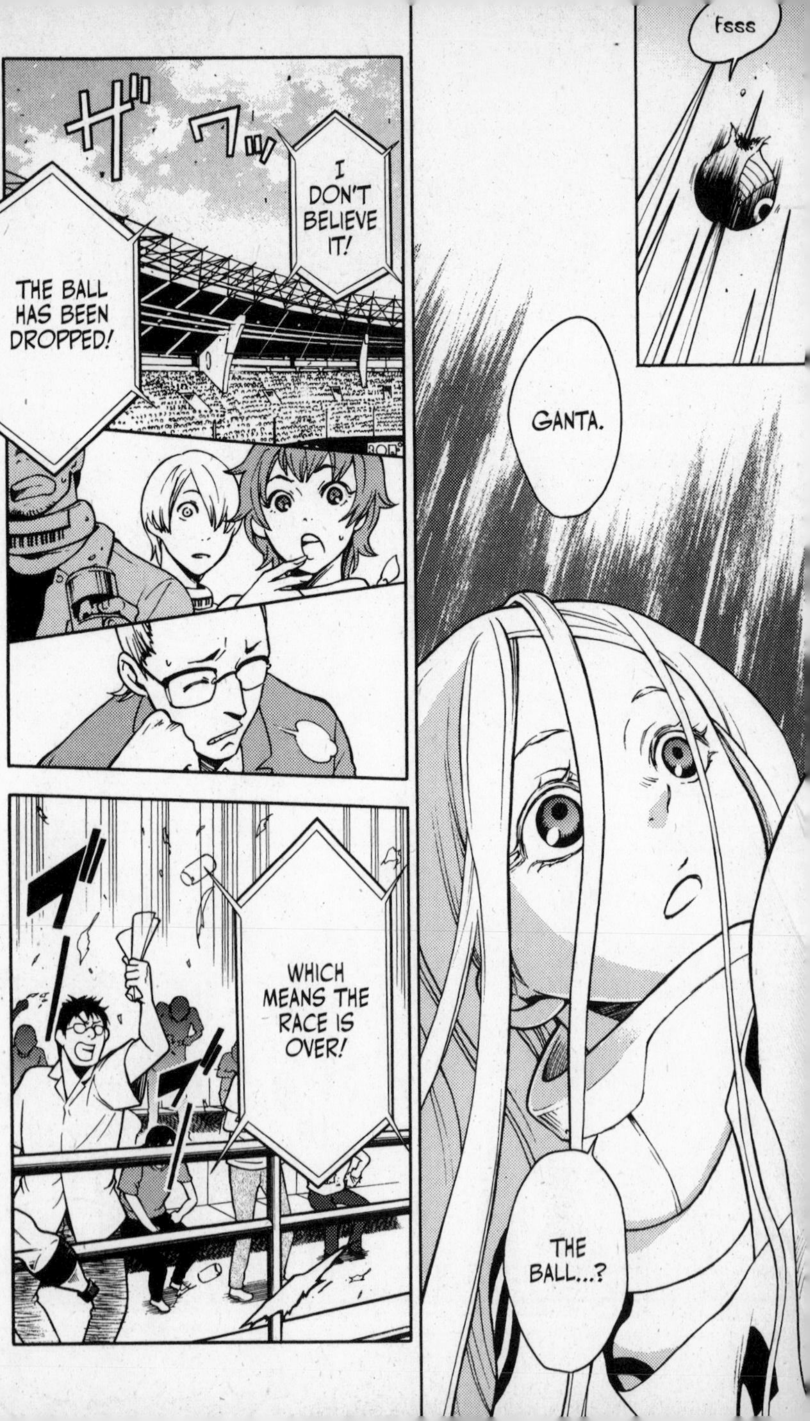
Fsss
GANTA.
THE BALL...?
ザワッ
I DON'T BELIEVE IT!
THE BALL HAS BEEN DROPPED!
WHICH MEANS THE RACE IS OVER!

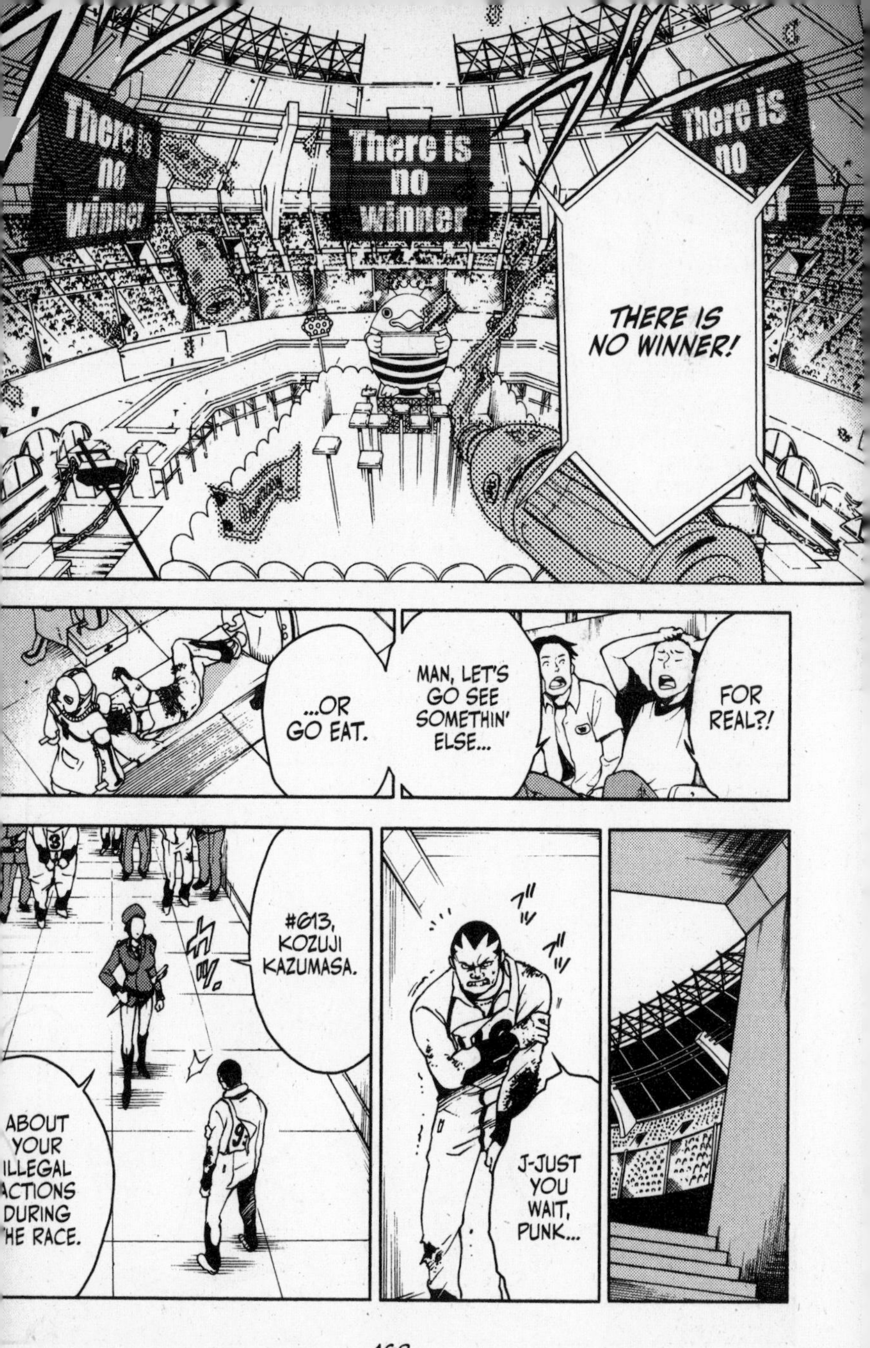
There is no winner
There is no winner
There is no winner
THERE IS NO WINNER!
FOR REAL?!
MAN, LET'S GO SEE SOMETHIN' ELSE...
...OR GO EAT.
J-JUST YOU WAIT, PUNK...
#613, KOZUJI KAZUMASA.
ABOUT YOUR ILLEGAL ACTIONS DURING THE RACE.

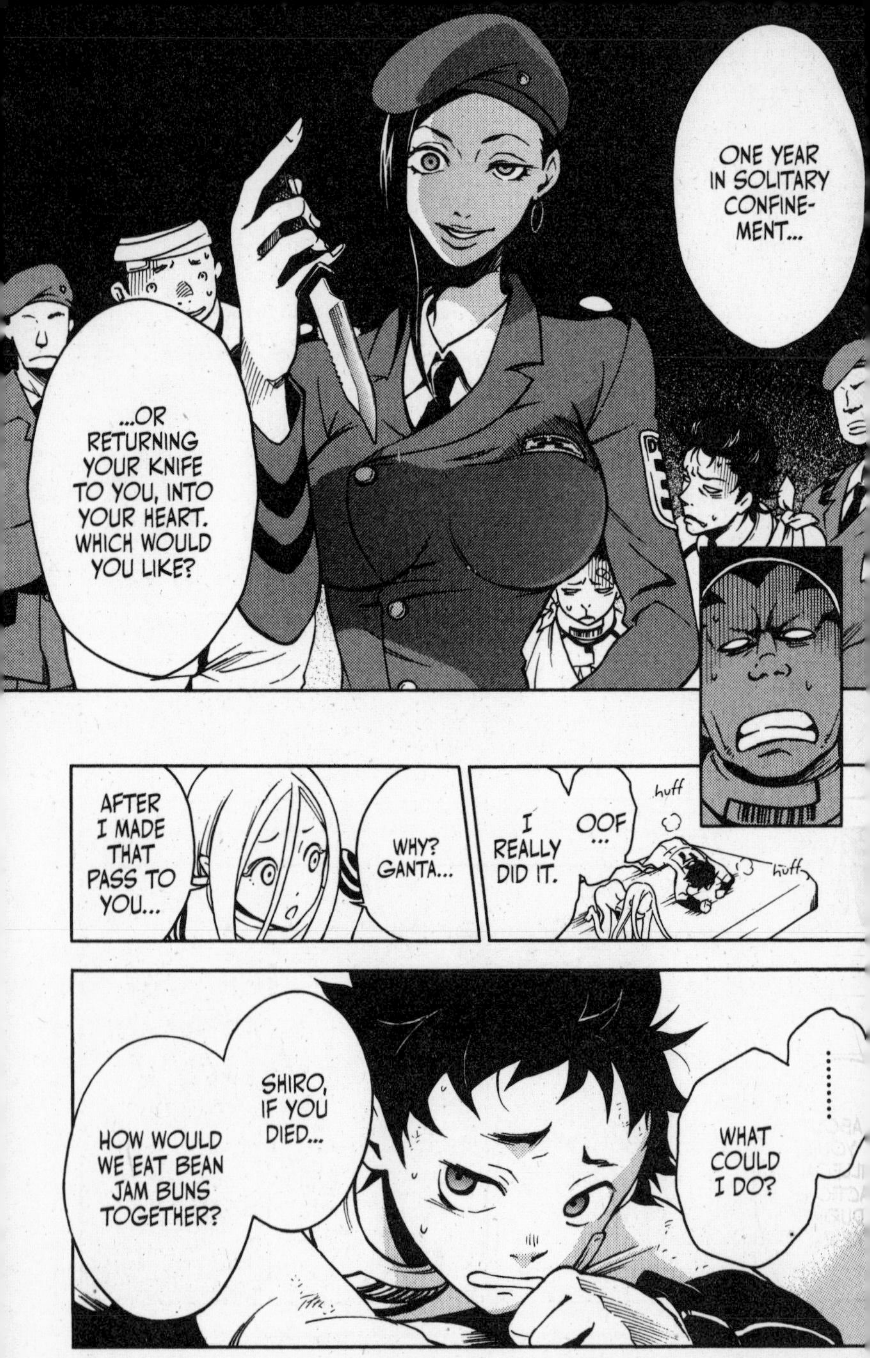
ONE YEAR IN SOLITARY CONFINE- MENT...
...OR RETURNING YOUR KNIFE TO YOU, INTO YOUR HEART. WHICH WOULD YOU LIKE?
huff
OOF...
I REALLY DID IT.
huff
WHY? GANTA...
AFTER I MADE THAT PASS TO YOU...
......
WHAT COULD I DO?
SHIRO, IF YOU DIED...
HOW WOULD WE EAT BEAN JAM BUNS TOGETHER?

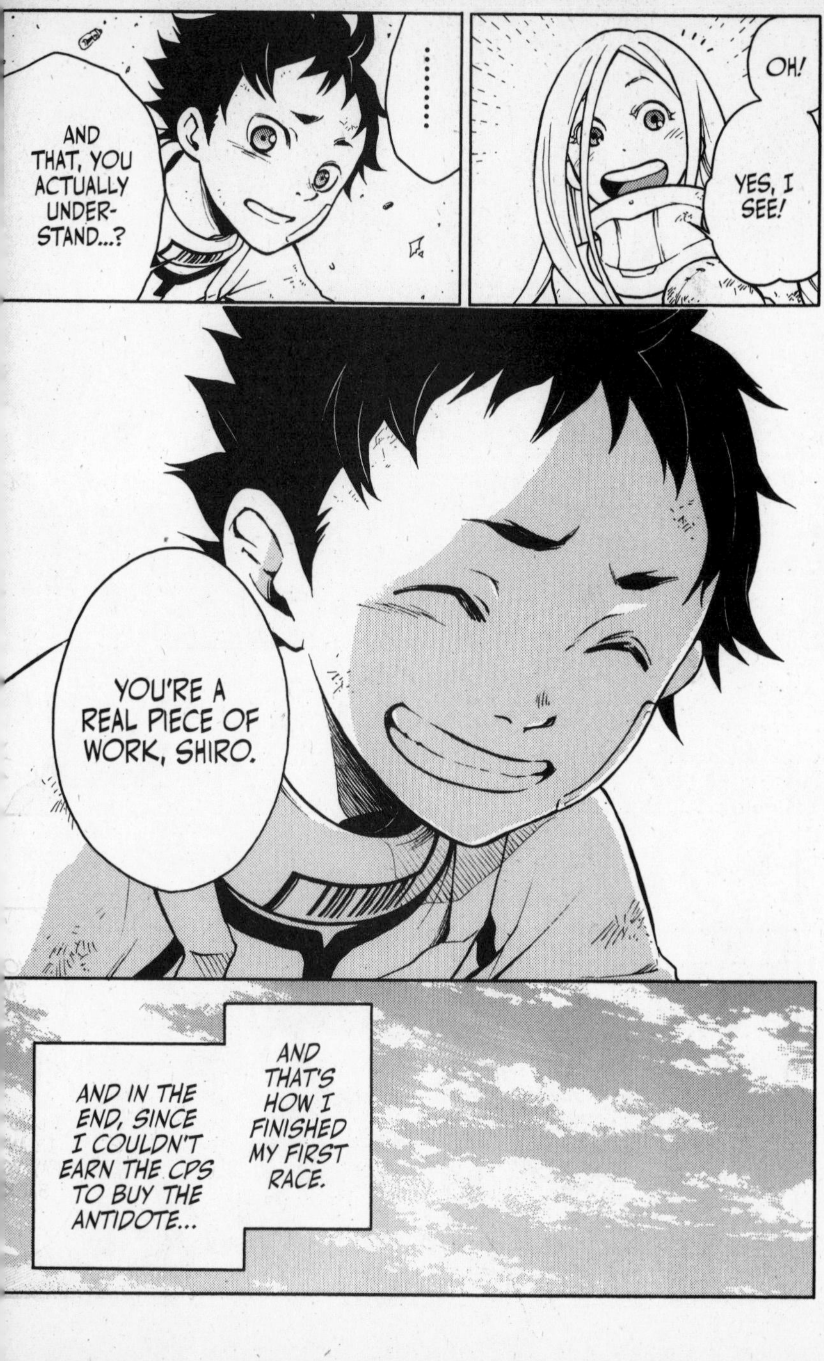
OH!
YES, I SEE!
......
AND THAT, YOU ACTUALLY UNDER-STAND...?
YOU'RE A REAL PIECE OF WORK, SHIRO.
AND THAT'S HOW I FINISHED MY FIRST RACE.
AND IN THE END, SINCE I COULDN'T EARN THE CPS TO BUY THE ANTIDOTE...

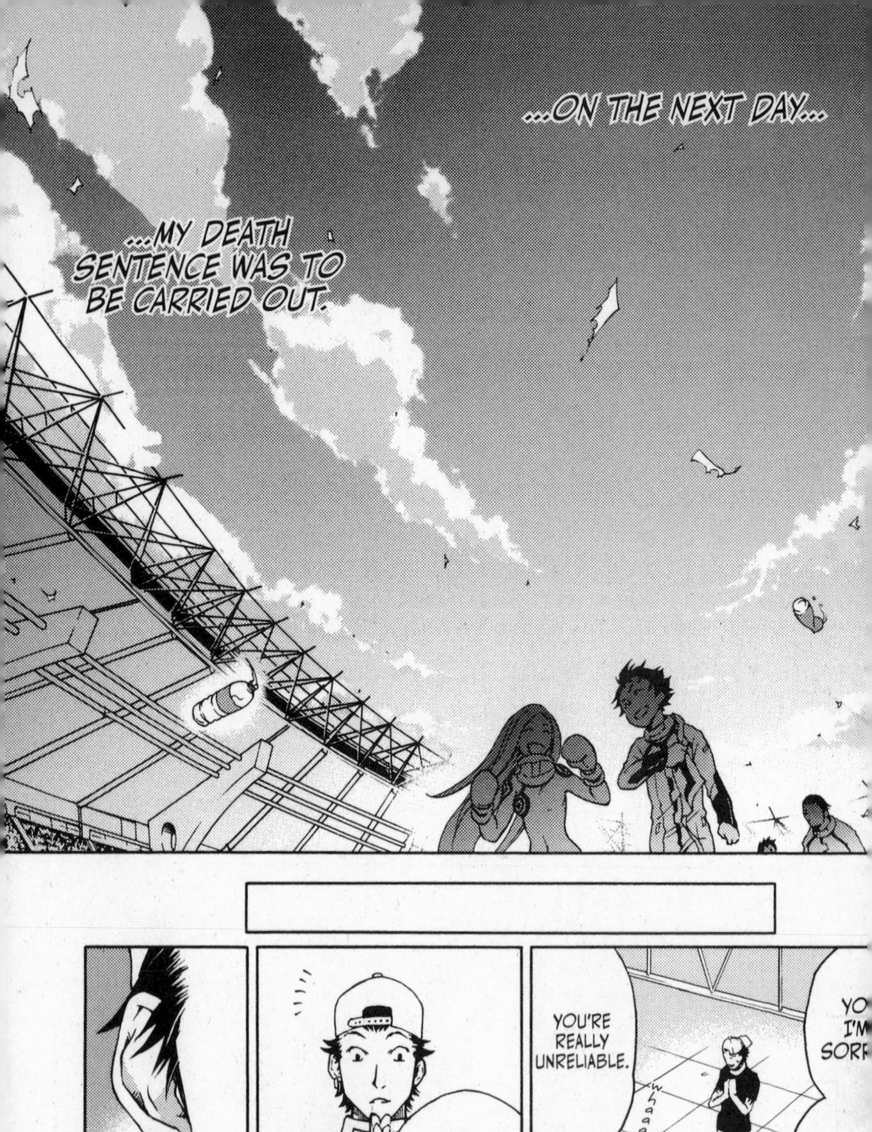
...ON THE NEXT DAY...
...MY DEATH SENTENCE WAS TO BE CARRIED OUT.
YO I'M SORR
I LOST I CAN' PAY YO BACK
YOU'RE REALLY UNRELIABLE.
whaaat?
THEN TODAY I'LL LET YOU OFF WITH JUST THE INTEREST.
INTEREST?

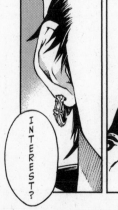

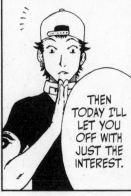

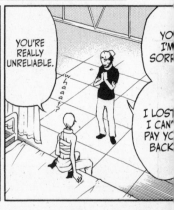

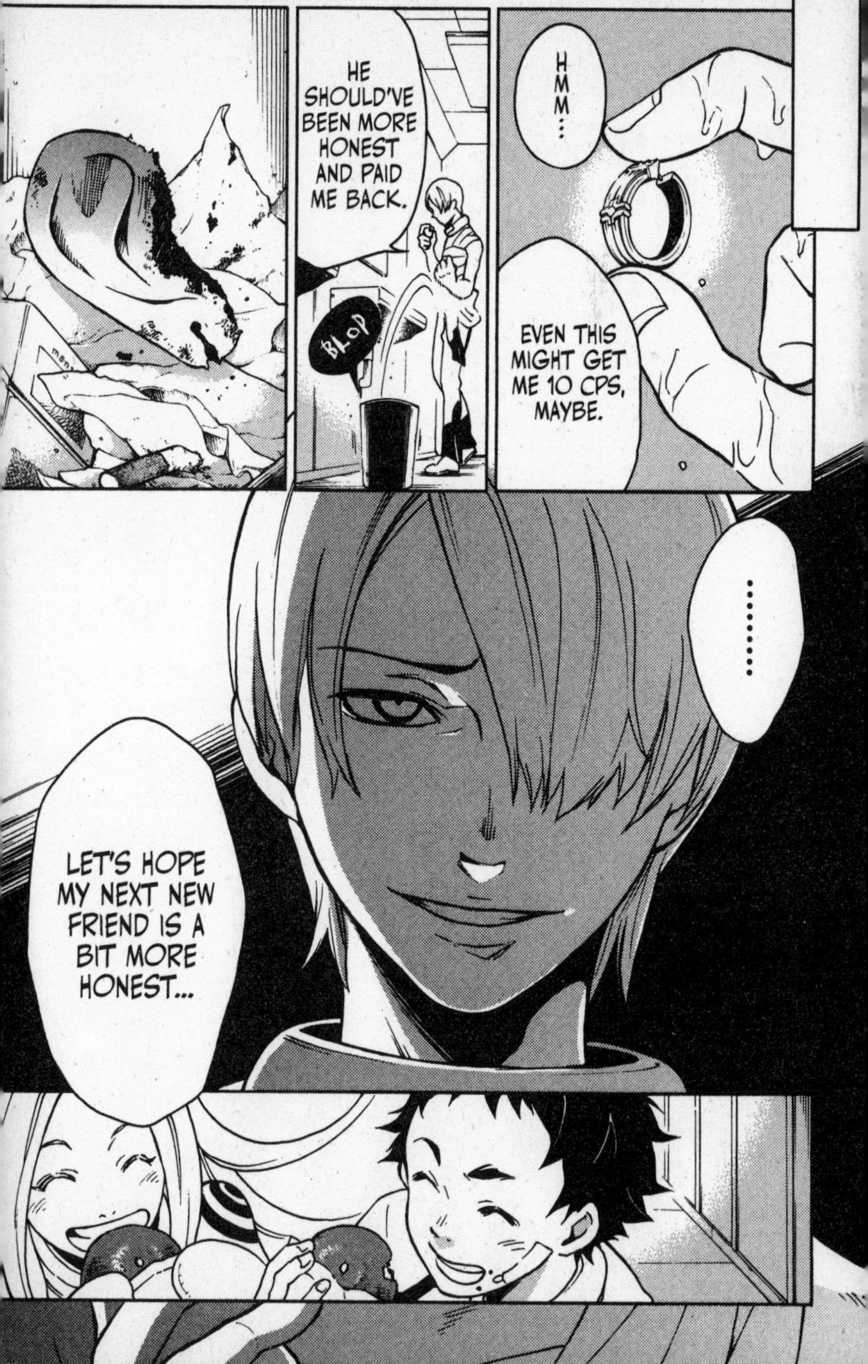
HMM...
EVEN THIS MIGHT GET ME 10 CPS, MAYBE.
HE SHOULD'VE BEEN MORE HONEST AND PAID ME BACK.
BLOP
......
LET'S HOPE MY NEXT NEW FRIEND IS A BIT MORE HONEST...

DEADMAN WONDERLAND

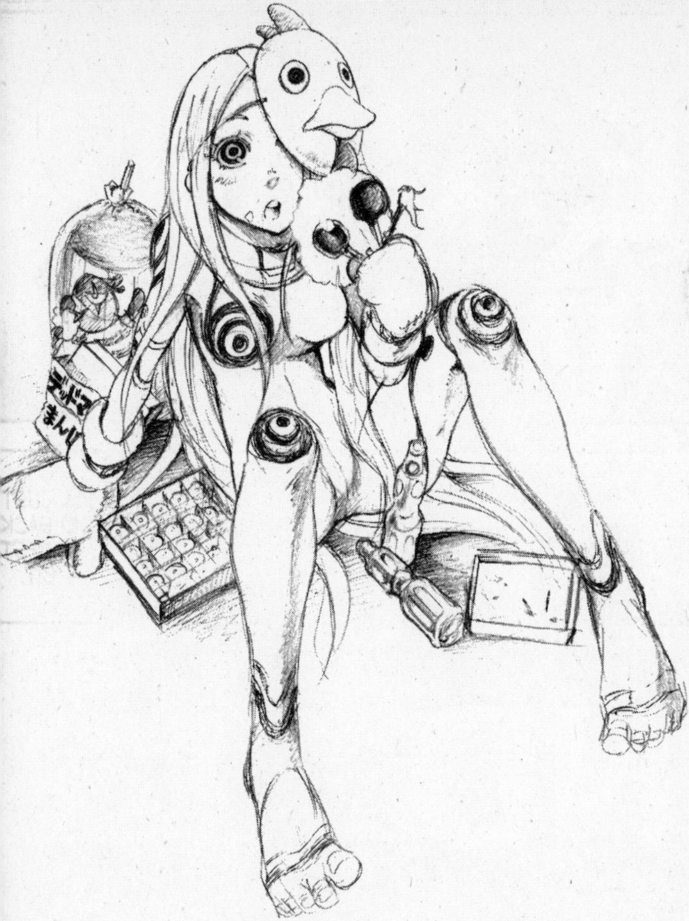
デッドマ
まん

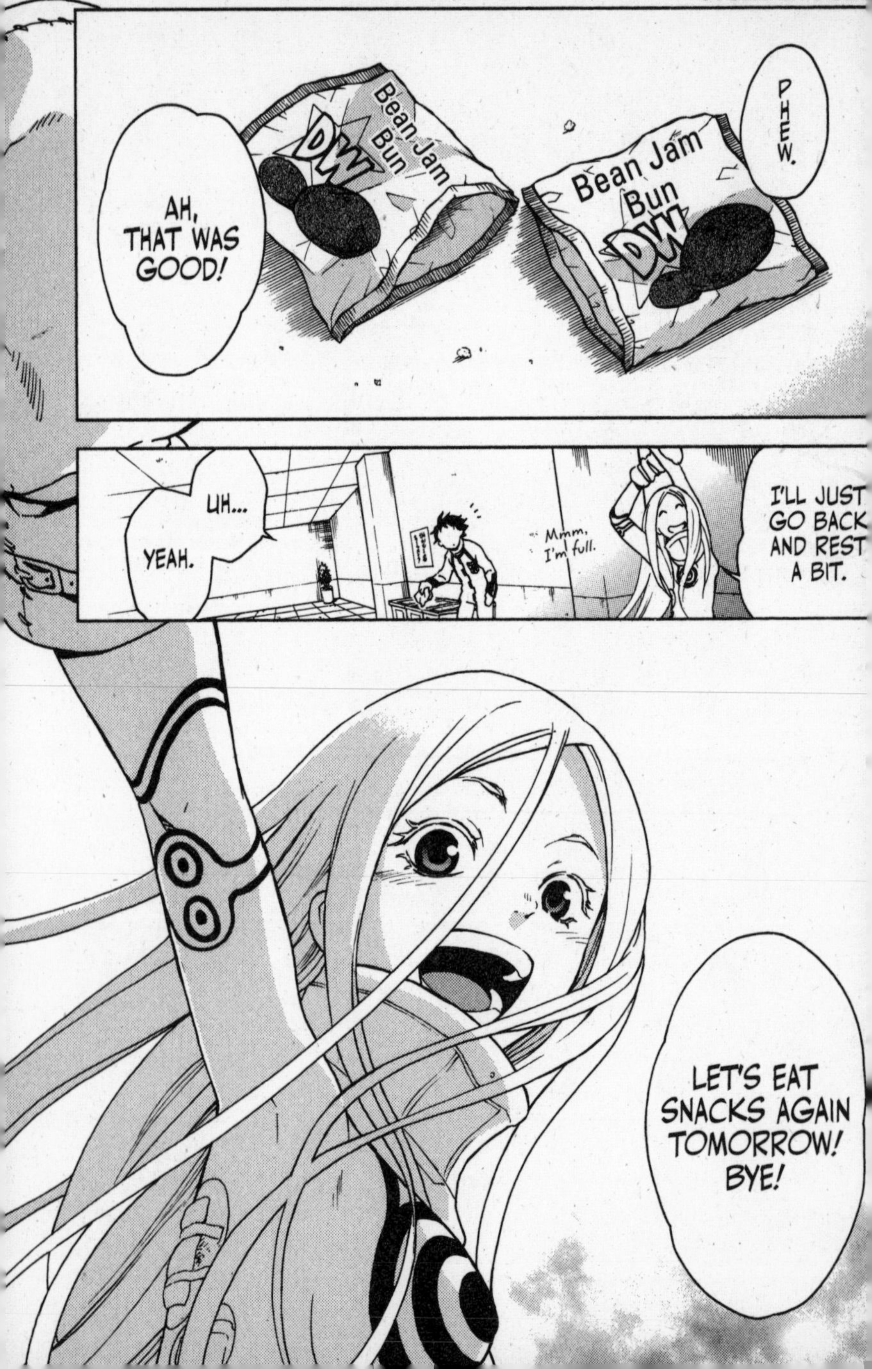
PHEW.
Bean Jam Bun DW
Bean Jam Bun DW
AH, THAT WAS GOOD!
I'LL JUST GO BACK AND REST A BIT.
Mmm, I'm full.
UH... YEAH.
LET'S EAT SNACKS AGAIN TOMORROW! BYE!

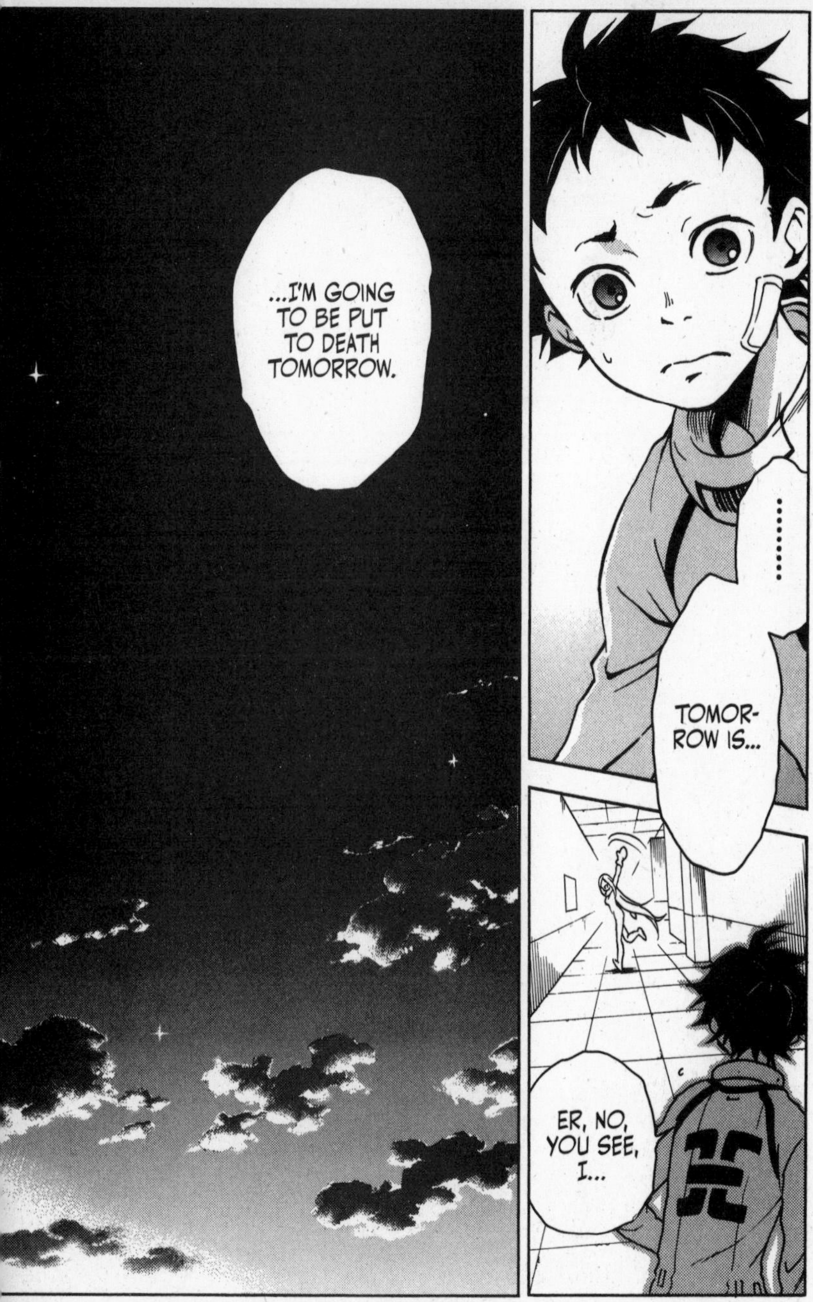
......
TOMORROW IS...
ER, NO, YOU SEE, I...
...I'M GOING TO BE PUT TO DEATH TOMORROW.

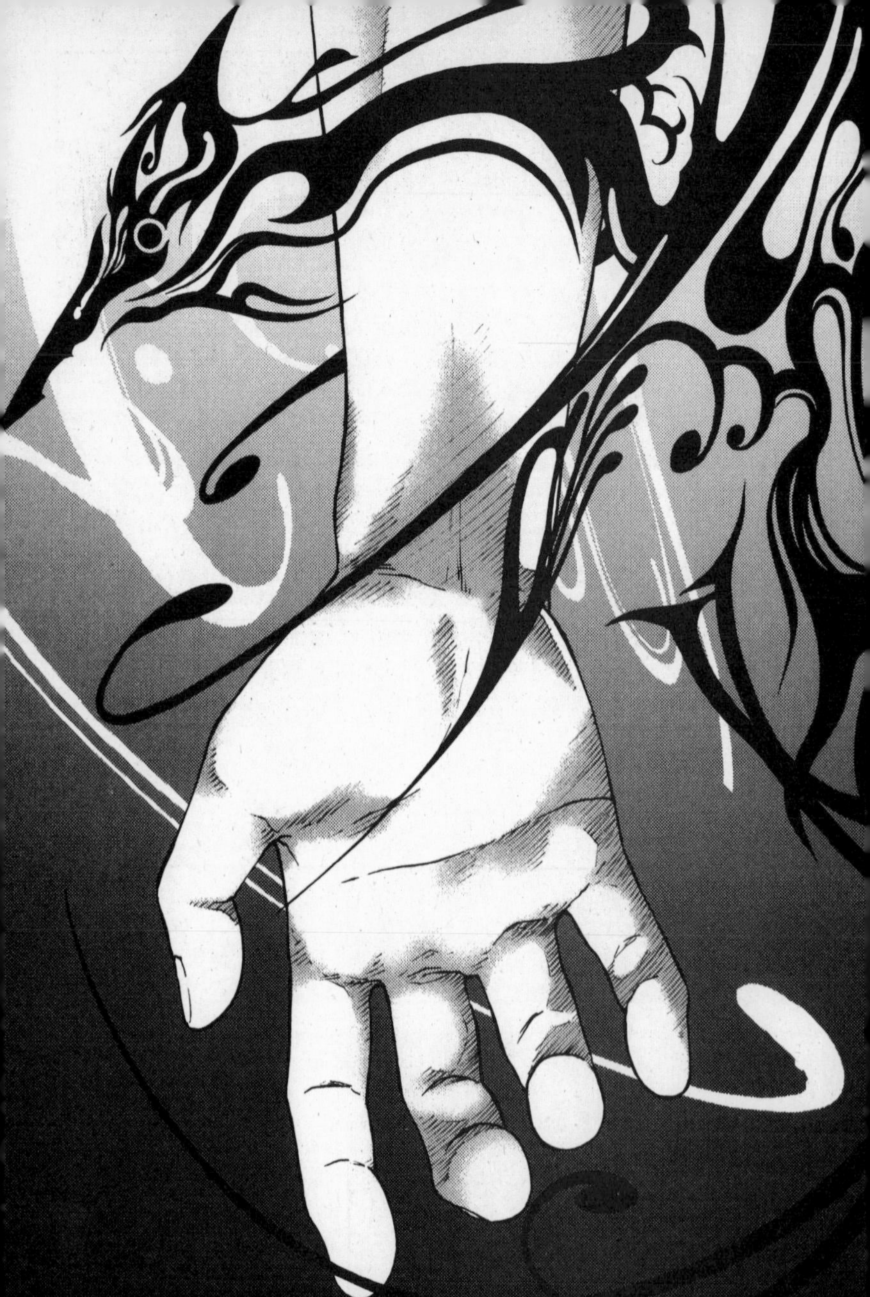

04 SLAYER'S SLAVE

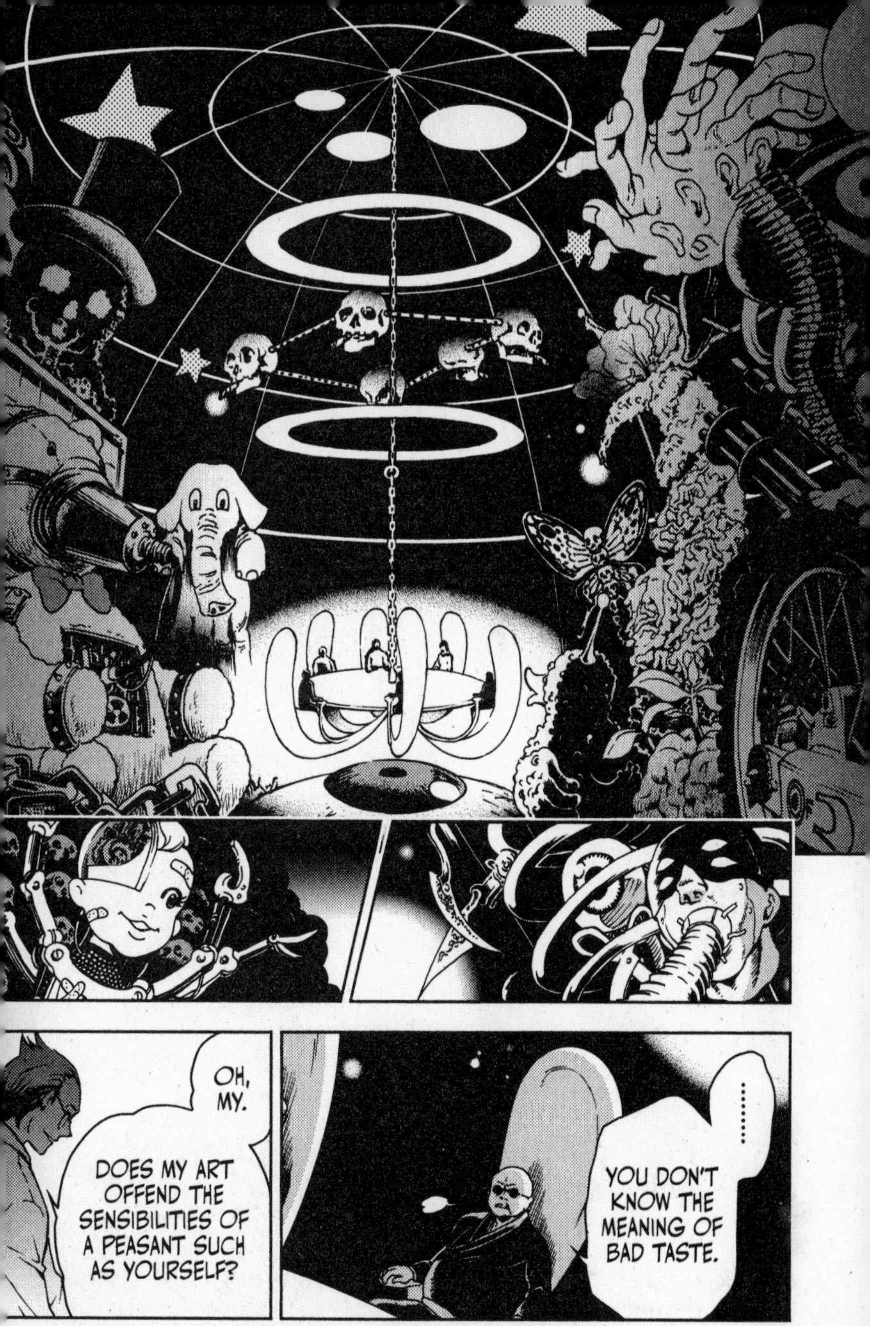

......
YOU DON'T KNOW THE MEANING OF BAD TASTE.
OH, MY.
DOES MY ART OFFEND THE SENSIBILITIES OF A PEASANT SUCH AS YOURSELF?

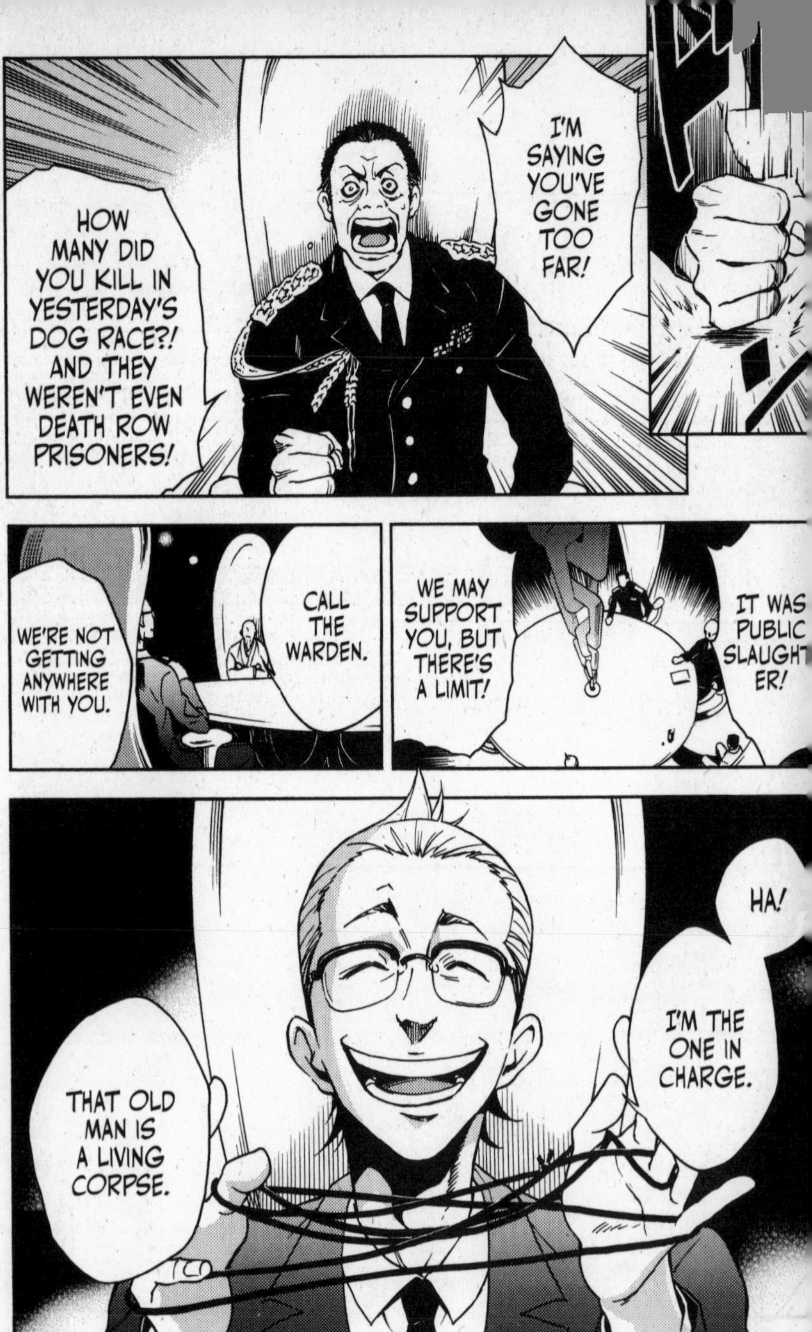
I'M SAYING YOU'VE GONE TOO FAR!
HOW MANY DID YOU KILL IN YESTERDAY'S DOG RACE?! AND THEY WEREN'T EVEN DEATH ROW PRISONERS!
IT WAS PUBLIC SLAUGHTER!
WE MAY SUPPORT YOU, BUT THERE'S A LIMIT!
CALL THE WARDEN.
WE'RE NOT GETTING ANYWHERE WITH YOU.
HA!
I'M THE ONE IN CHARGE.
THAT OLD MAN IS A LIVING CORPSE.

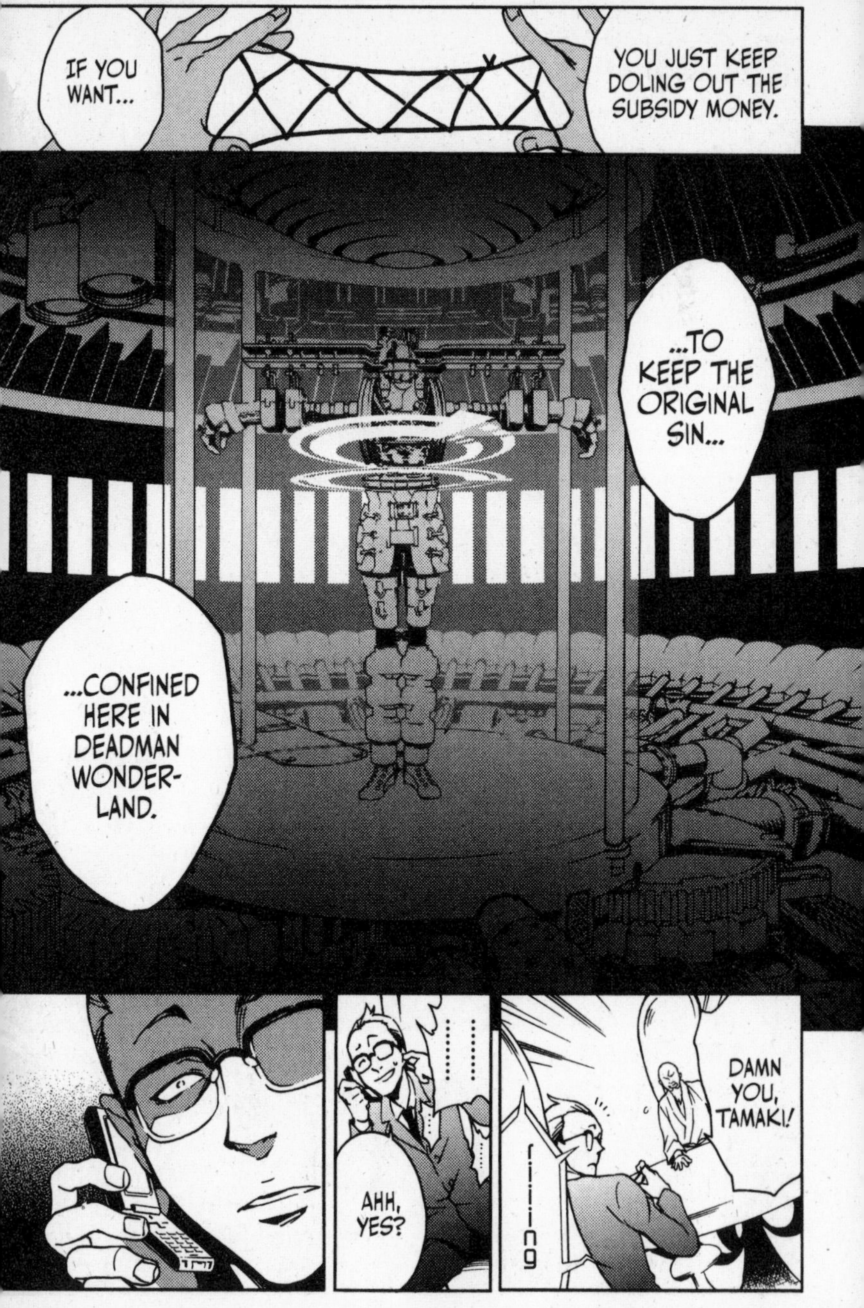
YOU JUST KEEP DOLING OUT THE SUBSIDY MONEY.
IF YOU WANT...
...TO KEEP THE ORIGINAL SIN...
...CONFINED HERE IN DEADMAN WONDERLAND.
DAMN YOU, TAMAKI!
riiing
......
......
AHH, YES?

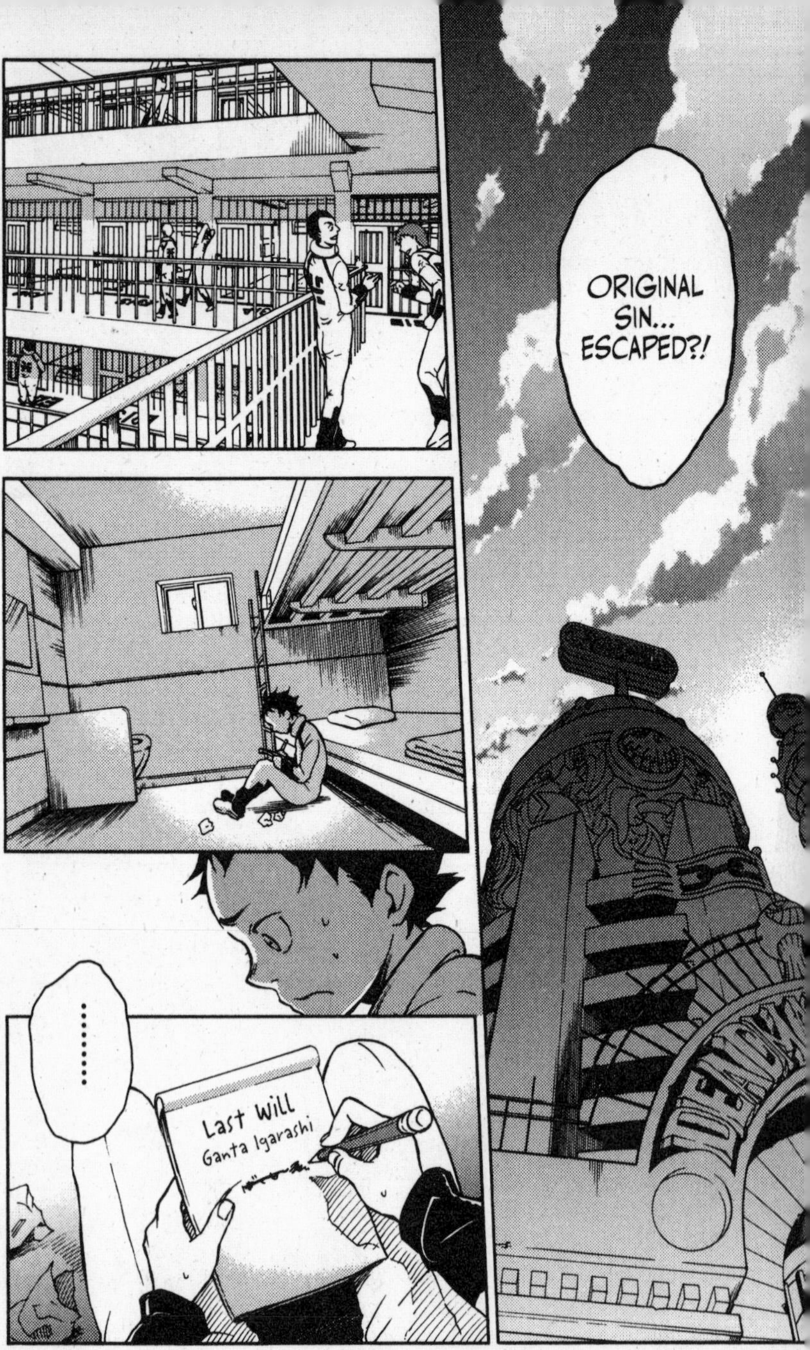
ORIGINAL SIN... ESCAPED?!
......
Last Will
Ganta Igarashi

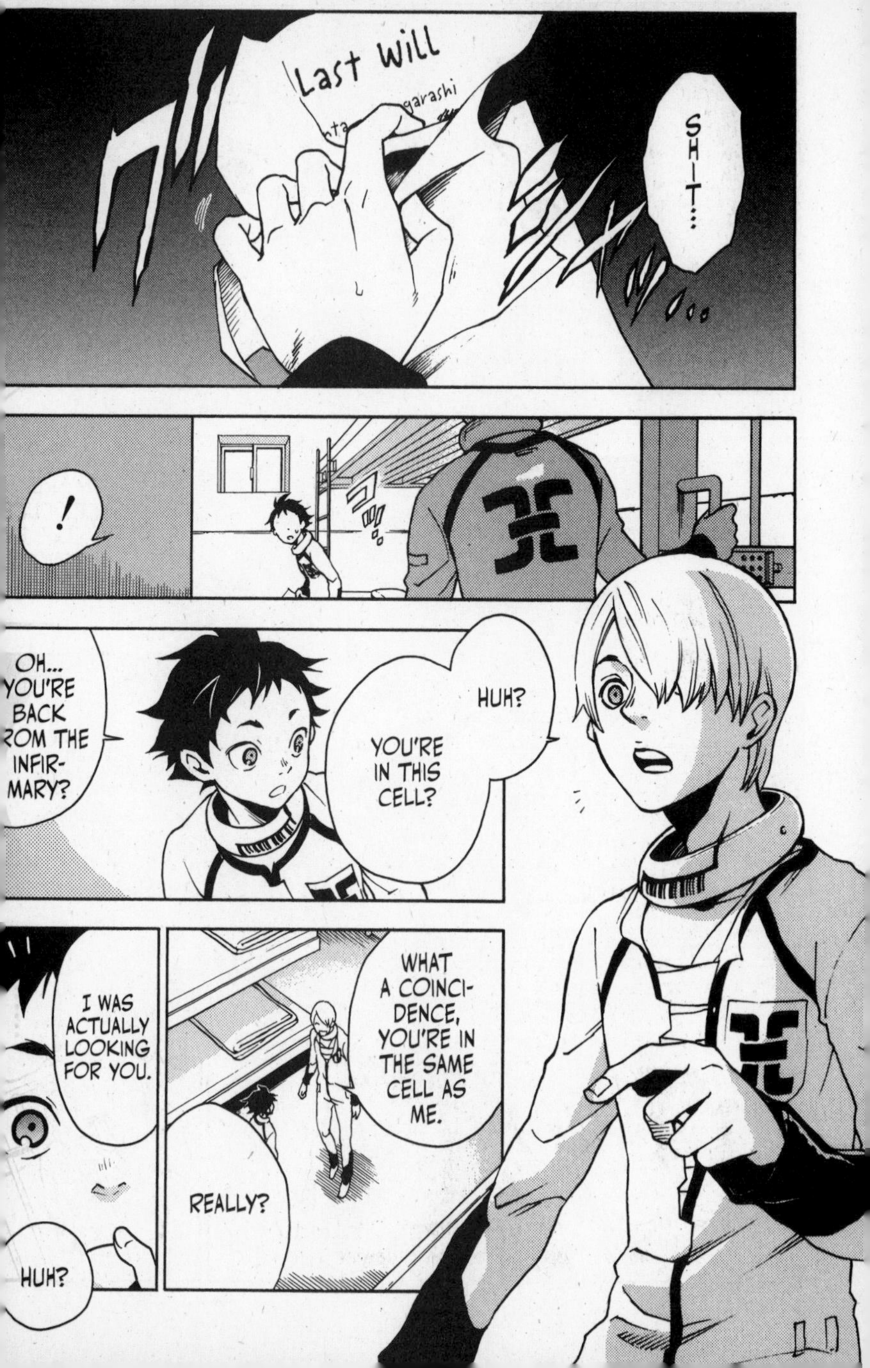
Last will
SHIT...
!
HUH?
YOU'RE IN THIS CELL?
OH... YOU'RE BACK ROM THE INFIR-MARY?
WHAT A COINCI-DENCE, YOU'RE IN THE SAME CELL AS ME.
REALLY?
I WAS ACTUALLY LOOKING FOR YOU.
HUH?

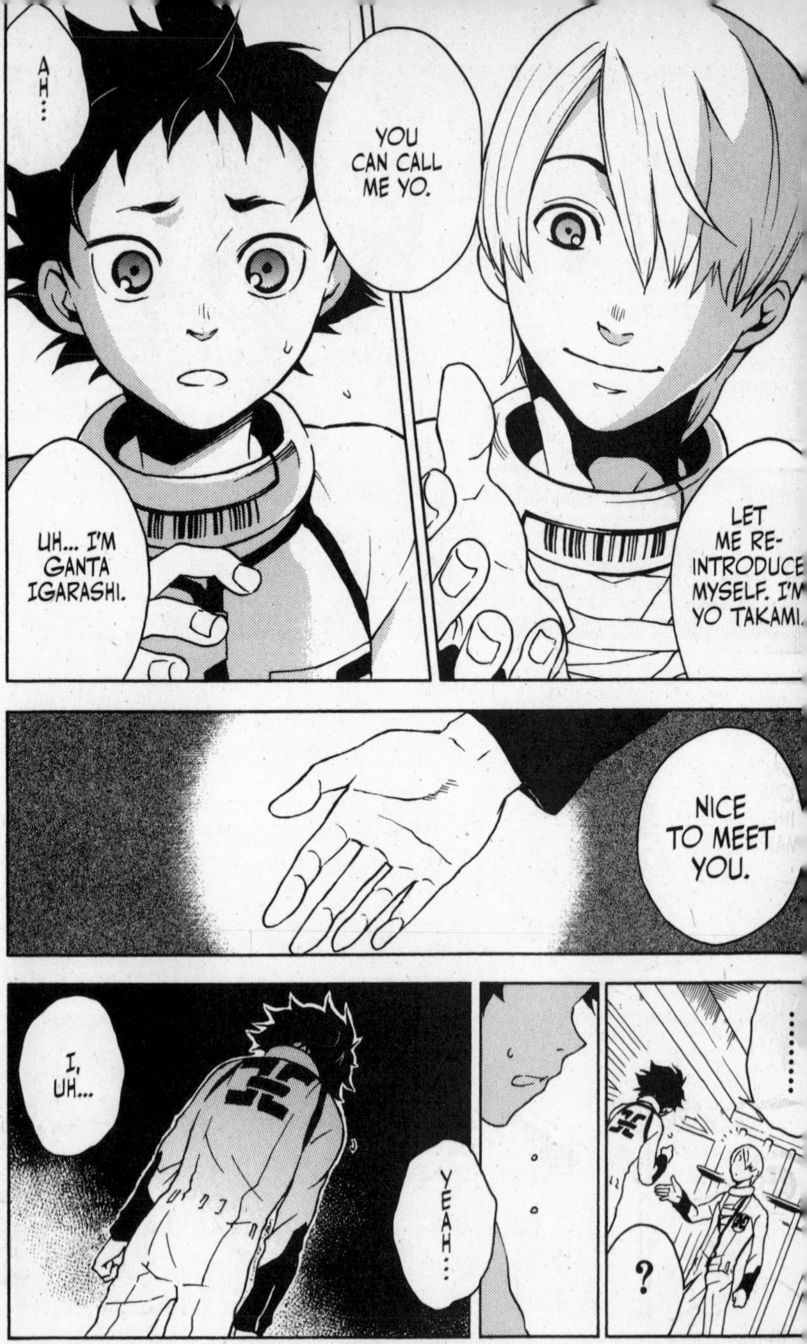
YOU CAN CALL ME YO.
AH...
LET ME RE-INTRODUCE MYSELF. I'M YO TAKAMI.
UH... I'M GANTA IGARASHI.
NICE TO MEET YOU.
......
?
YEAH...
I, UH...

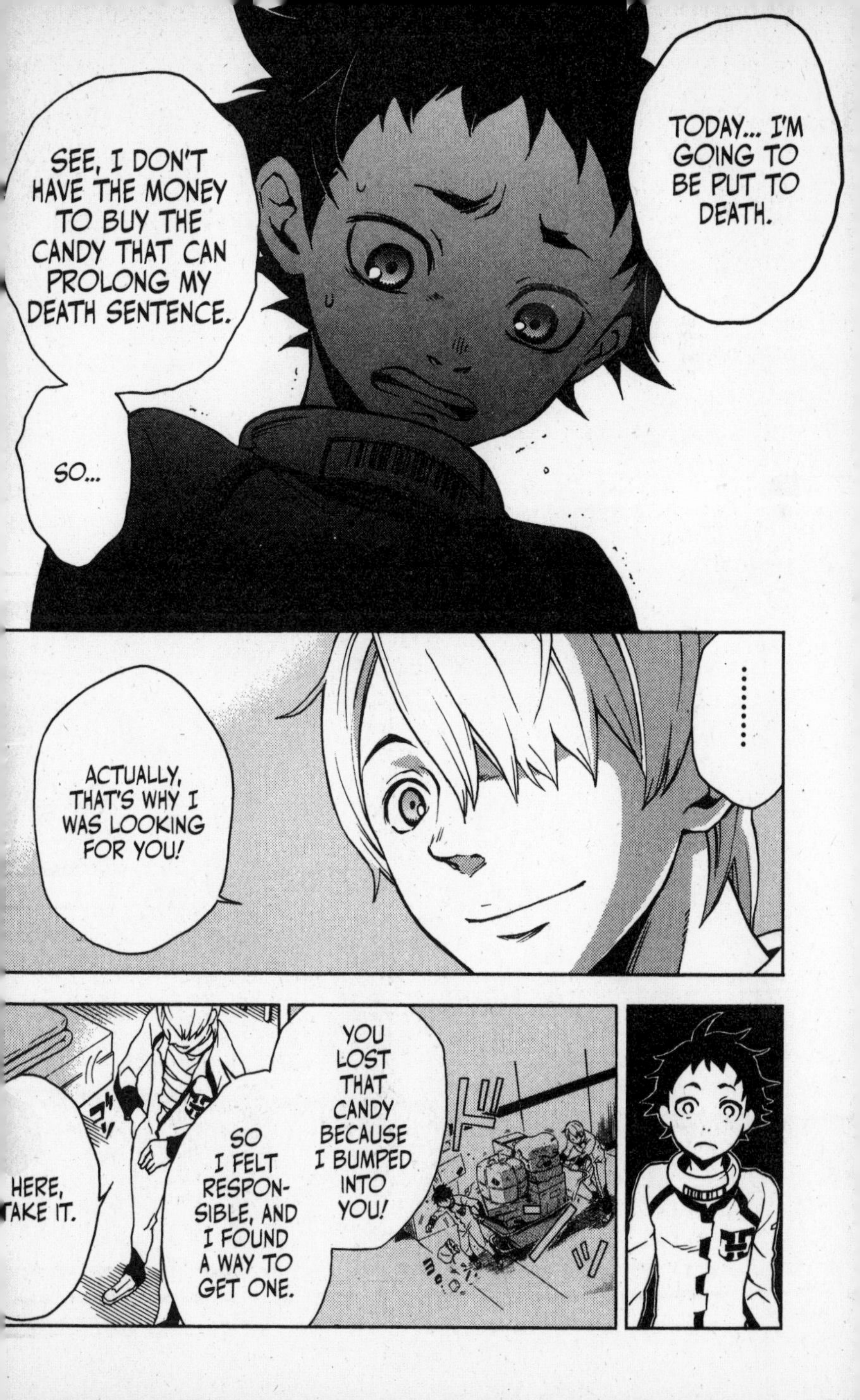
TODAY... I'M GOING TO BE PUT TO DEATH.
SEE, I DON'T HAVE THE MONEY TO BUY THE CANDY THAT CAN PROLONG MY DEATH SENTENCE.
SO...
......
ACTUALLY, THAT'S WHY I WAS LOOKING FOR YOU!
YOU LOST THAT CANDY BECAUSE I BUMPED INTO YOU!
SO I FELT RESPON-SIBLE, AND I FOUND A WAY TO GET ONE.
HERE, TAKE IT.

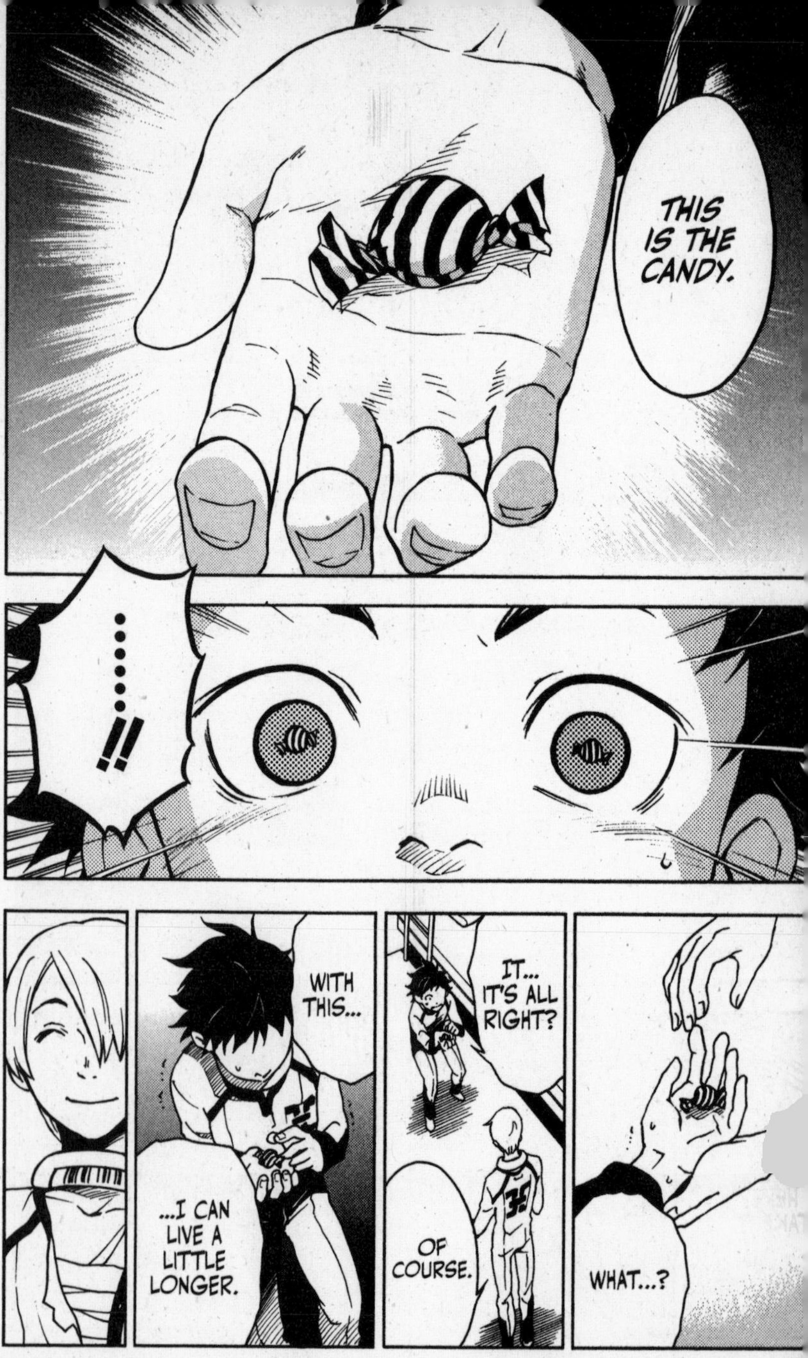
THIS IS THE CANDY.
......!!
WHAT...?
IT... IT'S ALL RIGHT?
OF COURSE.
WITH THIS...
...I CAN LIVE A LITTLE LONGER.

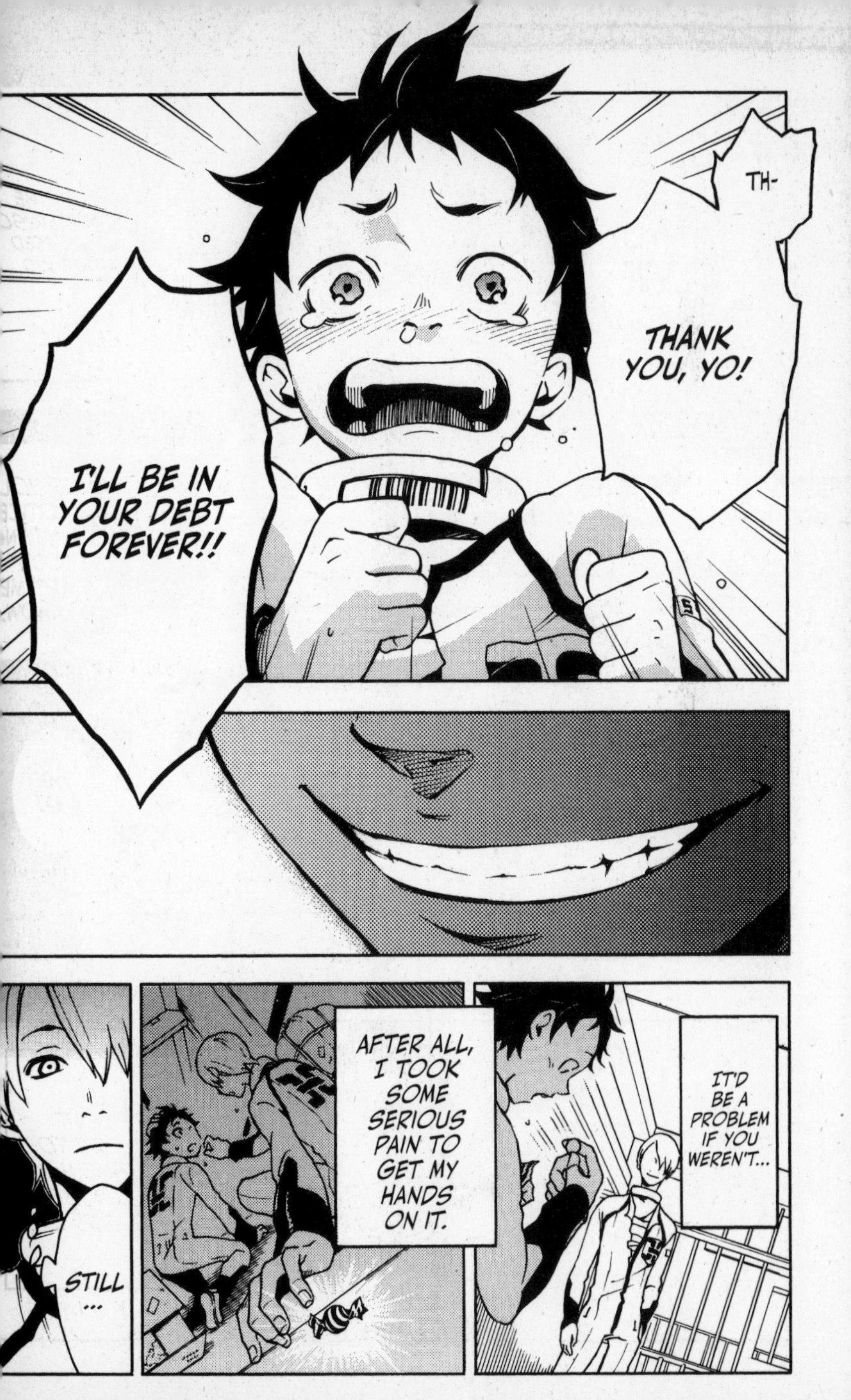
TH-
THANK YOU, YO!
I'LL BE IN YOUR DEBT FOREVER!!
IT'D BE A PROBLEM IF YOU WEREN'T...
AFTER ALL, I TOOK SOME SERIOUS PAIN TO GET MY HANDS ON IT.
STILL ...

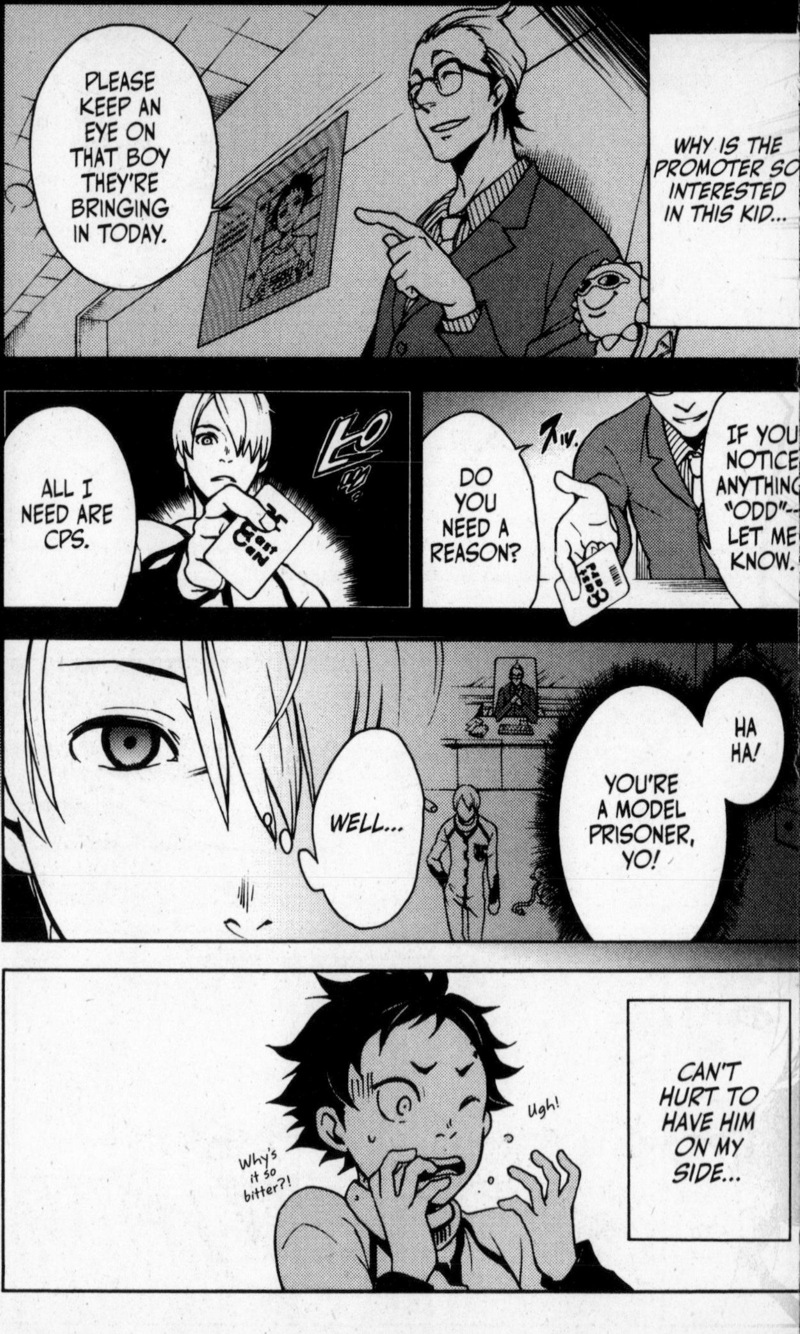
WHY IS THE PROMOTER SO INTERESTED IN THIS KID...
PLEASE KEEP AN EYE ON THAT BOY THEY'RE BRINGING IN TODAY.
IF YOU NOTICE ANYTHING "ODD"-- LET ME KNOW.
DO YOU NEED A REASON?
ALL I NEED ARE CPS.
HA HA!
YOU'RE A MODEL PRISONER, YO!
WELL...
CAN'T HURT TO HAVE HIM ON MY SIDE...
Ugh!
Why's it so bitter?!

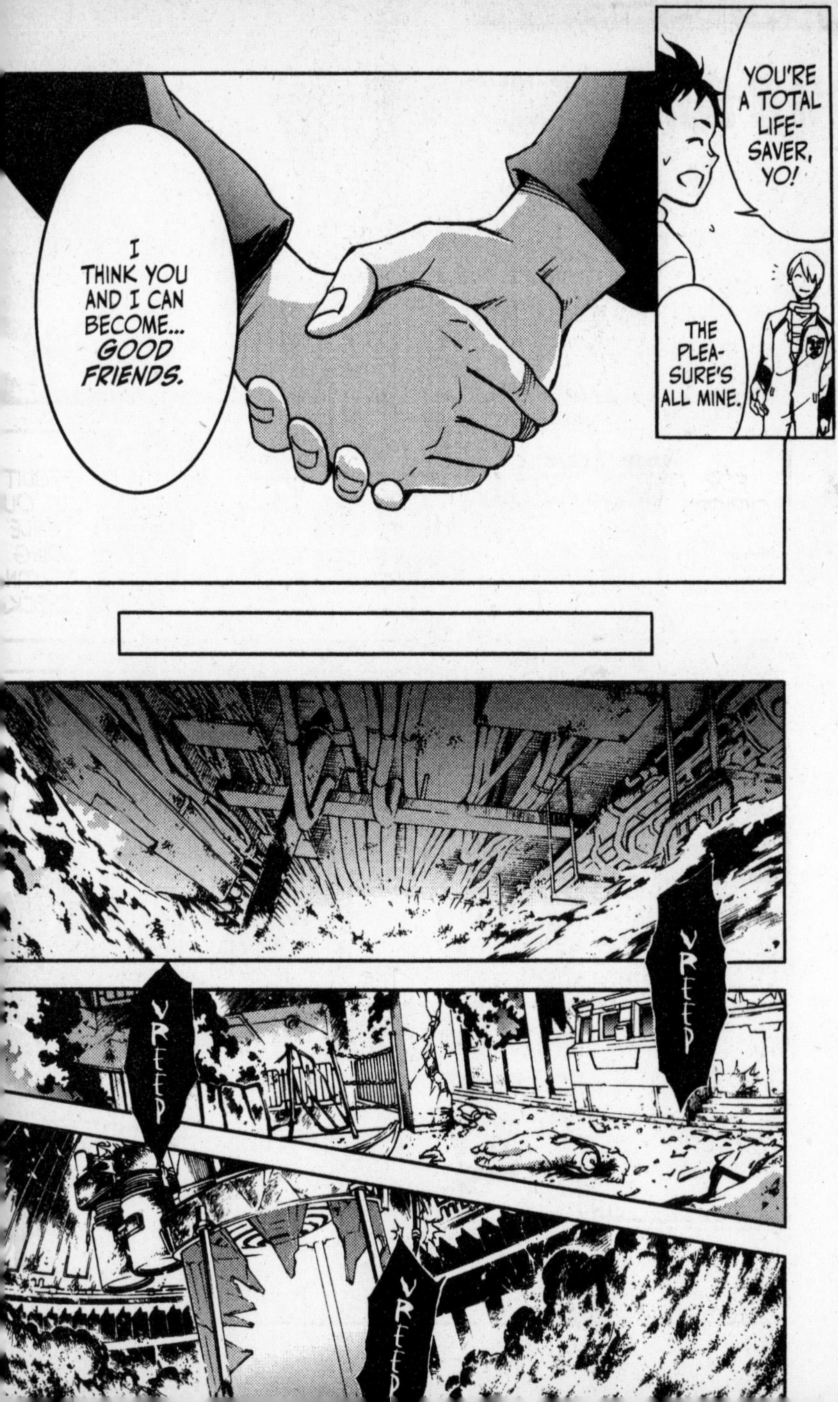
YOU'RE A TOTAL LIFE-SAVER, YO!
THE PLEA-SURE'S ALL MINE.
I THINK YOU AND I CAN BECOME... GOOD FRIENDS.
VREEP
VREEP
VREEP

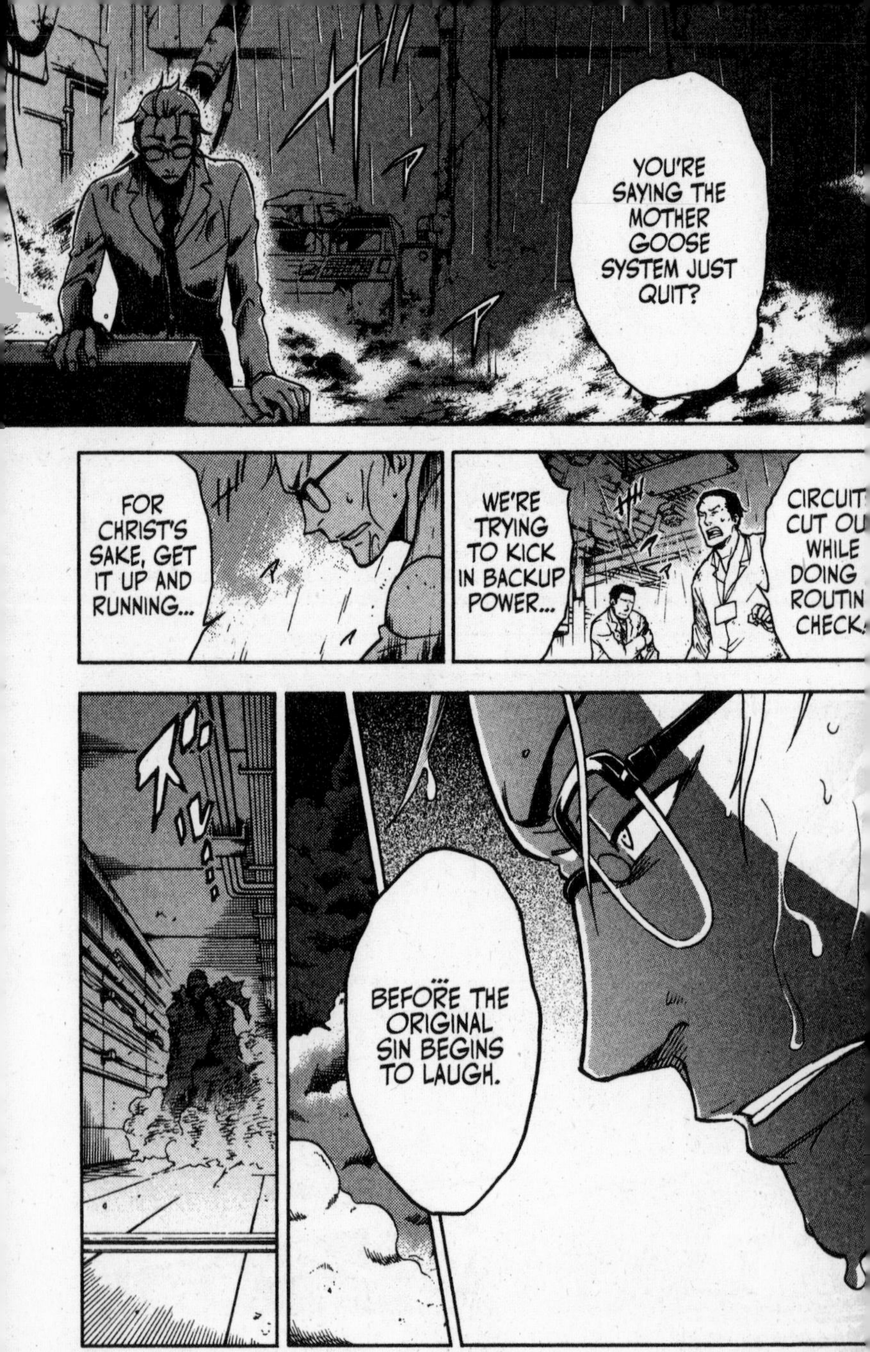
YOU'RE SAYING THE MOTHER GOOSE SYSTEM JUST QUIT?
CIRCUIT CUT OU WHILE DOING ROUTIN CHECK.
WE'RE TRYING TO KICK IN BACKUP POWER...
FOR CHRIST'S SAKE, GET IT UP AND RUNNING...
...BEFORE THE ORIGINAL SIN BEGINS TO LAUGH.

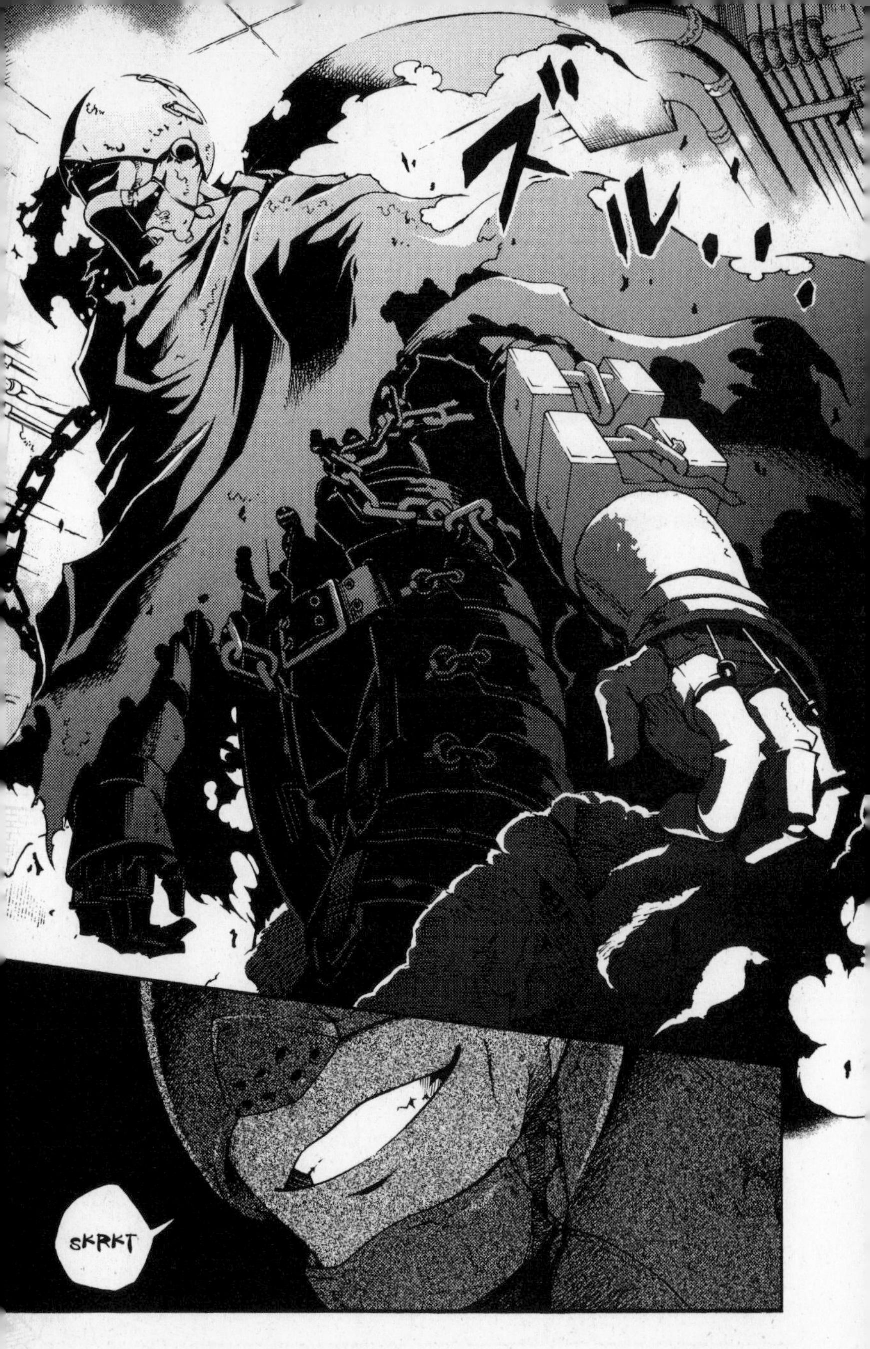
ズル…!
SKRKT

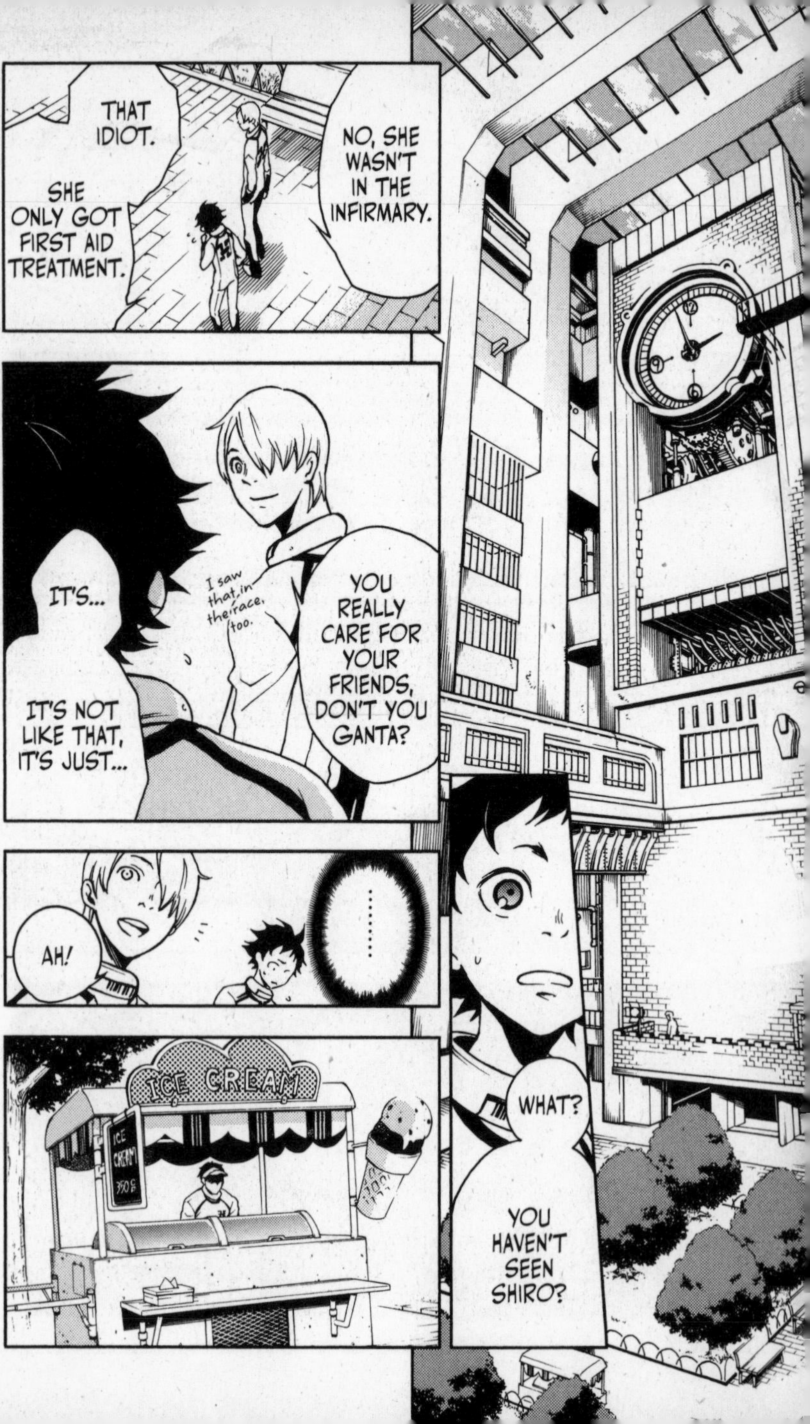
WHAT?
YOU HAVEN'T SEEN SHIRO?
NO, SHE WASN'T IN THE INFIRMARY.
THAT IDIOT.
SHE ONLY GOT FIRST AID TREATMENT.
YOU REALLY CARE FOR YOUR FRIENDS, DON'T YOU GANTA?
I saw that in the race, too.
IT'S...
IT'S NOT LIKE THAT, IT'S JUST...
......
AH!
ICE CREAM
ICE CREAM

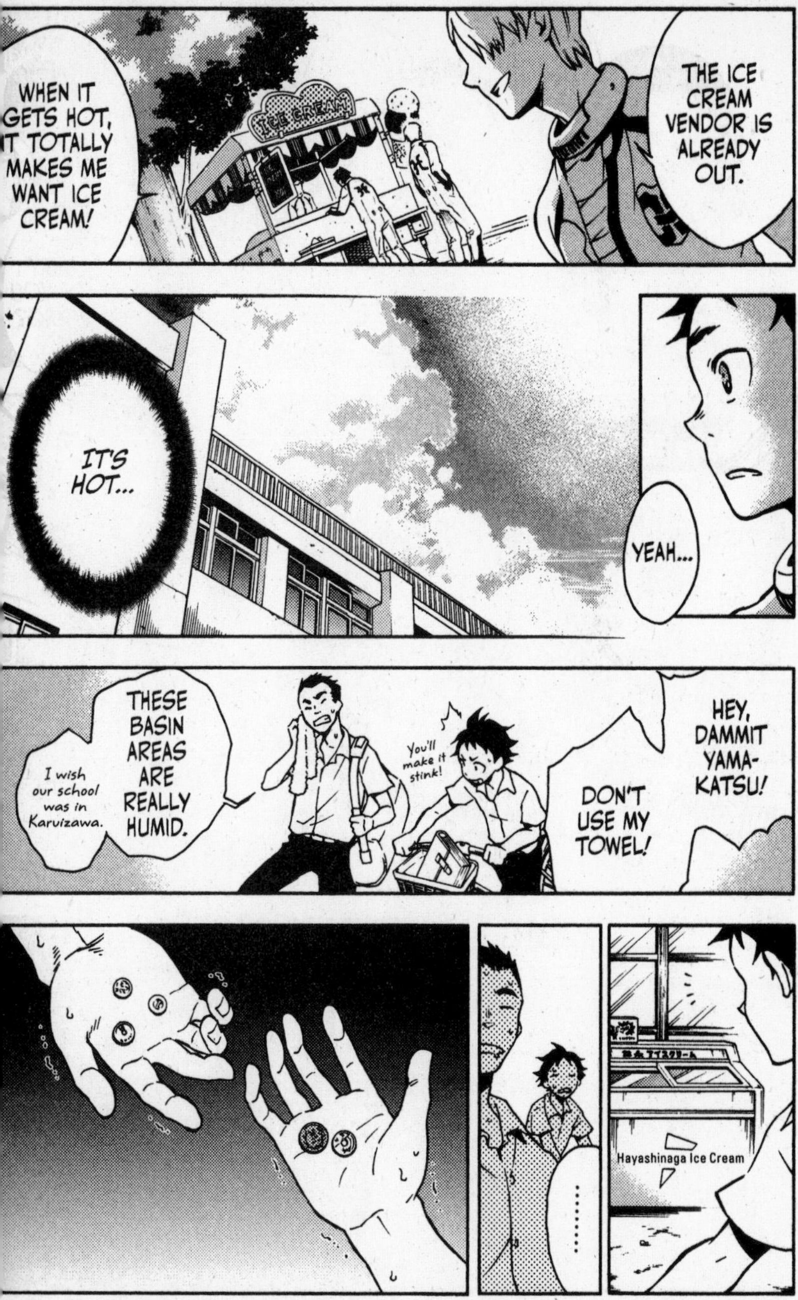
THE ICE CREAM VENDOR IS ALREADY OUT.
WHEN IT GETS HOT, IT TOTALLY MAKES ME WANT ICE CREAM!
YEAH...
IT'S HOT...
HEY, DAMMIT YAMA-KATSU!
DON'T USE MY TOWEL!
You'll make it stink!
THESE BASIN AREAS ARE REALLY HUMID.
I wish our school was in Karuizawa.
Hayashinaga Ice Cream
......

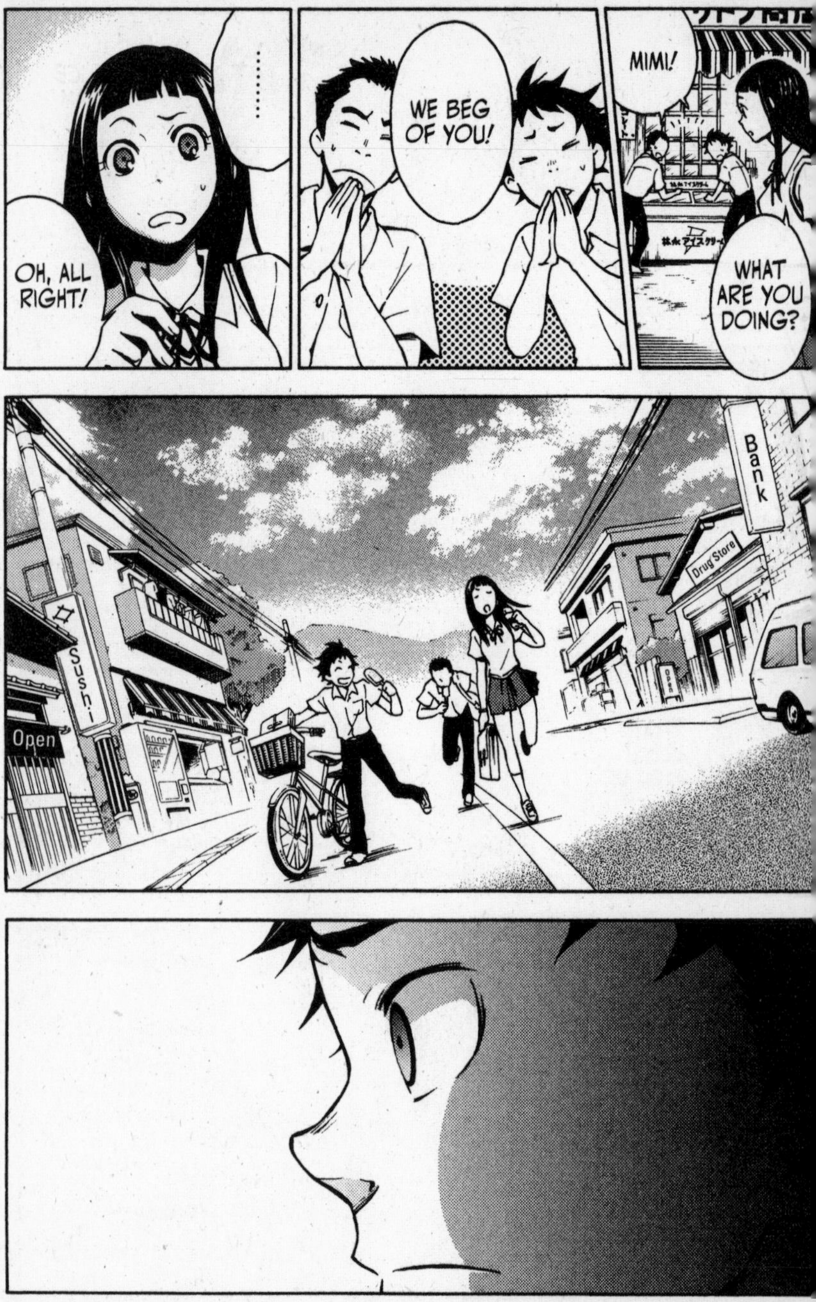
MIMI!
WHAT ARE YOU DOING?
WE BEG OF YOU!
......
OH, ALL RIGHT!
Bank
Drug Store
Sushi
Open

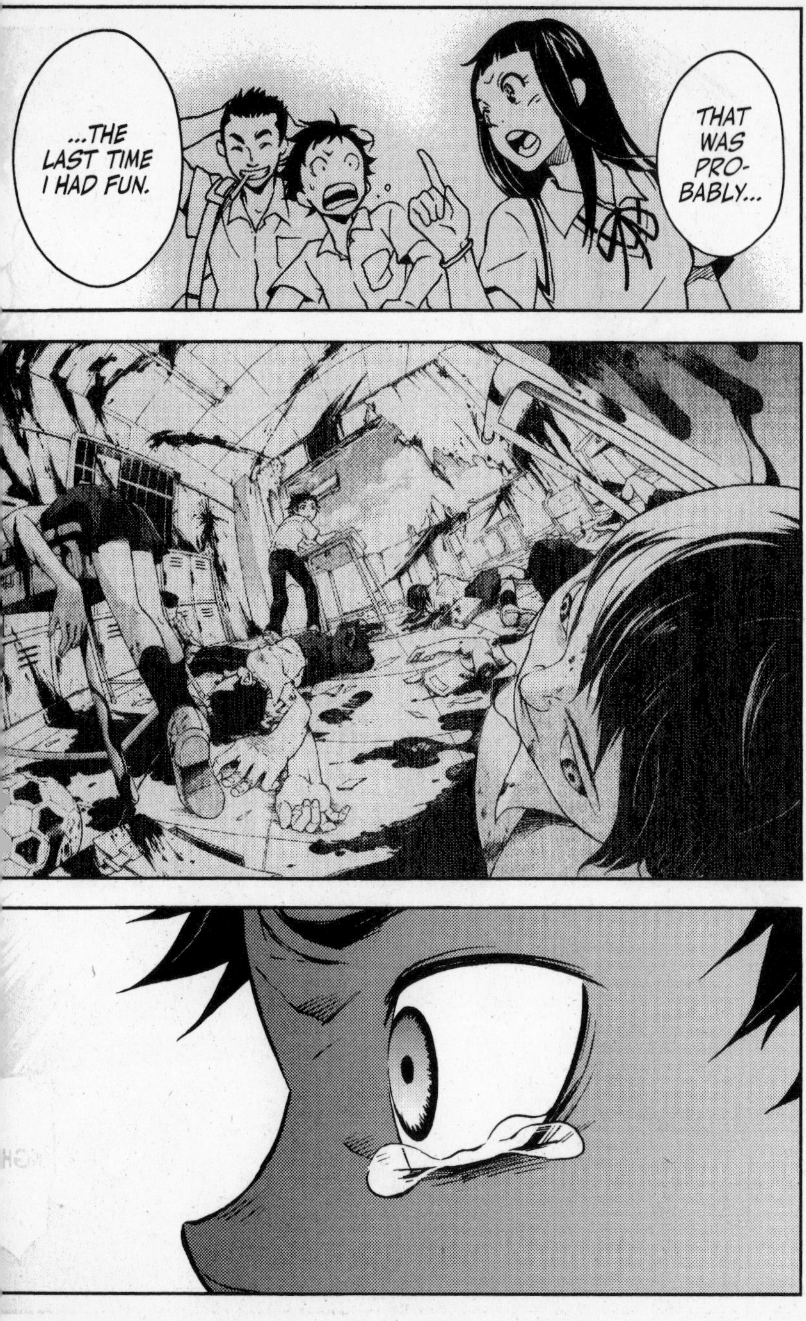
THAT WAS PRO-BABLY...
...THE LAST TIME I HAD FUN.

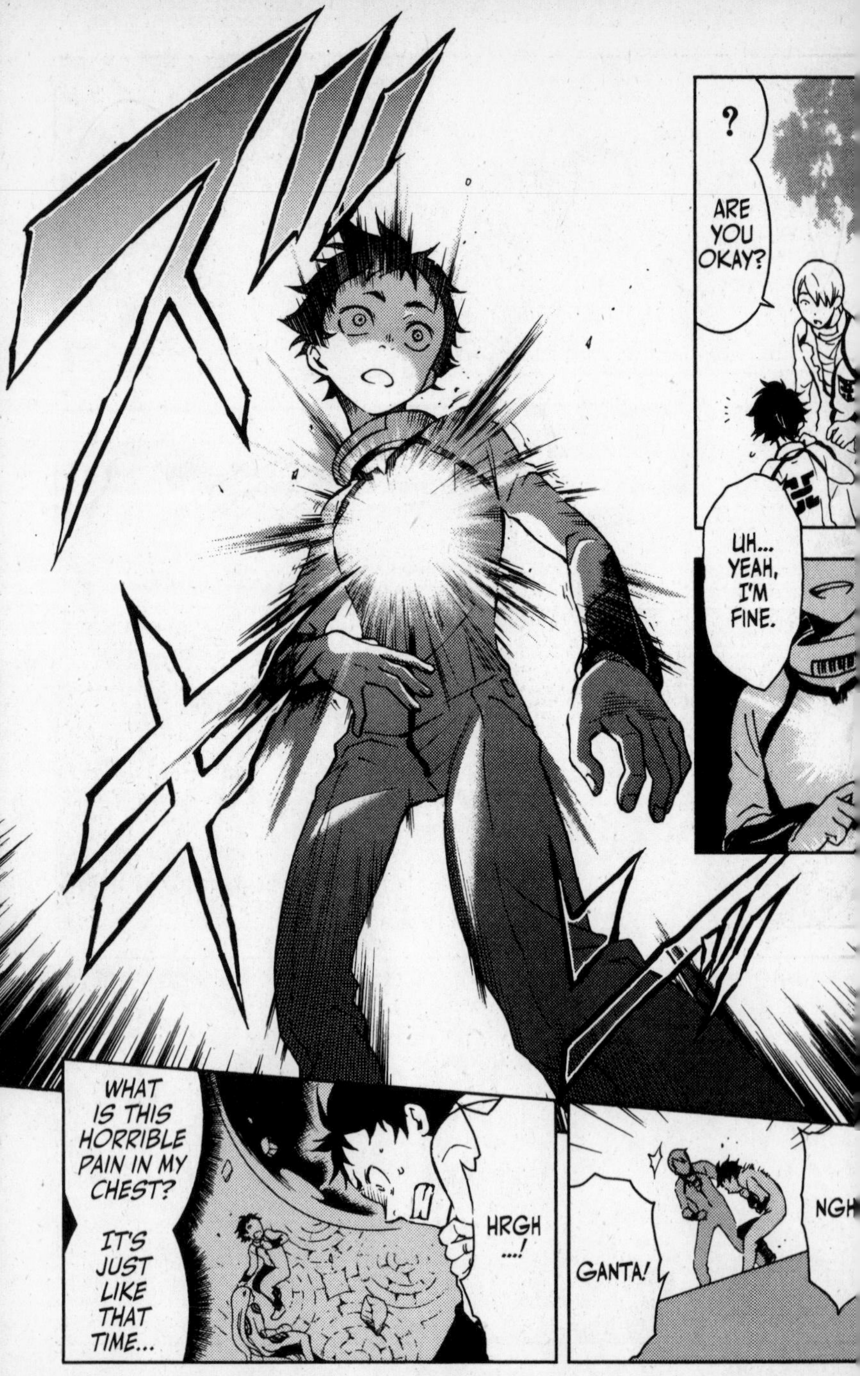
?
ARE YOU OKAY?
UH... YEAH, I'M FINE.
NGH
GANTA!
WHAT IS THIS HORRIBLE PAIN IN MY CHEST?
HRGH ...!
IT'S JUST LIKE THAT TIME...

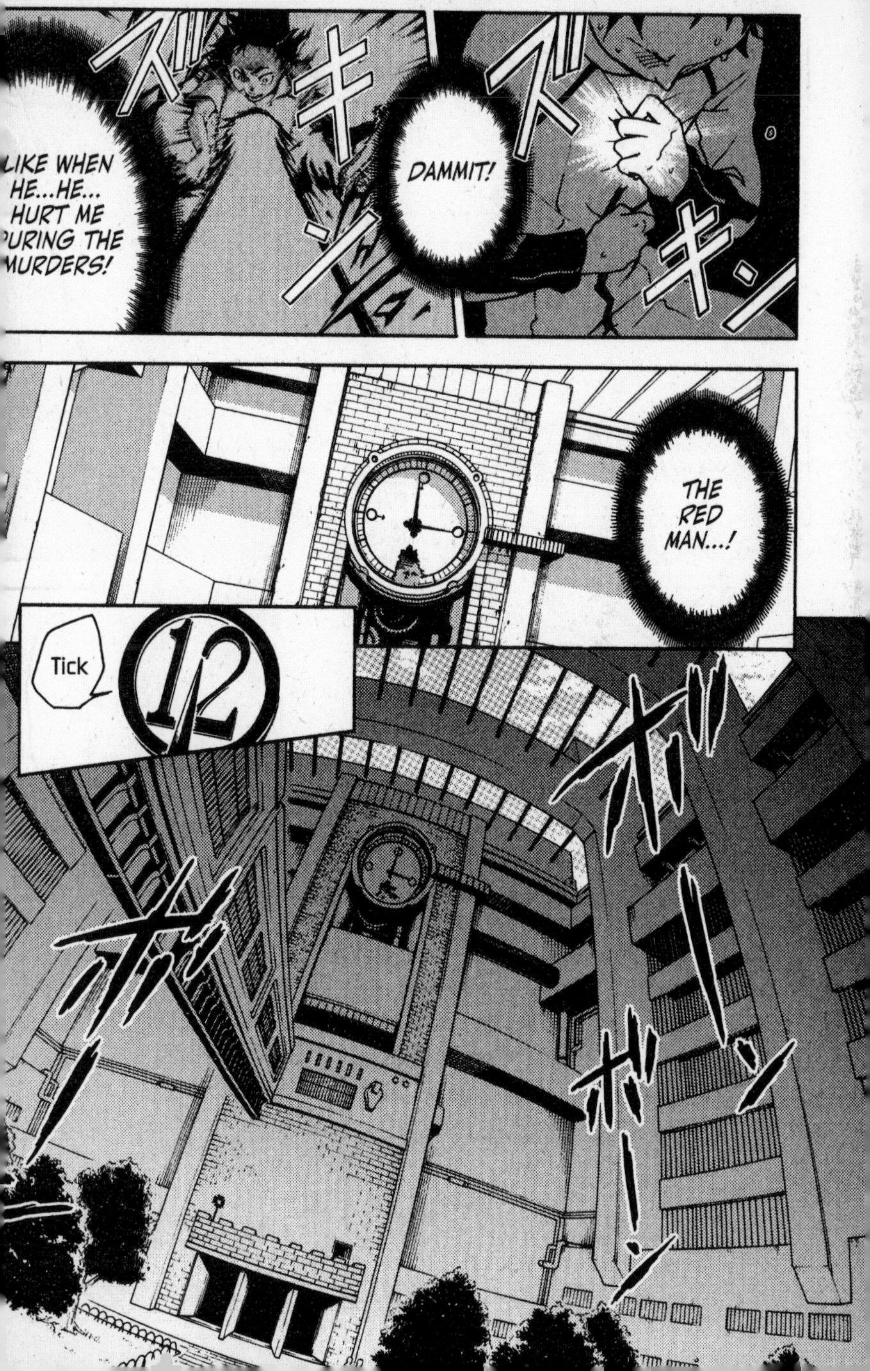
DAMMIT!
LIKE WHEN HE...HE... HURT ME DURING THE MURDERS!
THE RED MAN...!
Tick
12

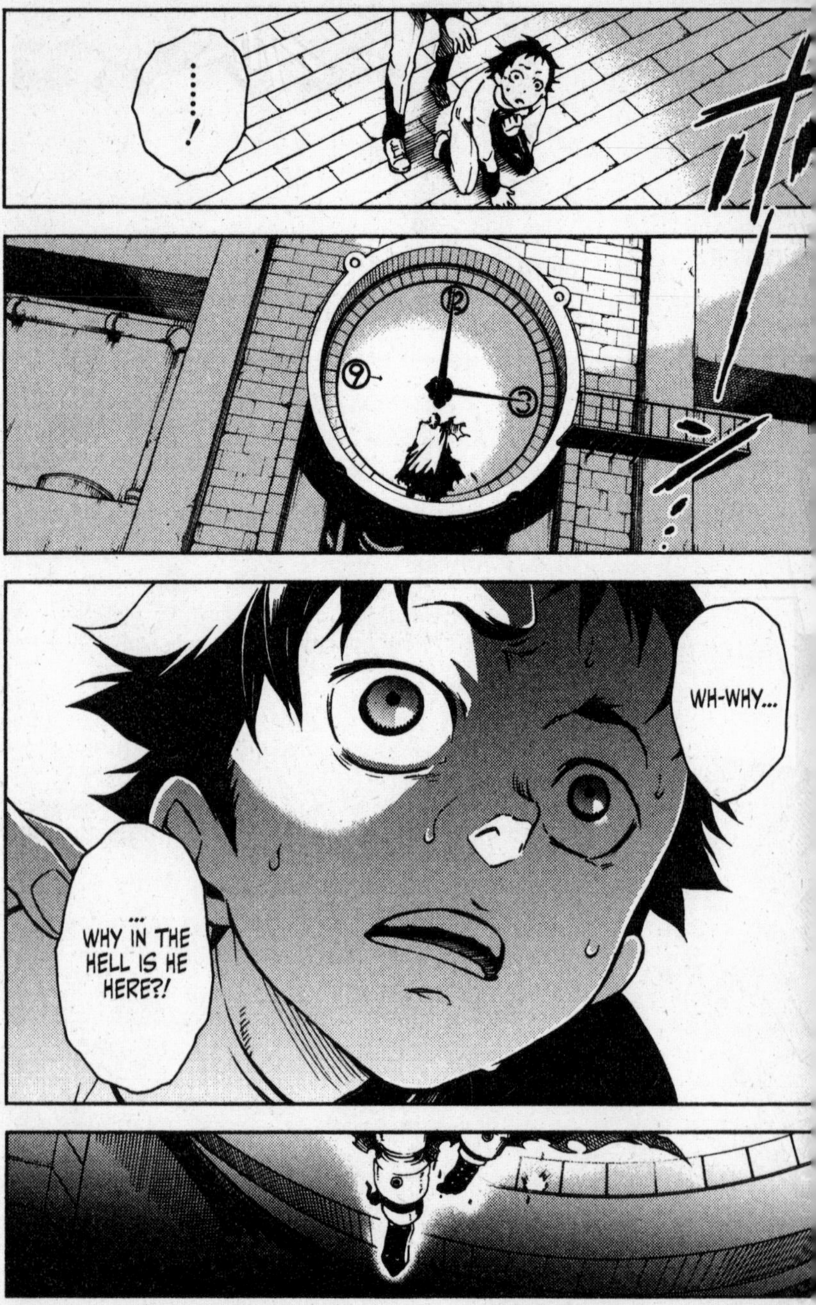

......!
WH-WHY...
...WHY IN THE HELL IS HE HERE?!

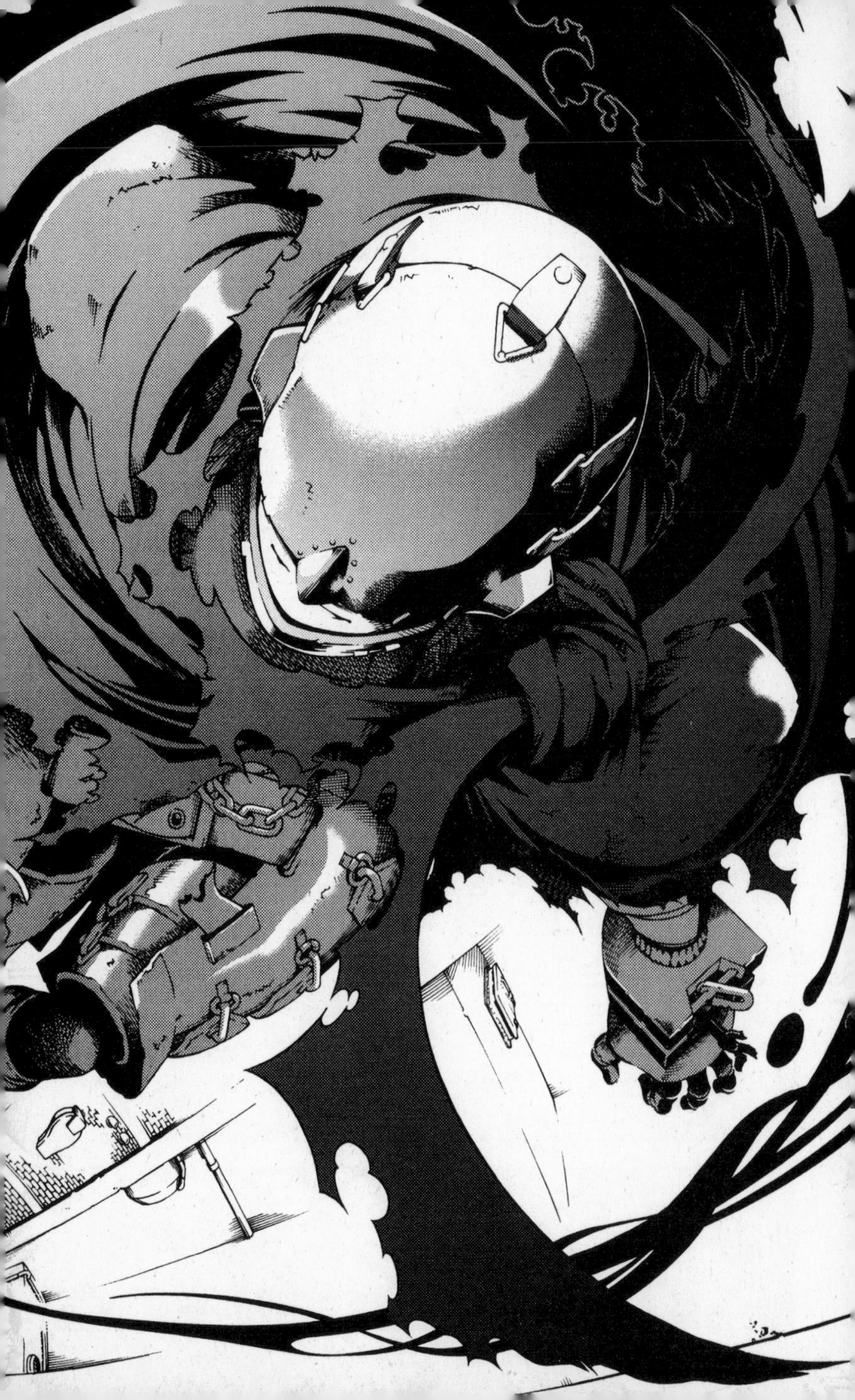

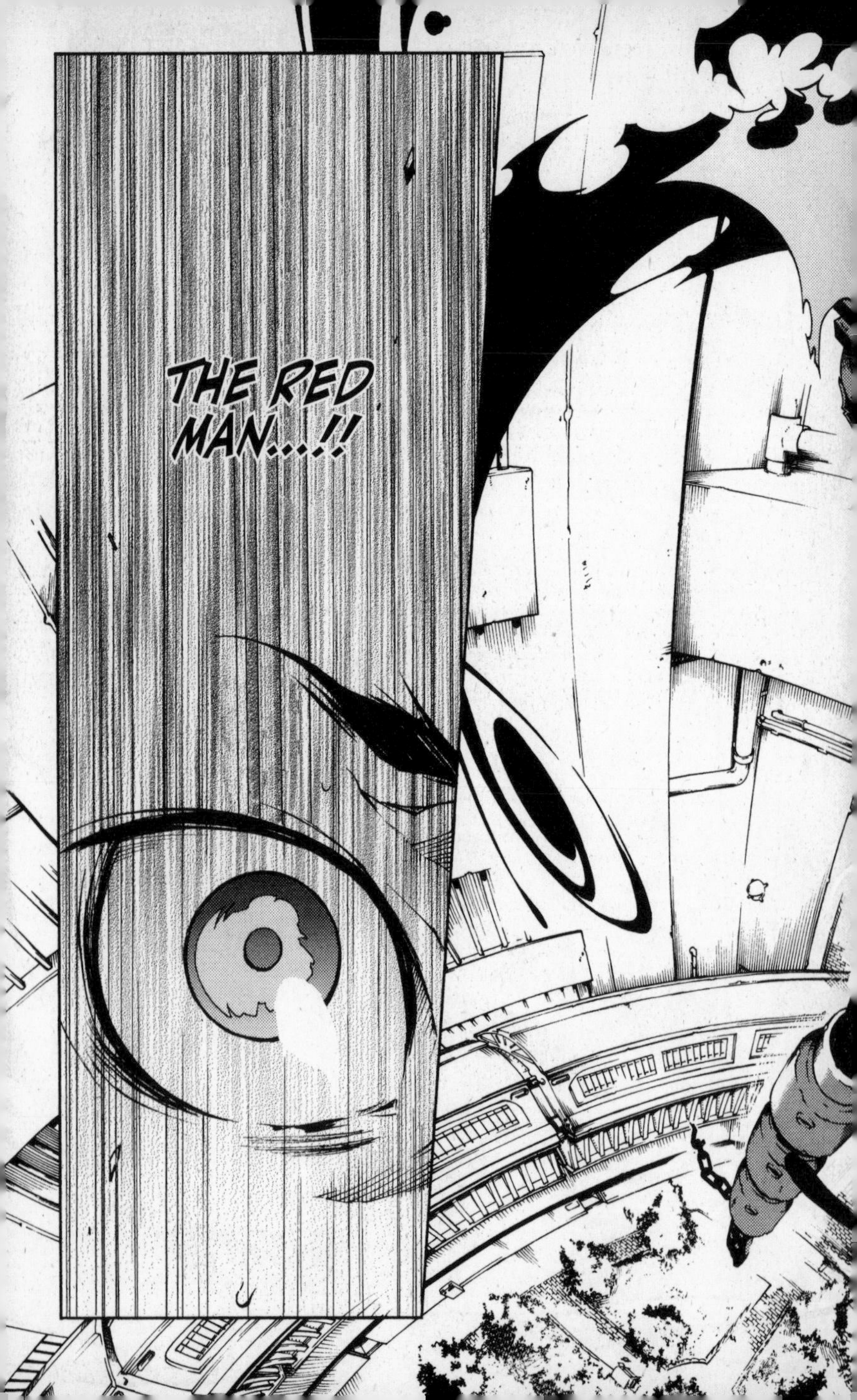
THE RED MAN...!!

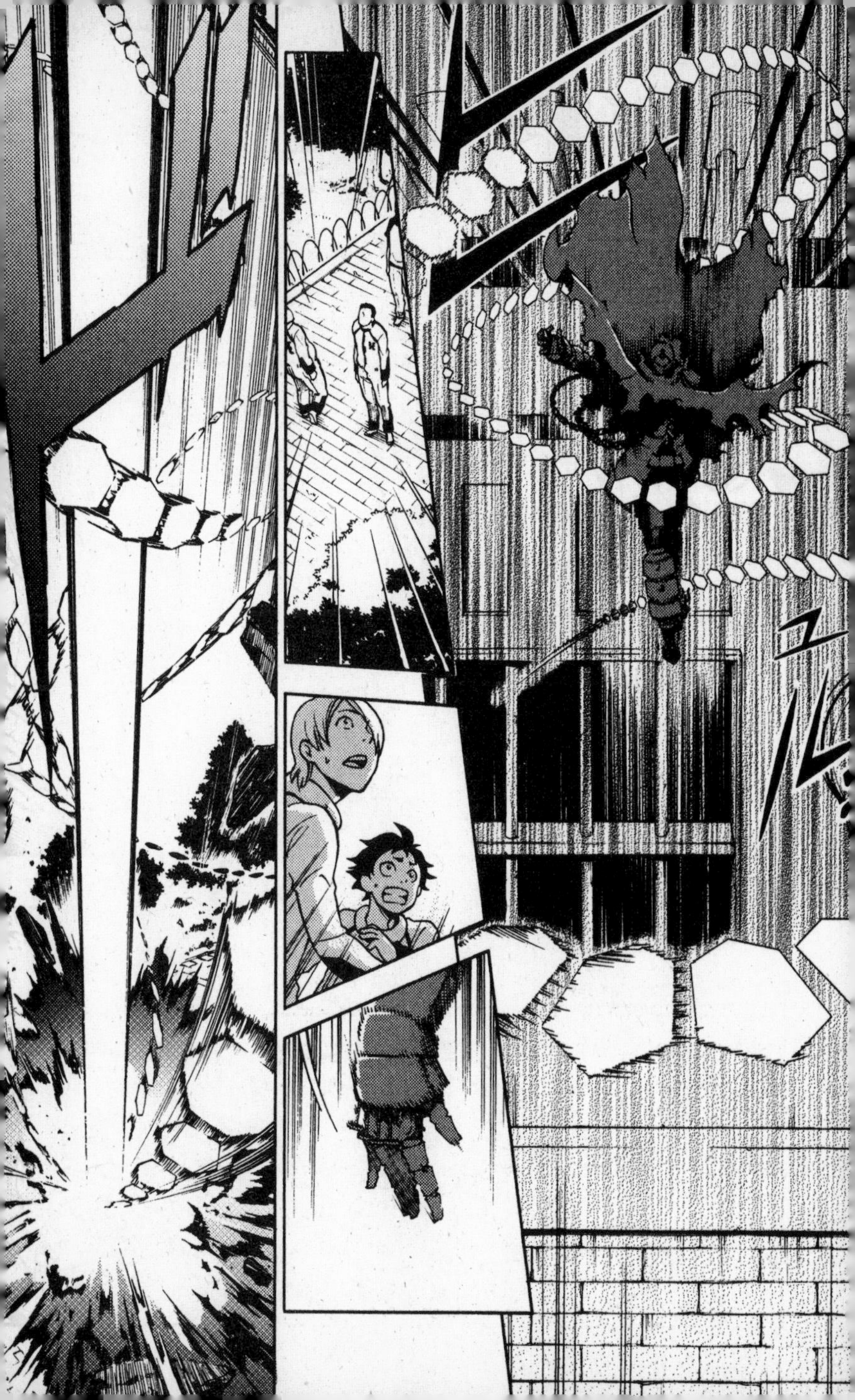

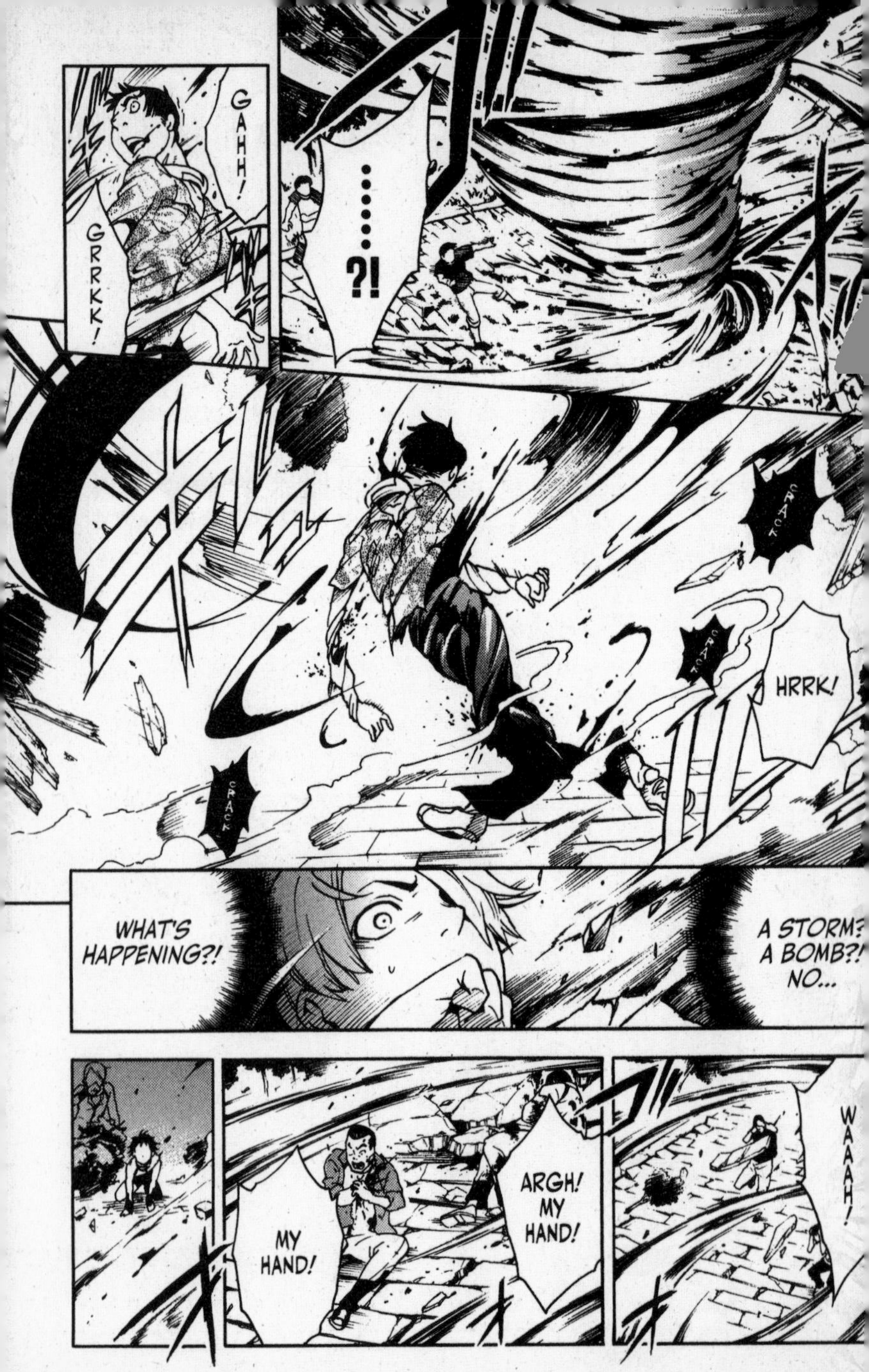
......
?!
GAHH!
GRRKK!
CRACK
CRACK
HRRK!
CRACK
A STORM? A BOMB?! NO...
WHAT'S HAPPENING?!
WAAAH!
ARGH! MY HAND!
MY HAND!

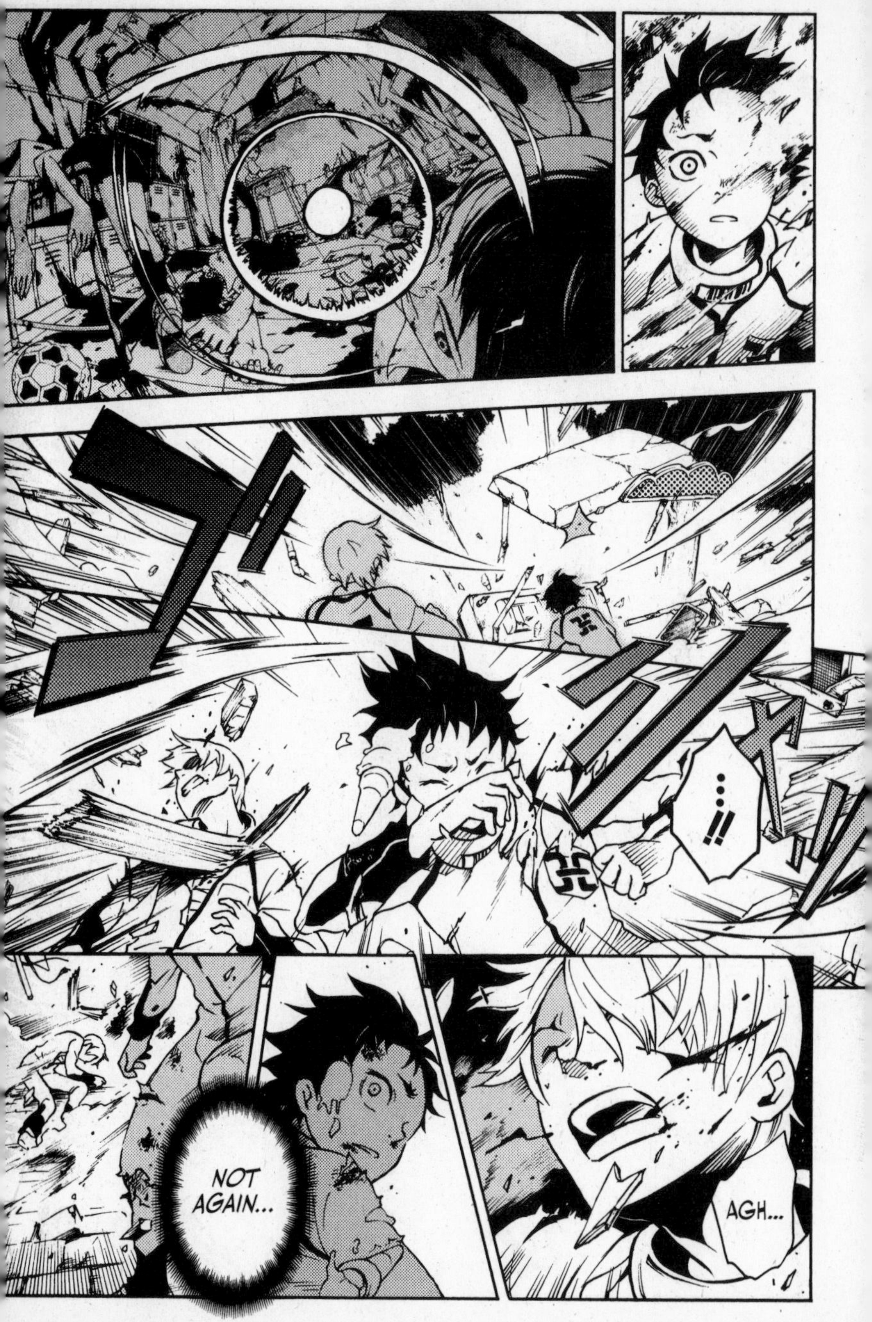
...!!
AGH...
NOT AGAIN...

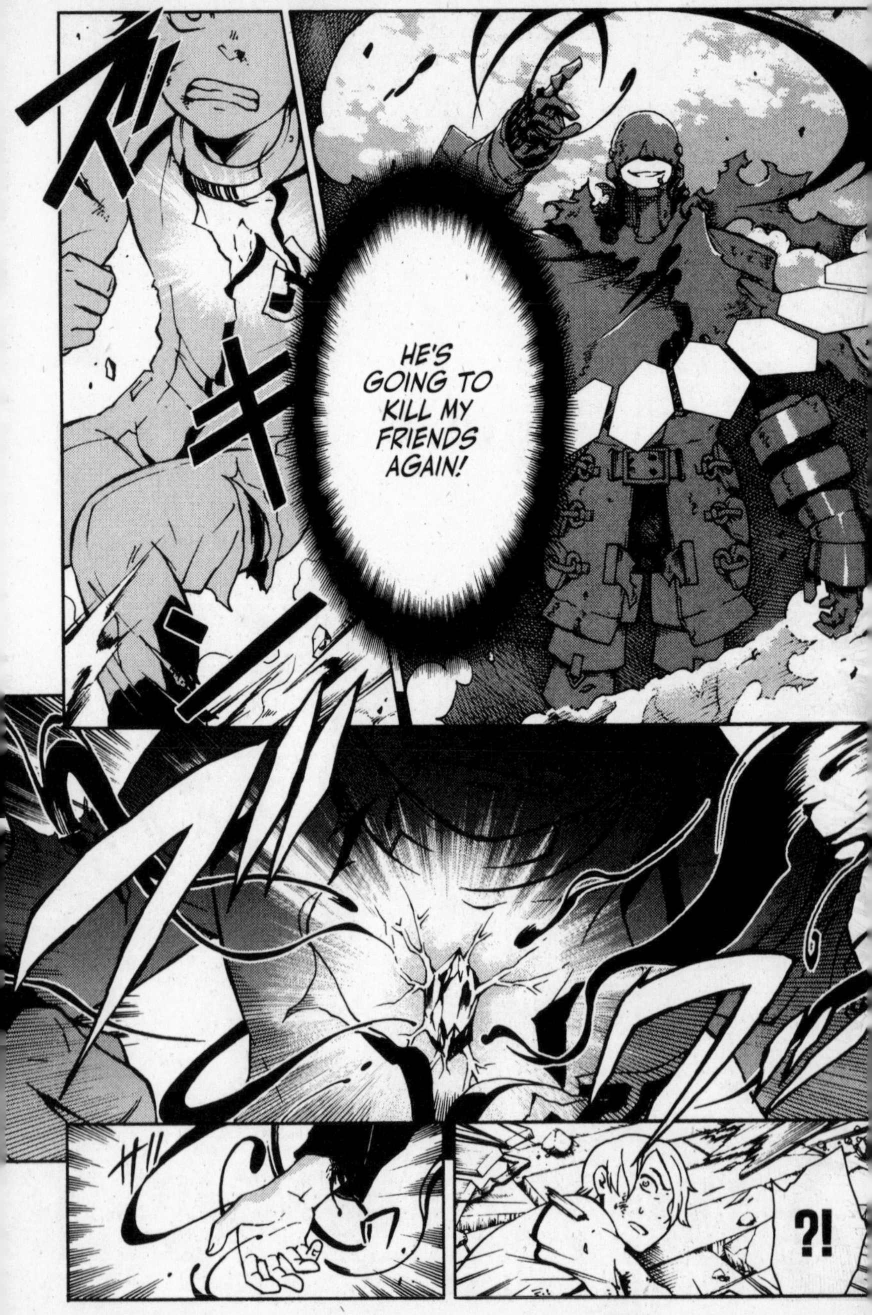
HE'S GOING TO KILL MY FRIENDS AGAIN!
?!

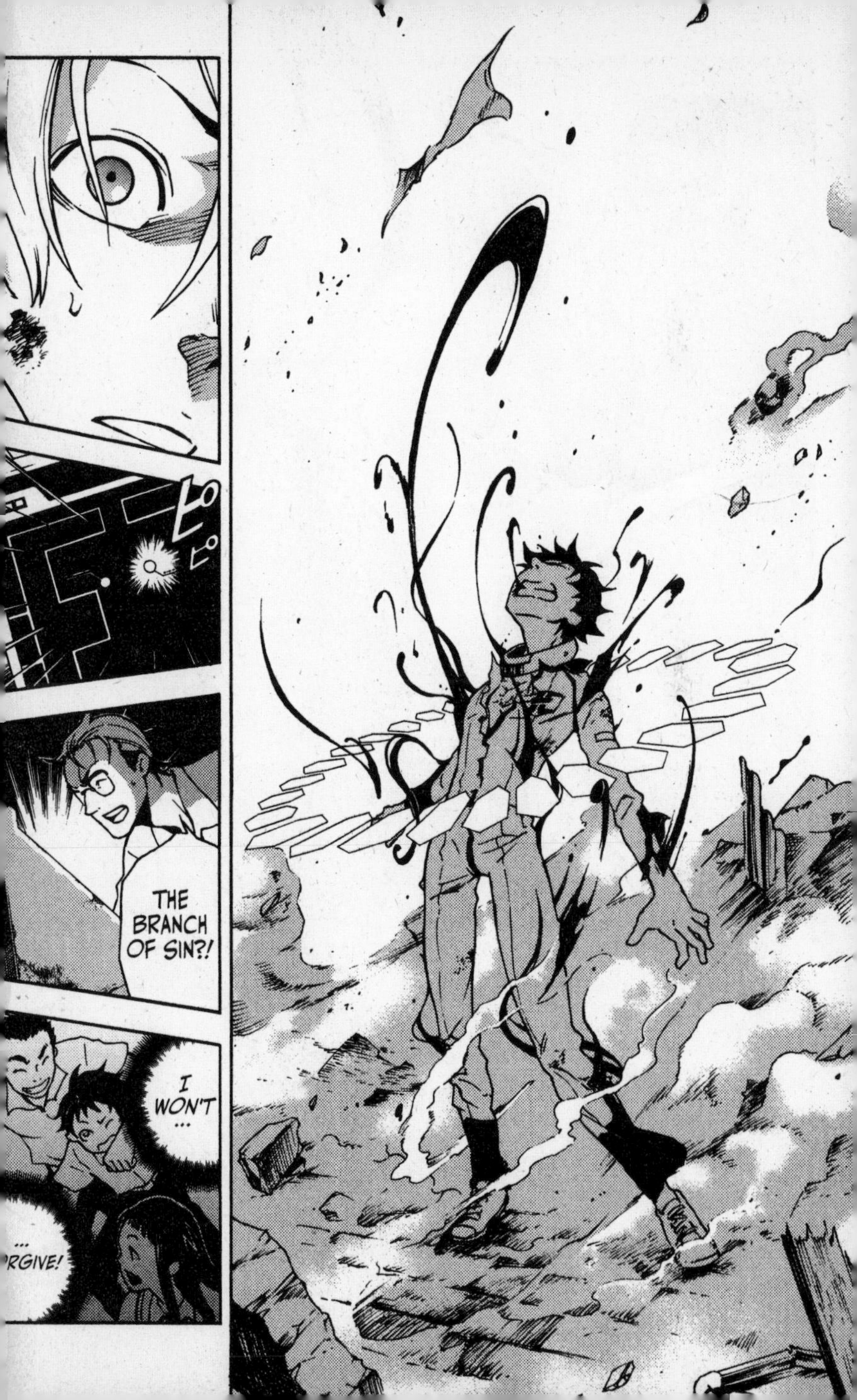
THE BRANCH OF SIN?!
I WON'T ...
... RGIVE!

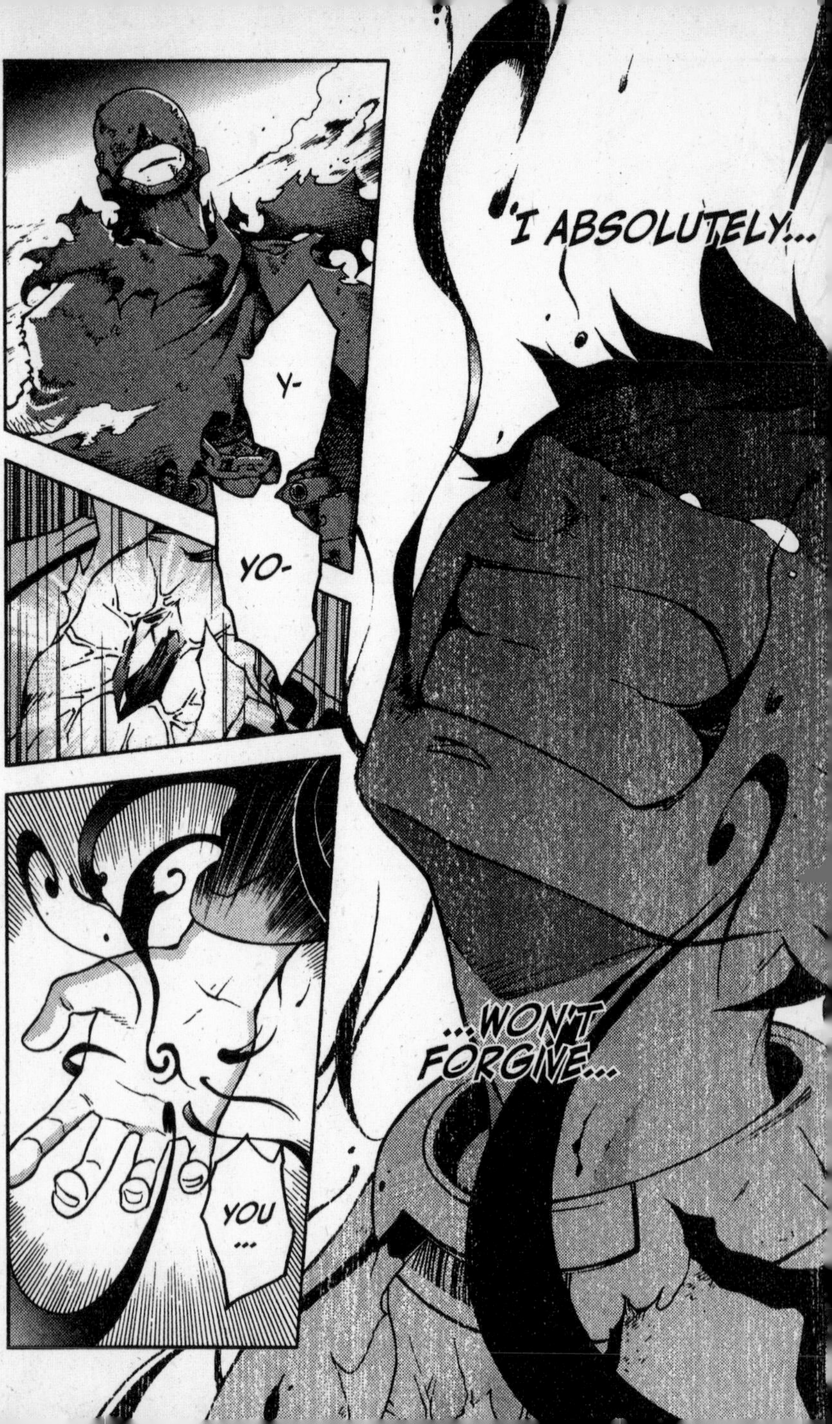
I ABSOLUTELY...
...WON'T FORGIVE...
Y-
YO-
YOU ...

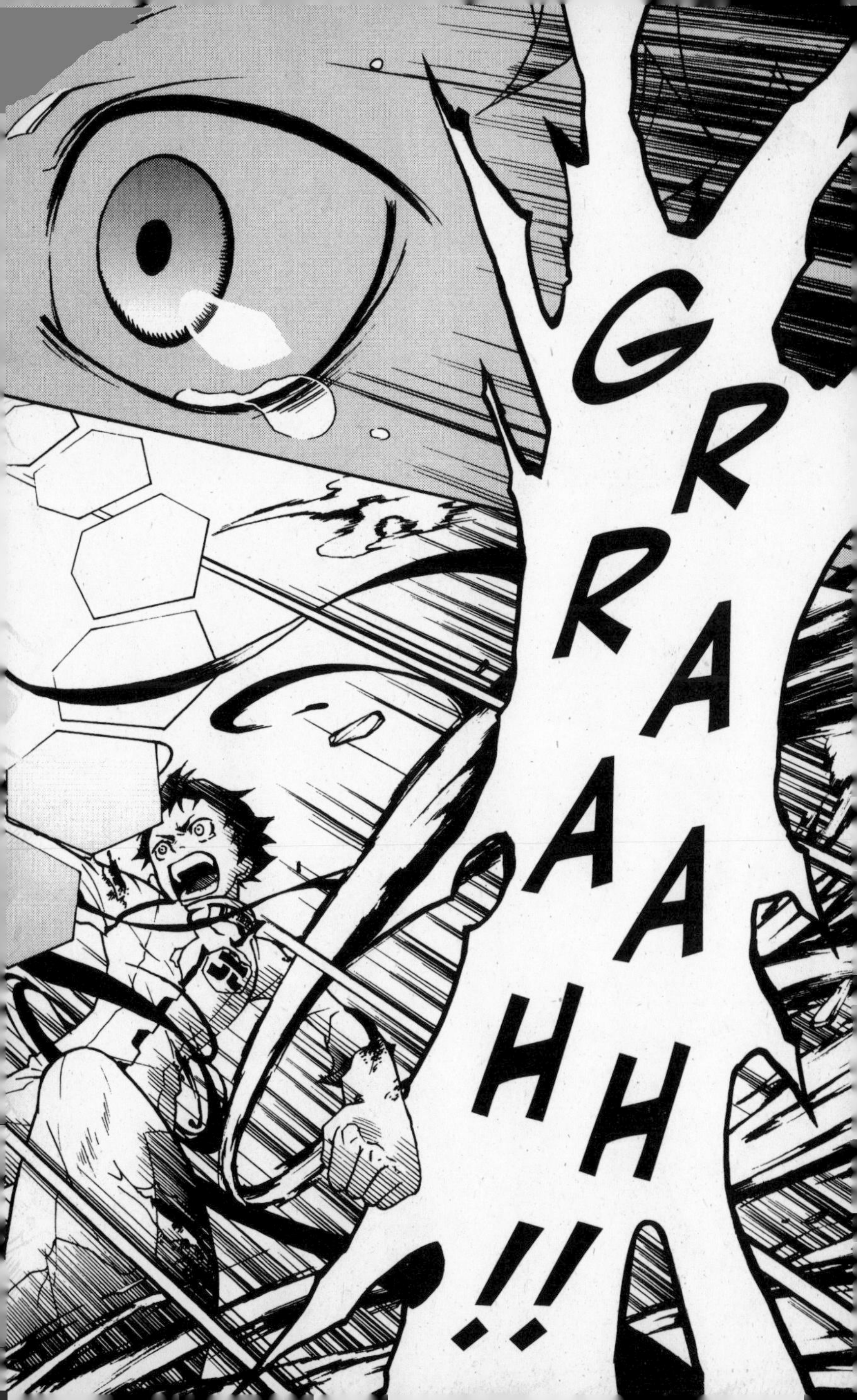
GRRAAAAHHH!!

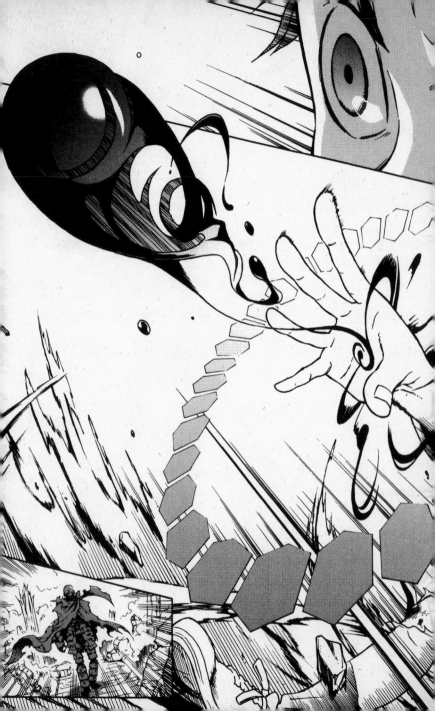

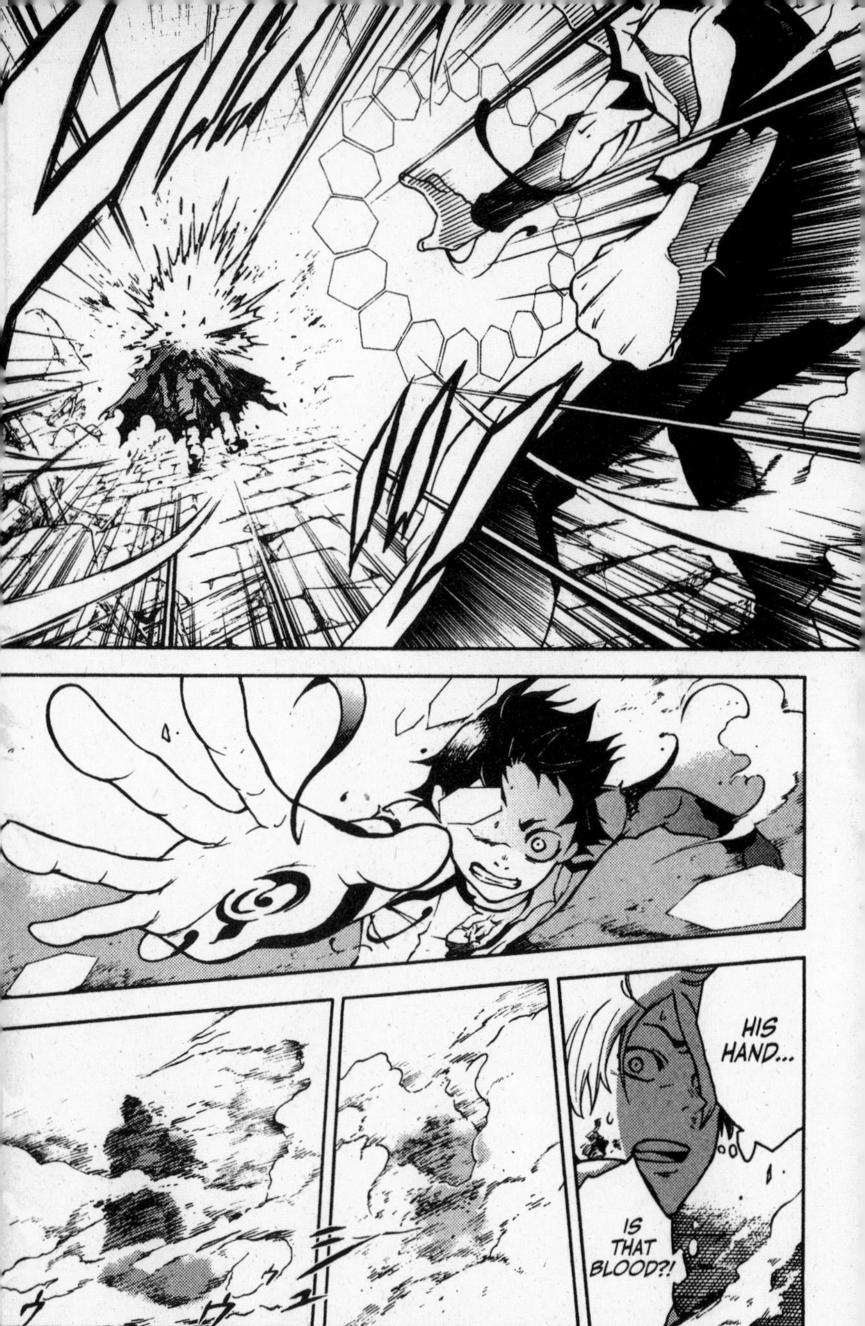
HIS HAND...
IS THAT BLOOD?!

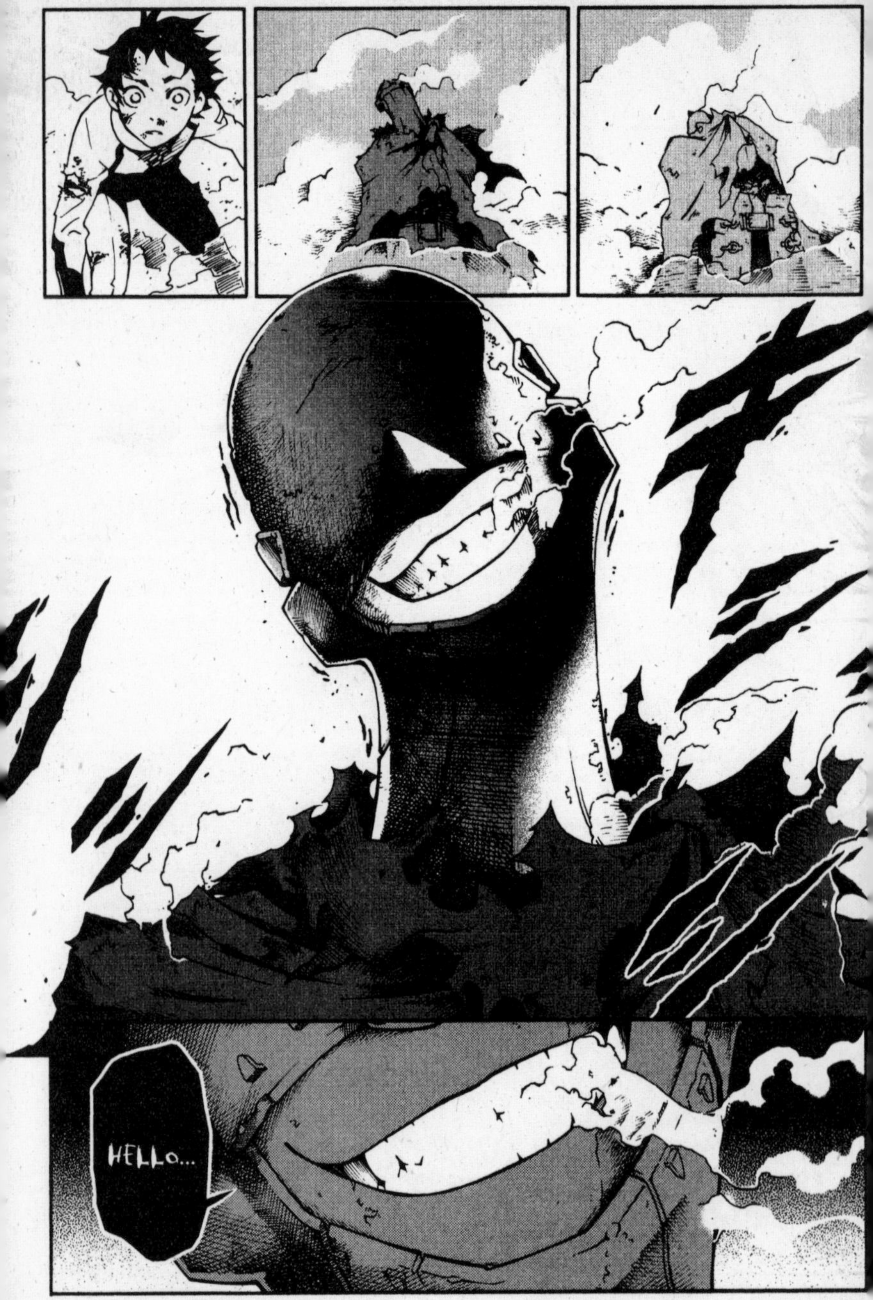
HELLO...

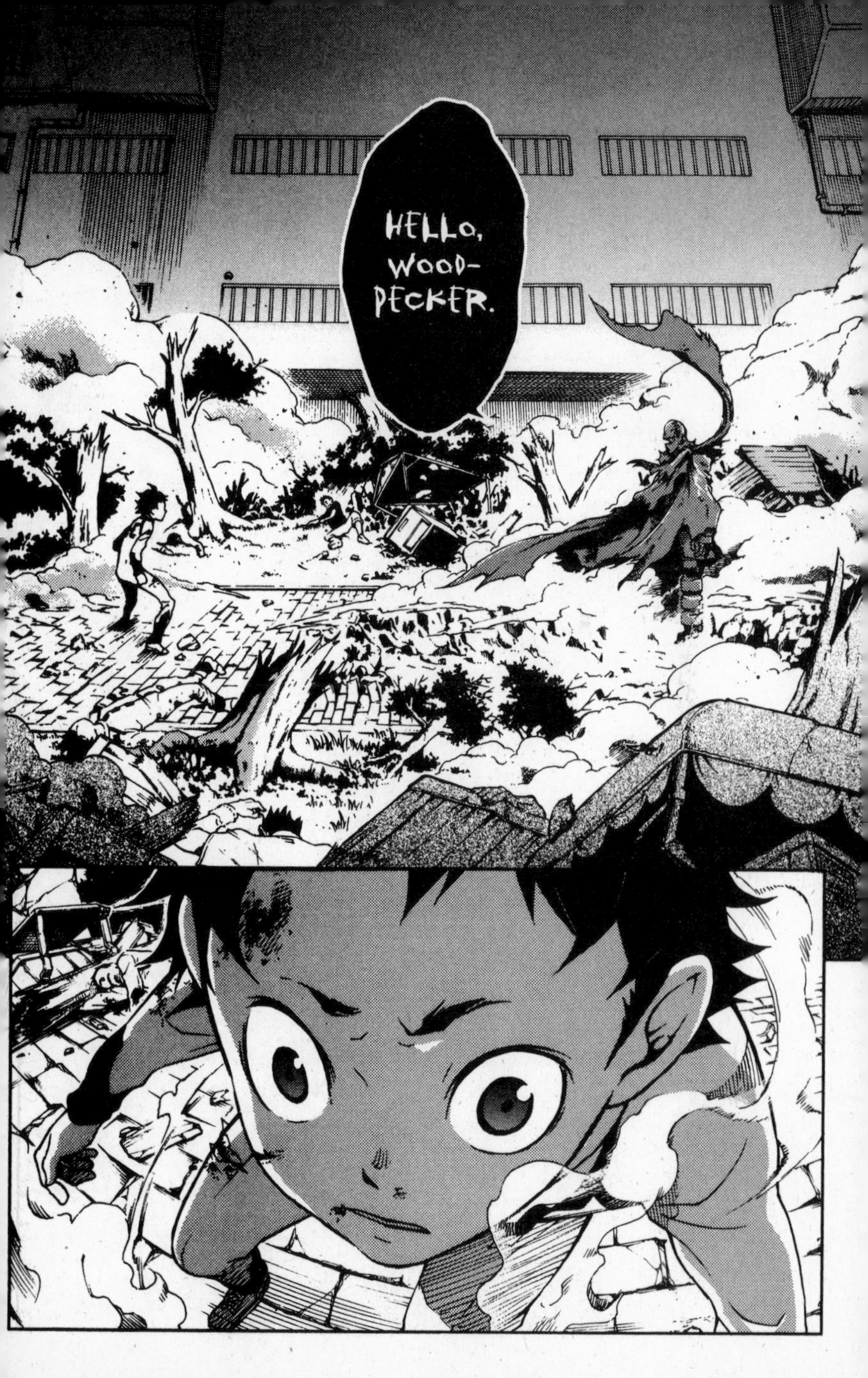
HELLO, WOOD-PECKER.

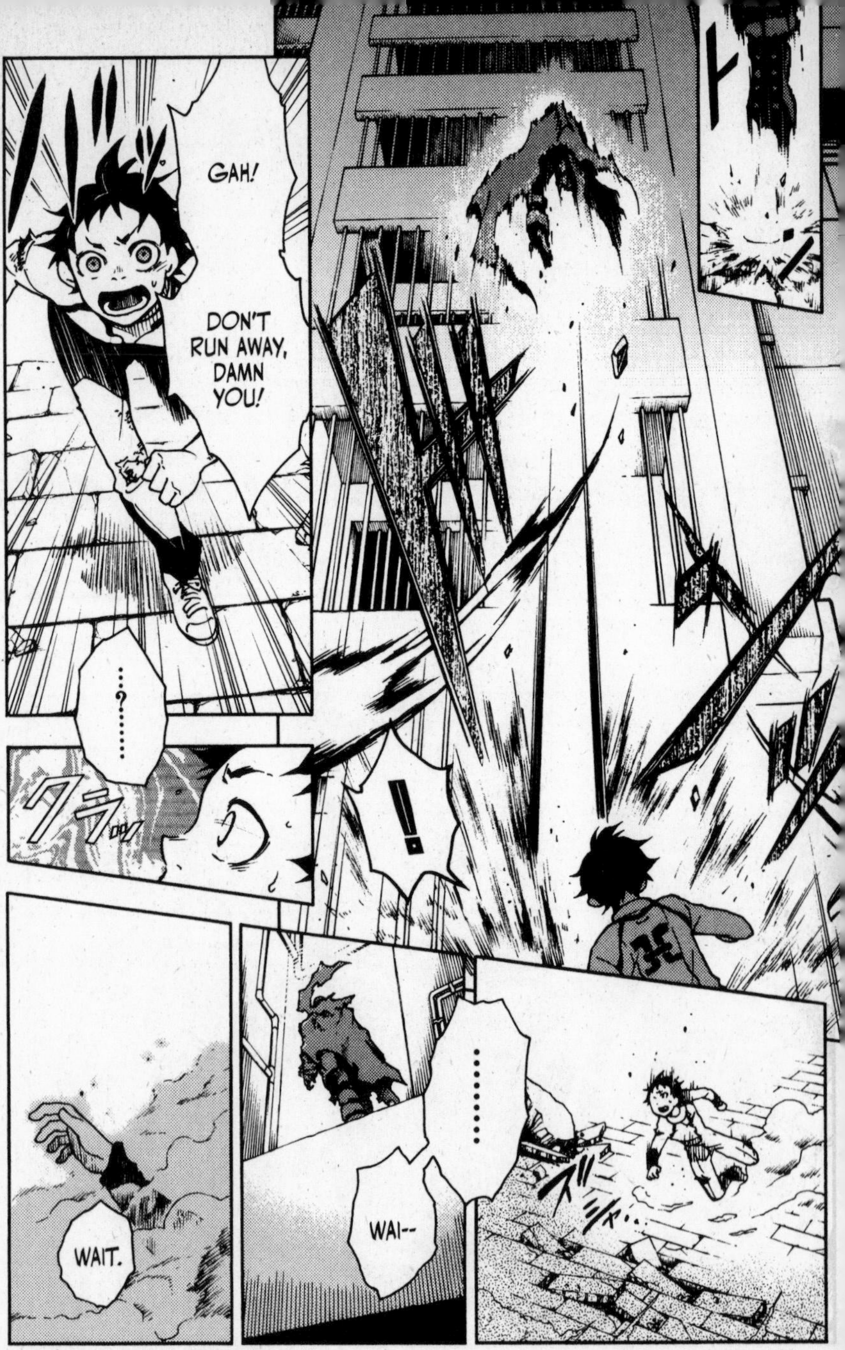
!
GAH!
DON'T RUN AWAY, DAMN YOU!
...?......
....
WAI--
WAIT.

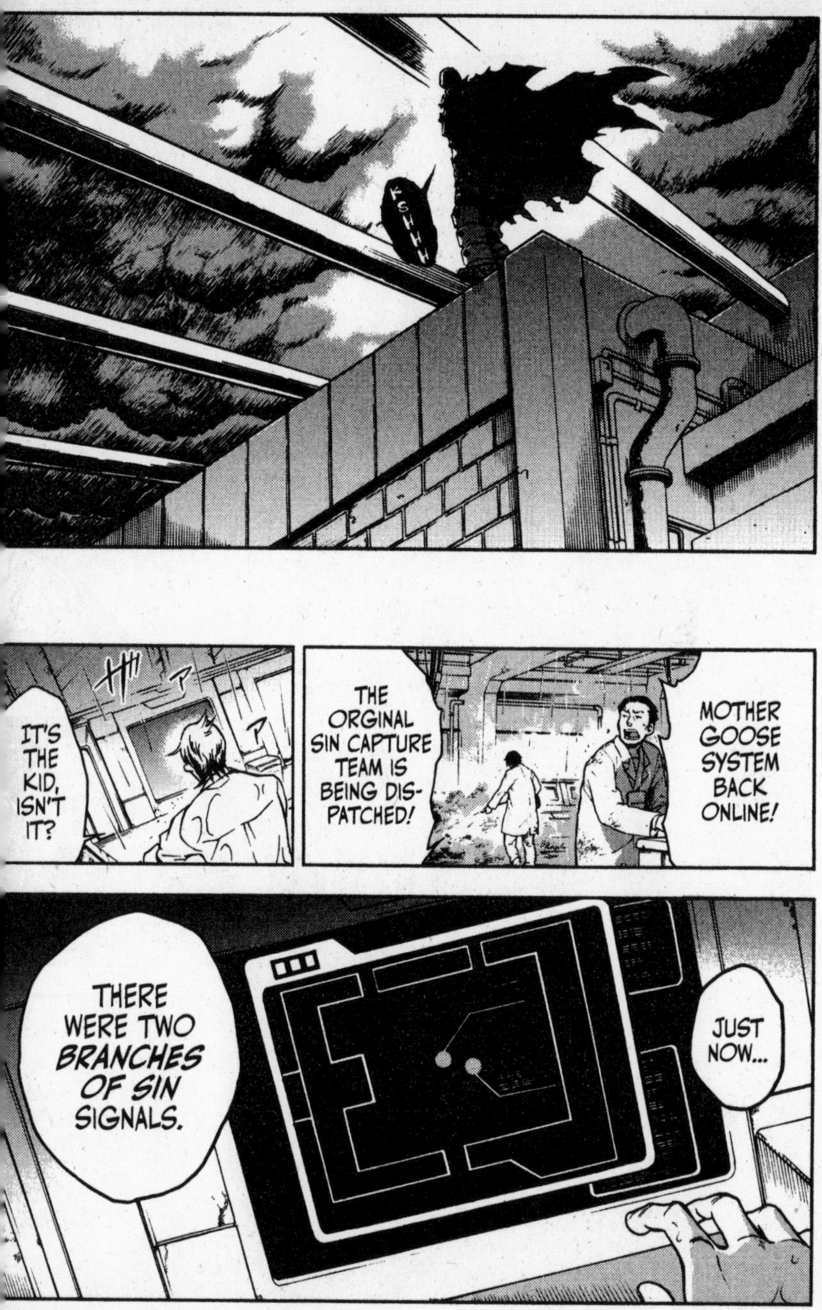
KSHHH
MOTHER GOOSE SYSTEM BACK ONLINE!
THE ORGINAL SIN CAPTURE TEAM IS BEING DISPATCHED!
IT'S THE KID, ISN'T IT?
JUST NOW...
THERE WERE TWO *BRANCHES OF SIN* SIGNALS.

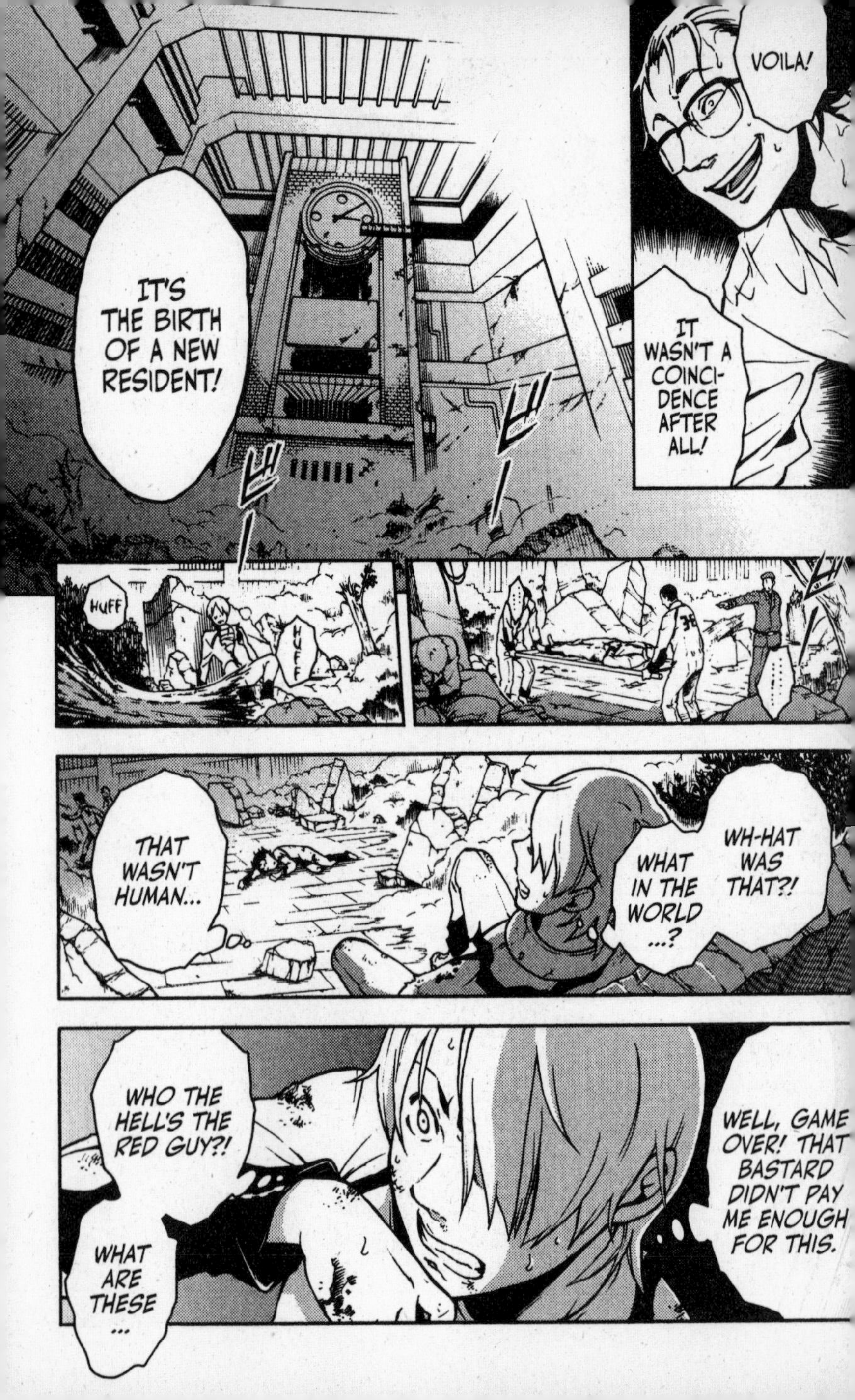
VOILA!
IT WASN'T A COINCIDENCE AFTER ALL!
IT'S THE BIRTH OF A NEW RESIDENT!
HUFF
HUFF
WH-HAT WAS THAT?!
WHAT IN THE WORLD ...?
THAT WASN'T HUMAN...
WELL, GAME OVER! THAT BASTARD DIDN'T PAY ME ENOUGH FOR THIS.
WHO THE HELL'S THE RED GUY?!
WHAT ARE THESE ...

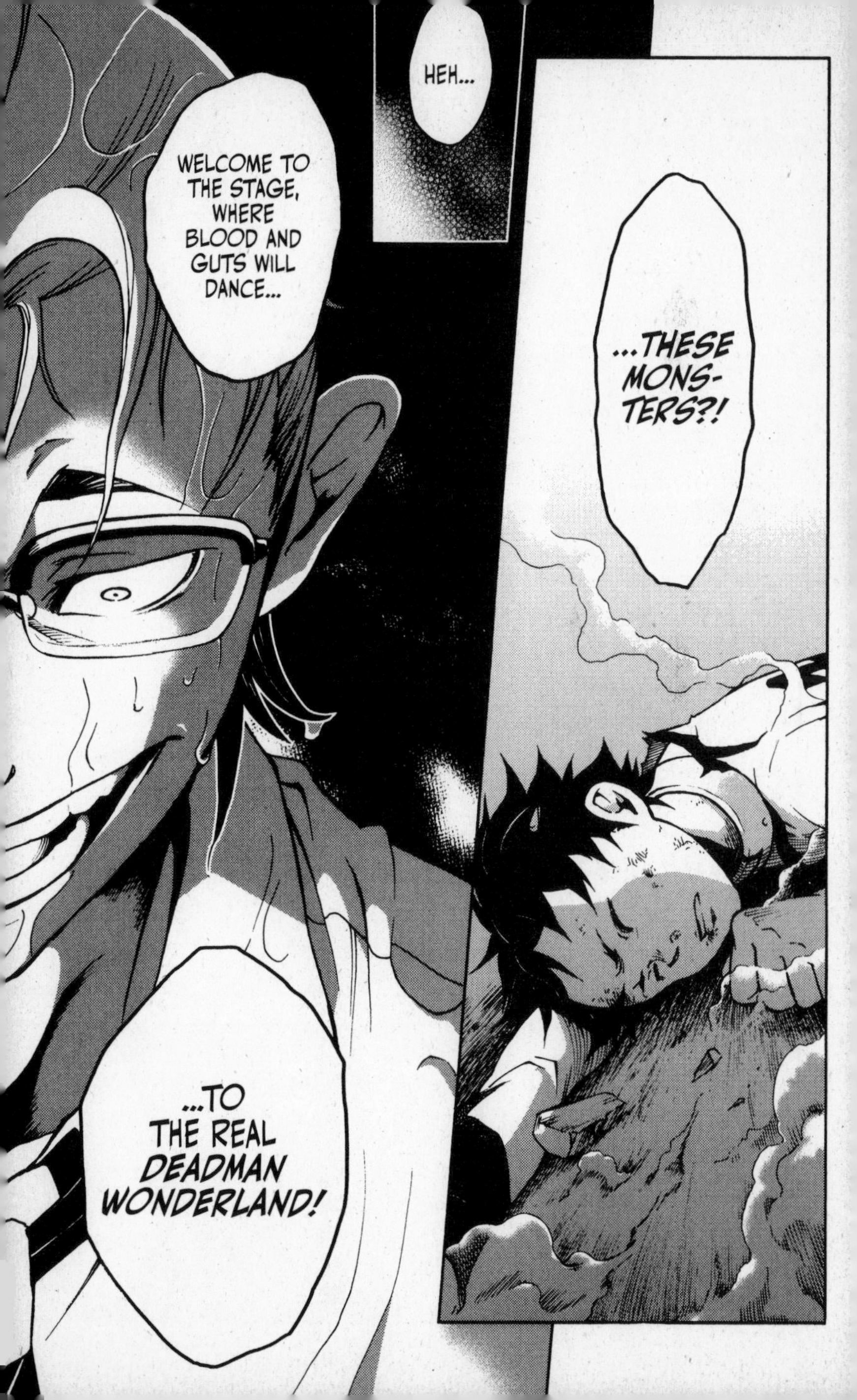
...THESE MONSTERS?!
HEH...
WELCOME TO THE STAGE, WHERE BLOOD AND GUTS WILL DANCE...
...TO THE REAL DEADMAN WONDERLAND!

DEADMAN WONDERLAND 1

CONTINUED TO VOLUME 02

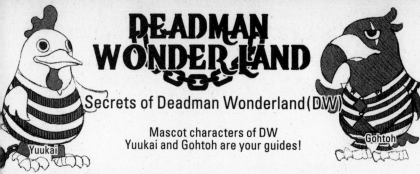

DEADMAN WONDERLAND

Secrets of Deadman Wonderland (DW)

Mascot characters of DW
Yuukai and Gohtoh are your guides!

Yuukai

Gohtoh

★ SINCE THE GREAT TOKYO EARTHQUAKE, DEADMAN WONDERLAND HAS BEEN ONE OF JAPAN'S PREEMINENT TOURIST ATTRACTIONS.

THERE ARE MANY WHO ARE PERPLEXED THAT DW HAS NO RATS... WHY IS THAT?

I ATE THEM!

★ DEADMAN WONDERLAND IS A THEME PARK PRISON.

SHOWS AND PERFORMANCES FEATURING REAL PRISONERS ARE VERY POPULAR.
THIS IS ONE WAY FOR PRISONERS TO CONTRIBUTE TO SOCIETY.
BEAR WITH IT, EVEN IF IT LOOKS DANGEROUS.
BUT ON THE OTHER HAND, THEY GET TO HAVE LOTS OF TATTOOS, SO IT'S FUN!

THERE ARE VIOLENT SHOWS FOR THE ENJOYMENT OF DEPRESSED _ULTS, AND BETTING RACES, SO BE CAREFUL ABOUT AGE RESTRICTIONS!

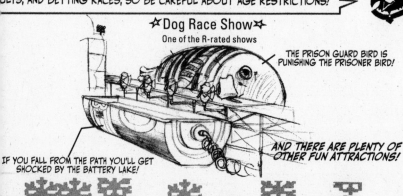

☆ Dog Race Show ☆
One of the R-rated shows

THE PRISON GUARD BIRD IS PUNISHING THE PRISONER BIRD!

IF YOU FALL FROM THE PATH YOU'LL GET SHOCKED BY THE BATTERY LAKE!

AND THERE ARE PLENTY OF OTHER FUN ATTRACTIONS!

★ There is a dedicated television channel, so watch that too!
PPV has no censorship!
"A former model female prisoner's secret room! Murder mystery – Why I killed?"
"Stubborn mob boss' Mossou rice cooking 365"...and so on!
Plenty of popular programs. So sign up today!

★Instead of money, prisoners use Cast Points(CPs), and spend their days trying to earn them.

DEPENDING ON HOW MANY CPS YOU POSSESS, YOU CAN EVEN EAT STEAK OR SASHIMI! IT'S MUCH EASIER TO UNDERSTAND THIS SYSTEM THAN THAT OF OTHER PRISONS WHICH ARE NOT PRIVATELY RUN -- THE HARDER YOU WORK THE BETTER YOUR LIFE BECOMES -- IT'S VERY POPULAR!

ON THE OTHER HAND, IF YOU DON'T WORK, YOU DON'T GET TO LIVE! IT IS WHAT IT IS!

★ Q & A Corner

Q: ISN'T IT DANGEROUS FOR PRISONERS TO BE IN SUCH CLOSE PROXIMITY OF THE GUESTS?
A: THEY'RE SEPARATED BY A SECURITY WALL, SO THAT THEY WON'T COME INTO CONTACT WITH THEM. IT'S NOOOO PROBLEM! AND NO MATTER HOW MUCH YOU TAUNT THEM, THEY CAN'T ATTACK YOU, SO IT'S ALL GOOD!

Q: IS IT TRUE THAT THERE ARE DEATH ROW INMATES?
A: IT'S TRUE. IN A NORMAL PRISON, WHICH IS NOT PRIVATELY OPERATED, DEATH ROW INMATES ARE "WAITING FOR THEIR SENTENCE" WHICH IS "DEATH BY EXECUTION," AND SO THEY ARE PLACED IN A HOLDING CENTER SEPARATE FROM OTHER PRISONERS. HOWEVER, AT DW, WE HAVE A SYSTEM WHEREBY DEATH ROW INMATES ARE SUBJECT TO A "CONSTANTLY EXECUTED DEATH SENTENCE," AND THUS, WE CAN TREAT THEM AS WE DO OTHER PRISONERS! THANKS TO THIS SYSTEM, THE PSYCHOLOGICAL STRESS BORNE BY EMPLOYEES WHO MUST NORMALLY EXECUTE A DEATH SENTENCE HAS BEEN GREATLY REDUCED. IT'S A FACT!

Q: WHAT KIND OF PLACE DO THEY LIVE IN?
A: THIS KIND OF PLACE. A MODIFIED PANOPTICON-TYPE PRISON FACILITY. WE MONITOR THE PRISONERS' HEALTH AND MOVEMENTS THROUGH THEIR COLLARS.

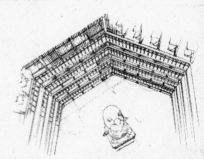

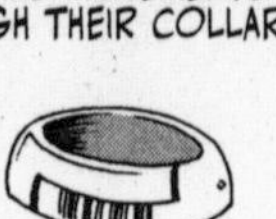

WHAT D'YOU THINK? DOESN'T DW SEEM LIKE A SAFE AND FUN PLACE? PLEASE COME AND VISIT!

PLEASE COME AND BE INCARCERATED!

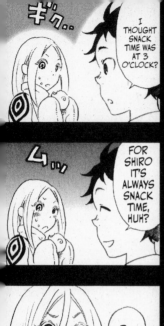

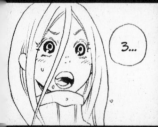

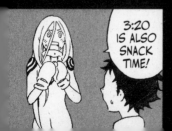

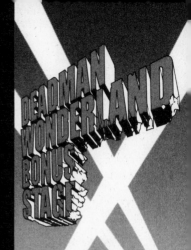

DEADMAN WONDERLAND BONUS STAGE

Jinsei Kataoka

Kazuma Kondou

ギク..
I THOUGHT SNACK TIME WAS AT 3 O'CLOCK?
FOR SHIRO IT'S ALWAYS SNACK TIME, HUH?
3...
3:20 IS ALSO SNACK TIME!

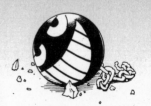

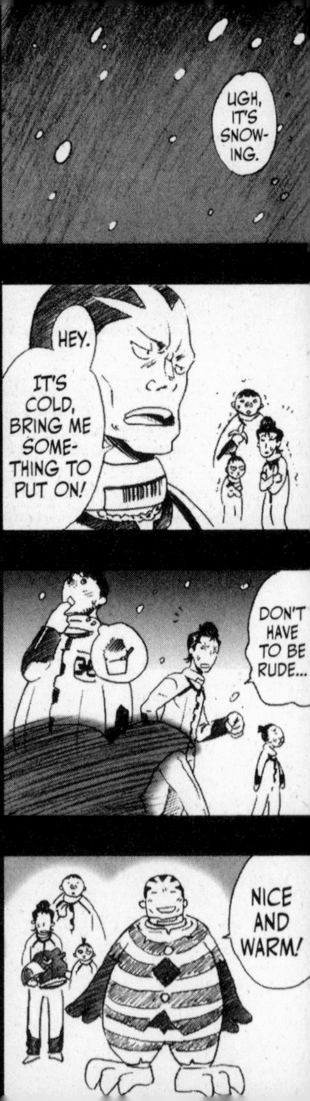
UGH, IT'S SNOW-ING.
HEY.
IT'S COLD, BRING ME SOME-THING TO PUT ON!
DON'T HAVE TO BE RUDE...
NICE AND WARM!
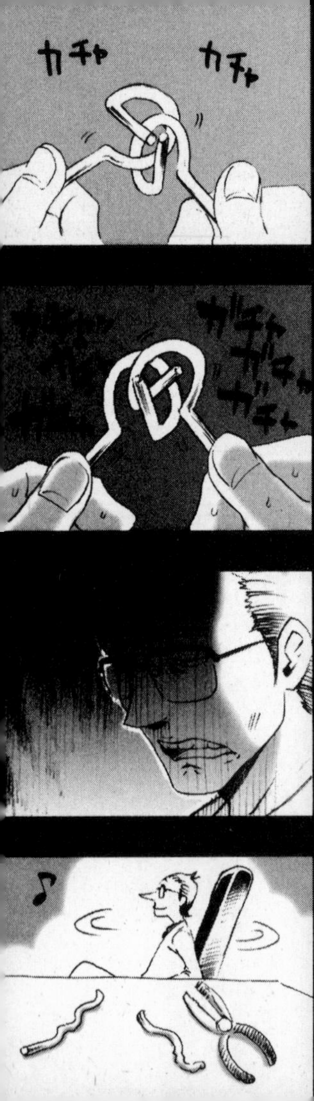
カチャ
カチャ
ガチャ
ガチャ
ガチャ

Z

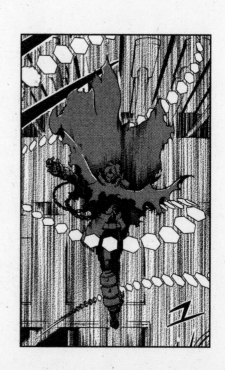

DEADMAN
WONDERLAND

AS GANTA DISCOVERS HIS NEW POWER, HE BECOMES MORE DETERMINED TO PURSUE THE RED MAN TO AVENGE HIS FRIENDS. AT THE SAME TIME, HIS STRANGE ABILITIES PROVE TO BE AN OBSTACLE TO CHIEF MAKINA WHO IS RESOLUTE IN MAINTAINING PEACE AND ORDER IN HER TERRITORY. WITH CONSPIRACY AND MONSTROUS ATTACKS COMING FROM EVERY ANGLE, GANTA MANAGES TO ARRIVE AT ZONE G, A MYSTERIOUS, DETACHED LOCATION IN DEADMAN WONDERLAND WHERE THE BLOODBATH CONTINUES...

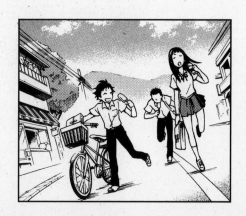

HANAKO 花子
AND THE TERROR OF ALLEGORY

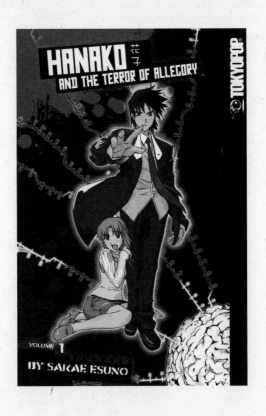

BY SAKAE ESUNO

AVAILABLE IN STORES MARCH 2010

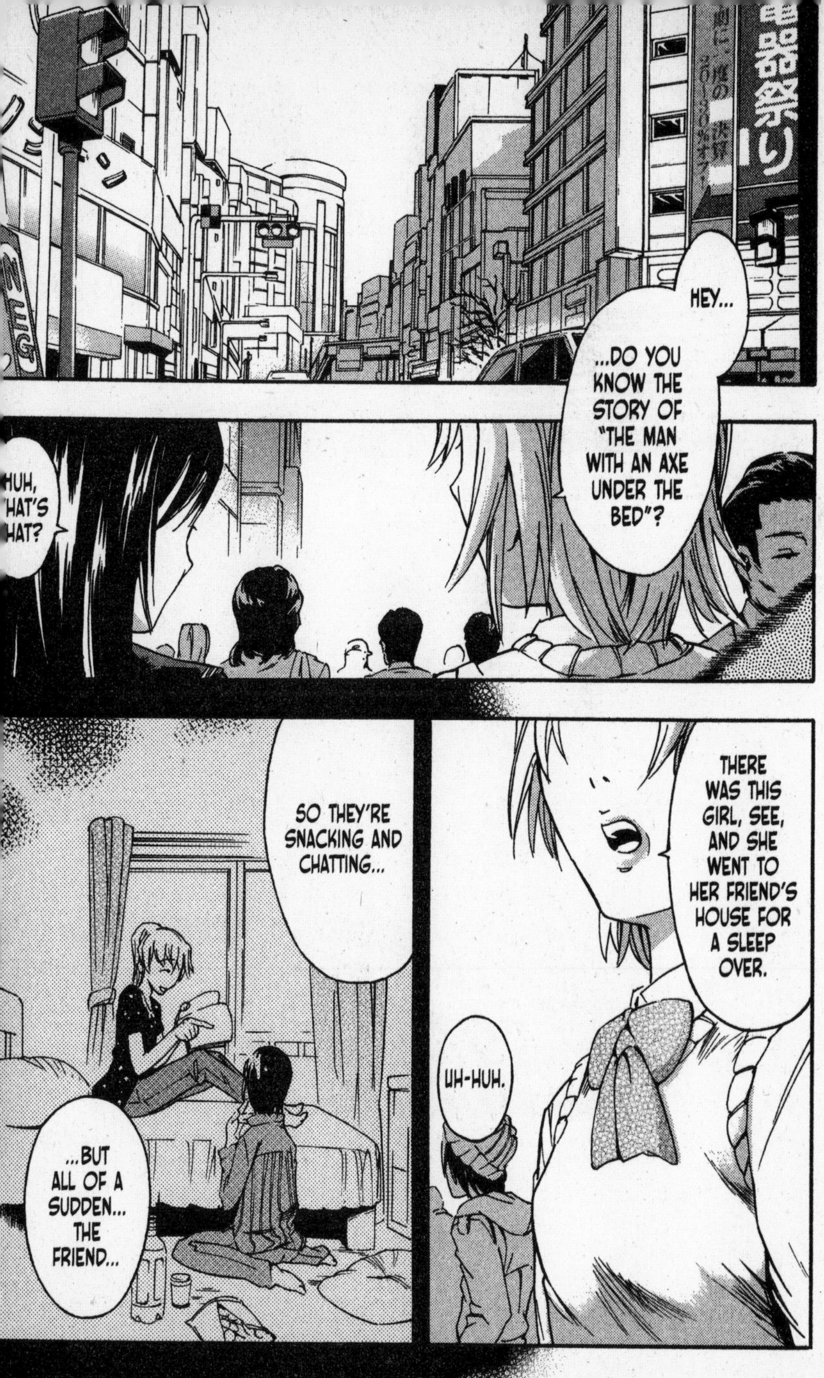
電器祭り
HEY...
...DO YOU KNOW THE STORY OF "THE MAN WITH AN AXE UNDER THE BED"?
HUH, HAT'S HAT?
THERE WAS THIS GIRL, SEE, AND SHE WENT TO HER FRIEND'S HOUSE FOR A SLEEP OVER.
UH-HUH.
SO THEY'RE SNACKING AND CHATTING...
...BUT ALL OF A SUDDEN... THE FRIEND...

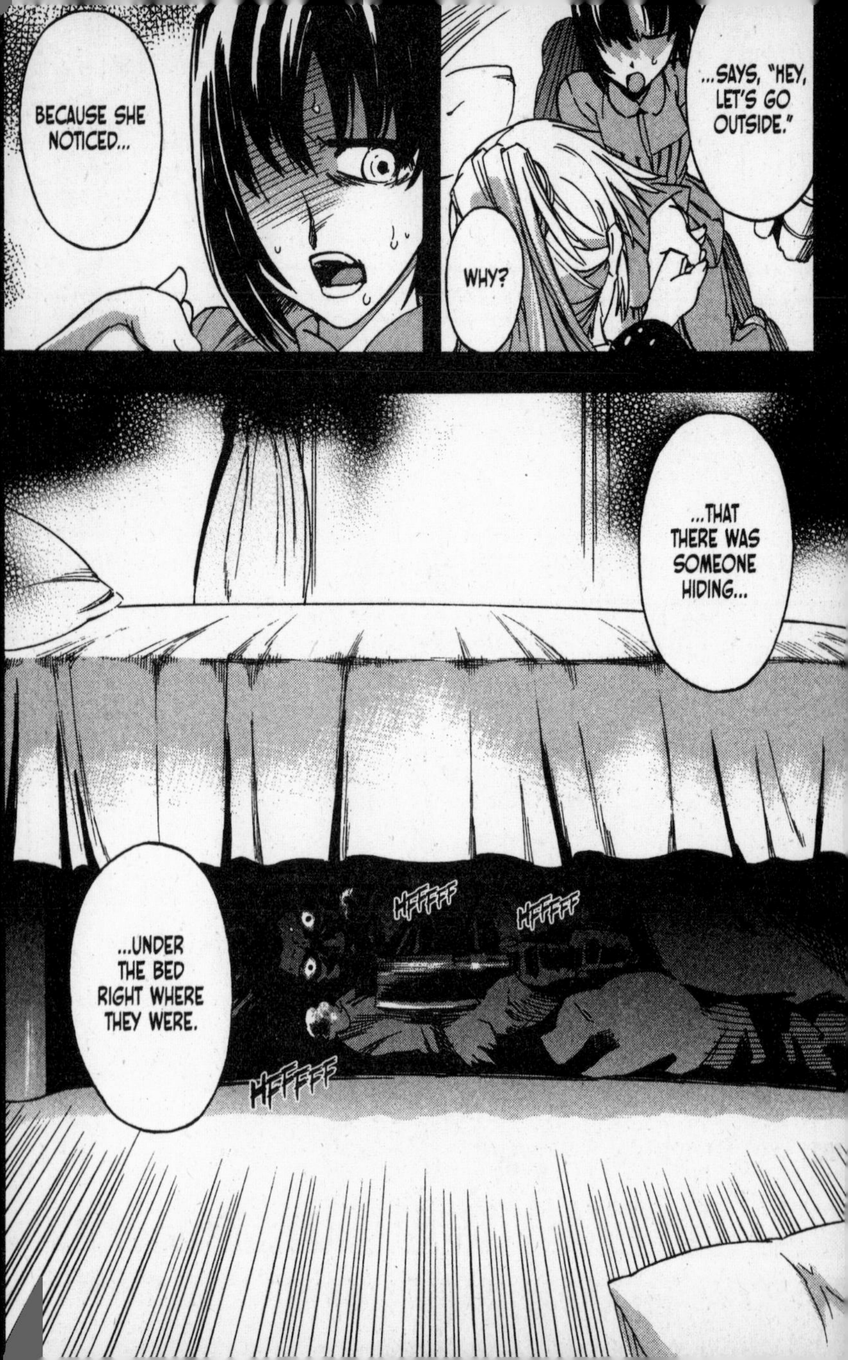
...SAYS, "HEY, LET'S GO OUTSIDE."
WHY?
BECAUSE SHE NOTICED...
...THAT THERE WAS SOMEONE HIDING...
HFFFFF
HFFFFF
...UNDER THE BED RIGHT WHERE THEY WERE.
HFFFFF

Folklore: The Man Under the Bed

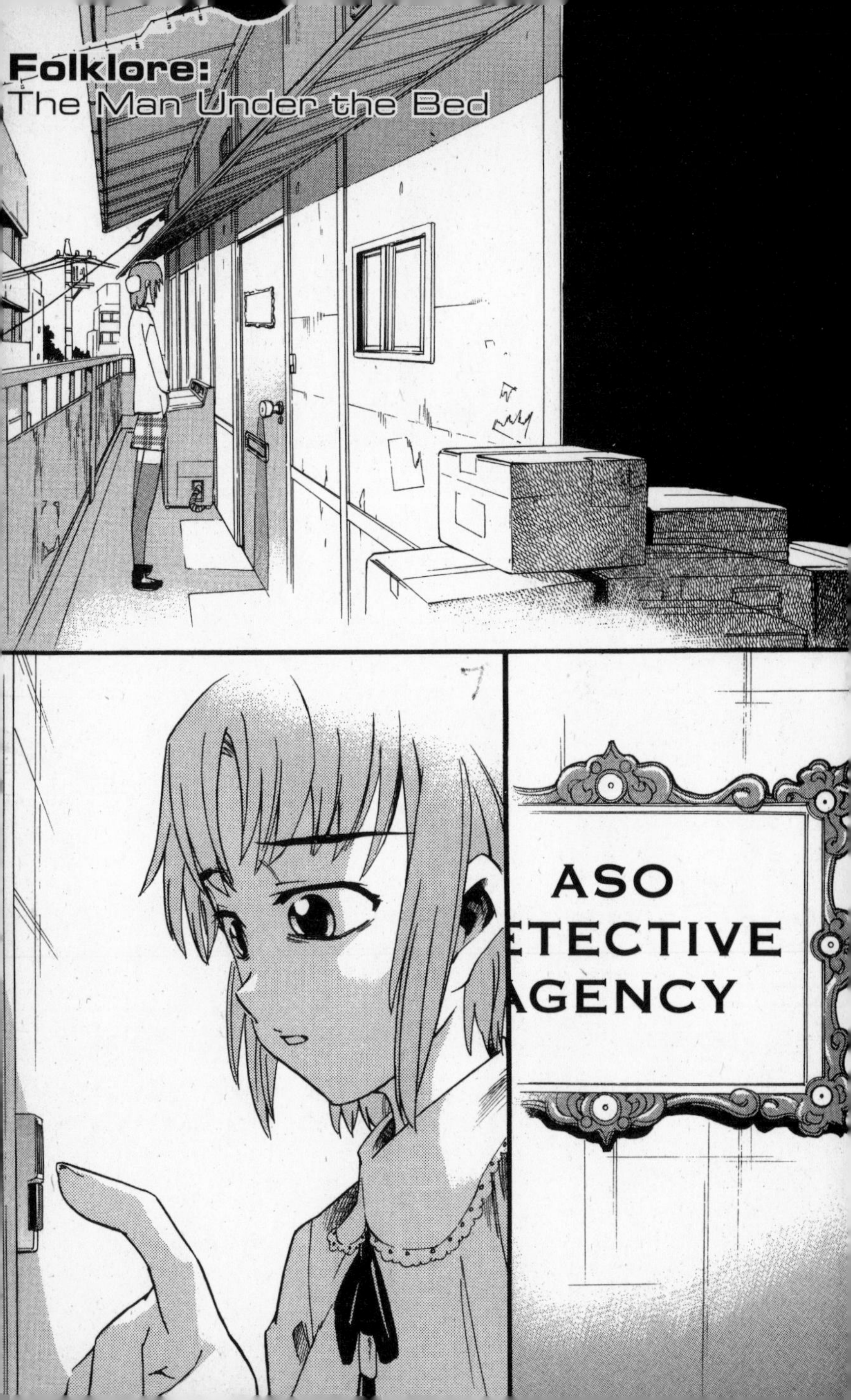
ASO
ETECTIVE
AGENCY

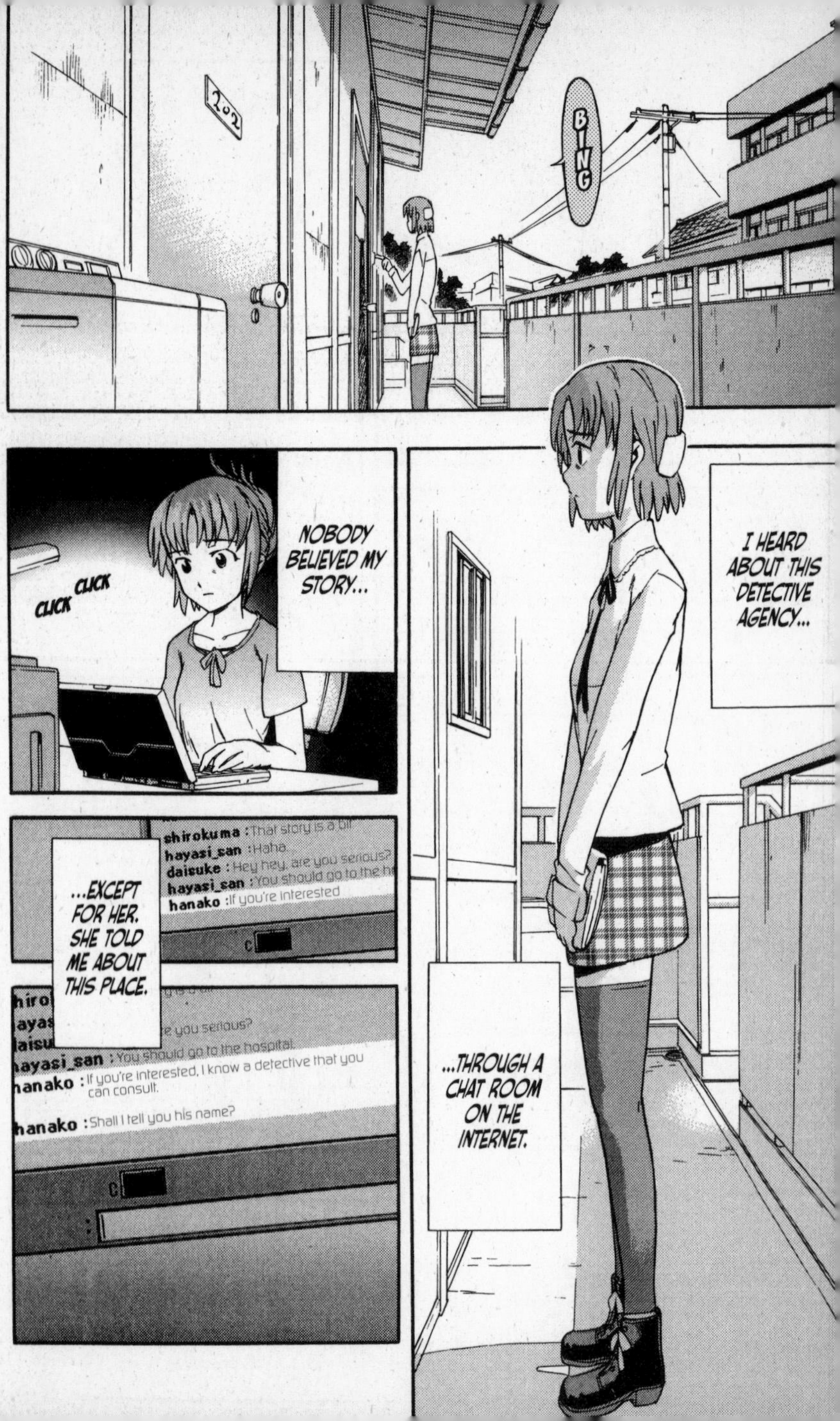
202
BING
I HEARD ABOUT THIS DETECTIVE AGENCY...
...THROUGH A CHAT ROOM ON THE INTERNET.
NOBODY BELIEVED MY STORY...
CLICK CLICK
shirokuma : That story is a bit
hayasi_san : Haha.
daisuke : Hey hey, are you serious?
hayasi_san : You should go to the h
hanako : If you're interested
...EXCEPT FOR HER. SHE TOLD ME ABOUT THIS PLACE.
re you serious?
hayasi_san : You should go to the hospital.
hanako : If you're interested, I know a detective that you can consult.
hanako : Shall I tell you his name?

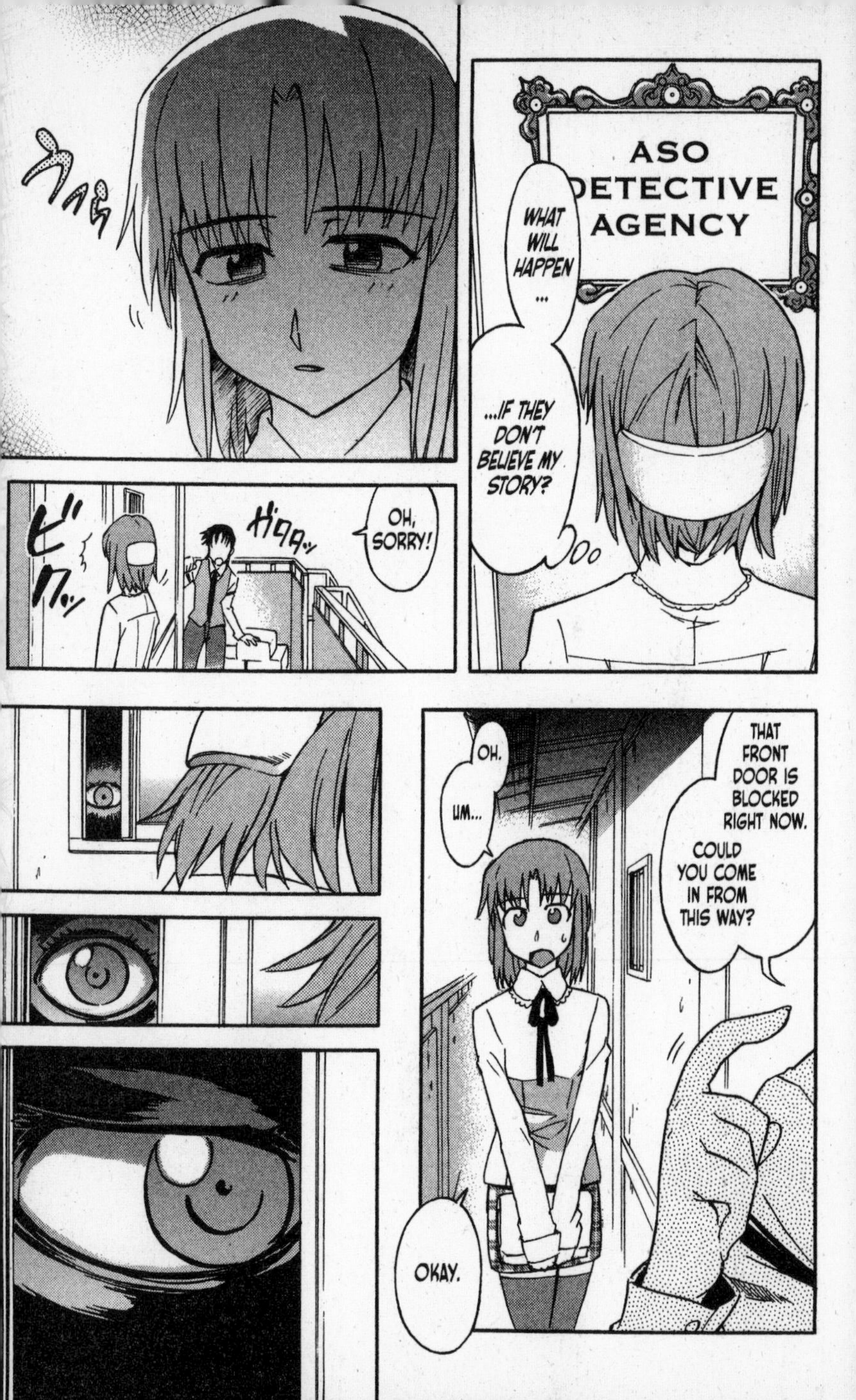
ASO DETECTIVE AGENCY
WHAT WILL HAPPEN ...
...IF THEY DON'T BELIEVE MY STORY?
OH, SORRY!
THAT FRONT DOOR IS BLOCKED RIGHT NOW.
COULD YOU COME IN FROM THIS WAY?
OH.
UM...
OKAY.

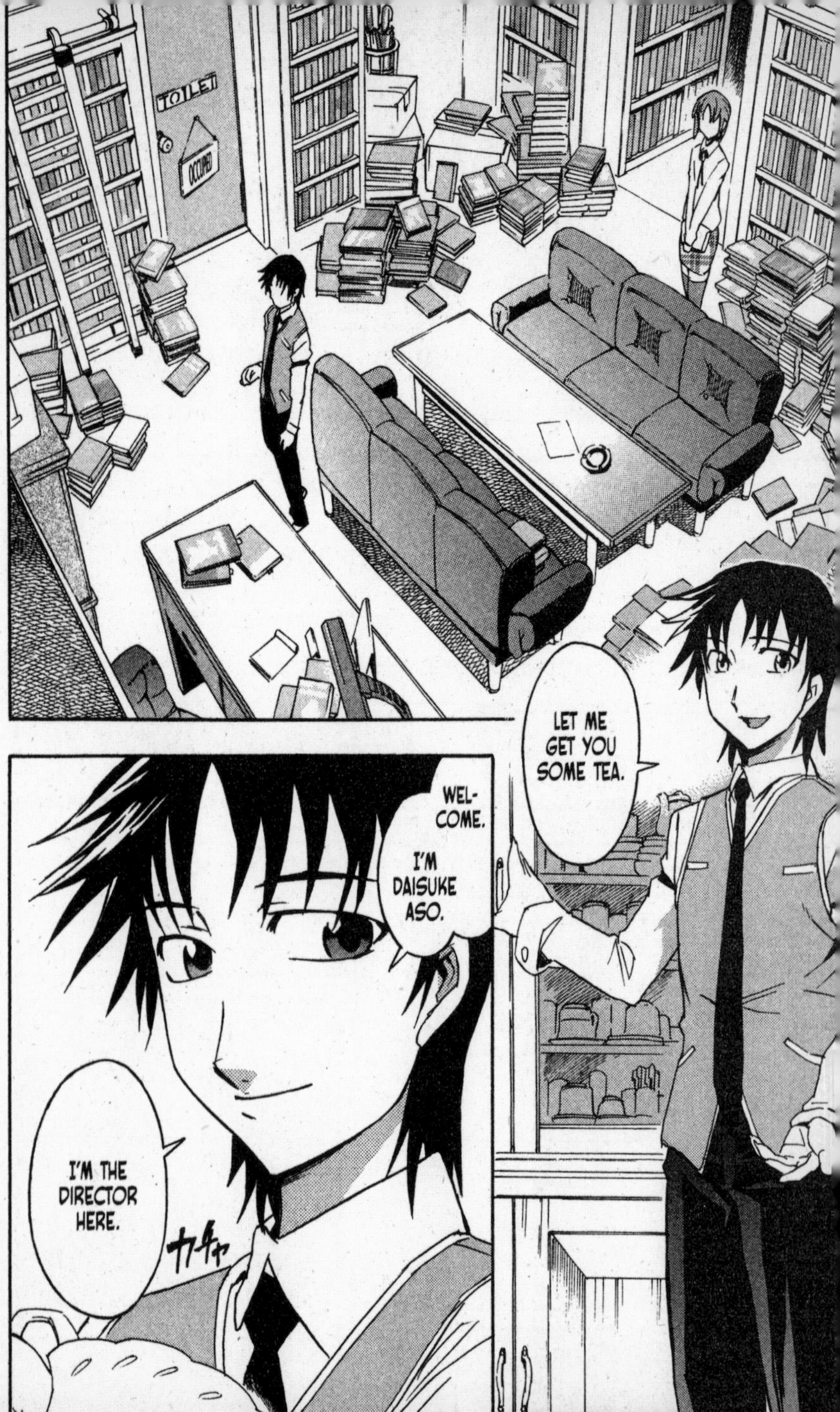
TOILET
OCCUPIED
LET ME GET YOU SOME TEA.
WEL-COME.
I'M DAISUKE ASO.
I'M THE DIRECTOR HERE.
カチャ

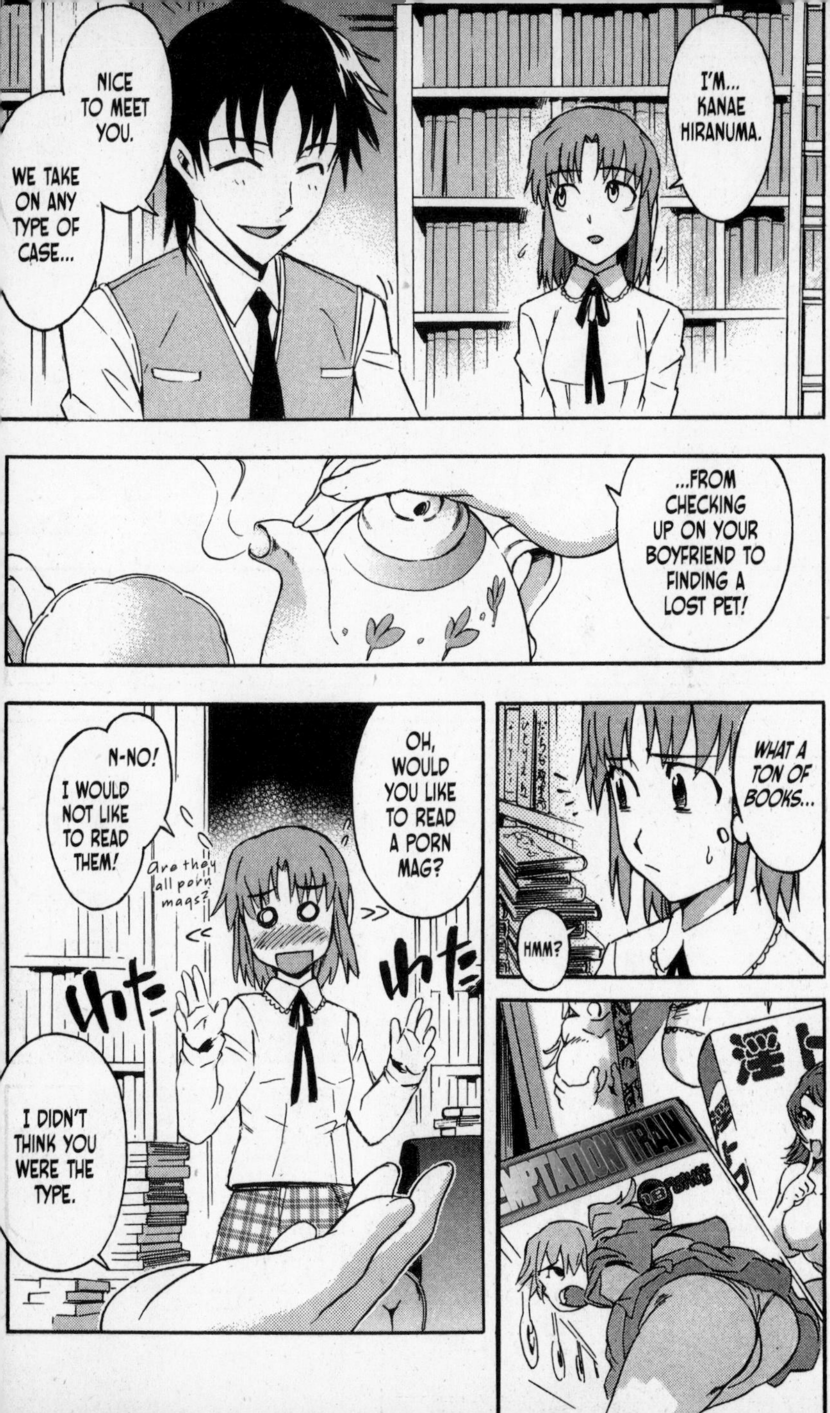
I'M... KANAE HIRANUMA.
NICE TO MEET YOU.
WE TAKE ON ANY TYPE OF CASE...
...FROM CHECKING UP ON YOUR BOYFRIEND TO FINDING A LOST PET!
WHAT A TON OF BOOKS...
HMM?
OH, WOULD YOU LIKE TO READ A PORN MAG?
N-NO! I WOULD NOT LIKE TO READ THEM!
Are they all porn mags?
I DIDN'T THINK YOU WERE THE TYPE.

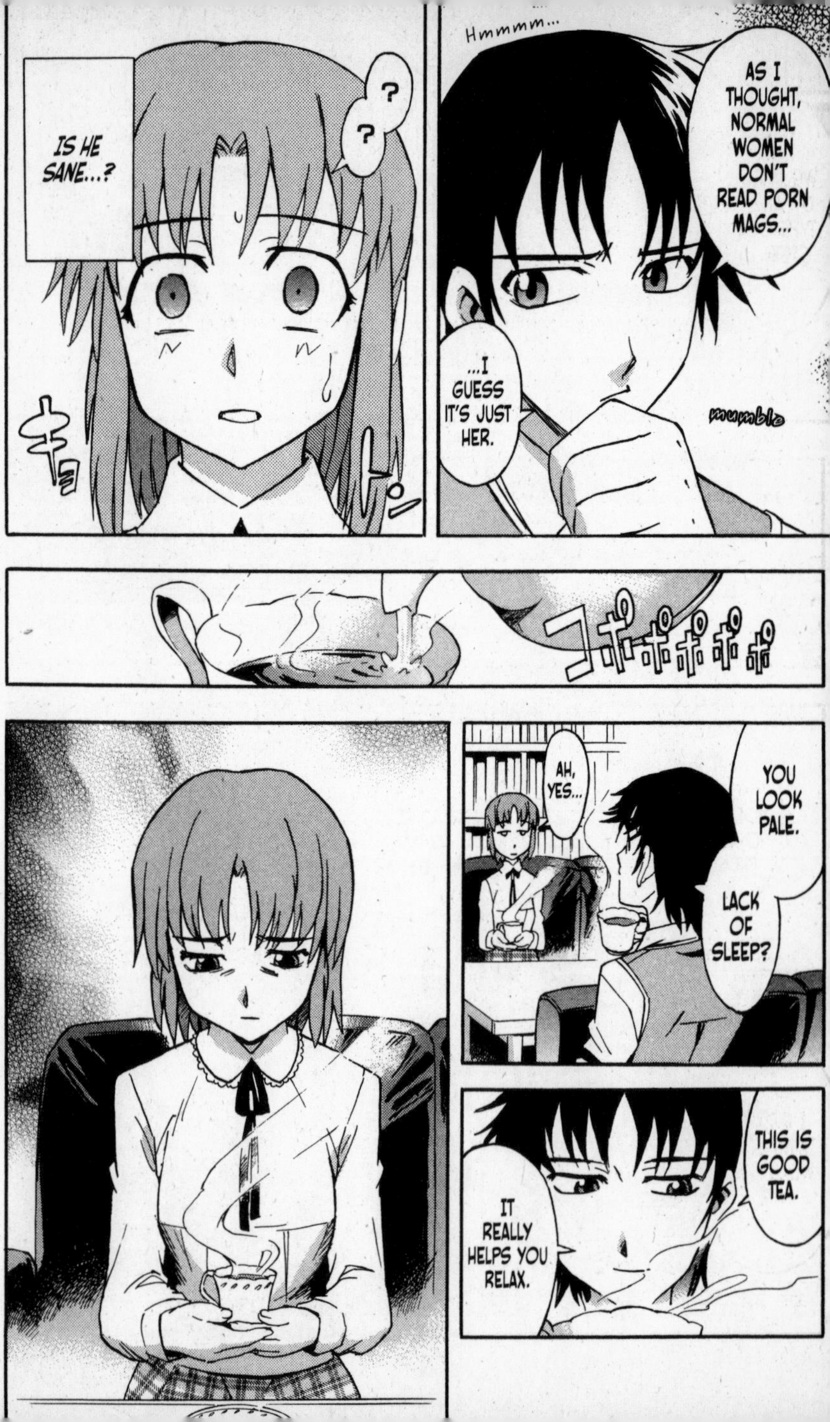
Hmmmm...
AS I THOUGHT, NORMAL WOMEN DON'T READ PORN MAGS...
...I GUESS IT'S JUST HER.
mumble
?
?
IS HE SANE...?
コポポポポポ
YOU LOOK PALE.
LACK OF SLEEP?
AH, YES...
THIS IS GOOD TEA.
IT REALLY HELPS YOU RELAX.

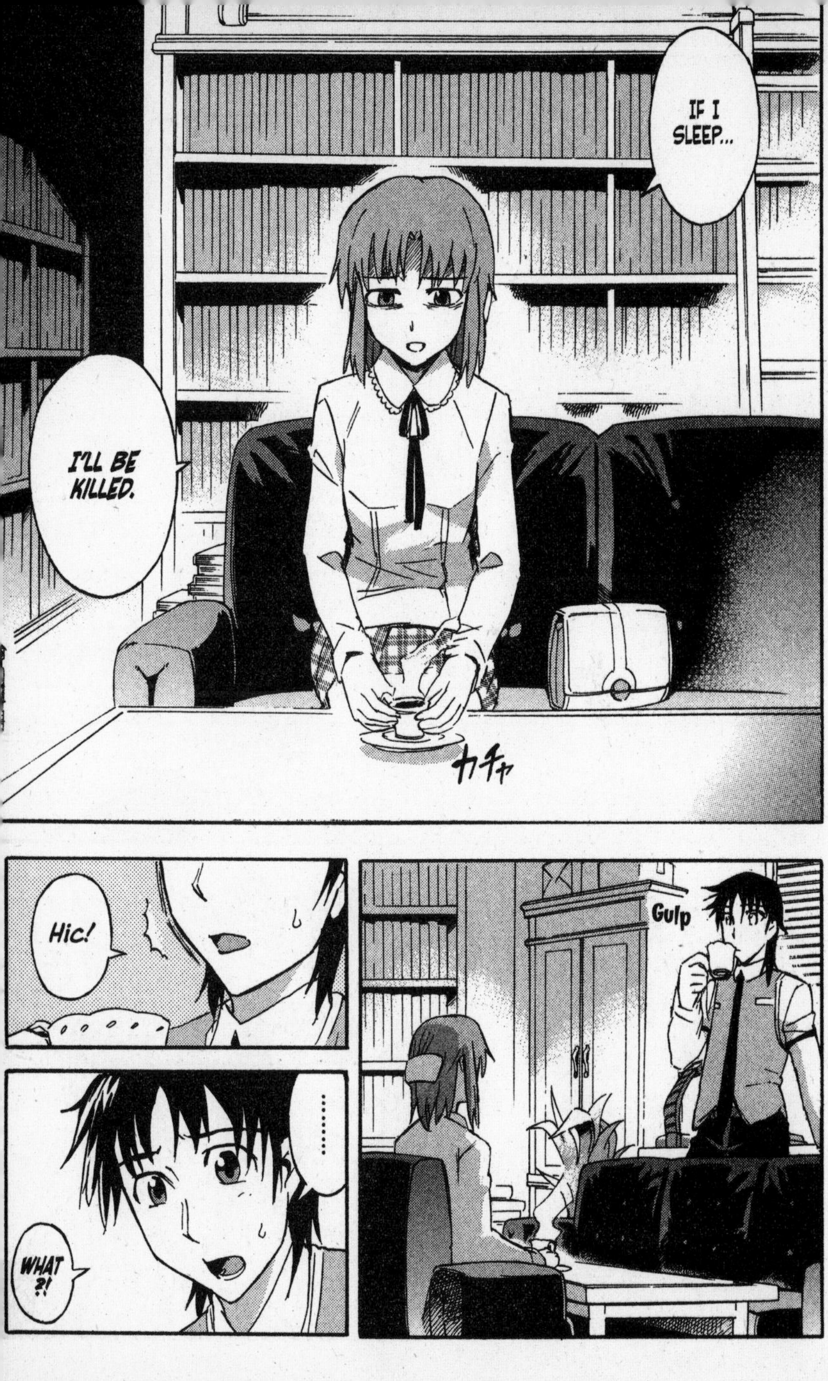
IF I SLEEP...
I'LL BE KILLED.
カチャ
Gulp
Hic!
......
WHAT ?!

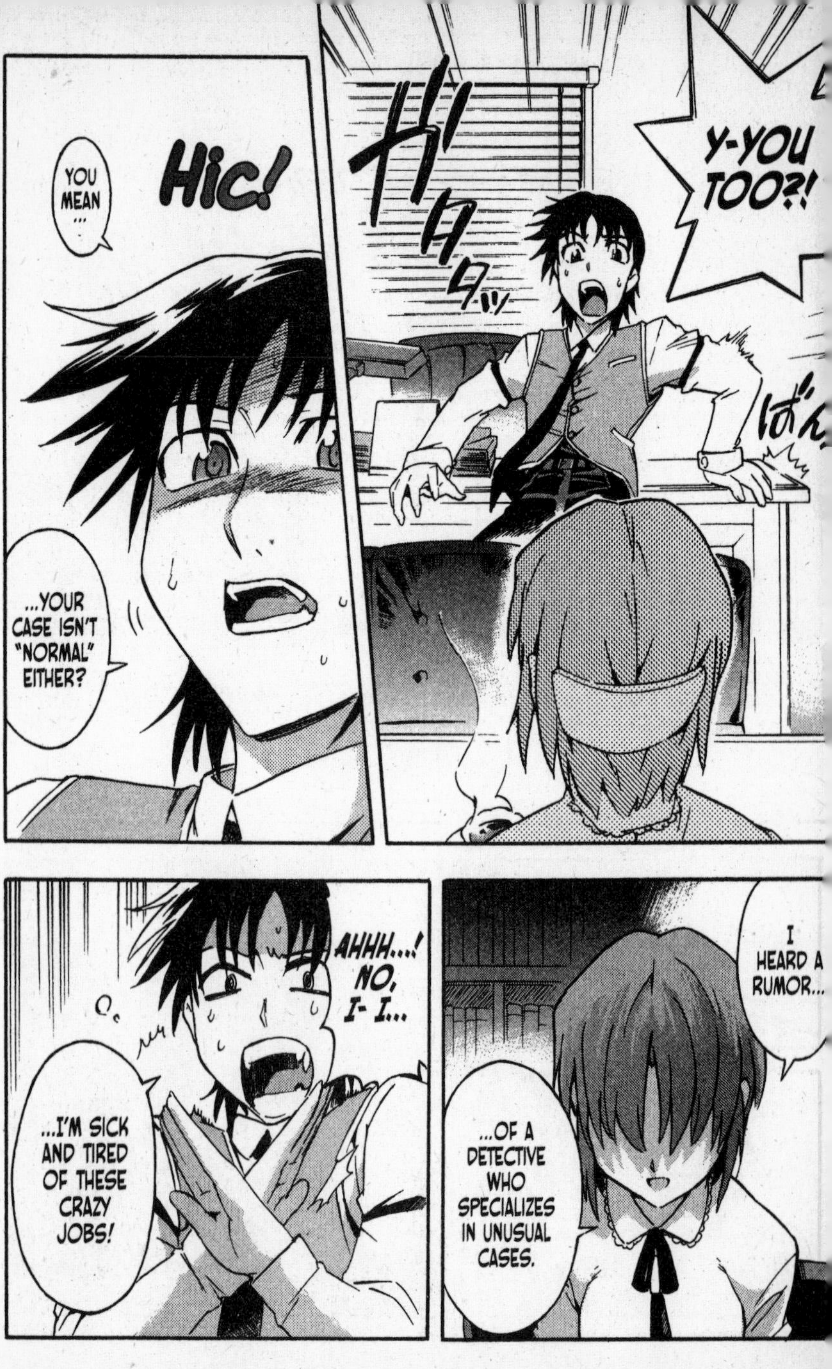
Y-YOU TOO?!
ばん
YOU MEAN...
Hic!
...YOUR CASE ISN'T "NORMAL" EITHER?
I HEARD A RUMOR...
...OF A DETECTIVE WHO SPECIALIZES IN UNUSUAL CASES.
AHHH...! NO, I- I...
...I'M SICK AND TIRED OF THESE CRAZY JOBS!

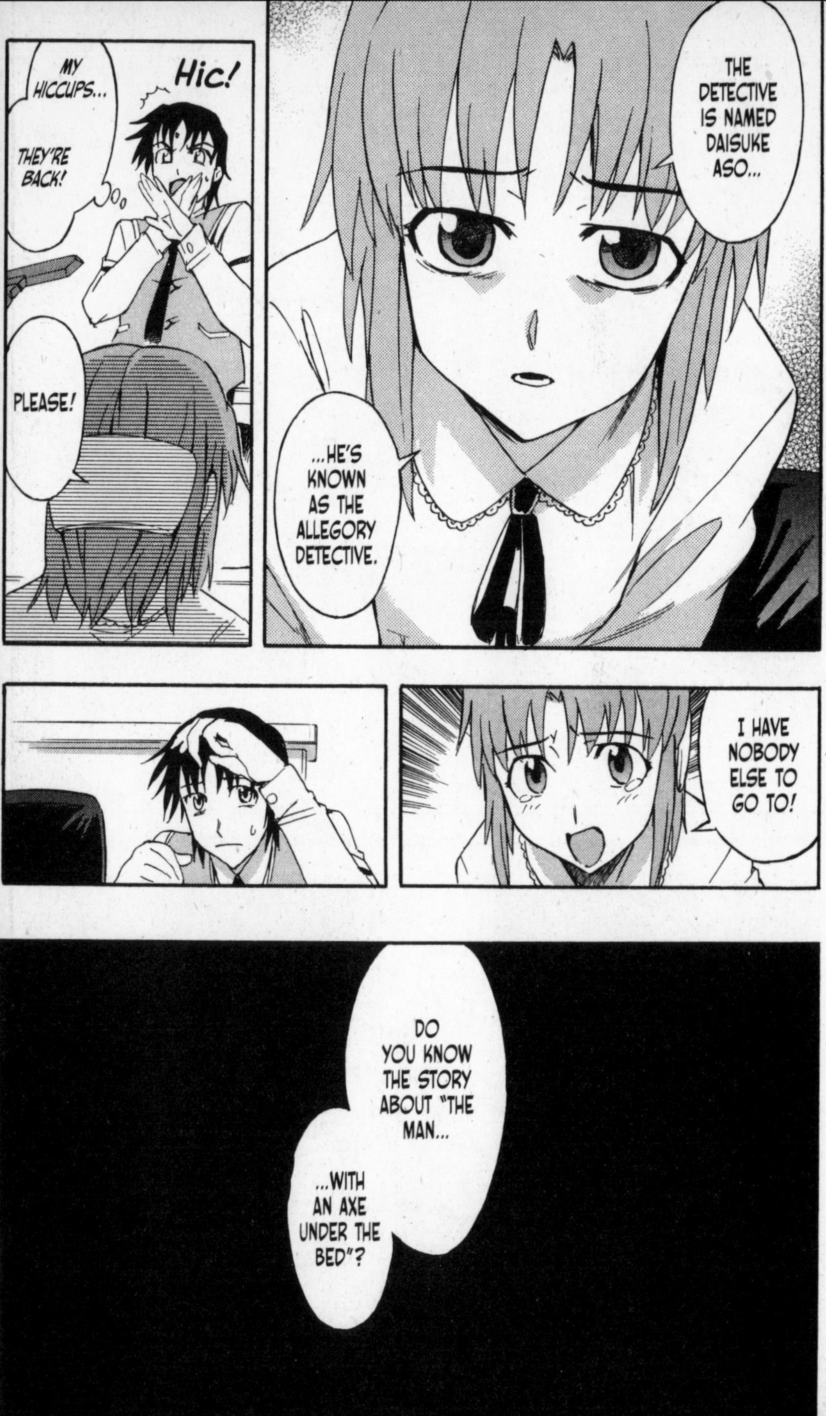
THE DETECTIVE IS NAMED DAISUKE ASO...
...HE'S KNOWN AS THE ALLEGORY DETECTIVE.
Hic!
MY HICCUPS...
THEY'RE BACK!
PLEASE!
I HAVE NOBODY ELSE TO GO TO!
DO YOU KNOW THE STORY ABOUT "THE MAN...
...WITH AN AXE UNDER THE BED"?

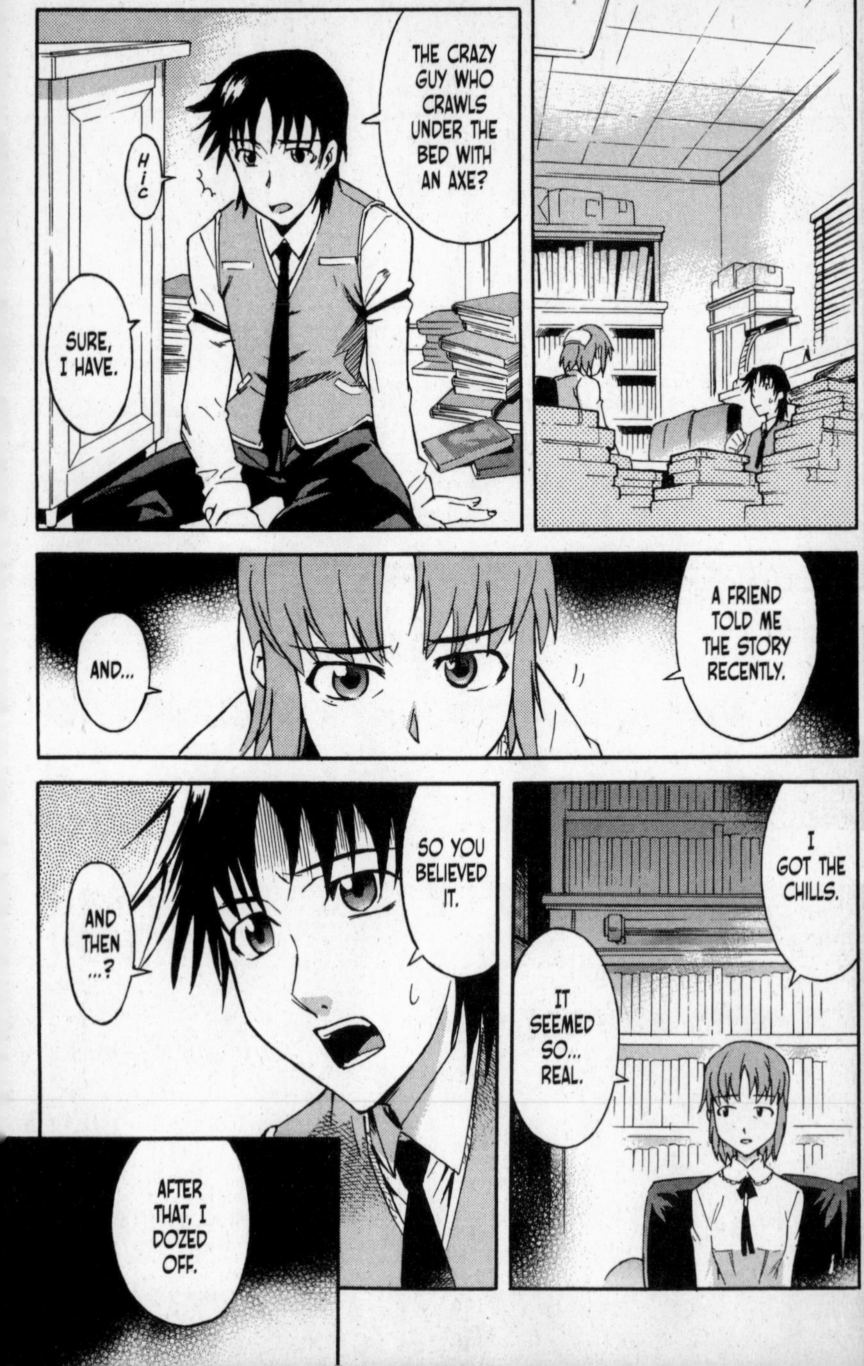
THE CRAZY GUY WHO CRAWLS UNDER THE BED WITH AN AXE?
Hic
SURE, I HAVE.
A FRIEND TOLD ME THE STORY RECENTLY.
AND...
I GOT THE CHILLS.
IT SEEMED SO... REAL.
SO YOU BELIEVED IT.
AND THEN ...?
AFTER THAT, I DOZED OFF.

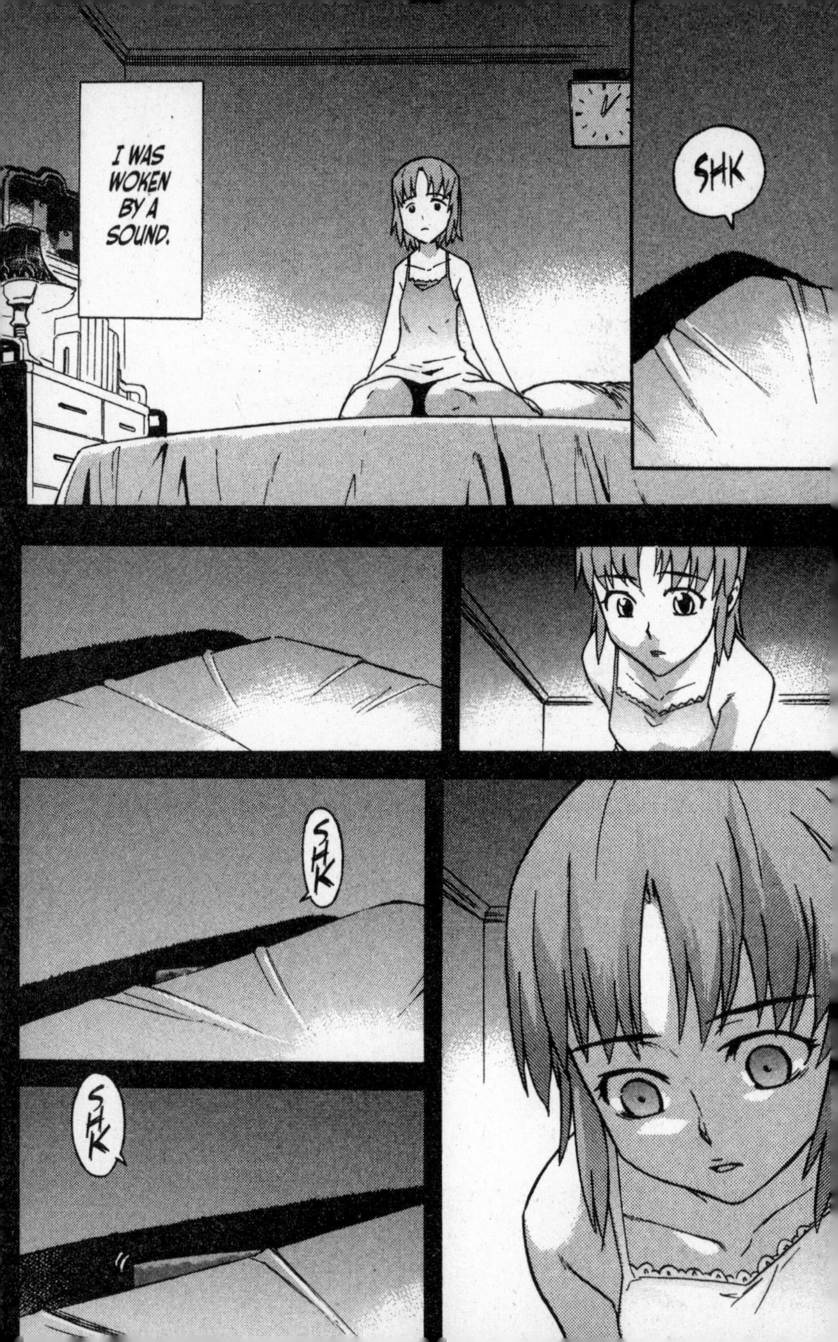
SHK
I WAS WOKEN BY A SOUND.
SHK
SHK

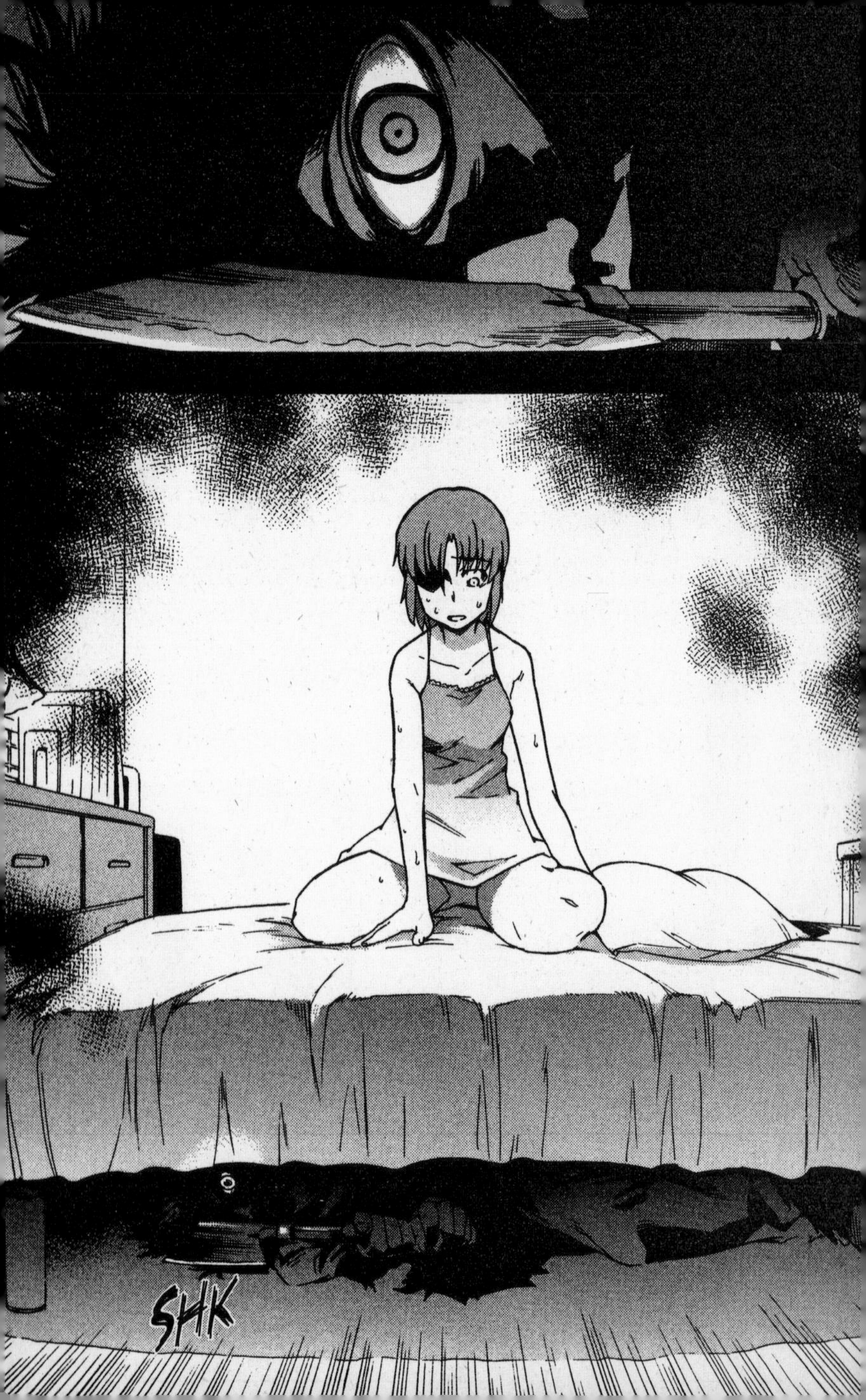
SHK

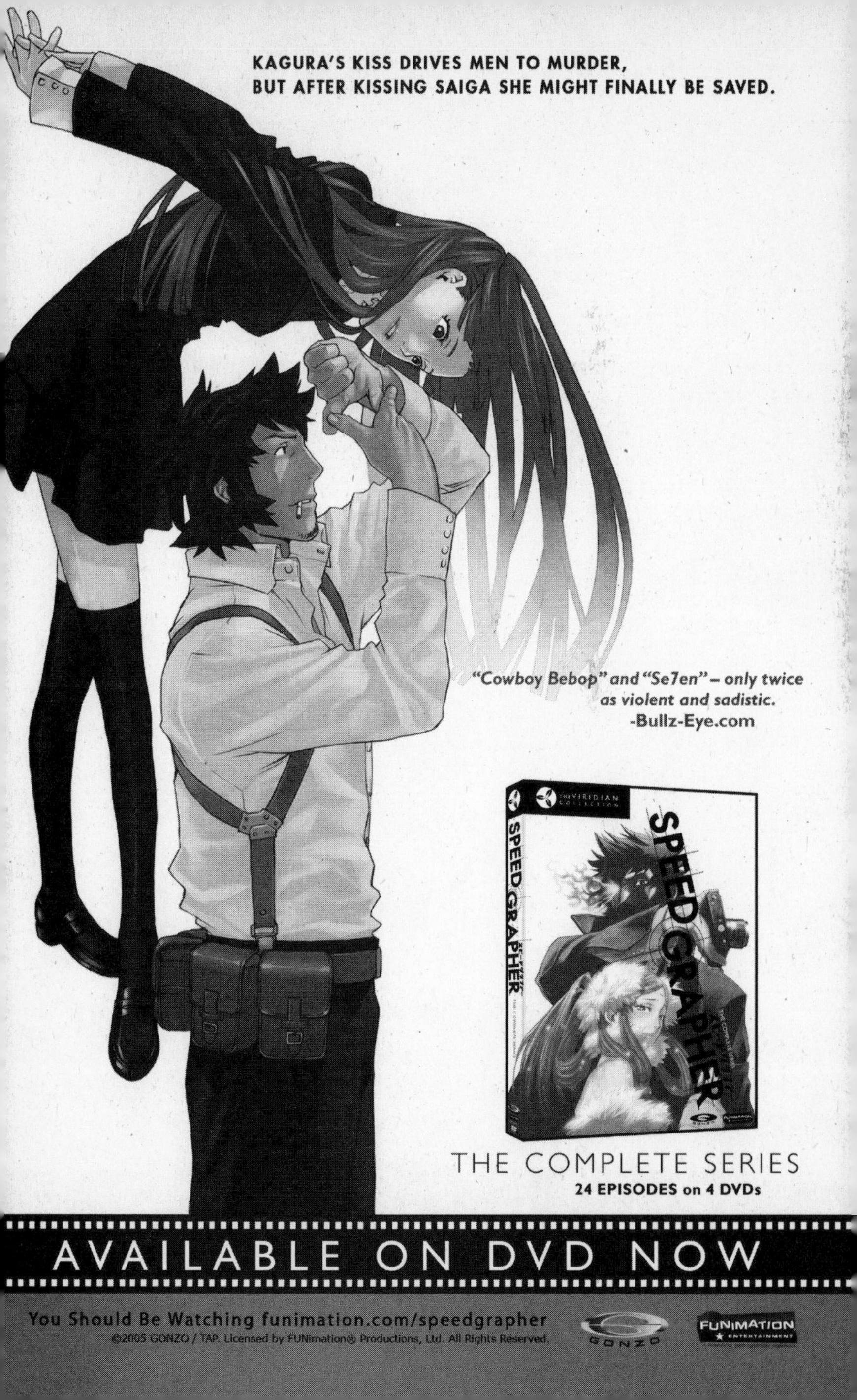
KAGURA'S KISS DRIVES MEN TO MURDER,
BUT AFTER KISSING SAIGA SHE MIGHT FINALLY BE SAVED.
"Cowboy Bebop" and "Se7en" – only twice as violent and sadistic.
-Bullz-Eye.com
THE VIRIDIAN COLLECTION
SPEED GRAPHER
THE COMPLETE SERIES
24 EPISODES on 4 DVDs
AVAILABLE ON DVD NOW
You Should Be Watching funimation.com/speedgrapher
©2005 GONZO / TAP. Licensed by FUNimation® Productions, Ltd. All Rights Reserved.
GONZO
FUNIMATION ENTERTAINMENT

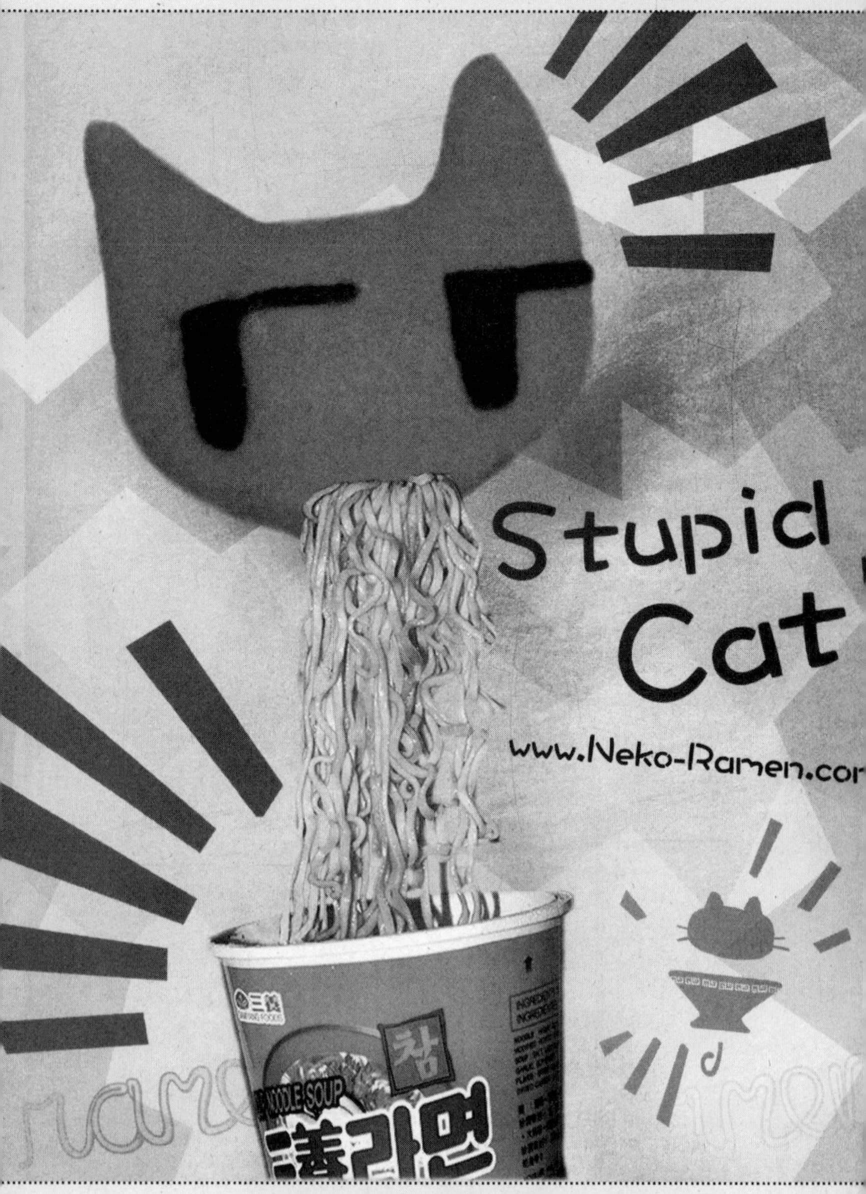
Stupid
Cat
www.Neko-Ramen.co
NOODLE SOUP
참
라면

The second epic trilogy continues!

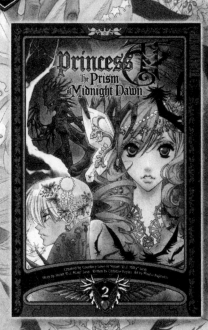

Ai fights to escape the clutches of her mysterious and malevolent captors, not knowing whether Kent, left behind on the Other Side, is even still alive. A frantic rescue mission commences, and in the end, even Ai's magical voice may not be enough to protect her from the trials of the Black Forest.

Dark secrets are revealed, and Ai must use all her strength and courage to face off against the new threat to Ai-Land. But will she ever see Kent again...?

"A very intriguing read that will satisfy old fans and create new fans, too."
– Bookloons

KARAKURI ODETTE

カラクリ オデット

VOL. 2

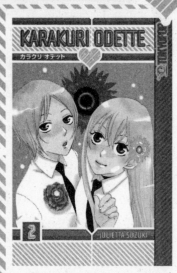

KARAKURI ODETTO © 2005 Julietta Suzuki / HAKUSENSHA, Inc.

She's a robot who wants to learn how to be a human... And what she learns will surprise everyone!

Odette is now a sophomore at her high school. She wants to be as close to human as she can, but finds out she still has a long way to go. From wanting to be "cute" by wearing nail polish, to making a "tasty" bento that people would be happy to eat, Odette faces each challenge head-on with the help of her friends Yoko, Chris, the Professor and, of course, Asao!

FROM THE CREATOR OF *AKUMA TO DOLCE*

"A SURPRISINGLY SENSITIVE, FUNNY AND THOUGHT-PROVOKING SCI-FI SHOJO SERIES ... AS GENUINELY CHARMING AND MEMORABLE AS ITS MECHANICAL HEROINE." —ABOUT.COM

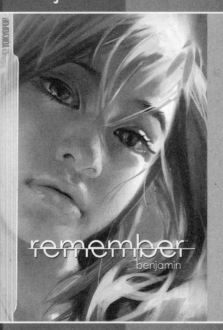
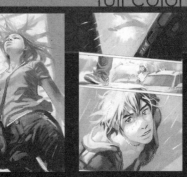

TOKYOPOP MANGA SUPPLEMENT

D•N•ANGEL

The secret of the Hikari/Niwa curse is revealed!

The time has come for Satoshi to reveal to Daisuke the history behind the Hikari/Niwa curse. How will Daisuke respond when he finds out why Satoshi is destined to die so young? Meanwhile, another fight breaks out against Argentine, sending Daisuke spiraling toward death as he tries to rescue Risa...

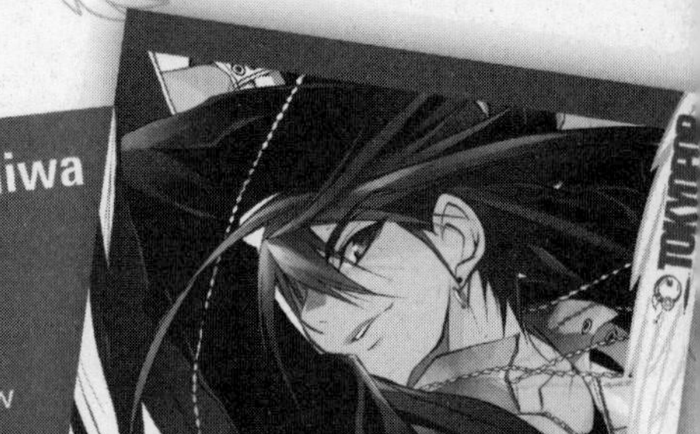
TOKYOPOP
D•N•ANGEL™
VOLUME 13 • YUKIRU SUGISAKI

FANTASY

T
TEEN AGE 13+

BE SURE TO VISIT WWW.TOKYOPOP.COM/SHOP FOR EVERYTHING YOU COULD EVER WANT!

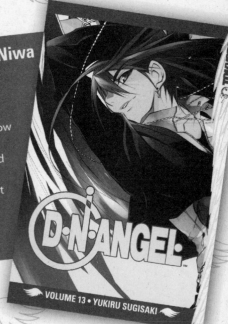

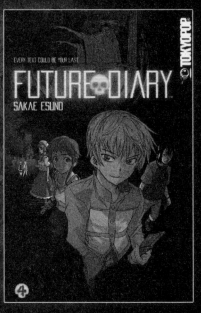

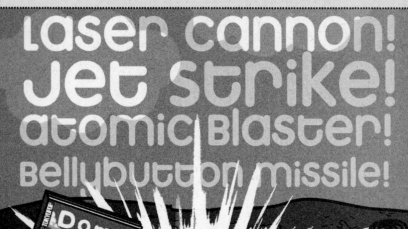
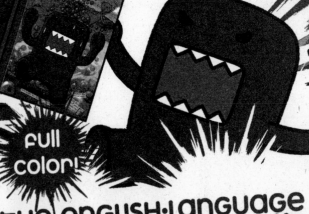
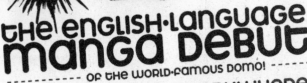

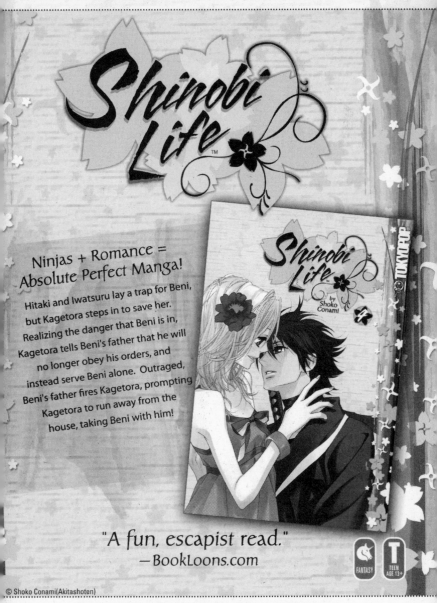

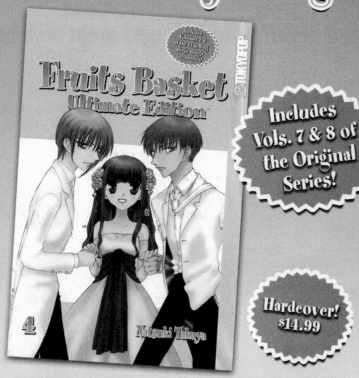

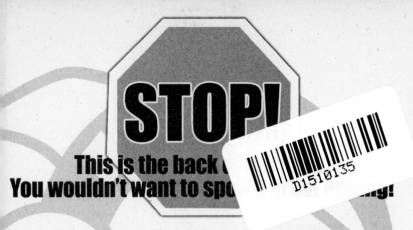

STOP!

This is the back
You wouldn't want to spo ... ng!

This book is printed "manga-style," in the authentic Japanese right-to-left format. Since none of the artwork has been flipped or altered, readers get to experience the story just as the creator intended. You've been asking for it, so TOKYOPOP® delivered: authentic, hot-off-the-press, and far more fun!

1
2
3
4
5
6
7
8
9
10

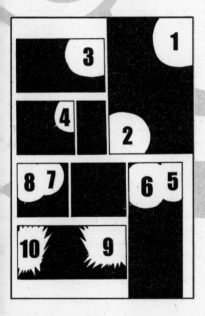

DIRECTIONS

If this is your first time reading manga-style, here's a quick guide to help you understand how it works.

It's easy... just start in the top right panel and follow the numbers. Have fun, and look for more 100% authentic manga from TOKYOPOP®!

THE MANGA REVOLUTION • LEADING THE MANGA REVOLUTION • LEADING
漫画革命

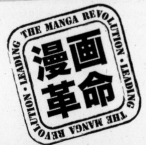